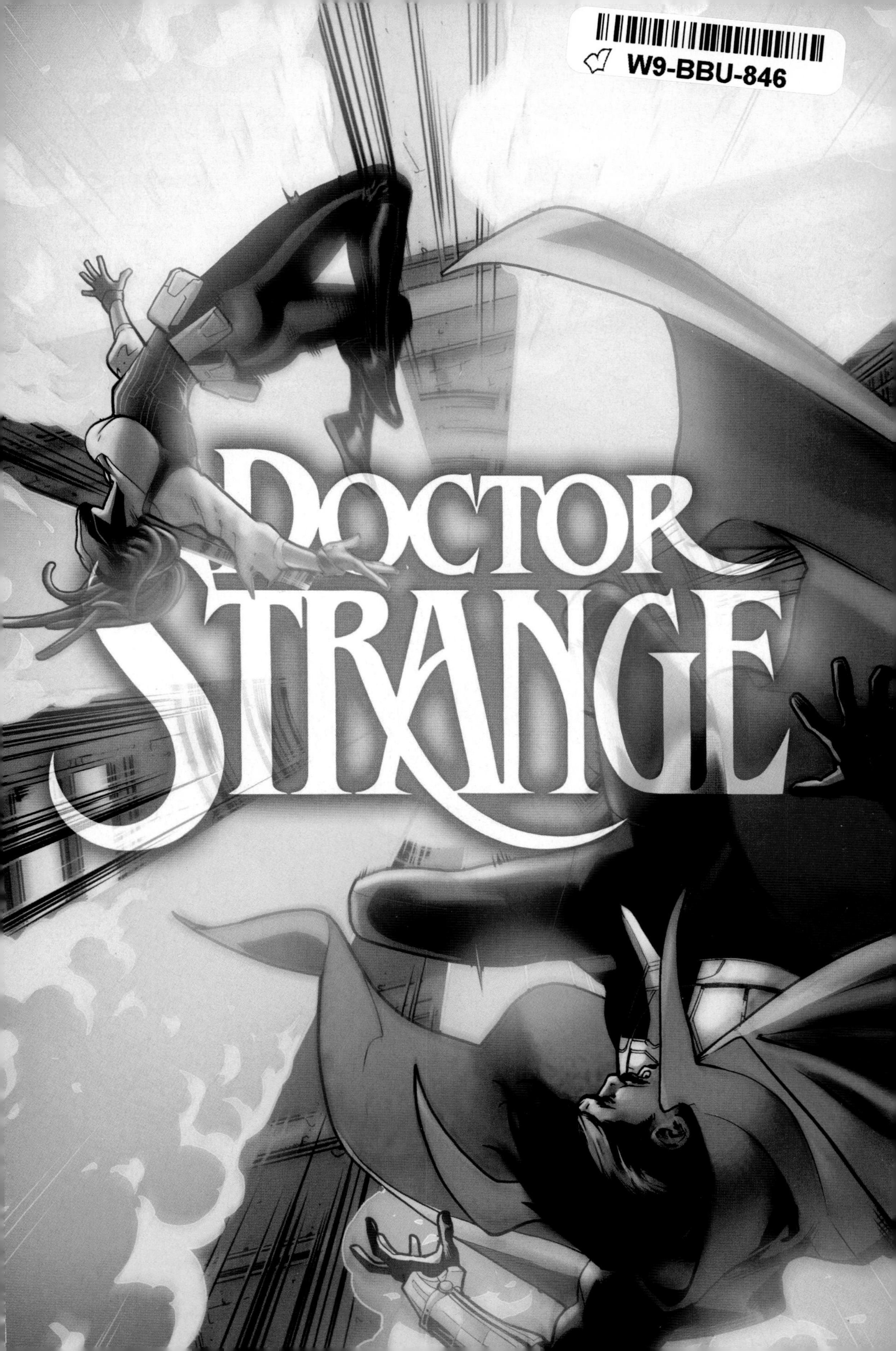
DOCTOR
STRANGE

LAST TIME...

WE OBSERVED THE ADVENTURES OF A MAN CALLING HIMSELF DOCTOR STRANGE, WHO HAD LOST TOUCH WITH MAGIC AND COULD NOT REMEMBER WHEN OR HOW. THAT MAN HAS RETURNED FROM A SABBATICAL IN SPACE, (ARGUABLY) BETTER THAN EVER. HE HAS A NEW ALLY, KANNA, AN ALIEN ARCANOLOGIST (EXPERT IN MAGICAL TECHNOLOGY/TECHNOLOGICAL MAGIC), AND HE HAS ACCESS TO THE FORGE--AN INTERDIMENSIONAL WORKSHOP FOR TOOLS OF SORCERY. THUS EQUIPPED, THIS STRANGE AND KANNA BARELY HAD TO ALTER THEIR ITINERARY TO FOIL A MAJESDANEAN ATTEMPT TO DESTROY EARTH. BUT AWAITING THEIR ARRIVAL IN THE SANCTUM SANCTORUM, ATTIRED AS WE SAW HIM ON HIS LAST ADVENTURES WITH THE AVENGERS, IS A MAN THE SORCERER SUPREME'S GHOST DOG, BATS, HAS BEEN CALLING "STEPHEN STRANGE"...

DOCTOR STRANGE CREATED BY STAN LEE & STEVE DITKO

COLLECTION EDITOR: **JENNIFER GRÜNWALD**
ASSISTANT EDITOR: **CAITLIN O'CONNELL**
ASSOCIATE MANAGING EDITOR: **KATERI WOODY**
EDITOR, SPECIAL PROJECTS: **MARK D. BEAZLEY**

VP PRODUCTION & SPECIAL PROJECTS: **JEFF YOUNGQUIST**
SVP PRINT, SALES & MARKETING: **DAVID GABRIEL**
BOOK DESIGN: **RODOLFO MURAGUCHI** WITH **STACIE ZUCKER**

EDITOR IN CHIEF: **C.B. CEBULSKI**
CHIEF CREATIVE OFFICER: **JOE QUESADA**
PRESIDENT: **DAN BUCKLEY**
EXECUTIVE PRODUCER: **ALAN FINE**

DOCTOR STRANGE BY MARK WAID VOL. 2: REMITTANCE. Contains material originally published in magazine form as DOCTOR STRANGE #6-11. First printing 2019. ISBN 978-1-302-91234-5. Published by MARVEL WORLDWIDE, INC., a subsidiary of MARVEL ENTERTAINMENT, LLC. OFFICE OF PUBLICATION: 135 West 50th Street, New York, NY 10020. © 2019 MARVEL No similarity between any of the names, characters, persons, and/or institutions in this magazine with those of any living or dead person or institution is intended, and any such similarity which may exist is purely coincidental. **Printed in the U.S.A.** DAN BUCKLEY, President, Marvel Entertainment; JOHN NEE, Publisher; JOE QUESADA, Chief Creative Officer; TOM BREVOORT, SVP of Publishing; DAVID BOGART, Associate Publisher & SVP of Talent Affairs; DAVID GABRIEL, SVP of Sales & Marketing, Publishing; JEFF YOUNGQUIST, VP of Production & Special Projects; DAN CARR, Executive Director of Publishing Technology; ALEX MORALES, Director of Publishing Operations; DAN EDINGTON, Managing Editor; SUSAN CRESPI, Production Manager; STAN LEE, Chairman Emeritus. For information regarding advertising in Marvel Comics or on Marvel.com, please contact Vit DeBellis, Custom Solutions & Integrated Advertising Manager, at vdebellis@marvel.com. For Marvel subscription inquiries, please call 888-511-5480. **Manufactured between 3/8/2019 and 4/9/2019 by LSC COMMUNICATIONS INC., KENDALLVILLE, IN, USA.**

10 9 8 7 6 5 4 3 2 1

Remittance

WRITER
Mark Waid

Issues #6-8

PENCILERS
Javier Pina (#6-8) & Andres Guinaldo (#7-8)

INKERS
Javier Pina (#6-8), JP Mayer (#7), Andy Owens (#7-8),
Roberto Poggi (#7) & Keith Champagne (#7)

COLOR ARTISTS
Brian Reber (#6-7), Jim Campbell (#7), Andrew Crossley (#7) & Carlos Lopez (#8)

COVER ART
Kevin Nowlan

Issues #9-11

ARTISTS
Jesús Saiz with Javier Pina (#11)

COLOR ARTISTS
Jesús Saiz with Rachelle Rosenberg (#11)

COVER ART
Jesús Saiz

#10 Anniversary Stories

ARTISTS
Kevin Nowlan & Jim Campbell; Butch Guice & Carlos Lopez;
AND Daniel Acuña

CELEBRATORY SPREAD ART
Tom Palmer

LETTERER
VC's Cory Petit

T EDITORS
i & Annalise Bissa

EDITOR
Nick Lowe

6

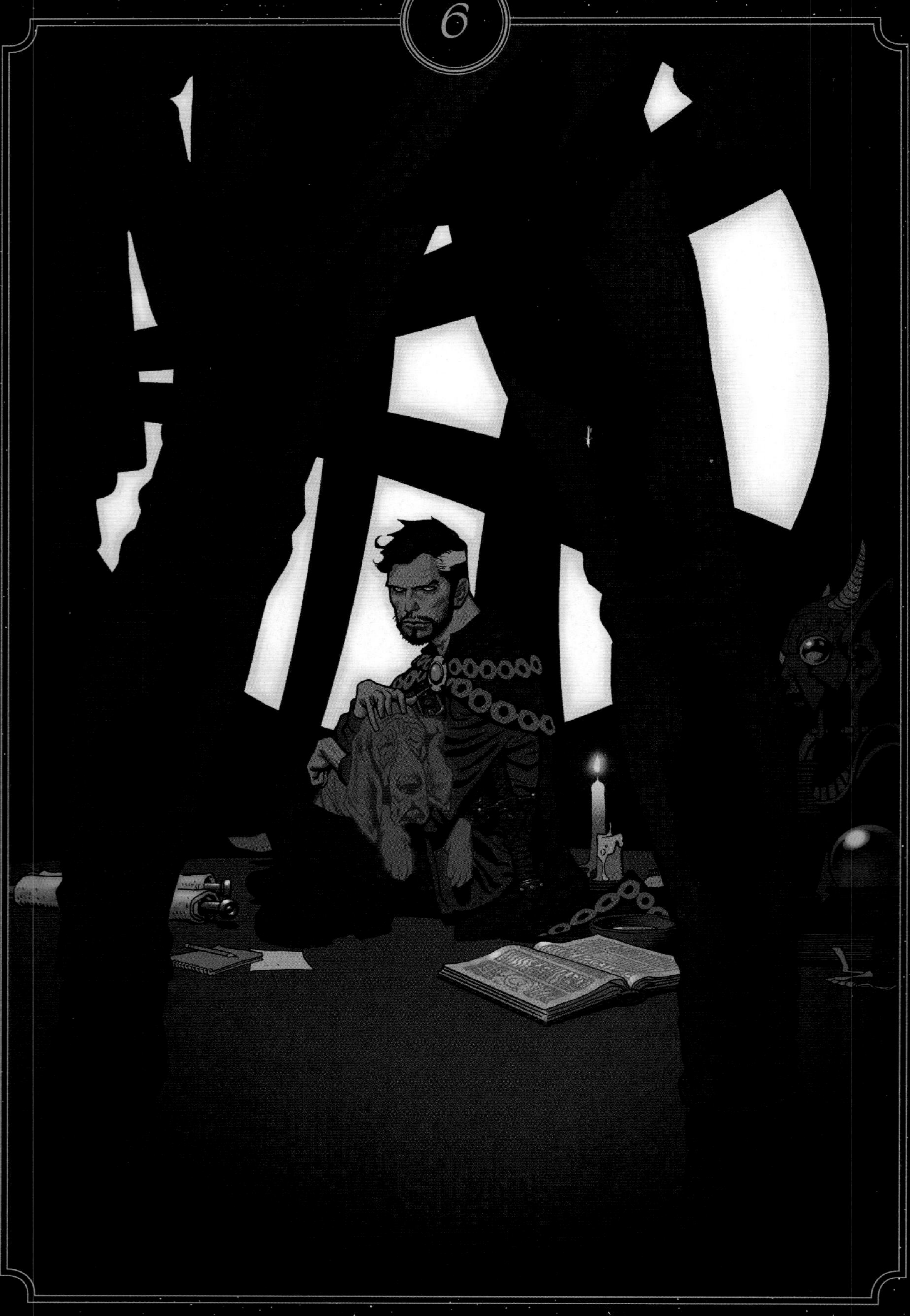

The Two Doctors PART ONE

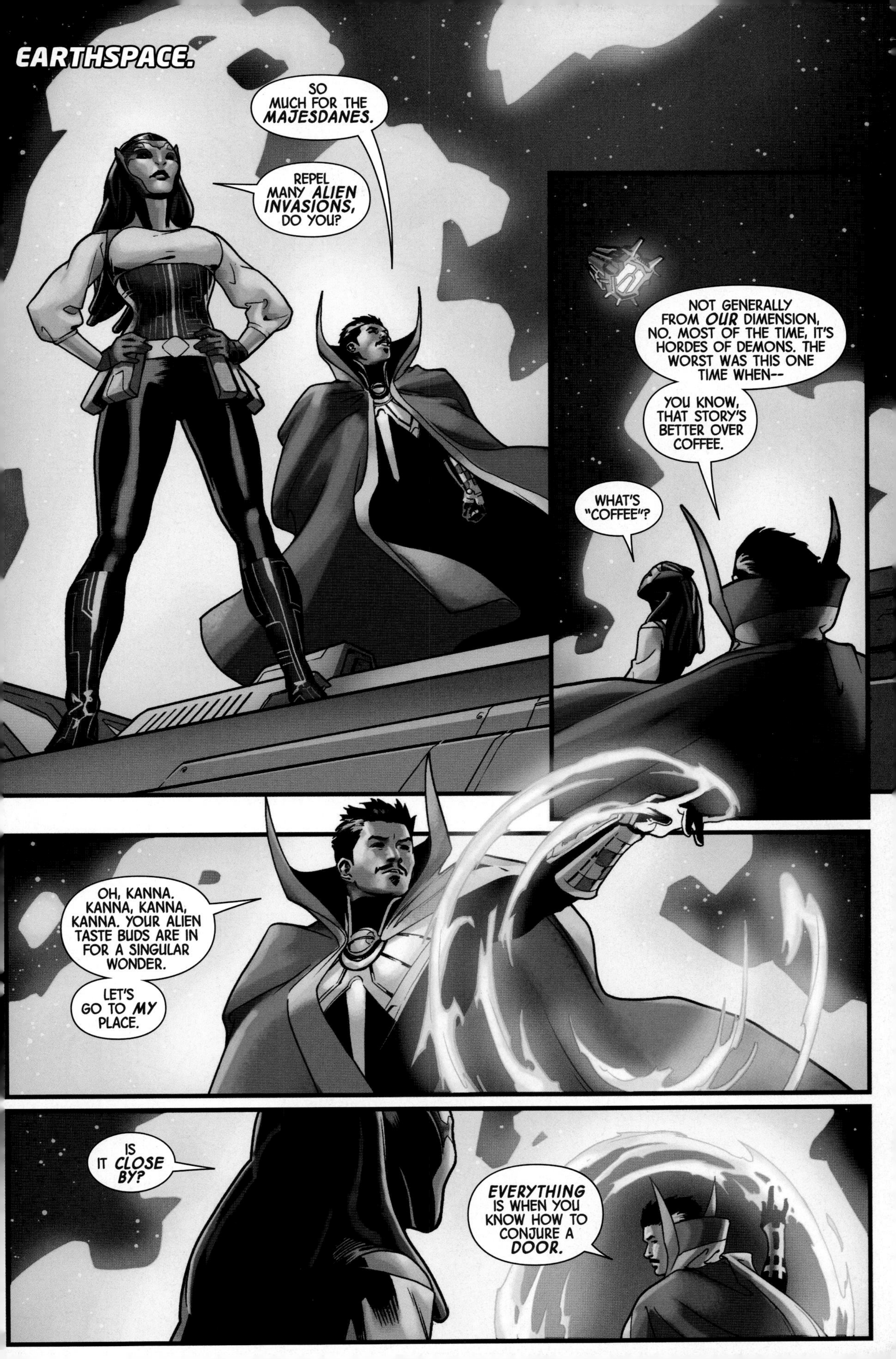
EARTHSPACE.
SO MUCH FOR THE MAJESDANES.
REPEL MANY ALIEN INVASIONS, DO YOU?
NOT GENERALLY FROM OUR DIMENSION, NO. MOST OF THE TIME, IT'S HORDES OF DEMONS. THE WORST WAS THIS ONE TIME WHEN--
YOU KNOW, THAT STORY'S BETTER OVER COFFEE.
WHAT'S "COFFEE"?
OH, KANNA. KANNA, KANNA, KANNA. YOUR ALIEN TASTE BUDS ARE IN FOR A SINGULAR WONDER.
LET'S GO TO MY PLACE.
IS IT CLOSE BY?
EVERYTHING IS WHEN YOU KNOW HOW TO CONJURE A DOOR.

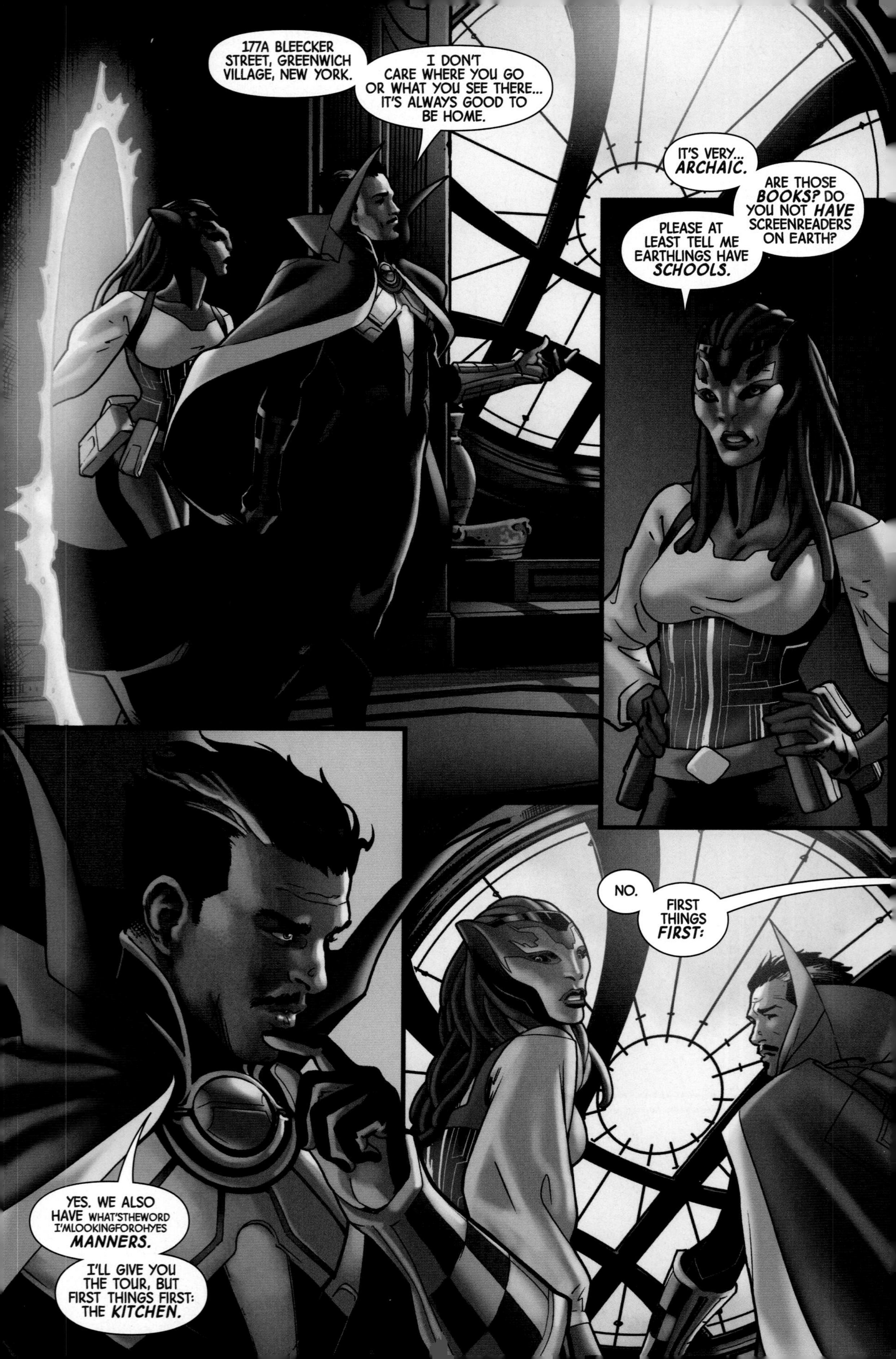
177A BLEECKER STREET, GREENWICH VILLAGE, NEW YORK.
I DON'T CARE WHERE YOU GO OR WHAT YOU SEE THERE... IT'S ALWAYS GOOD TO BE HOME.
IT'S VERY... ARCHAIC.
ARE THOSE BOOKS? DO YOU NOT HAVE SCREENREADERS ON EARTH?
PLEASE AT LEAST TELL ME EARTHLINGS HAVE SCHOOLS.
YES. WE ALSO HAVE WHAT'STHEWORD I'MLOOKINGFOROHYES MANNERS.
I'LL GIVE YOU THE TOUR, BUT FIRST THINGS FIRST: THE KITCHEN.
NO.
FIRST THINGS FIRST:

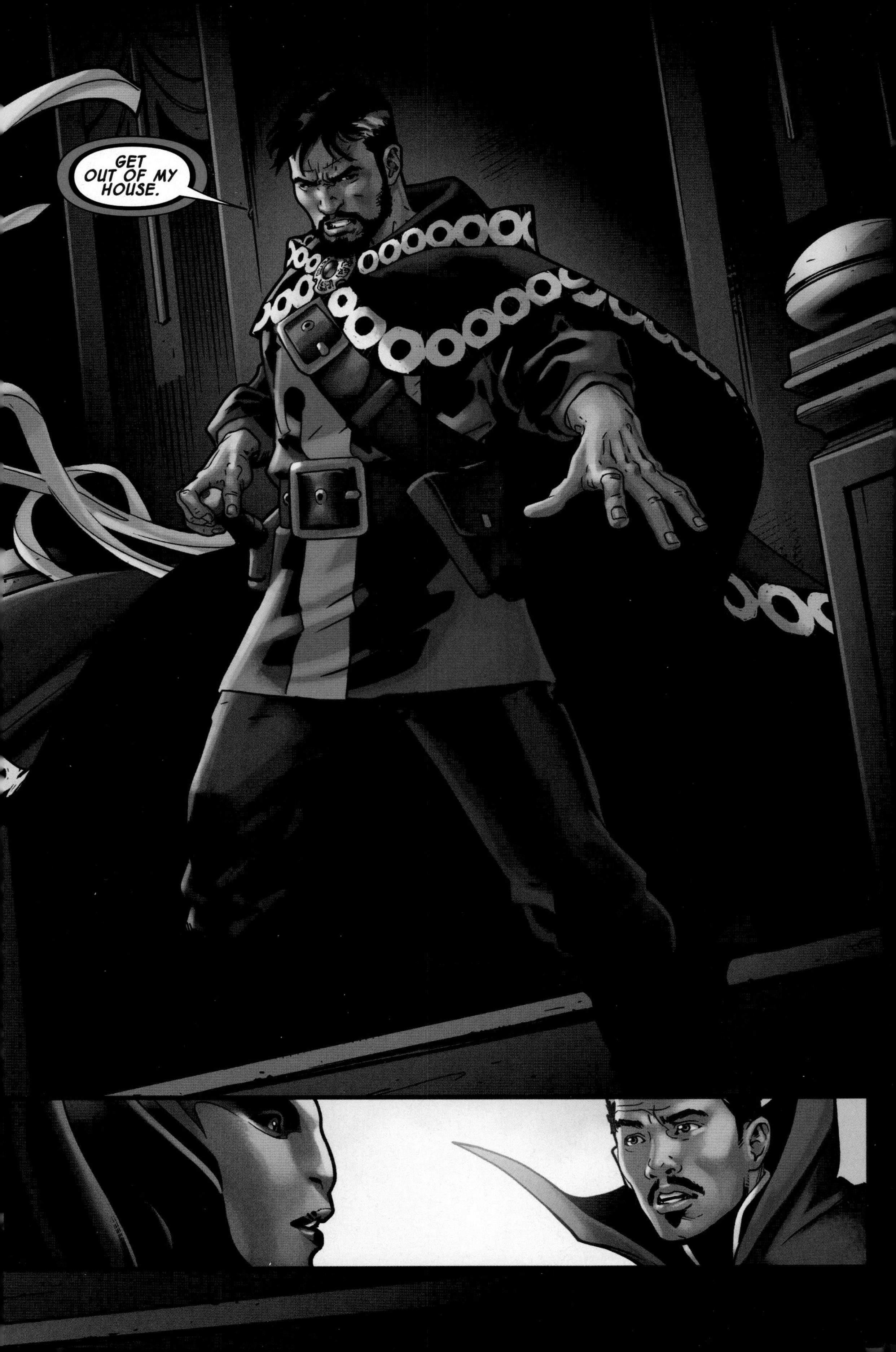
GET OUT OF MY HOUSE.

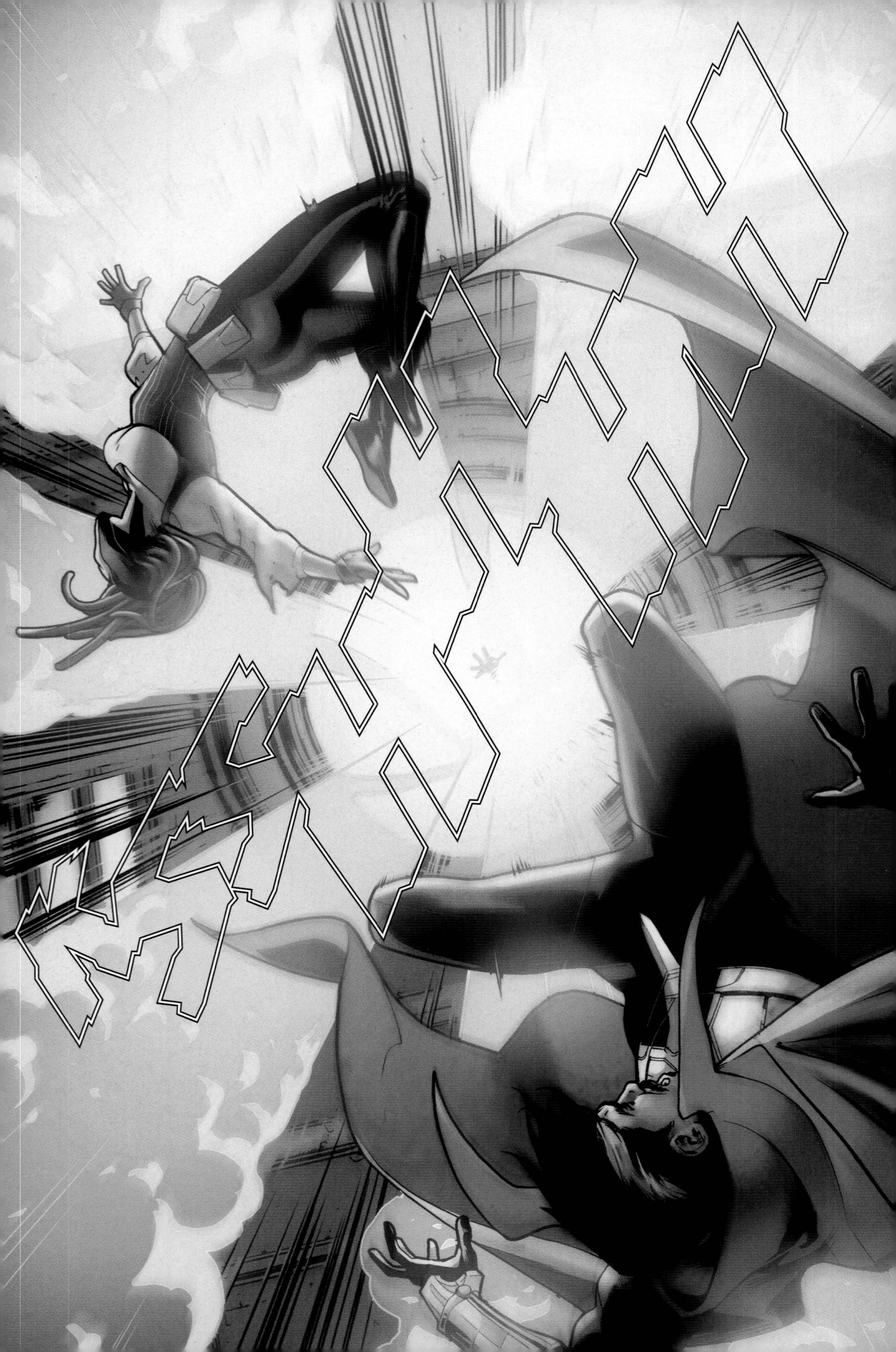

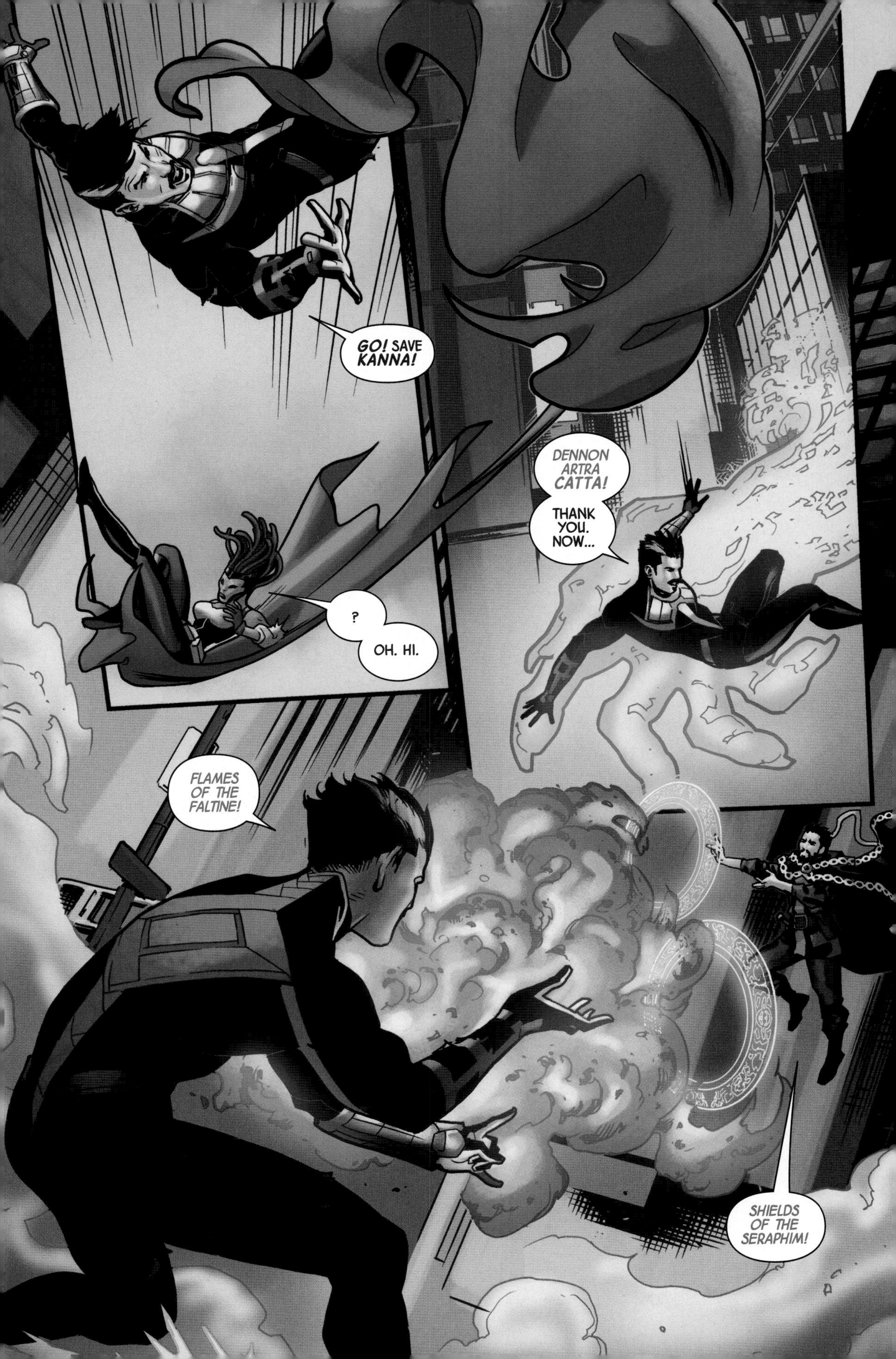
GO! SAVE KANNA!
DENNON ARTRA CATTA!
THANK YOU. NOW...
?
OH. HI.
FLAMES OF THE FALTINE!
SHIELDS OF THE SERAPHIM!

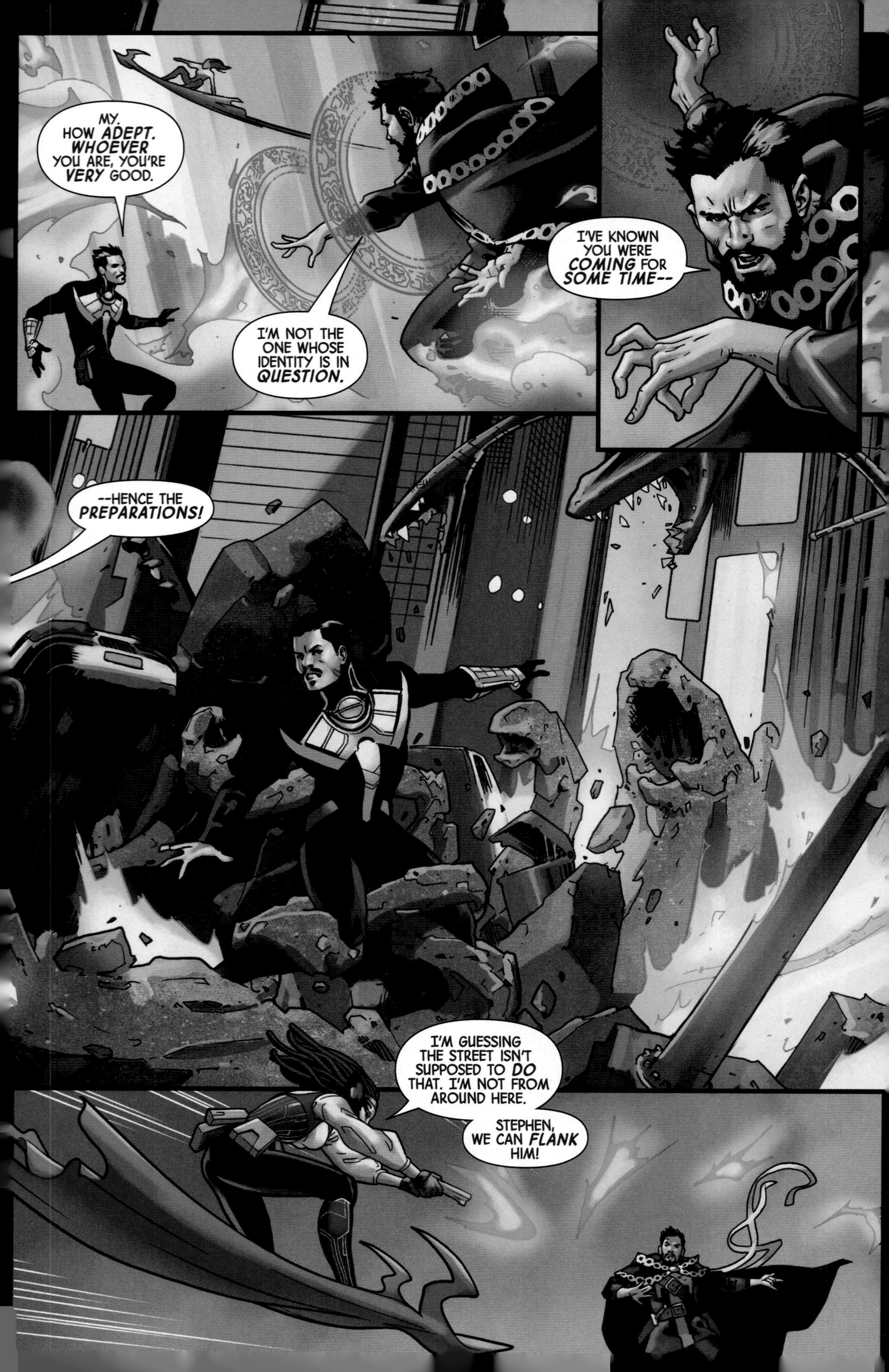
MY. HOW ADEPT. WHOEVER YOU ARE, YOU'RE VERY GOOD.
I'M NOT THE ONE WHOSE IDENTITY IS IN QUESTION.
I'VE KNOWN YOU WERE COMING FOR SOME TIME--
--HENCE THE PREPARATIONS!
I'M GUESSING THE STREET ISN'T SUPPOSED TO DO THAT. I'M NOT FROM AROUND HERE.
STEPHEN, WE CAN FLANK HIM!

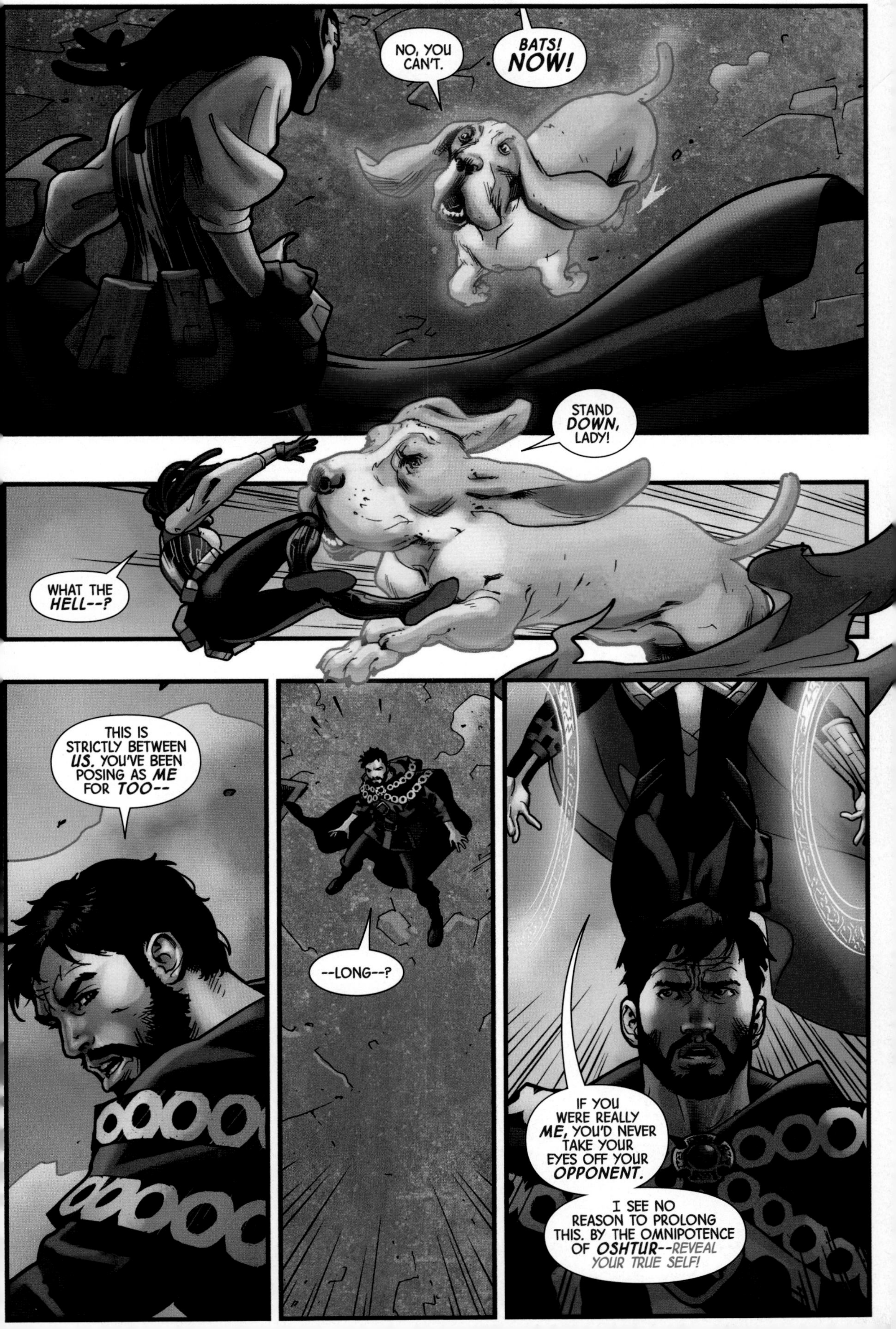
NO, YOU CAN'T.
BATS! NOW!
STAND DOWN, LADY!
WHAT THE HELL--?
THIS IS STRICTLY BETWEEN US. YOU'VE BEEN POSING AS ME FOR TOO--
--LONG--?
IF YOU WERE REALLY ME, YOU'D NEVER TAKE YOUR EYES OFF YOUR OPPONENT.
I SEE NO REASON TO PROLONG THIS. BY THE OMNIPOTENCE OF OSHTUR--REVEAL YOUR TRUE SELF!

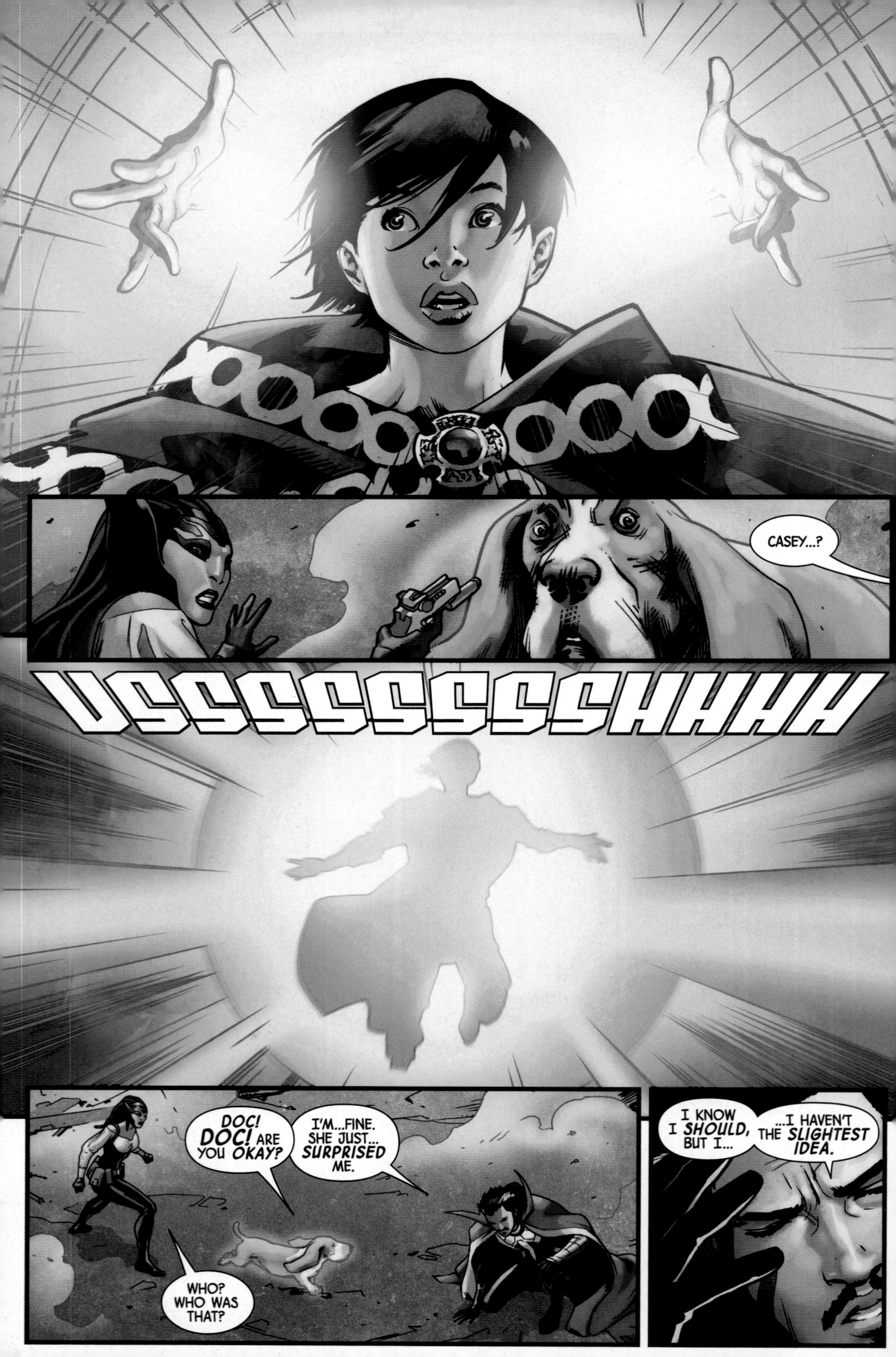
CASEY...?
VSSSSSSSSHHHH
DOC! DOC! ARE YOU OKAY?
I'M...FINE. SHE JUST... SURPRISED ME.
WHO? WHO WAS THAT?
I KNOW I SHOULD, BUT I...
...I HAVEN'T THE SLIGHTEST IDEA.

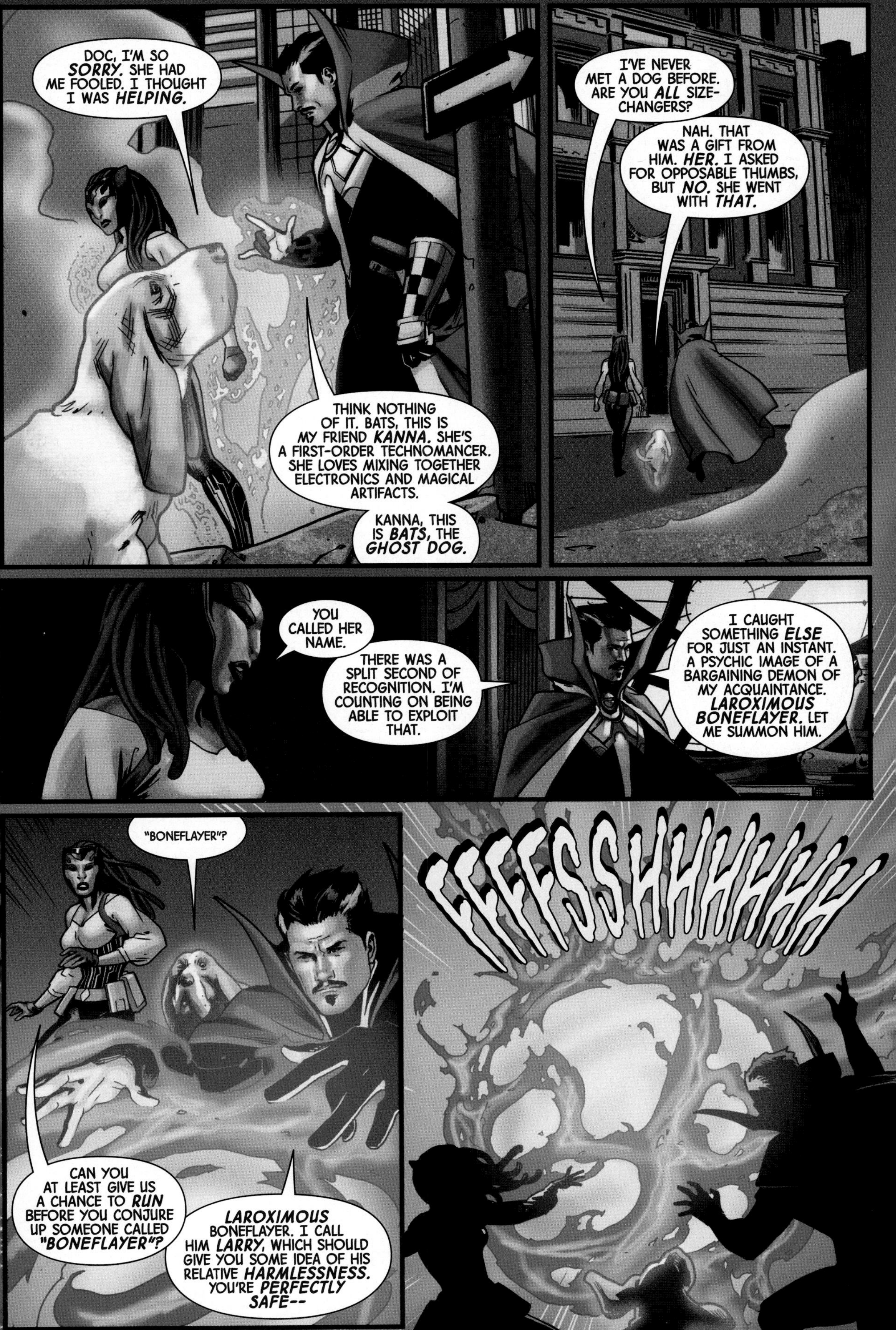
DOC, I'M SO SORRY. SHE HAD ME FOOLED. I THOUGHT I WAS HELPING.
THINK NOTHING OF IT. BATS, THIS IS MY FRIEND KANNA. SHE'S A FIRST-ORDER TECHNOMANCER. SHE LOVES MIXING TOGETHER ELECTRONICS AND MAGICAL ARTIFACTS.
KANNA, THIS IS BATS, THE GHOST DOG.
I'VE NEVER MET A DOG BEFORE. ARE YOU ALL SIZE-CHANGERS?
NAH. THAT WAS A GIFT FROM HIM. HER. I ASKED FOR OPPOSABLE THUMBS, BUT NO. SHE WENT WITH THAT.
YOU CALLED HER NAME.
THERE WAS A SPLIT SECOND OF RECOGNITION. I'M COUNTING ON BEING ABLE TO EXPLOIT THAT.
I CAUGHT SOMETHING ELSE FOR JUST AN INSTANT. A PSYCHIC IMAGE OF A BARGAINING DEMON OF MY ACQUAINTANCE. LAROXIMOUS BONEFLAYER. LET ME SUMMON HIM.
"BONEFLAYER"?
CAN YOU AT LEAST GIVE US A CHANCE TO RUN BEFORE YOU CONJURE UP SOMEONE CALLED "BONEFLAYER"?
LAROXIMOUS BONEFLAYER. I CALL HIM LARRY, WHICH SHOULD GIVE YOU SOME IDEA OF HIS RELATIVE HARMLESSNESS. YOU'RE PERFECTLY SAFE--
FFFFSSHHHHHH

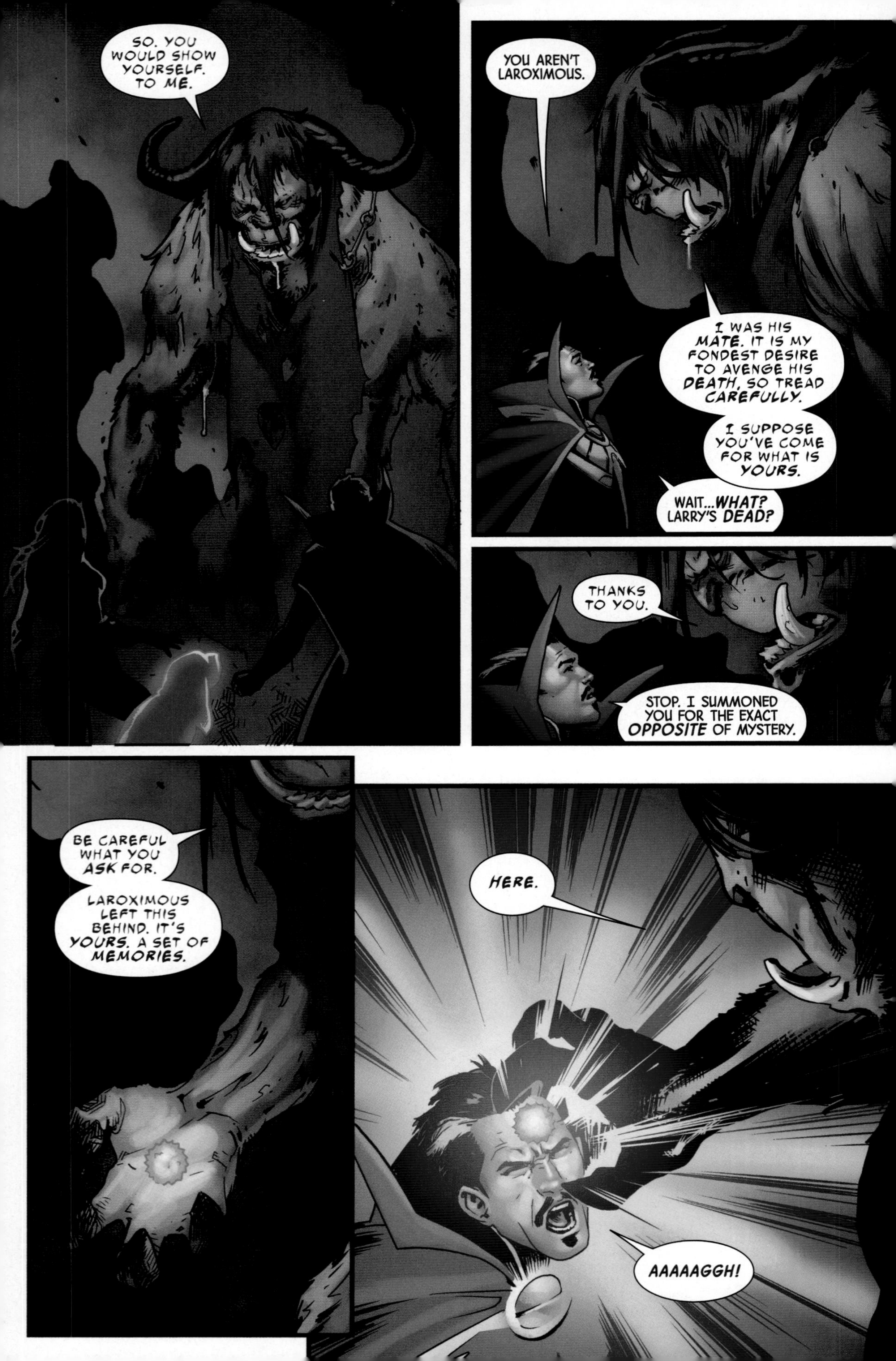
SO. YOU WOULD SHOW YOURSELF. TO ME.
YOU AREN'T LAROXIMOUS.
I WAS HIS MATE. IT IS MY FONDEST DESIRE TO AVENGE HIS DEATH, SO TREAD CAREFULLY.
I SUPPOSE YOU'VE COME FOR WHAT IS YOURS.
WAIT...WHAT? LARRY'S DEAD?
THANKS TO YOU.
STOP. I SUMMONED YOU FOR THE EXACT OPPOSITE OF MYSTERY.
BE CAREFUL WHAT YOU ASK FOR.
LAROXIMOUS LEFT THIS BEHIND. IT'S YOURS. A SET OF MEMORIES.
HERE.
AAAAAGGH!

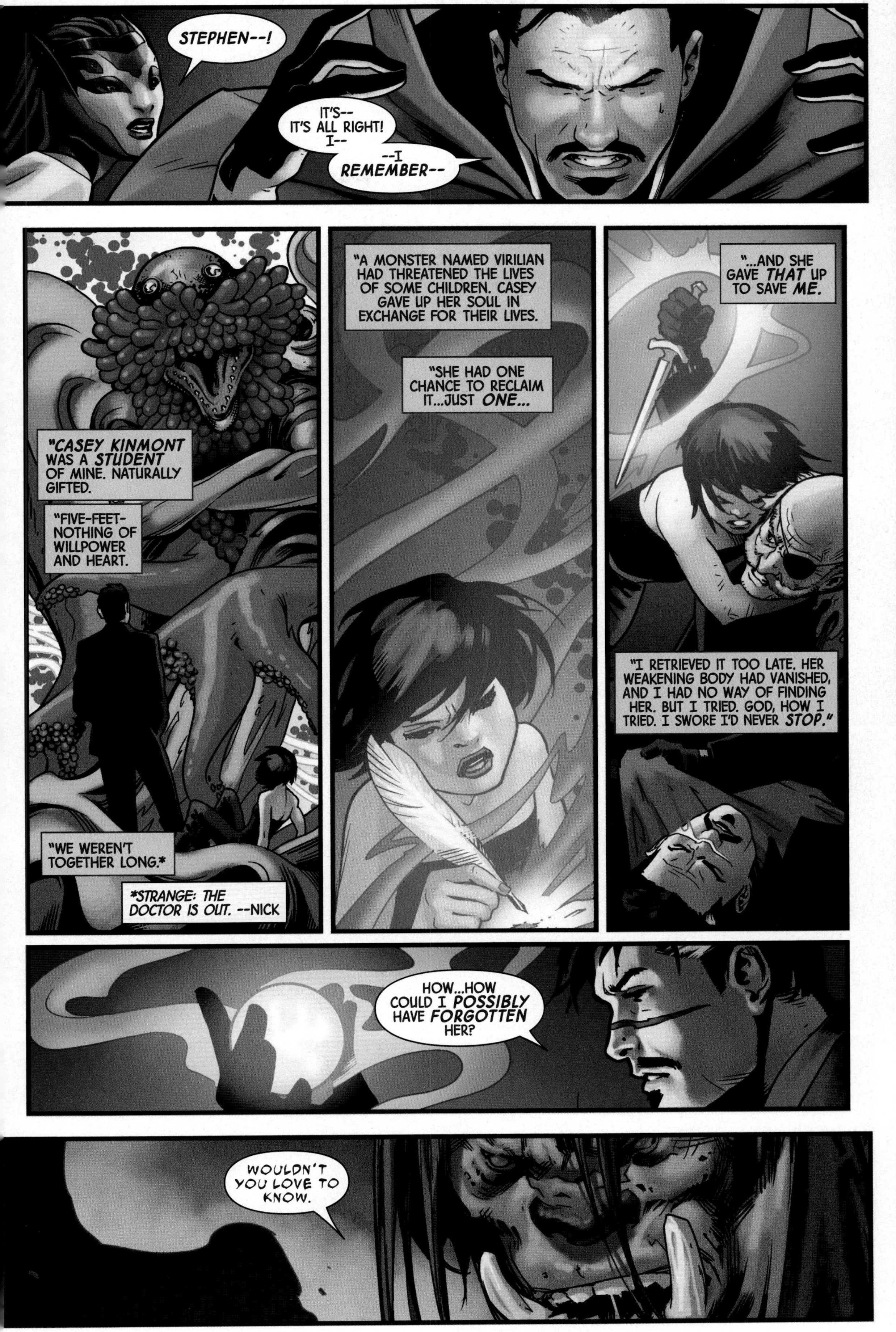
STEPHEN--!
IT'S-- IT'S ALL RIGHT! I--
--I REMEMBER--
"CASEY KINMONT WAS A STUDENT OF MINE. NATURALLY GIFTED.
"FIVE-FEET-NOTHING OF WILLPOWER AND HEART.
"WE WEREN'T TOGETHER LONG.*
*STRANGE: THE DOCTOR IS OUT. --NICK
"A MONSTER NAMED VIRILIAN HAD THREATENED THE LIVES OF SOME CHILDREN. CASEY GAVE UP HER SOUL IN EXCHANGE FOR THEIR LIVES.
"SHE HAD ONE CHANCE TO RECLAIM IT...JUST ONE...
"...AND SHE GAVE THAT UP TO SAVE ME.
"I RETRIEVED IT TOO LATE. HER WEAKENING BODY HAD VANISHED, AND I HAD NO WAY OF FINDING HER. BUT I TRIED. GOD, HOW I TRIED. I SWORE I'D NEVER STOP."
HOW...HOW COULD I POSSIBLY HAVE FORGOTTEN HER?
WOULDN'T YOU LOVE TO KNOW.

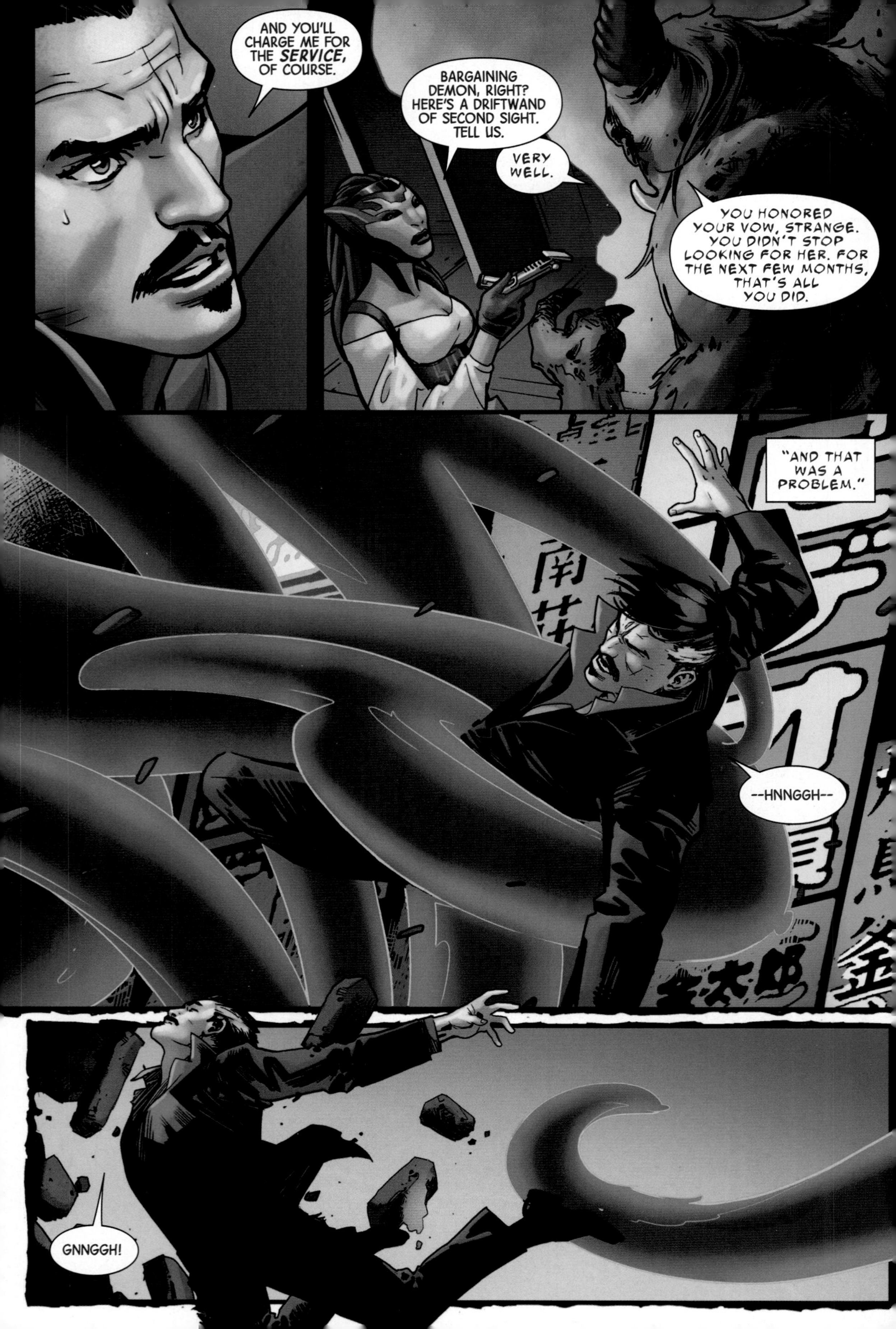
AND YOU'LL CHARGE ME FOR THE SERVICE, OF COURSE.
BARGAINING DEMON, RIGHT? HERE'S A DRIFTWAND OF SECOND SIGHT. TELL US.
VERY WELL.
YOU HONORED YOUR VOW, STRANGE. YOU DIDN'T STOP LOOKING FOR HER. FOR THE NEXT FEW MONTHS, THAT'S ALL YOU DID.
"AND THAT WAS A PROBLEM."
--HNNGGH--
GNNGGH!

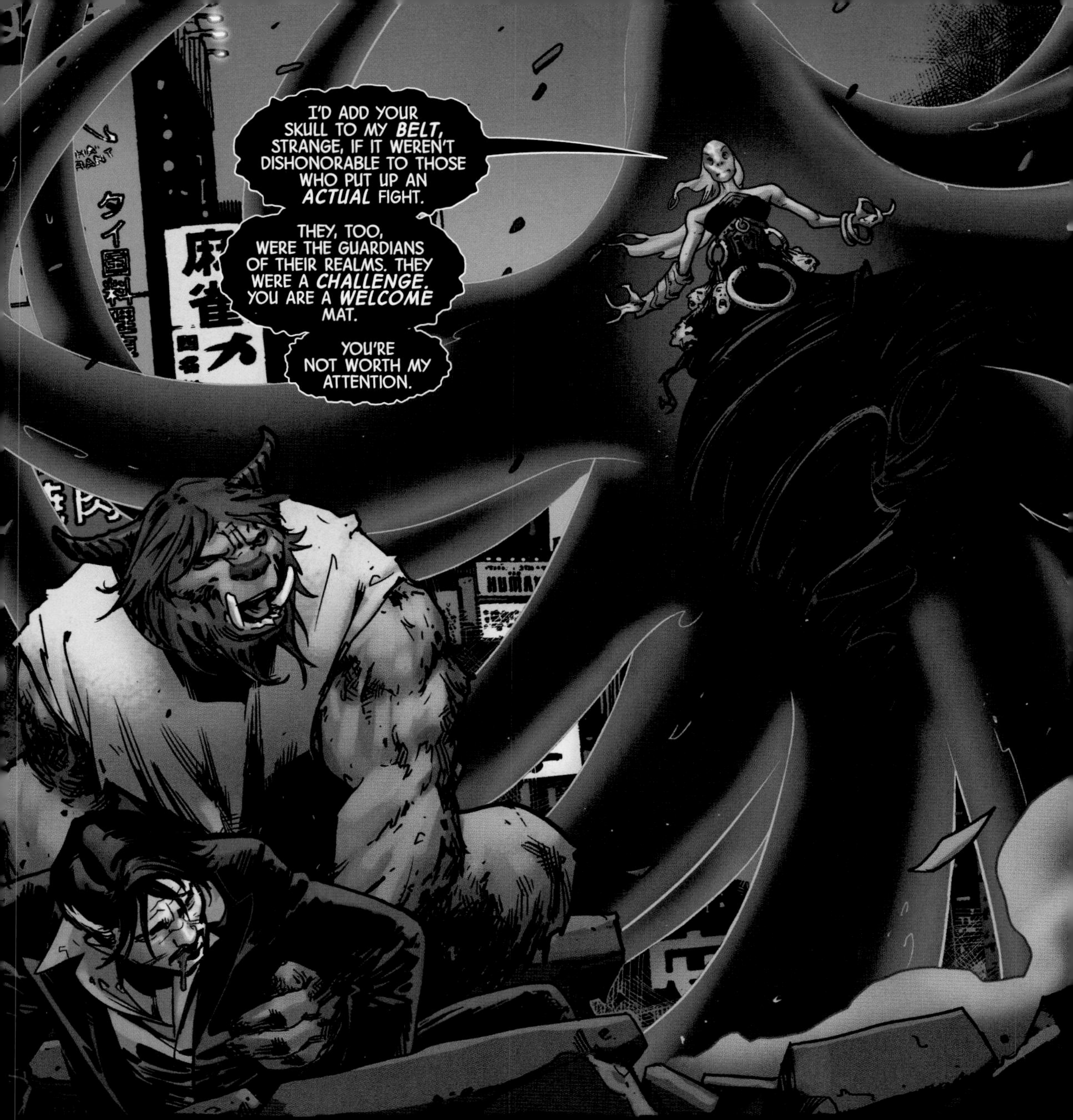
I'D ADD YOUR SKULL TO MY BELT, STRANGE, IF IT WEREN'T DISHONORABLE TO THOSE WHO PUT UP AN ACTUAL FIGHT.
THEY, TOO, WERE THE GUARDIANS OF THEIR REALMS. THEY WERE A CHALLENGE. YOU ARE A WELCOME MAT.
YOU'RE NOT WORTH MY ATTENTION.
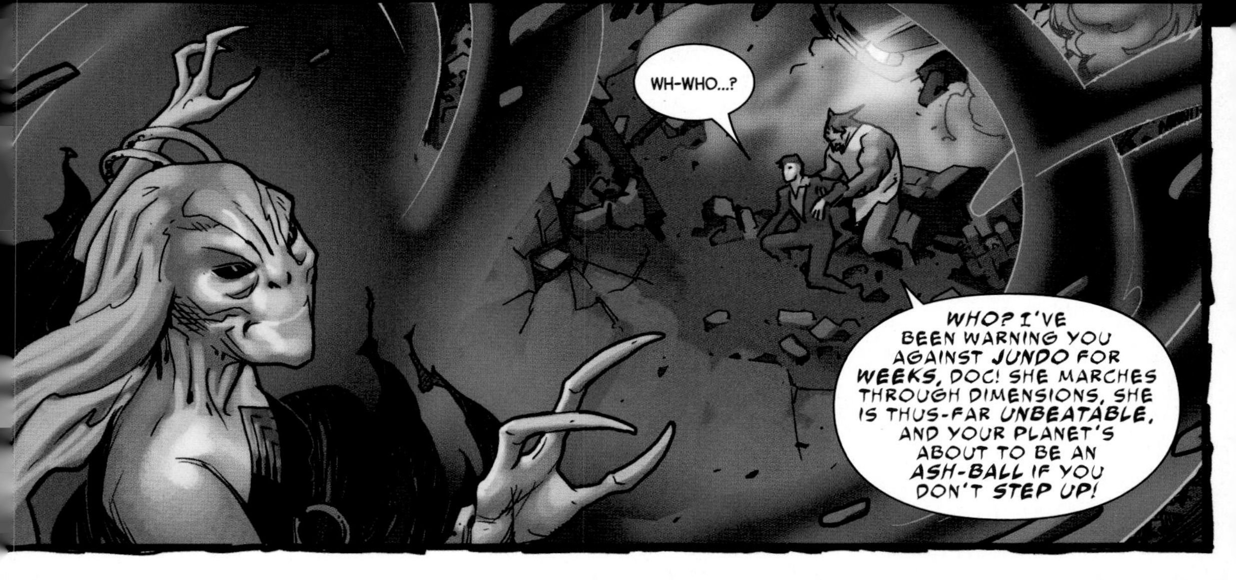
WH-WHO...?
WHO? I'VE BEEN WARNING YOU AGAINST JUNDO FOR WEEKS, DOC! SHE MARCHES THROUGH DIMENSIONS, SHE IS THUS-FAR UNBEATABLE, AND YOUR PLANET'S ABOUT TO BE AN ASH-BALL IF YOU DON'T STEP UP!

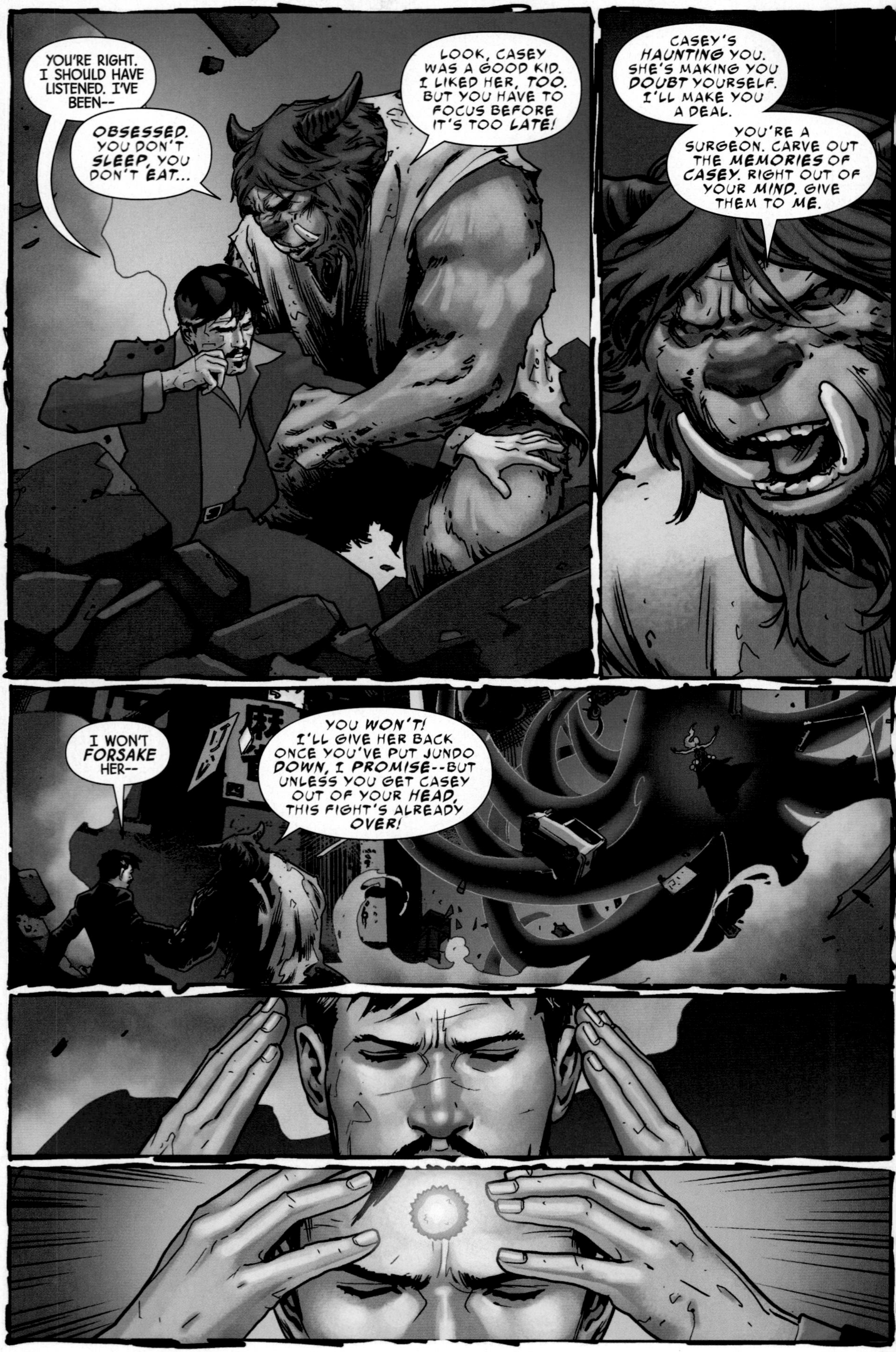
YOU'RE RIGHT. I SHOULD HAVE LISTENED. I'VE BEEN--
OBSESSED. YOU DON'T SLEEP, YOU DON'T EAT...
LOOK, CASEY WAS A GOOD KID. I LIKED HER, TOO. BUT YOU HAVE TO FOCUS BEFORE IT'S TOO LATE!
CASEY'S HAUNTING YOU. SHE'S MAKING YOU DOUBT YOURSELF. I'LL MAKE YOU A DEAL.
YOU'RE A SURGEON. CARVE OUT THE MEMORIES OF CASEY. RIGHT OUT OF YOUR MIND. GIVE THEM TO ME.
I WON'T FORSAKE HER--
YOU WON'T! I'LL GIVE HER BACK ONCE YOU'VE PUT JUNDO DOWN, I PROMISE--BUT UNLESS YOU GET CASEY OUT OF YOUR HEAD, THIS FIGHT'S ALREADY OVER!

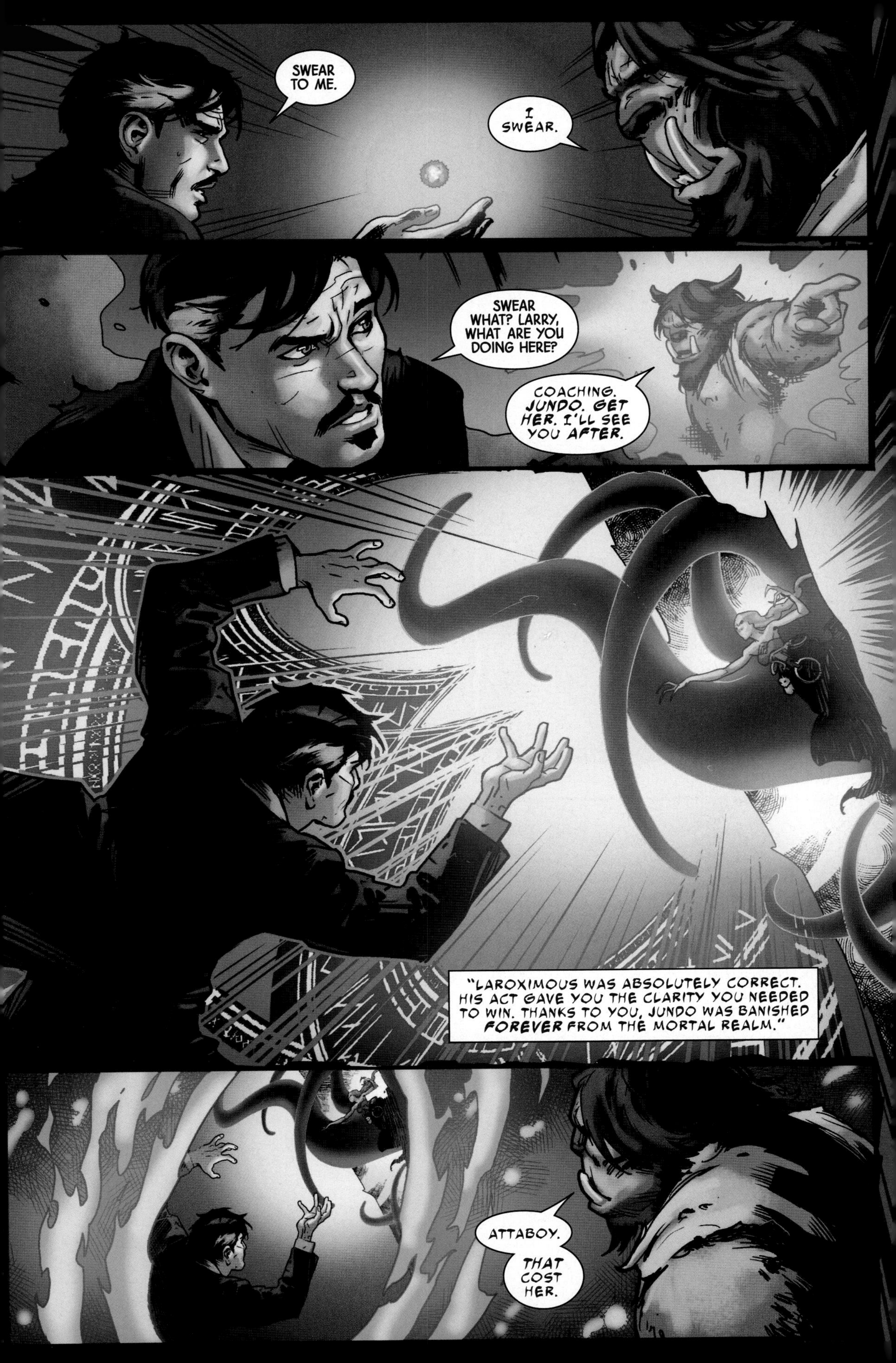
SWEAR TO ME.
I SWEAR.
SWEAR WHAT? LARRY, WHAT ARE YOU DOING HERE?
COACHING. JUNDO. GET HER. I'LL SEE YOU AFTER.
"LAROXIMOUS WAS ABSOLUTELY CORRECT. HIS ACT GAVE YOU THE CLARITY YOU NEEDED TO WIN. THANKS TO YOU, JUNDO WAS BANISHED FOREVER FROM THE MORTAL REALM."
ATTABOY.
THAT COST HER.

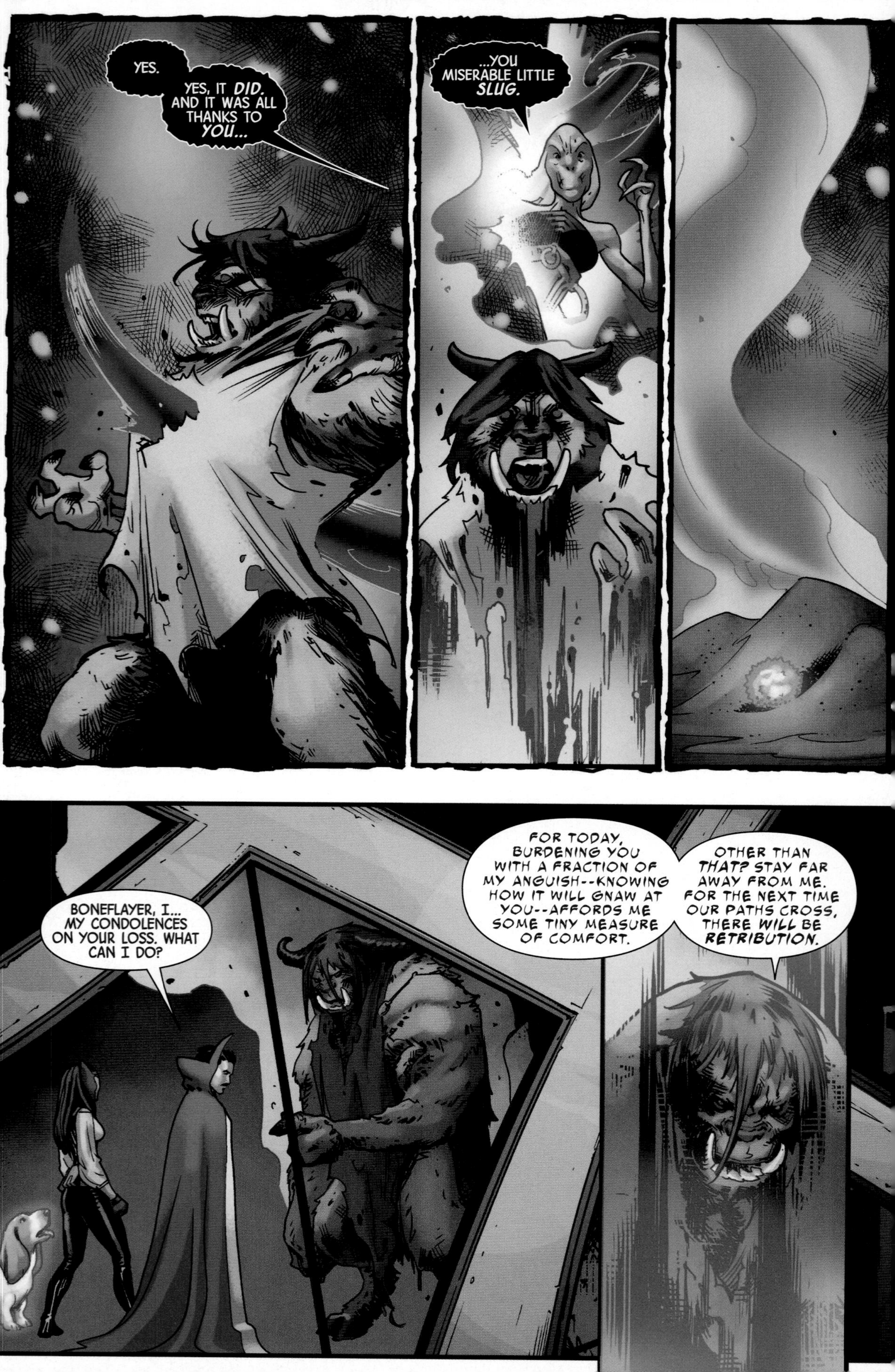
YES.
YES, IT DID. AND IT WAS ALL THANKS TO YOU...
...YOU MISERABLE LITTLE SLUG.
BONEFLAYER, I... MY CONDOLENCES ON YOUR LOSS. WHAT CAN I DO?
FOR TODAY, BURDENING YOU WITH A FRACTION OF MY ANGUISH--KNOWING HOW IT WILL GNAW AT YOU--AFFORDS ME SOME TINY MEASURE OF COMFORT.
OTHER THAN THAT? STAY FAR AWAY FROM ME. FOR THE NEXT TIME OUR PATHS CROSS, THERE WILL BE RETRIBUTION.

THAT WAS SOME TIME AGO. LARRY NEVER GOT THE **OPPORTUNITY** TO GIVE ME MY MEMORIES BACK.

NO **WONDER** CASEY IS ACTING OUT. SHE BELIEVES I **ABANDONED** HER-- AND WHO COULD BLAME HER?

WHAT HAPPENED TO HER IN ALL THAT TIME? HOW DID SHE **RETURN?**

YOU SAID HER BODY HAD VANISHED?

HAD BEEN **ACQUIRED,** MORE ACCURATELY. BY A DEMON NAMED **BAROSHTOK** WHOM SHE'D CROSSED. HE SEALED THE BRIDGE BETWEEN OUR REALM AND HIS, LEFT ME NO PATH OF RETRIEVAL--

BUT IF SHE'S **BACK,** IT'S NO LONGER **SEALED.** WHY DON'T I INVESTIGATE THAT LEAD-- SEE IF THIS "BAROSHTOK" CAN GIVE US ANY ANSWERS.

THANK YOU. HE'S UNPLEASANT, BUT HE WOULD HAVE BEEN THE LAST TO SEE CASEY BEFORE THIS.

HERE ARE DIRECTIONS THAT SHOULD TAKE YOU TO HIM.

GOT IT. YOU WANT TO COME **WITH** IN CASE I NEED SOME BACKUP?

IT'S THE LEAST I CAN DO. GIVEN THAT I AM A **DOG,** THAT'S A LOW BAR, BUT...

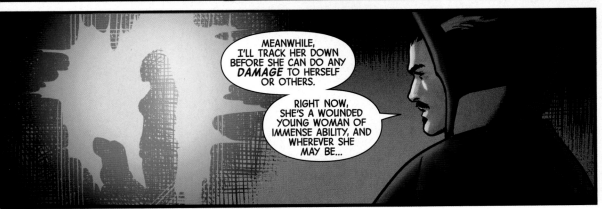

MEANWHILE, I'LL TRACK HER DOWN BEFORE SHE CAN DO ANY **DAMAGE** TO HERSELF OR OTHERS.

RIGHT NOW, SHE'S A WOUNDED YOUNG WOMAN OF IMMENSE ABILITY, AND WHEREVER SHE MAY BE...

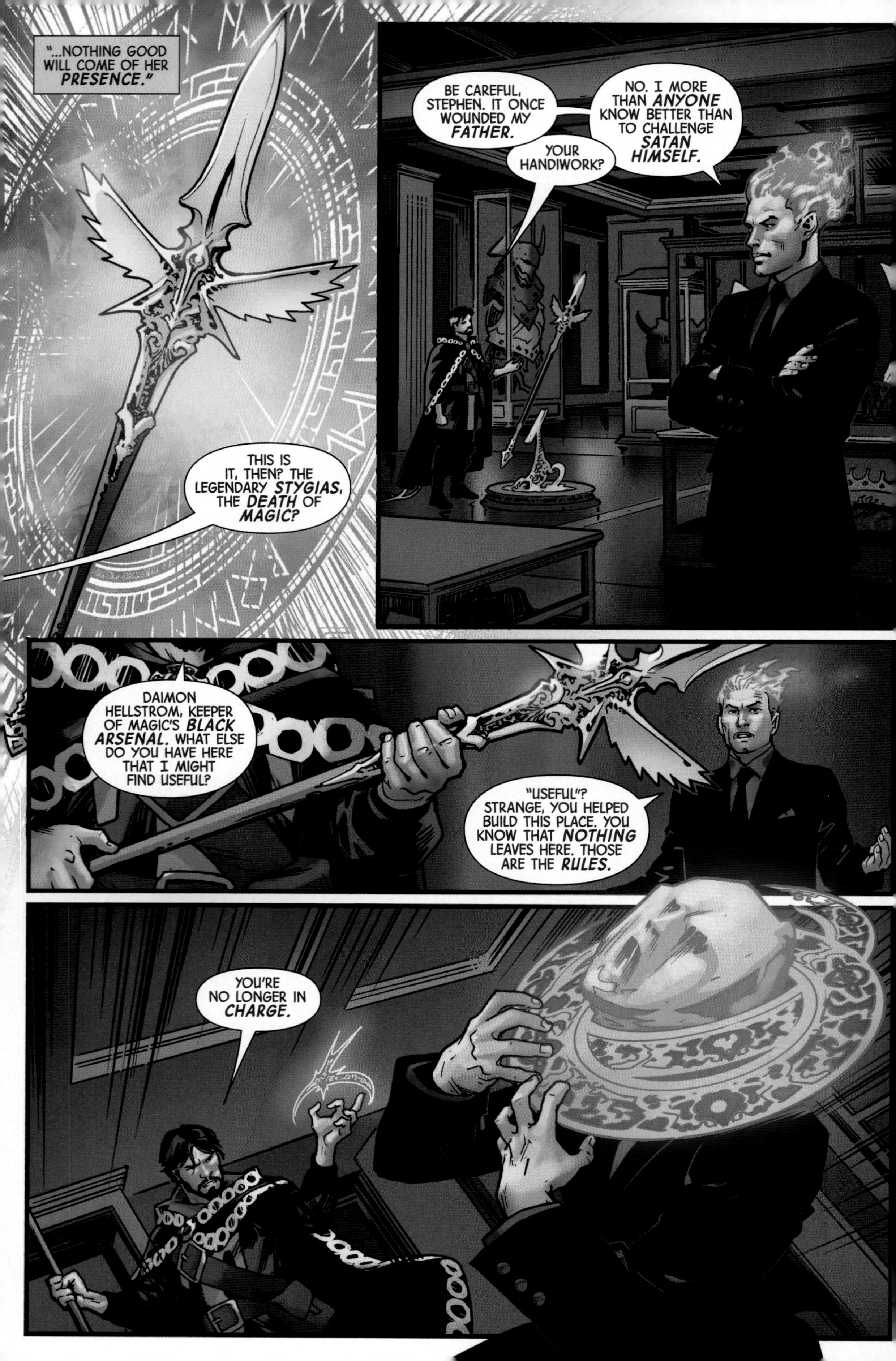
"...NOTHING GOOD WILL COME OF HER PRESENCE."
BE CAREFUL, STEPHEN. IT ONCE WOUNDED MY FATHER.
NO. I MORE THAN ANYONE KNOW BETTER THAN TO CHALLENGE SATAN HIMSELF.
YOUR HANDIWORK?
THIS IS IT, THEN? THE LEGENDARY STYGIAS, THE DEATH OF MAGIC?
DAIMON HELLSTROM, KEEPER OF MAGIC'S BLACK ARSENAL. WHAT ELSE DO YOU HAVE HERE THAT I MIGHT FIND USEFUL?
"USEFUL"? STRANGE, YOU HELPED BUILD THIS PLACE. YOU KNOW THAT NOTHING LEAVES HERE. THOSE ARE THE RULES.
YOU'RE NO LONGER IN CHARGE.

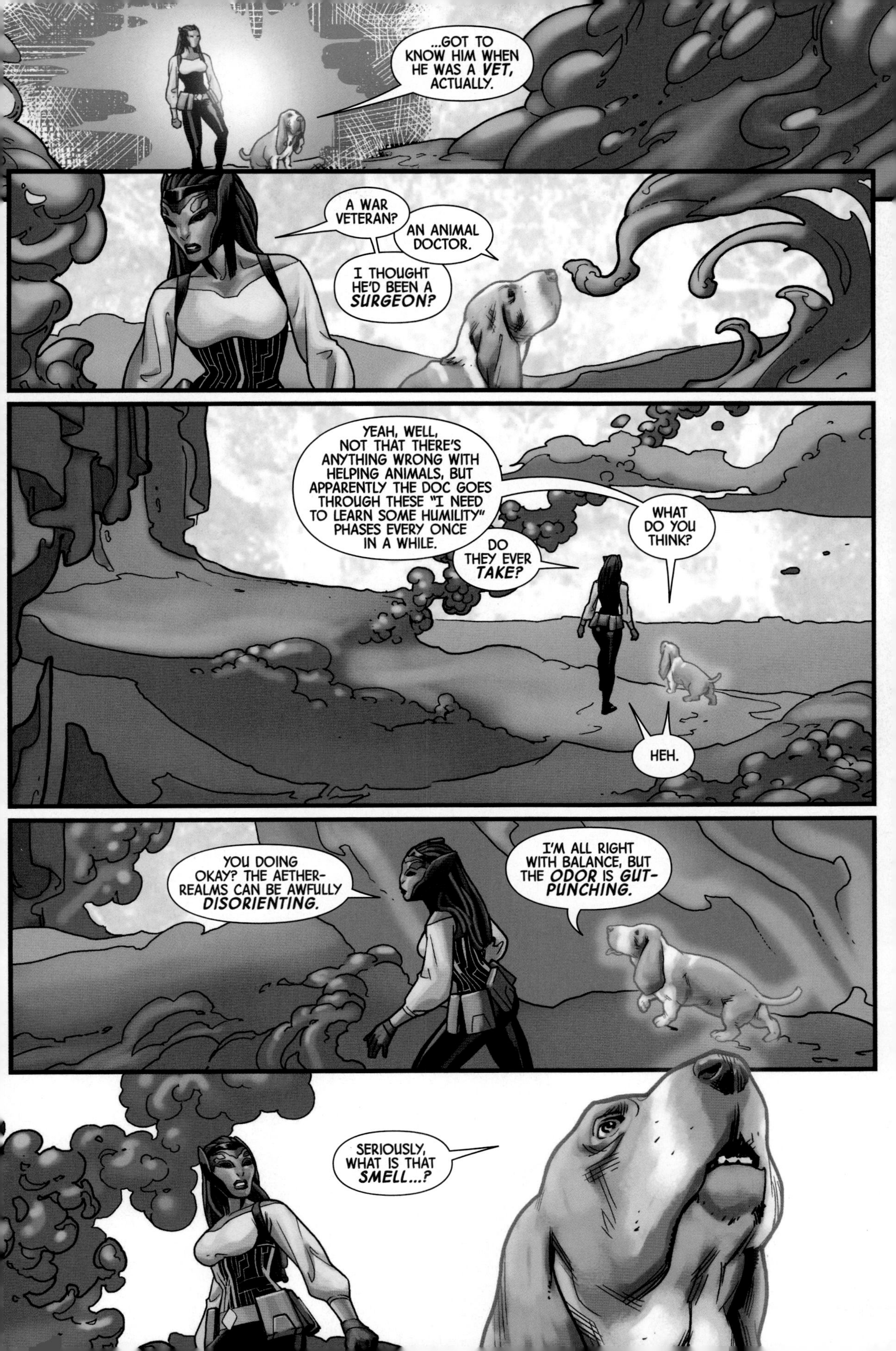
...GOT TO KNOW HIM WHEN HE WAS A VET, ACTUALLY.
A WAR VETERAN?
AN ANIMAL DOCTOR.
I THOUGHT HE'D BEEN A SURGEON?
YEAH, WELL, NOT THAT THERE'S ANYTHING WRONG WITH HELPING ANIMALS, BUT APPARENTLY THE DOC GOES THROUGH THESE "I NEED TO LEARN SOME HUMILITY" PHASES EVERY ONCE IN A WHILE.
DO THEY EVER TAKE?
WHAT DO YOU THINK?
HEH.
YOU DOING OKAY? THE AETHER-REALMS CAN BE AWFULLY DISORIENTING.
I'M ALL RIGHT WITH BALANCE, BUT THE ODOR IS GUT-PUNCHING.
SERIOUSLY, WHAT IS THAT SMELL...?

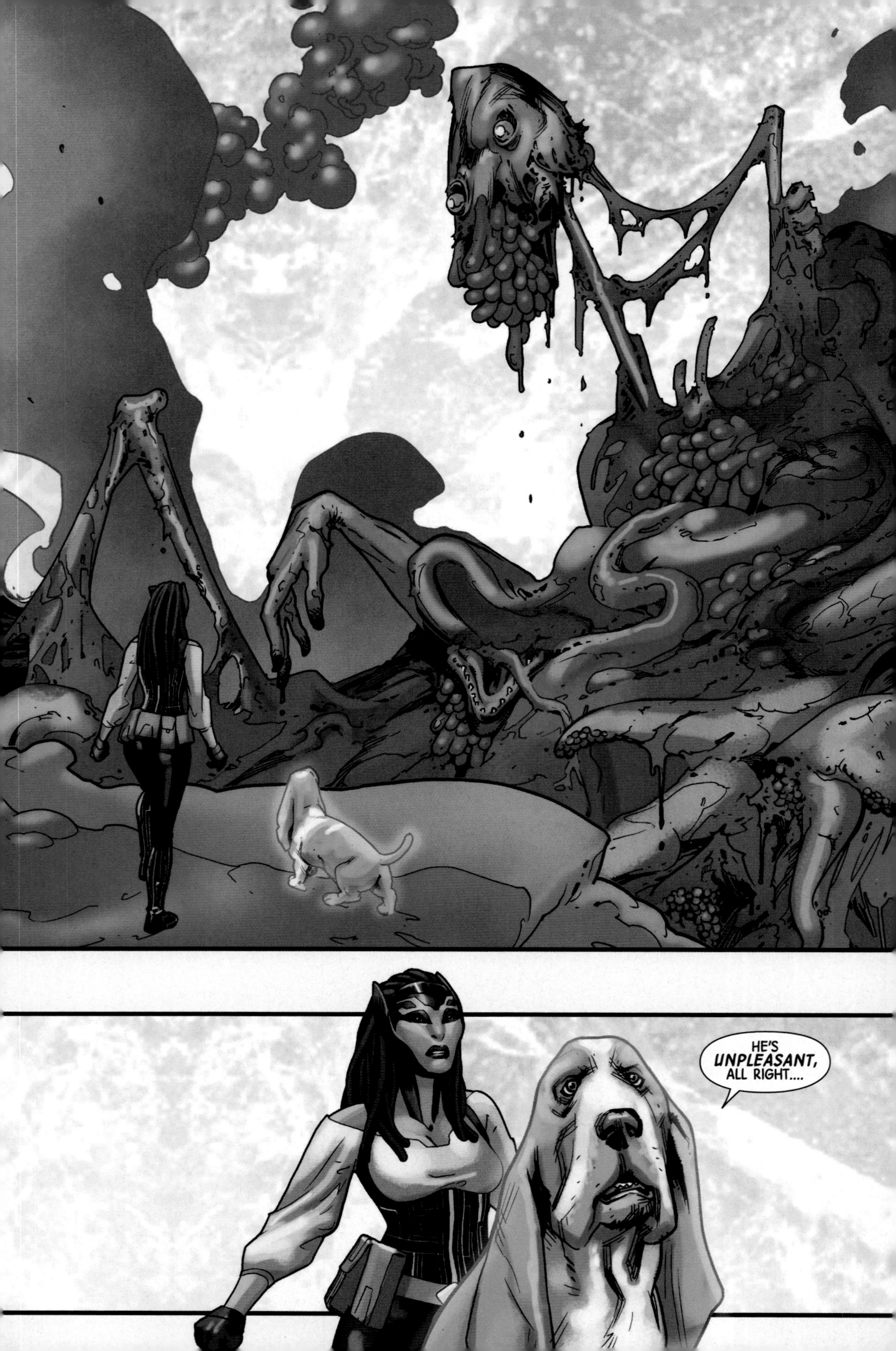
HE'S *UNPLEASANT,* ALL RIGHT....

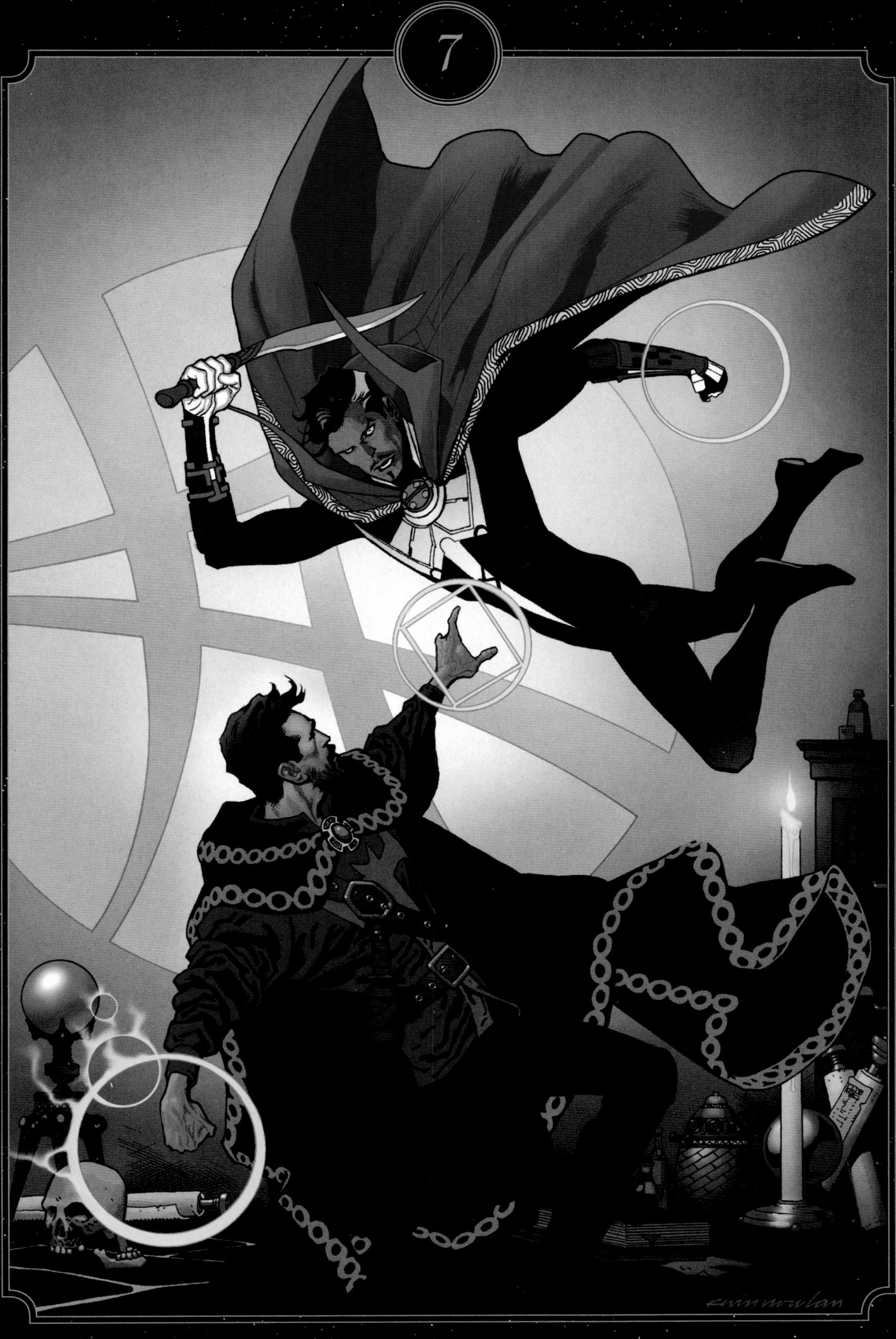
7
kevin nowlan

The Two Doctors PART TWO

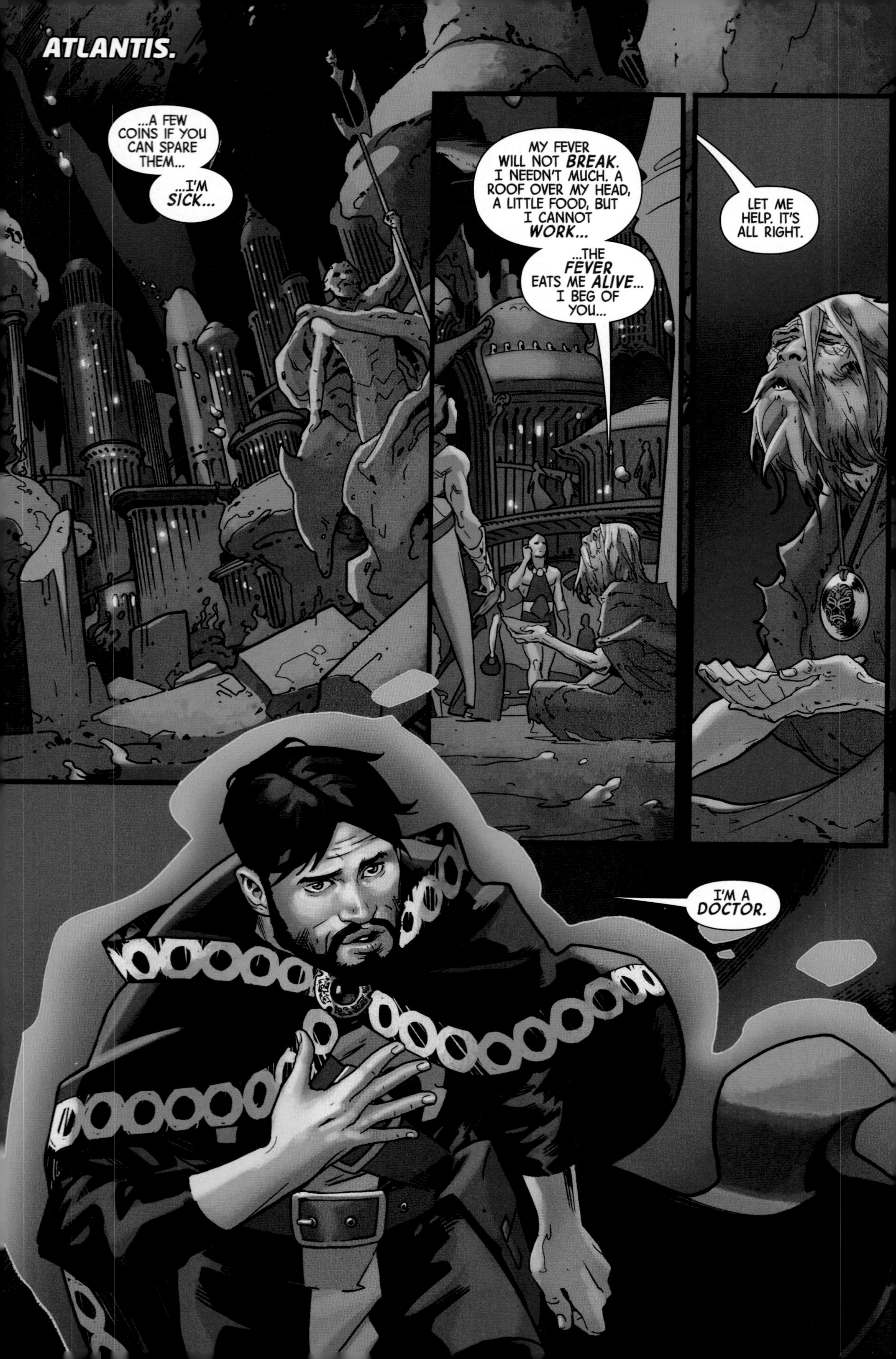
ATLANTIS.
...A FEW COINS IF YOU CAN SPARE THEM...
...I'M SICK...
MY FEVER WILL NOT BREAK. I NEEDN'T MUCH. A ROOF OVER MY HEAD, A LITTLE FOOD, BUT I CANNOT WORK...
...THE FEVER EATS ME ALIVE... I BEG OF YOU...
LET ME HELP. IT'S ALL RIGHT.
I'M A DOCTOR.

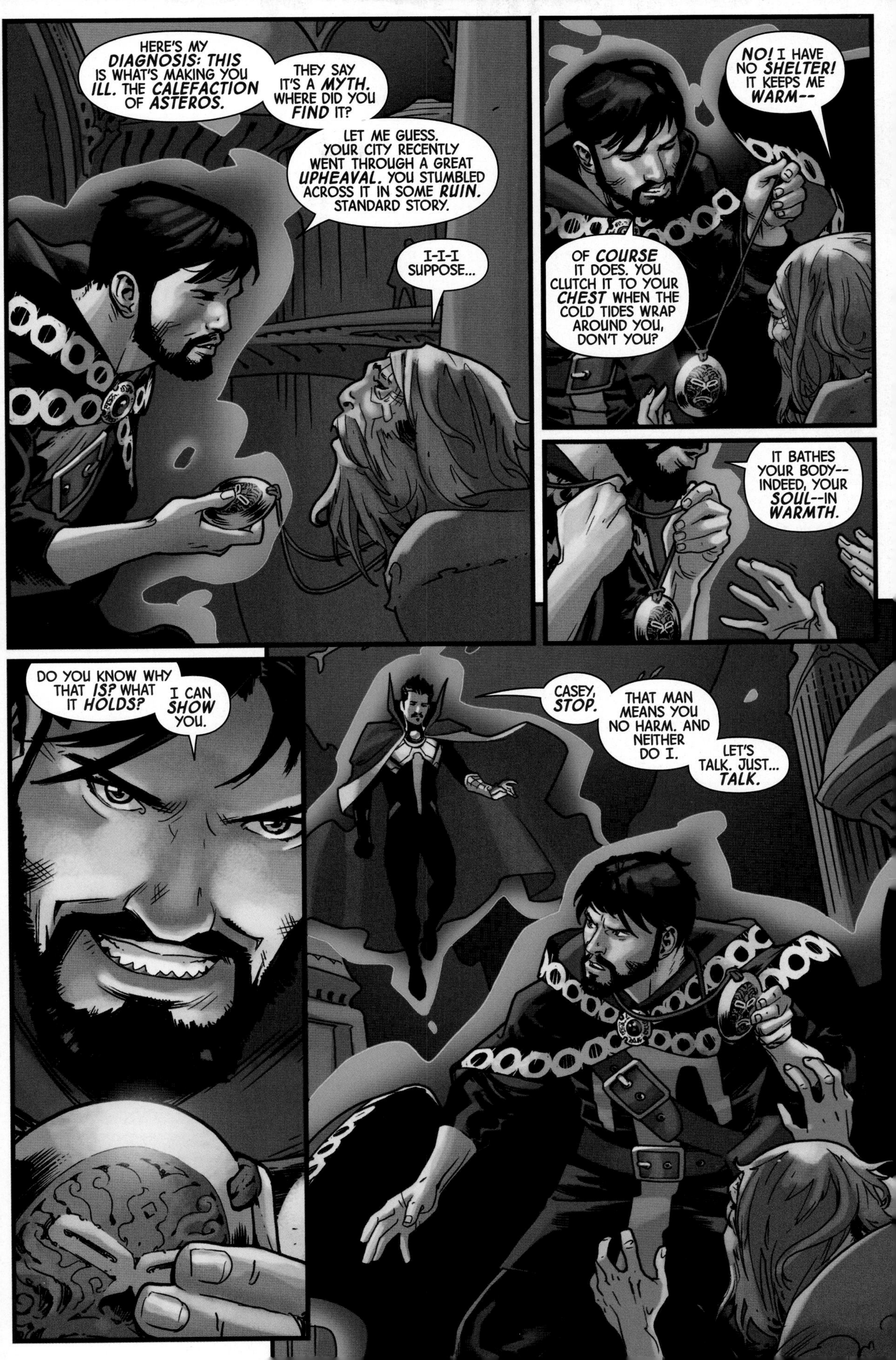
HERE'S MY DIAGNOSIS: THIS IS WHAT'S MAKING YOU ILL. THE CALEFACTION OF ASTEROS.
THEY SAY IT'S A MYTH. WHERE DID YOU FIND IT?
LET ME GUESS. YOUR CITY RECENTLY WENT THROUGH A GREAT UPHEAVAL. YOU STUMBLED ACROSS IT IN SOME RUIN. STANDARD STORY.
I-I-I SUPPOSE...
NO! I HAVE NO SHELTER! IT KEEPS ME WARM--
OF COURSE IT DOES. YOU CLUTCH IT TO YOUR CHEST WHEN THE COLD TIDES WRAP AROUND YOU, DON'T YOU?
IT BATHES YOUR BODY-- INDEED, YOUR SOUL--IN WARMTH.
DO YOU KNOW WHY THAT IS? WHAT IT HOLDS?
I CAN SHOW YOU.
CASEY, STOP.
THAT MAN MEANS YOU NO HARM. AND NEITHER DO I.
LET'S TALK. JUST... TALK.

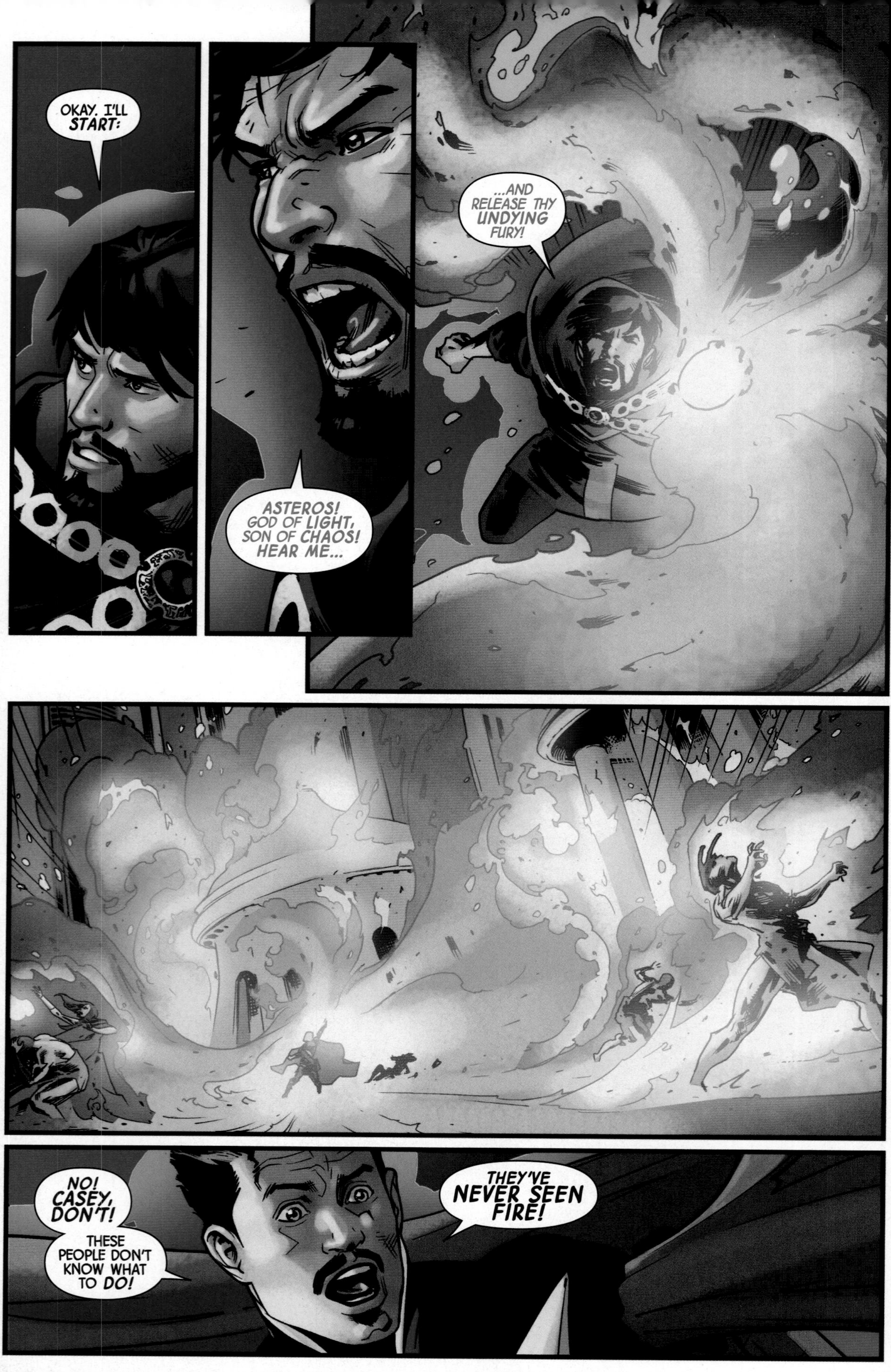
OKAY. I'LL START:
ASTEROS! GOD OF LIGHT, SON OF CHAOS! HEAR ME...
...AND RELEASE THY UNDYING FURY!
NO! CASEY, DON'T!
THESE PEOPLE DON'T KNOW WHAT TO DO!
THEY'VE NEVER SEEN FIRE!

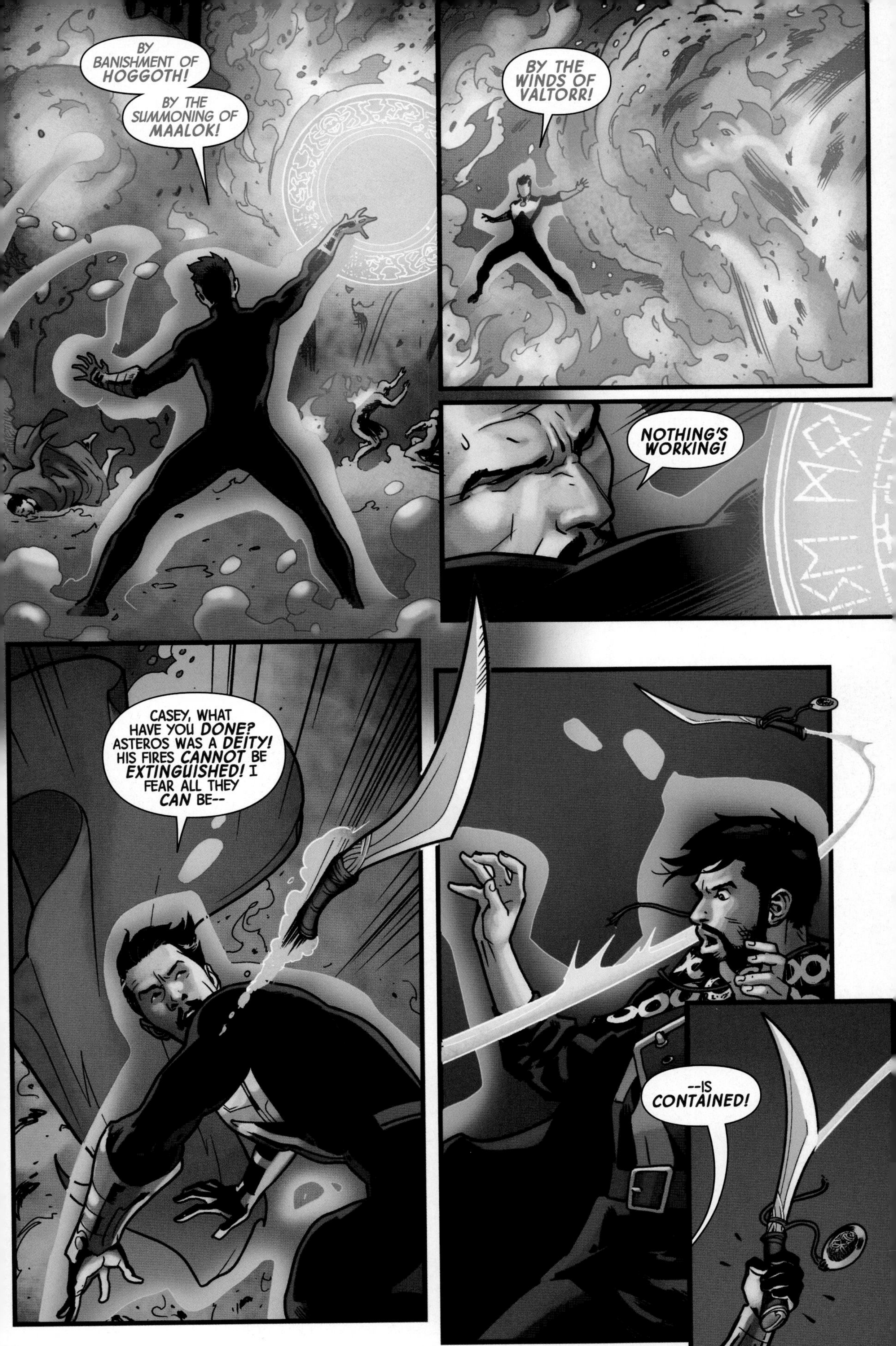
BY BANISHMENT OF HOGGOTH!
BY THE SUMMONING OF MAALOK!
BY THE WINDS OF VALTORR!
NOTHING'S WORKING!
CASEY, WHAT HAVE YOU DONE? ASTEROS WAS A DEITY! HIS FIRES CANNOT BE EXTINGUISHED! I FEAR ALL THEY CAN BE--
--IS CONTAINED!

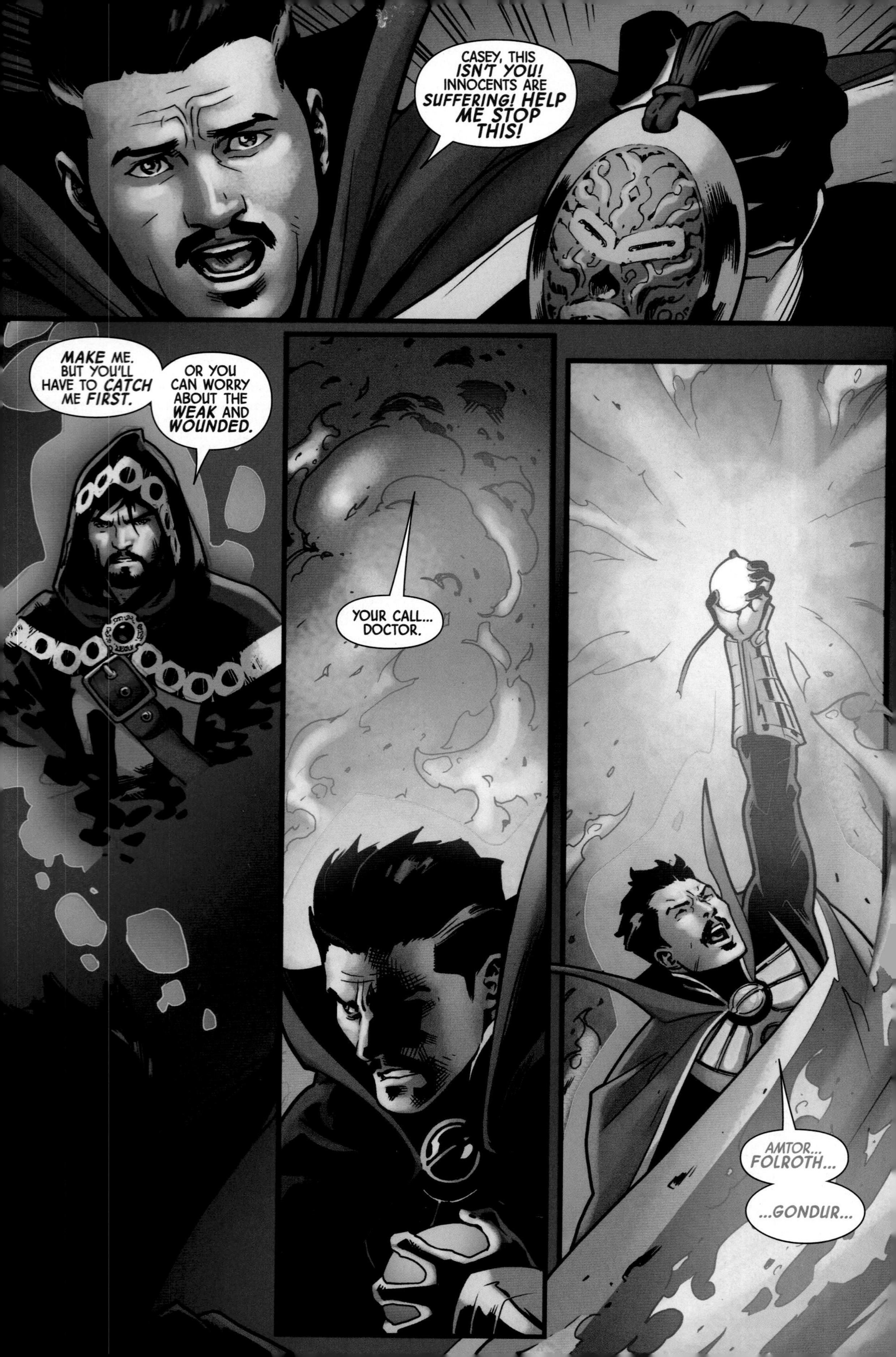
CASEY, THIS ISN'T YOU! INNOCENTS ARE SUFFERING! HELP ME STOP THIS!
MAKE ME. BUT YOU'LL HAVE TO CATCH ME FIRST.
OR YOU CAN WORRY ABOUT THE WEAK AND WOUNDED.
YOUR CALL... DOCTOR.
AMTOR... FOLROTH...
...GONDUR...

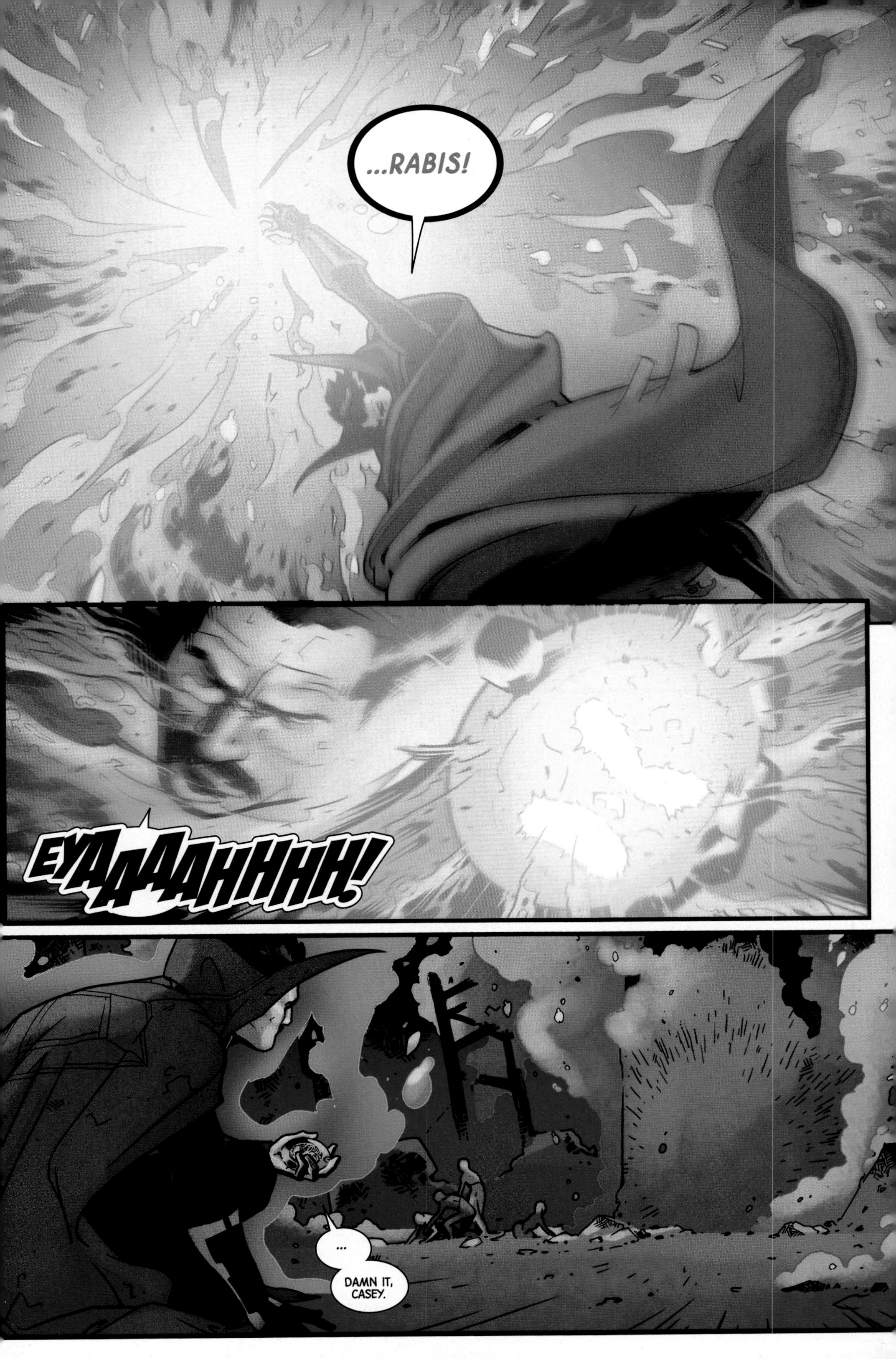
...RABIS!
EYAAAAHHHH!
...
DAMN IT, CASEY.

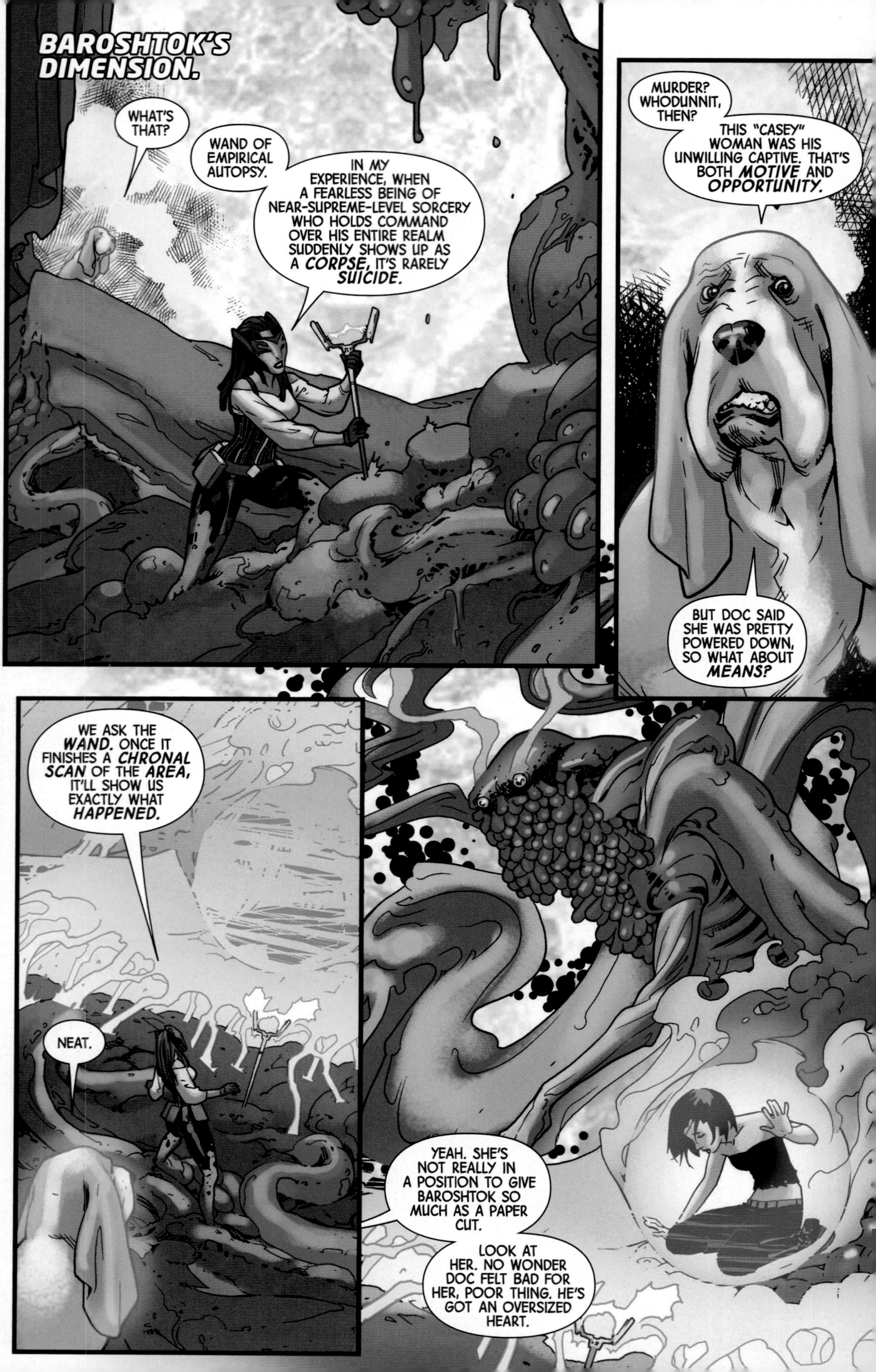
BAROSHTOK'S DIMENSION.
WHAT'S THAT?
WAND OF EMPIRICAL AUTOPSY.
IN MY EXPERIENCE, WHEN A FEARLESS BEING OF NEAR-SUPREME-LEVEL SORCERY WHO HOLDS COMMAND OVER HIS ENTIRE REALM SUDDENLY SHOWS UP AS A CORPSE, IT'S RARELY SUICIDE.
MURDER? WHODUNNIT, THEN?
THIS "CASEY" WOMAN WAS HIS UNWILLING CAPTIVE. THAT'S BOTH MOTIVE AND OPPORTUNITY.
BUT DOC SAID SHE WAS PRETTY POWERED DOWN, SO WHAT ABOUT MEANS?
WE ASK THE WAND. ONCE IT FINISHES A CHRONAL SCAN OF THE AREA, IT'LL SHOW US EXACTLY WHAT HAPPENED.
NEAT.
YEAH. SHE'S NOT REALLY IN A POSITION TO GIVE BAROSHTOK SO MUCH AS A PAPER CUT.
LOOK AT HER. NO WONDER DOC FELT BAD FOR HER, POOR THING. HE'S GOT AN OVERSIZED HEART.

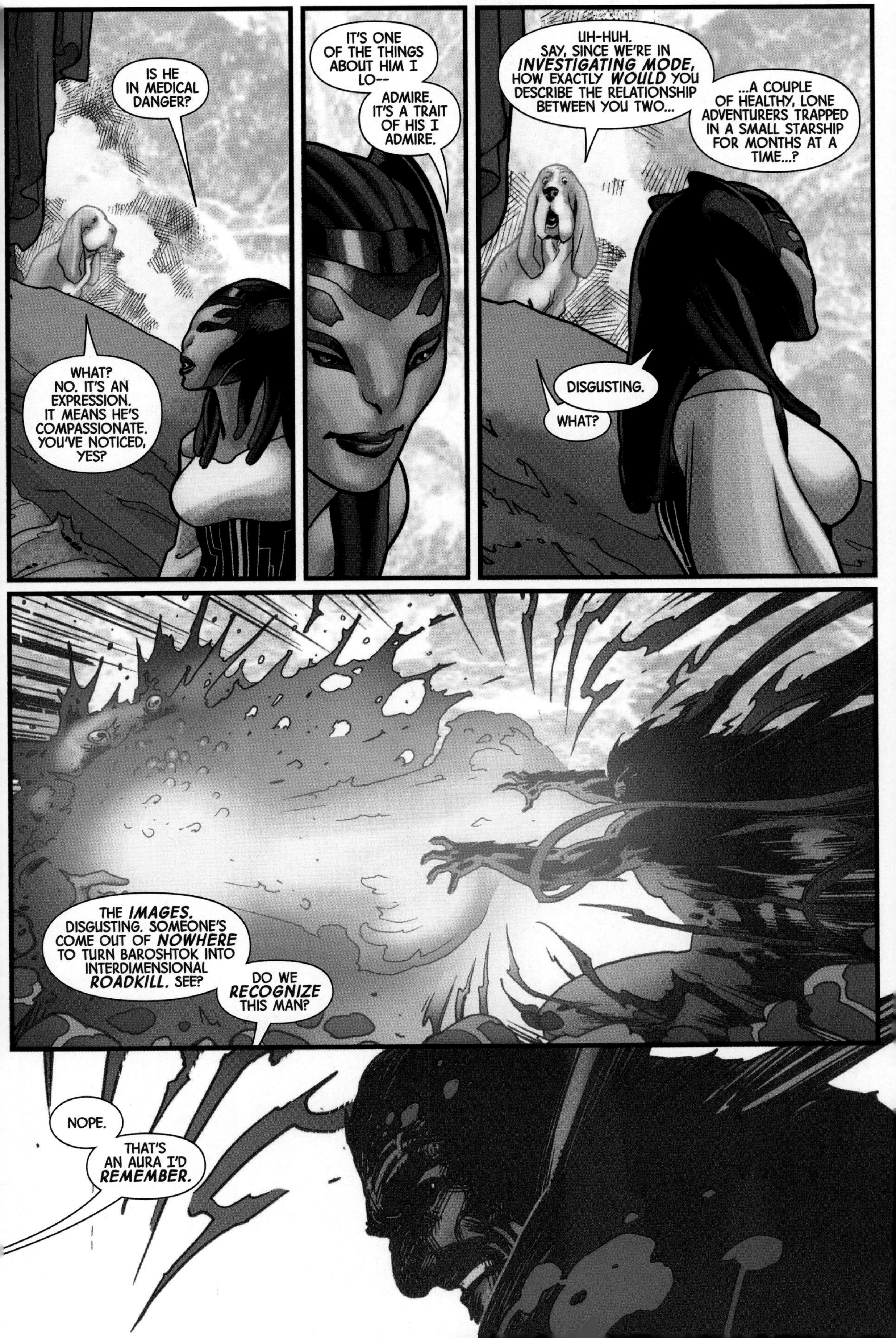
IS HE IN MEDICAL DANGER?
WHAT? NO. IT'S AN EXPRESSION. IT MEANS HE'S COMPASSIONATE. YOU'VE NOTICED, YES?
IT'S ONE OF THE THINGS ABOUT HIM I LO--
ADMIRE. IT'S A TRAIT OF HIS I ADMIRE.
UH-HUH. SAY, SINCE WE'RE IN INVESTIGATING MODE, HOW EXACTLY WOULD YOU DESCRIBE THE RELATIONSHIP BETWEEN YOU TWO...
...A COUPLE OF HEALTHY, LONE ADVENTURERS TRAPPED IN A SMALL STARSHIP FOR MONTHS AT A TIME...?
DISGUSTING.
WHAT?
THE IMAGES. DISGUSTING. SOMEONE'S COME OUT OF NOWHERE TO TURN BAROSHTOK INTO INTERDIMENSIONAL ROADKILL. SEE?
DO WE RECOGNIZE THIS MAN?
NOPE.
THAT'S AN AURA I'D REMEMBER.

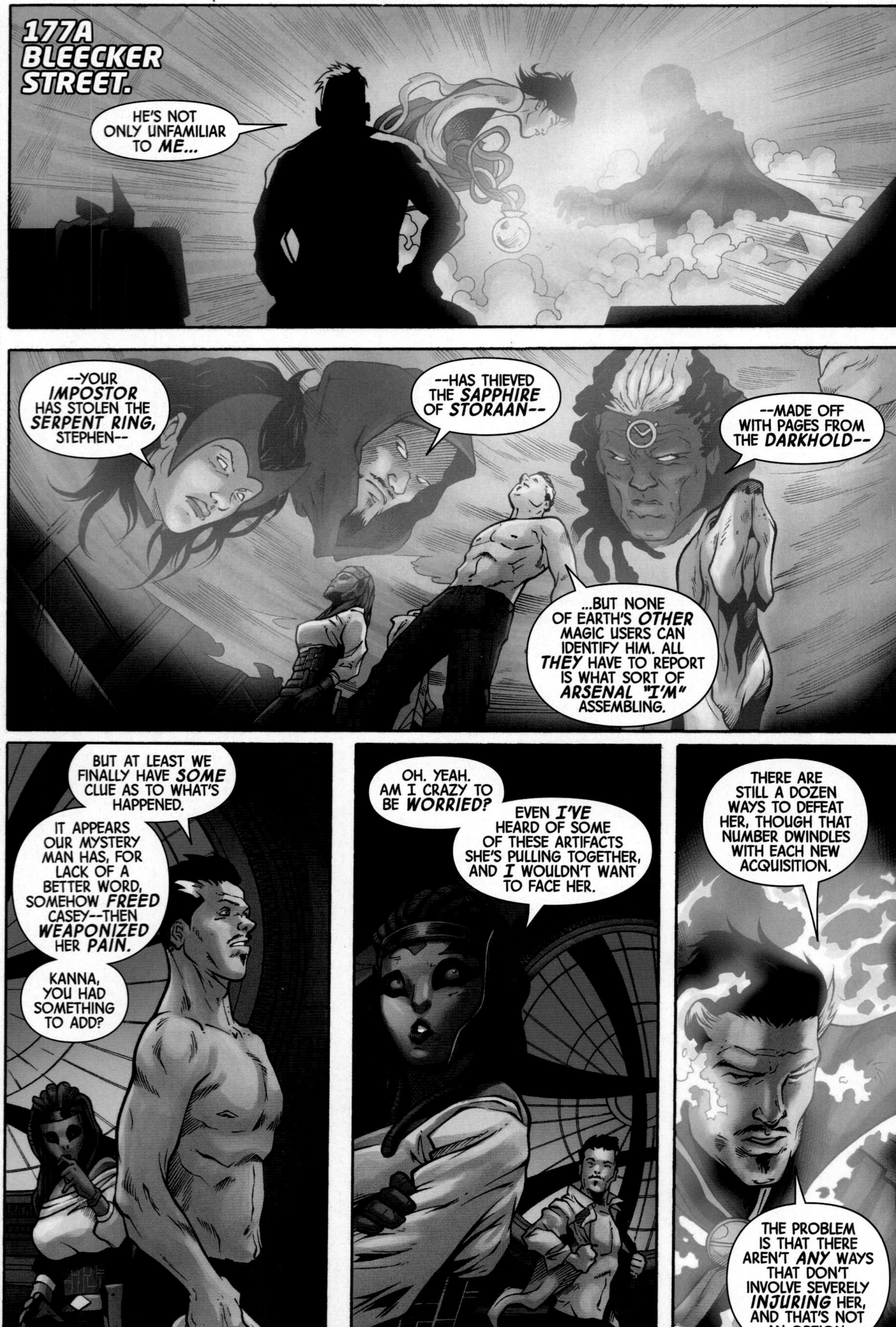
177A BLEECKER STREET.
HE'S NOT ONLY UNFAMILIAR TO ME...
--YOUR IMPOSTOR HAS STOLEN THE SERPENT RING, STEPHEN--
--HAS THIEVED THE SAPPHIRE OF STORAAN--
--MADE OFF WITH PAGES FROM THE DARKHOLD--
...BUT NONE OF EARTH'S OTHER MAGIC USERS CAN IDENTIFY HIM. ALL THEY HAVE TO REPORT IS WHAT SORT OF ARSENAL "I'M" ASSEMBLING.
BUT AT LEAST WE FINALLY HAVE SOME CLUE AS TO WHAT'S HAPPENED.
IT APPEARS OUR MYSTERY MAN HAS, FOR LACK OF A BETTER WORD, SOMEHOW FREED CASEY--THEN WEAPONIZED HER PAIN.
KANNA, YOU HAD SOMETHING TO ADD?
OH. YEAH. AM I CRAZY TO BE WORRIED?
EVEN I'VE HEARD OF SOME OF THESE ARTIFACTS SHE'S PULLING TOGETHER, AND I WOULDN'T WANT TO FACE HER.
THERE ARE STILL A DOZEN WAYS TO DEFEAT HER, THOUGH THAT NUMBER DWINDLES WITH EACH NEW ACQUISITION.
THE PROBLEM IS THAT THERE AREN'T ANY WAYS THAT DON'T INVOLVE SEVERELY INJURING HER, AND THAT'S NOT AN OPTION.

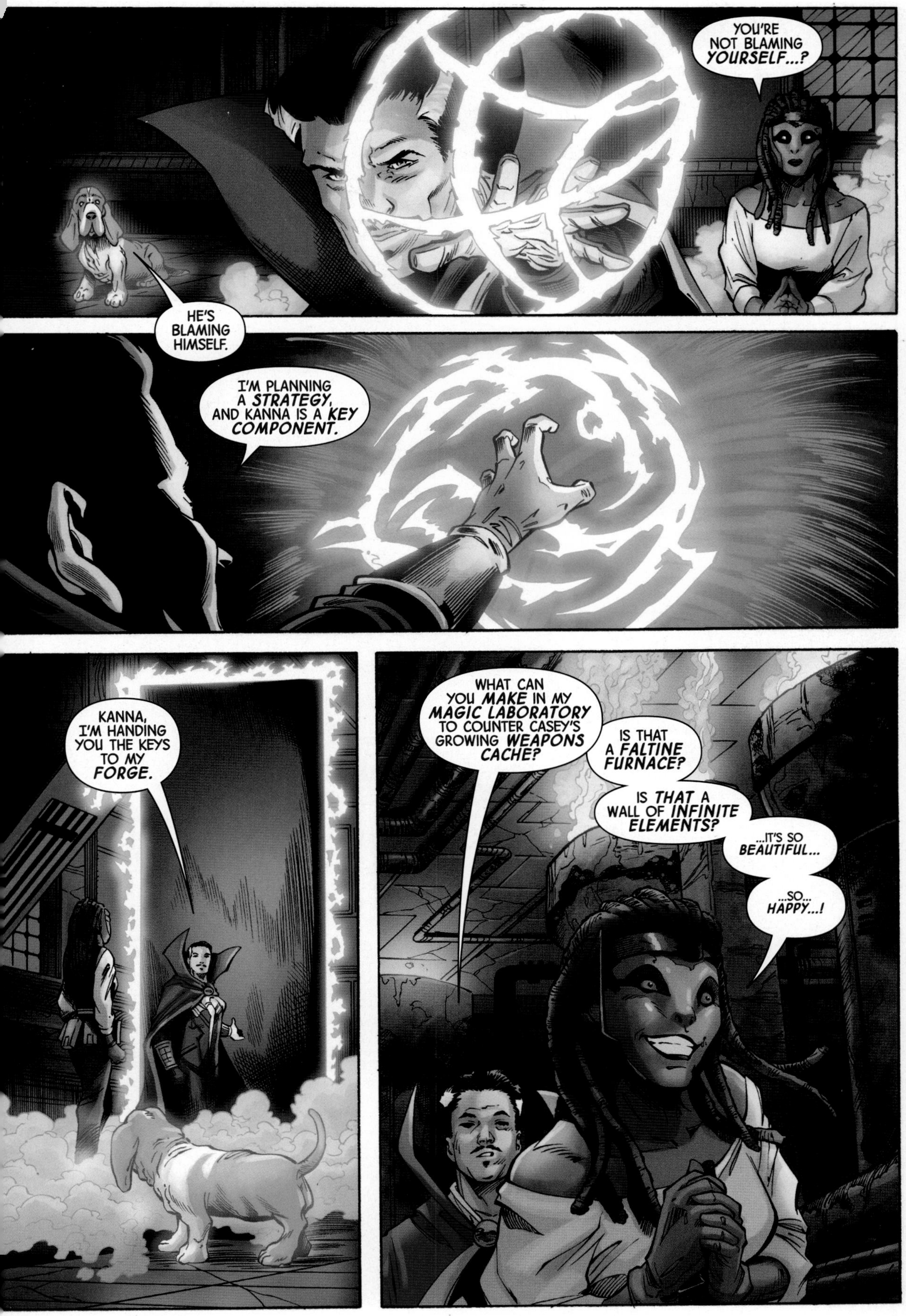
YOU'RE NOT BLAMING YOURSELF...?
HE'S BLAMING HIMSELF.
I'M PLANNING A STRATEGY, AND KANNA IS A KEY COMPONENT.
KANNA, I'M HANDING YOU THE KEYS TO MY FORGE.
WHAT CAN YOU MAKE IN MY MAGIC LABORATORY TO COUNTER CASEY'S GROWING WEAPONS CACHE?
IS THAT A FALTINE FURNACE?
IS THAT A WALL OF INFINITE ELEMENTS?
...IT'S SO BEAUTIFUL...
...SO... HAPPY...!

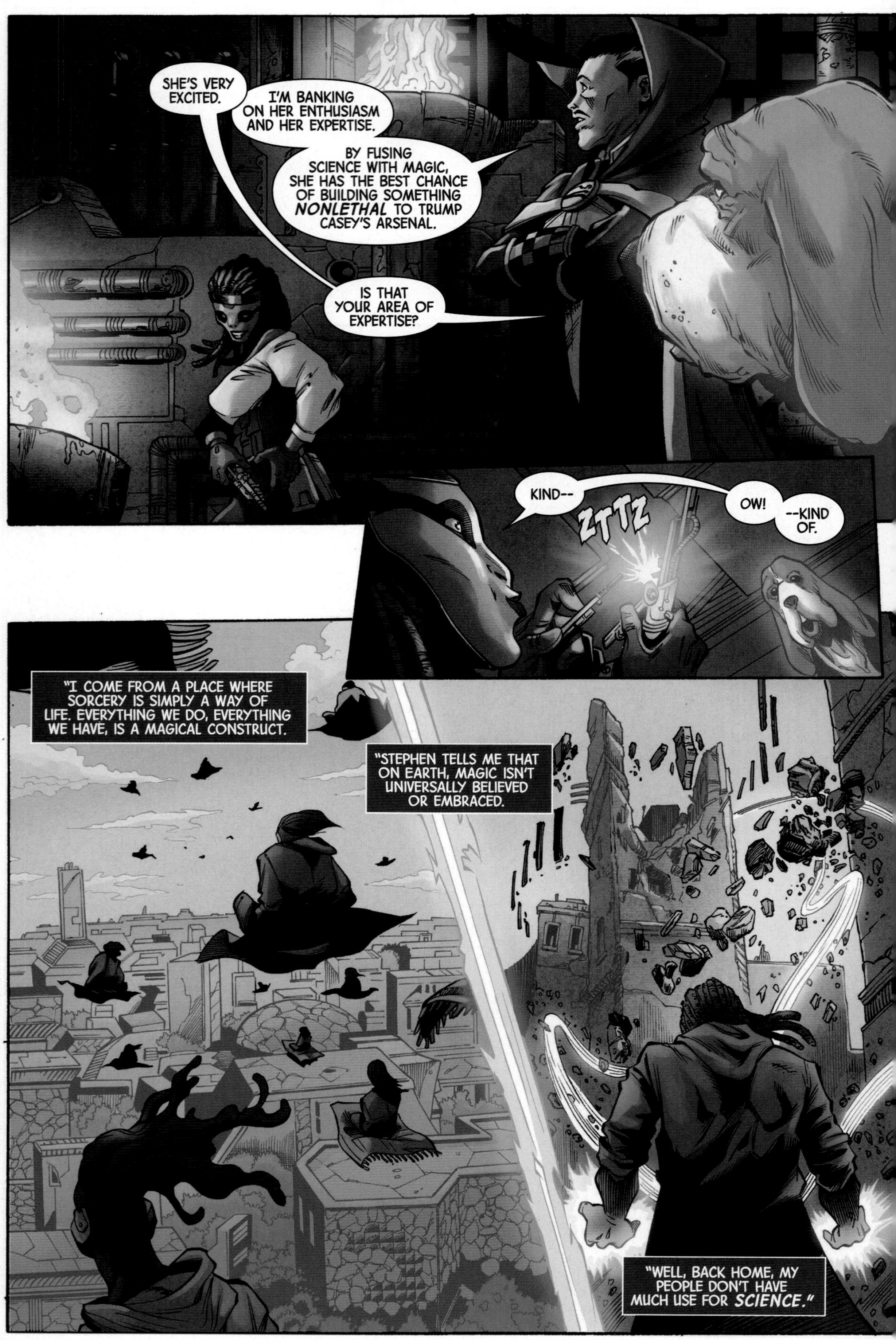
SHE'S VERY EXCITED.
I'M BANKING ON HER ENTHUSIASM AND HER EXPERTISE.
BY FUSING SCIENCE WITH MAGIC, SHE HAS THE BEST CHANCE OF BUILDING SOMETHING NONLETHAL TO TRUMP CASEY'S ARSENAL.
IS THAT YOUR AREA OF EXPERTISE?
KIND--
ZTTZ
OW!
--KIND OF.
"I COME FROM A PLACE WHERE SORCERY IS SIMPLY A WAY OF LIFE. EVERYTHING WE DO, EVERYTHING WE HAVE, IS A MAGICAL CONSTRUCT.
"STEPHEN TELLS ME THAT ON EARTH, MAGIC ISN'T UNIVERSALLY BELIEVED OR EMBRACED.
"WELL, BACK HOME, MY PEOPLE DON'T HAVE MUCH USE FOR SCIENCE."

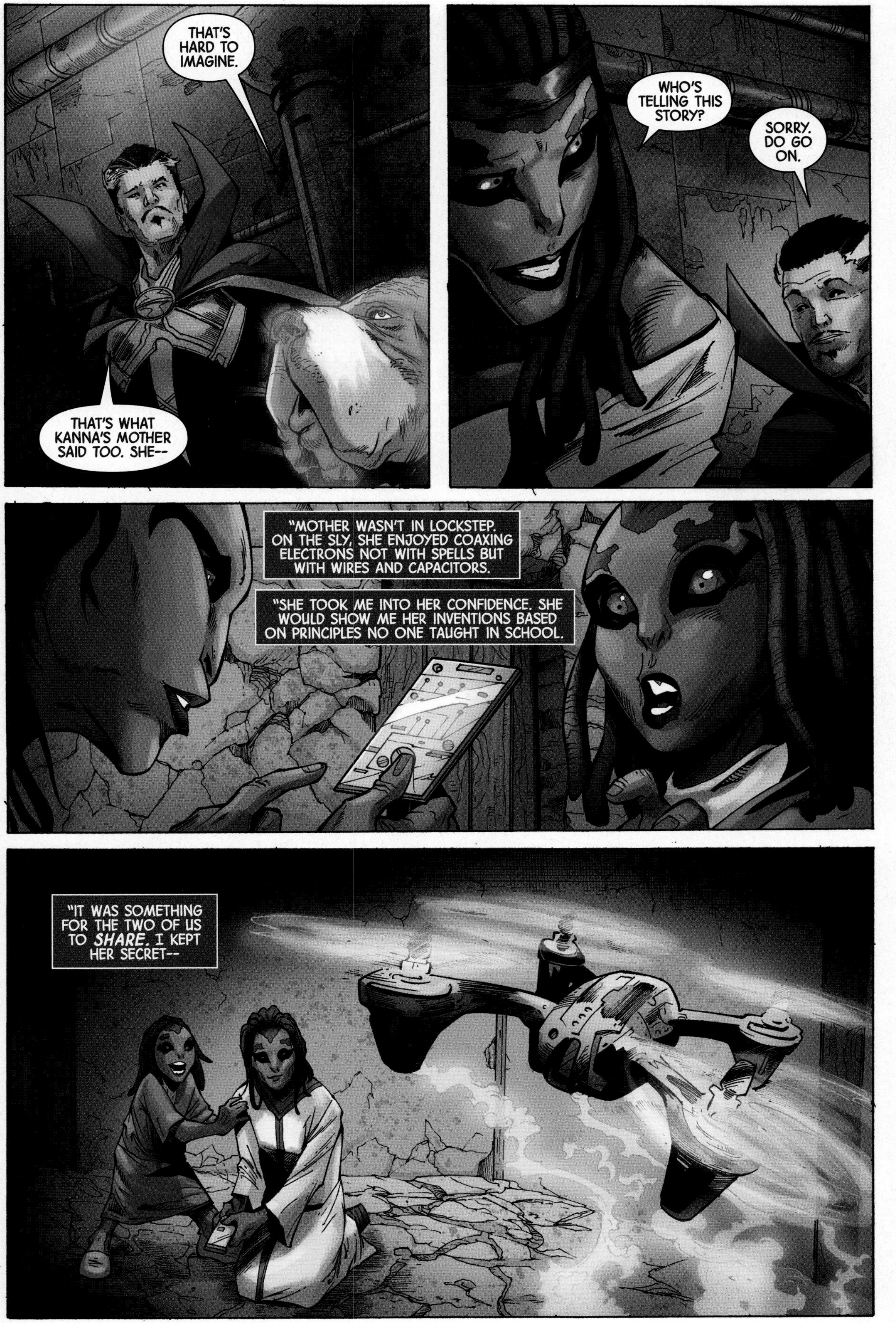
THAT'S HARD TO IMAGINE.
THAT'S WHAT KANNA'S MOTHER SAID TOO. SHE--
WHO'S TELLING THIS STORY?
SORRY. DO GO ON.
"MOTHER WASN'T IN LOCKSTEP. ON THE SLY, SHE ENJOYED COAXING ELECTRONS NOT WITH SPELLS BUT WITH WIRES AND CAPACITORS.
"SHE TOOK ME INTO HER CONFIDENCE. SHE WOULD SHOW ME HER INVENTIONS BASED ON PRINCIPLES NO ONE TAUGHT IN SCHOOL.
"IT WAS SOMETHING FOR THE TWO OF US TO SHARE. I KEPT HER SECRET--

"--BUT DAD *DIDN'T*, HE TURNED HIS *OWN WIFE* IN TO THE *CONJURE PARLIAMENT* FOR *HERESY*."

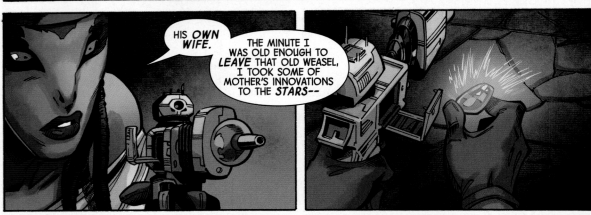

HIS *OWN WIFE.*

THE MINUTE I WAS OLD ENOUGH TO *LEAVE* THAT OLD WEASEL, I TOOK SOME OF MOTHER'S INNOVATIONS TO THE *STARS*--

--AND FIGURED OUT HOW TO MAKE THEM WORK *WITH* MAGIC RATHER THAN *BESIDE* IT.

I FIGURE THAT ONE OF THESE DAYS, I'M GOING TO GET GOOD ENOUGH TO RETURN HOME AND SHOVE A *NEUTRON ORB OF CHAOS* UP THE PARLIAMENT'S COLLECTIVE--

I →YAWN← GET THE DRIFT.

NO OFFENSE. THAT WASN'T A YAWN OF *BOREDOM.*

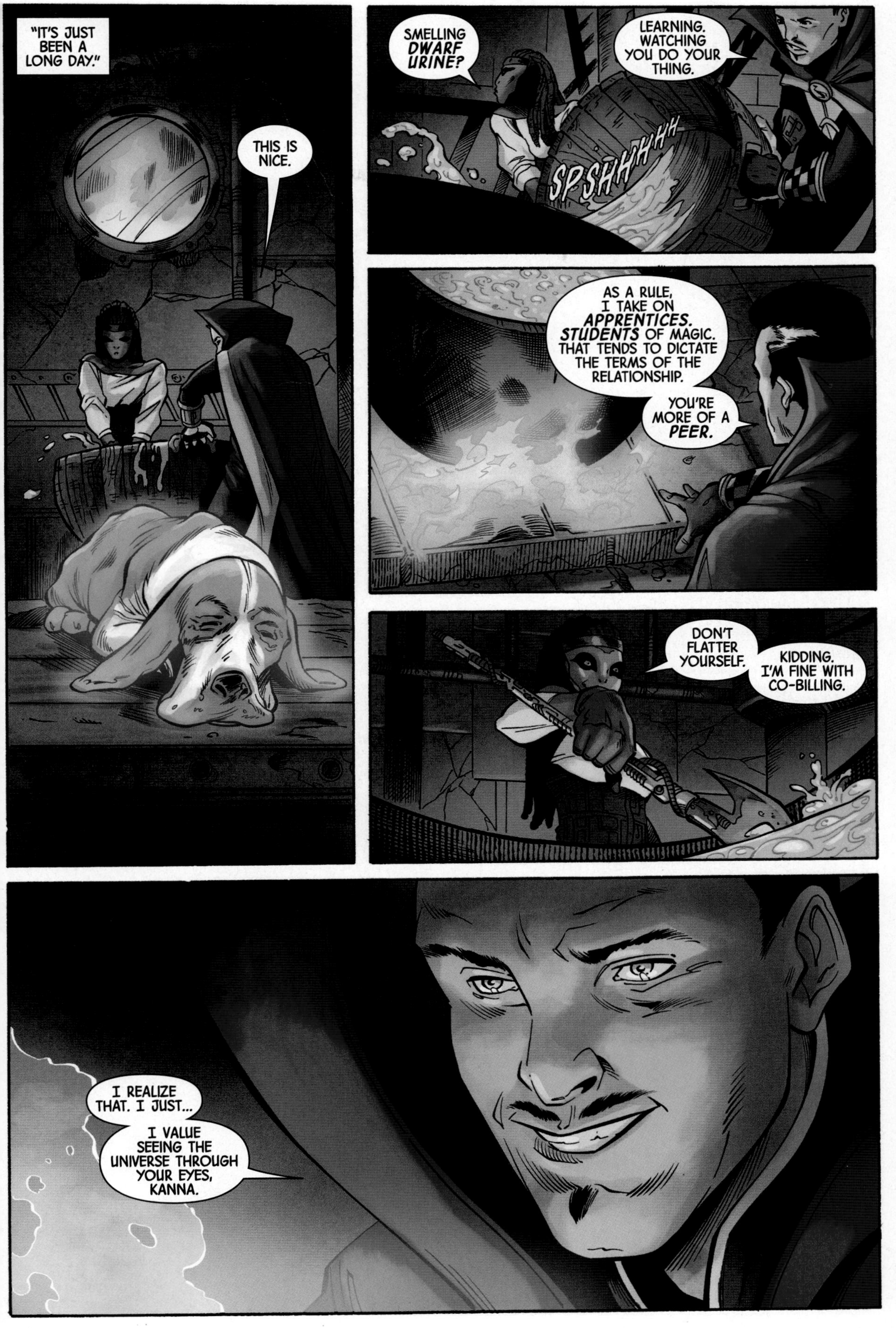
"IT'S JUST BEEN A LONG DAY."
THIS IS NICE.
SMELLING DWARF URINE?
LEARNING. WATCHING YOU DO YOUR THING.
SPSHHHHH
AS A RULE, I TAKE ON APPRENTICES. STUDENTS OF MAGIC. THAT TENDS TO DICTATE THE TERMS OF THE RELATIONSHIP.
YOU'RE MORE OF A PEER.
DON'T FLATTER YOURSELF.
KIDDING. I'M FINE WITH CO-BILLING.
I REALIZE THAT. I JUST...
I VALUE SEEING THE UNIVERSE THROUGH YOUR EYES, KANNA.

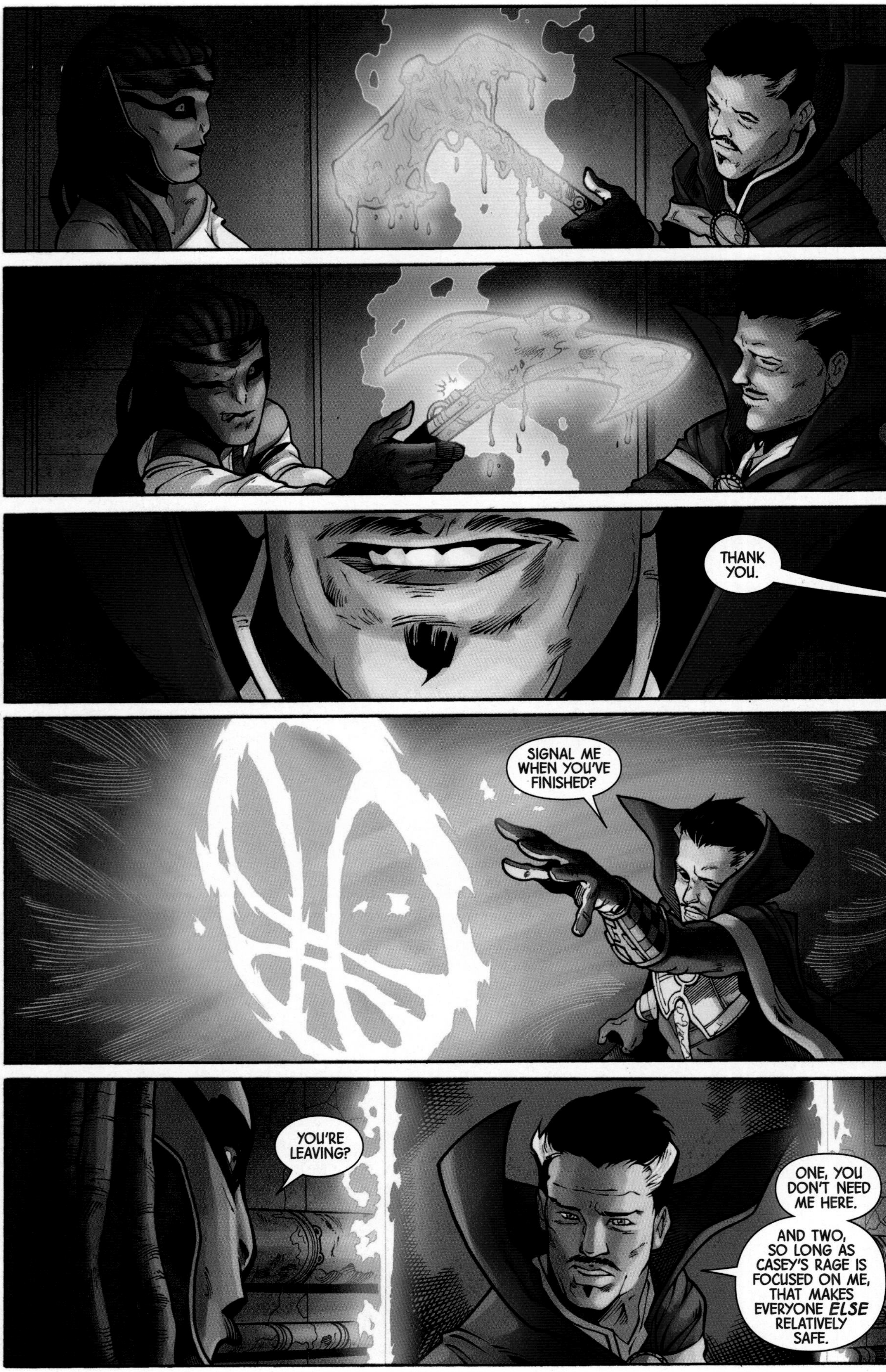
THANK YOU.
SIGNAL ME WHEN YOU'VE FINISHED?
YOU'RE LEAVING?
ONE, YOU DON'T NEED ME HERE.
AND TWO, SO LONG AS CASEY'S RAGE IS FOCUSED ON ME, THAT MAKES EVERYONE *ELSE* RELATIVELY SAFE.

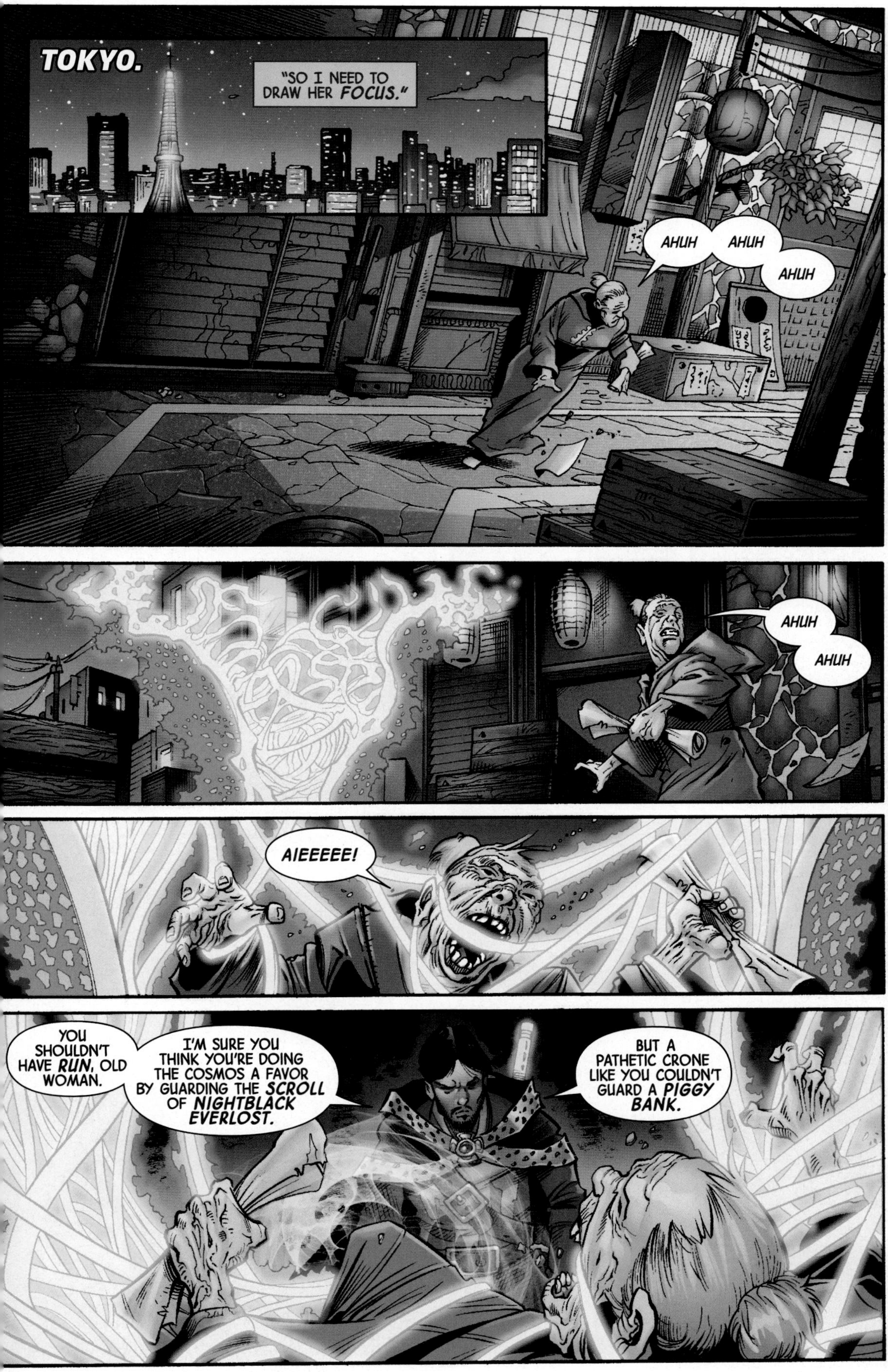
TOKYO.
"SO I NEED TO DRAW HER FOCUS."
AHUH
AHUH
AHUH
AHUH
AHUH
AIEEEEE!
YOU SHOULDN'T HAVE RUN, OLD WOMAN.
I'M SURE YOU THINK YOU'RE DOING THE COSMOS A FAVOR BY GUARDING THE SCROLL OF NIGHTBLACK EVERLOST.
BUT A PATHETIC CRONE LIKE YOU COULDN'T GUARD A PIGGY BANK.

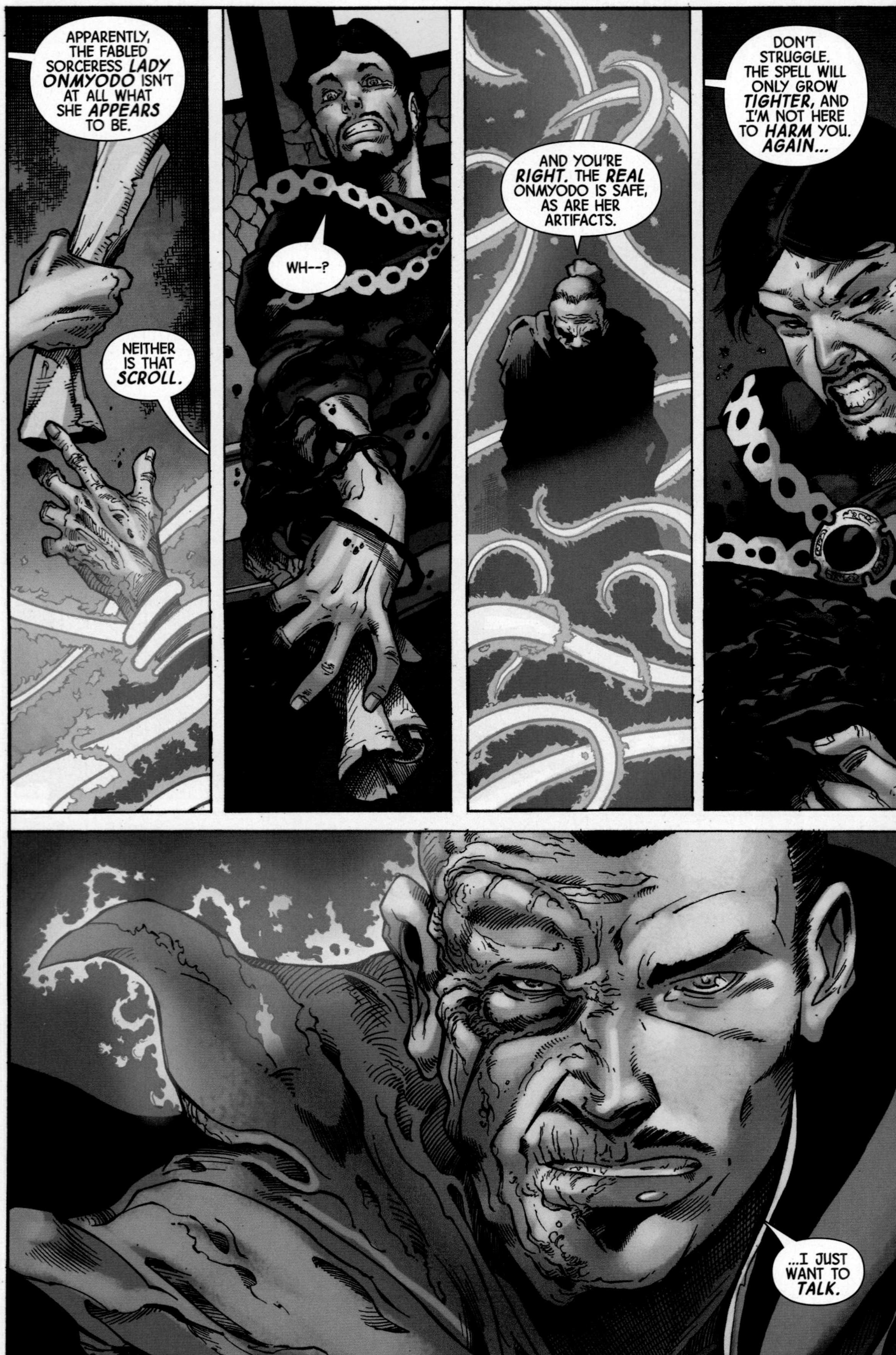
APPARENTLY, THE FABLED SORCERESS LADY ONMYODO ISN'T AT ALL WHAT SHE APPEARS TO BE.
NEITHER IS THAT SCROLL.
WH--?
AND YOU'RE RIGHT. THE REAL ONMYODO IS SAFE, AS ARE HER ARTIFACTS.
DON'T STRUGGLE. THE SPELL WILL ONLY GROW TIGHTER, AND I'M NOT HERE TO HARM YOU. AGAIN...
...I JUST WANT TO TALK.

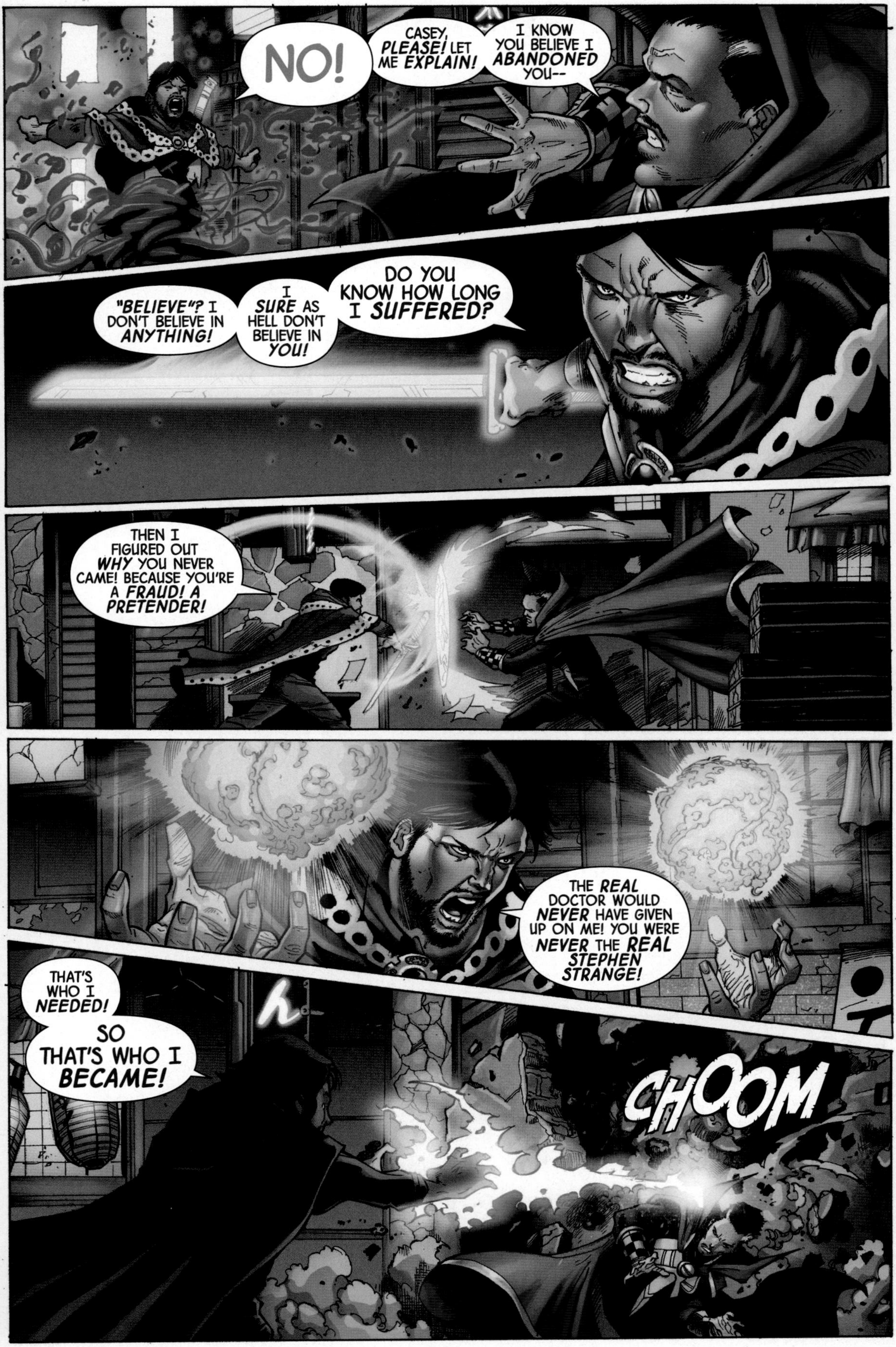
NO!
CASEY, PLEASE! LET ME EXPLAIN!
I KNOW YOU BELIEVE I ABANDONED YOU--
DO YOU KNOW HOW LONG I SUFFERED?
I SURE AS HELL DON'T BELIEVE IN YOU!
"BELIEVE"? I DON'T BELIEVE IN ANYTHING!
THEN I FIGURED OUT WHY YOU NEVER CAME! BECAUSE YOU'RE A FRAUD! A PRETENDER!
THE REAL DOCTOR WOULD NEVER HAVE GIVEN UP ON ME! YOU WERE NEVER THE REAL STEPHEN STRANGE!
THAT'S WHO I NEEDED!
SO THAT'S WHO I BECAME!
CHOOM

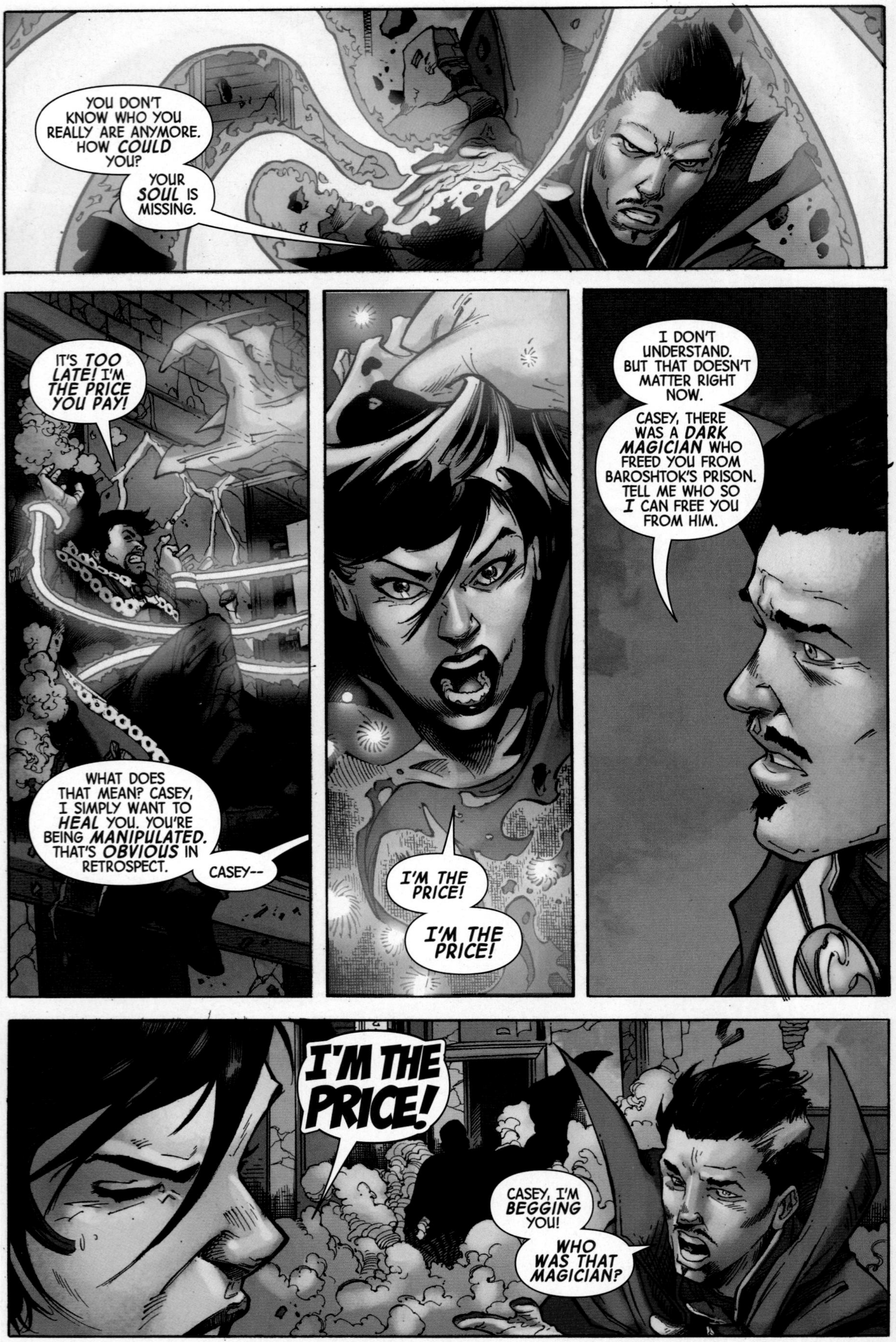
YOU DON'T KNOW WHO YOU REALLY ARE ANYMORE. HOW COULD YOU?
YOUR SOUL IS MISSING.
IT'S TOO LATE! I'M THE PRICE YOU PAY!
WHAT DOES THAT MEAN? CASEY, I SIMPLY WANT TO HEAL YOU. YOU'RE BEING MANIPULATED. THAT'S OBVIOUS IN RETROSPECT.
CASEY--
I'M THE PRICE!
I'M THE PRICE!
I DON'T UNDERSTAND. BUT THAT DOESN'T MATTER RIGHT NOW.
CASEY, THERE WAS A DARK MAGICIAN WHO FREED YOU FROM BAROSHTOK'S PRISON. TELL ME WHO SO I CAN FREE YOU FROM HIM.
I'M THE PRICE!
CASEY, I'M BEGGING YOU!
WHO WAS THAT MAGICIAN?

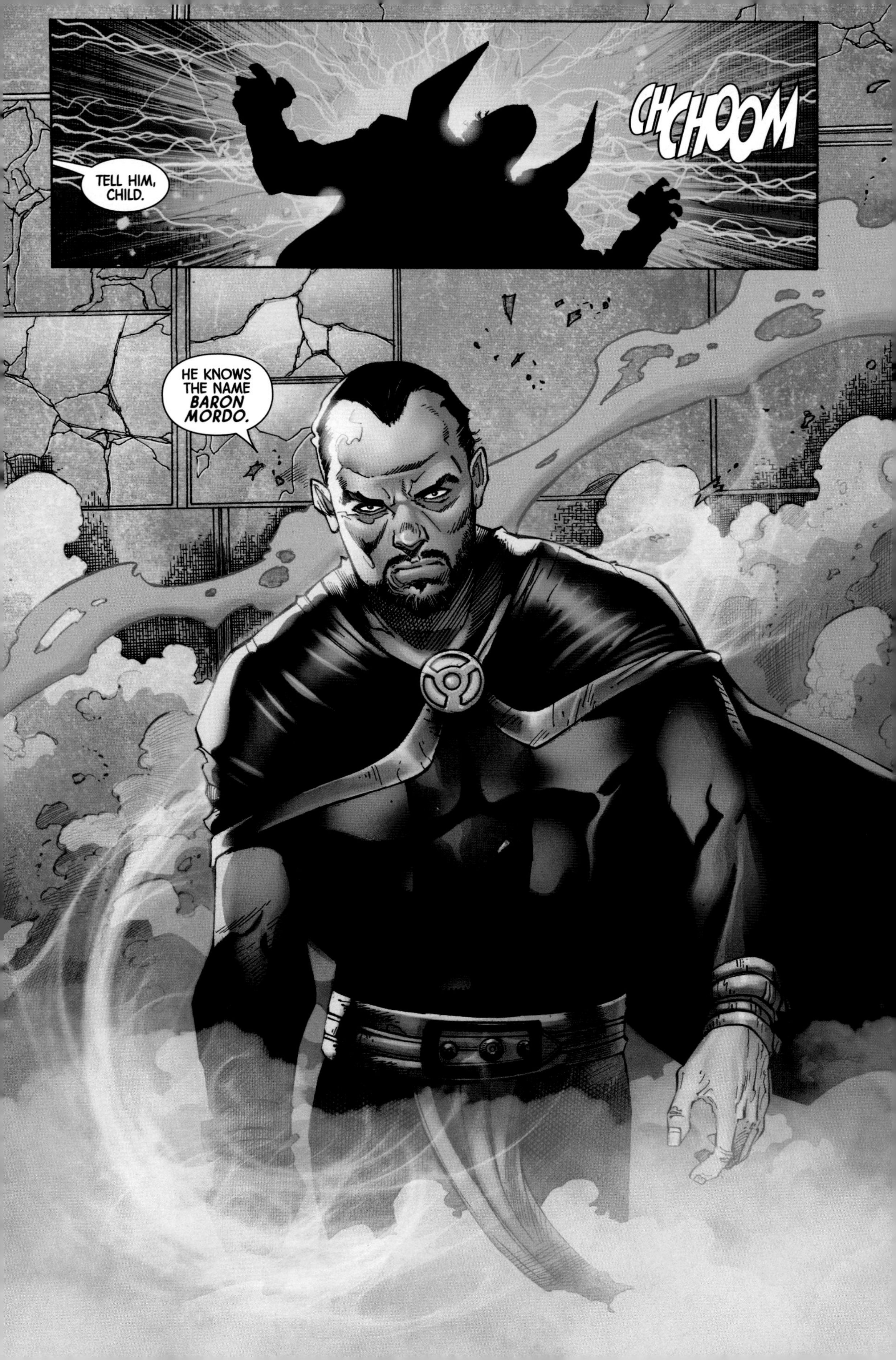
CHCHOOM
TELL HIM, CHILD.
HE KNOWS THE NAME BARON MORDO.

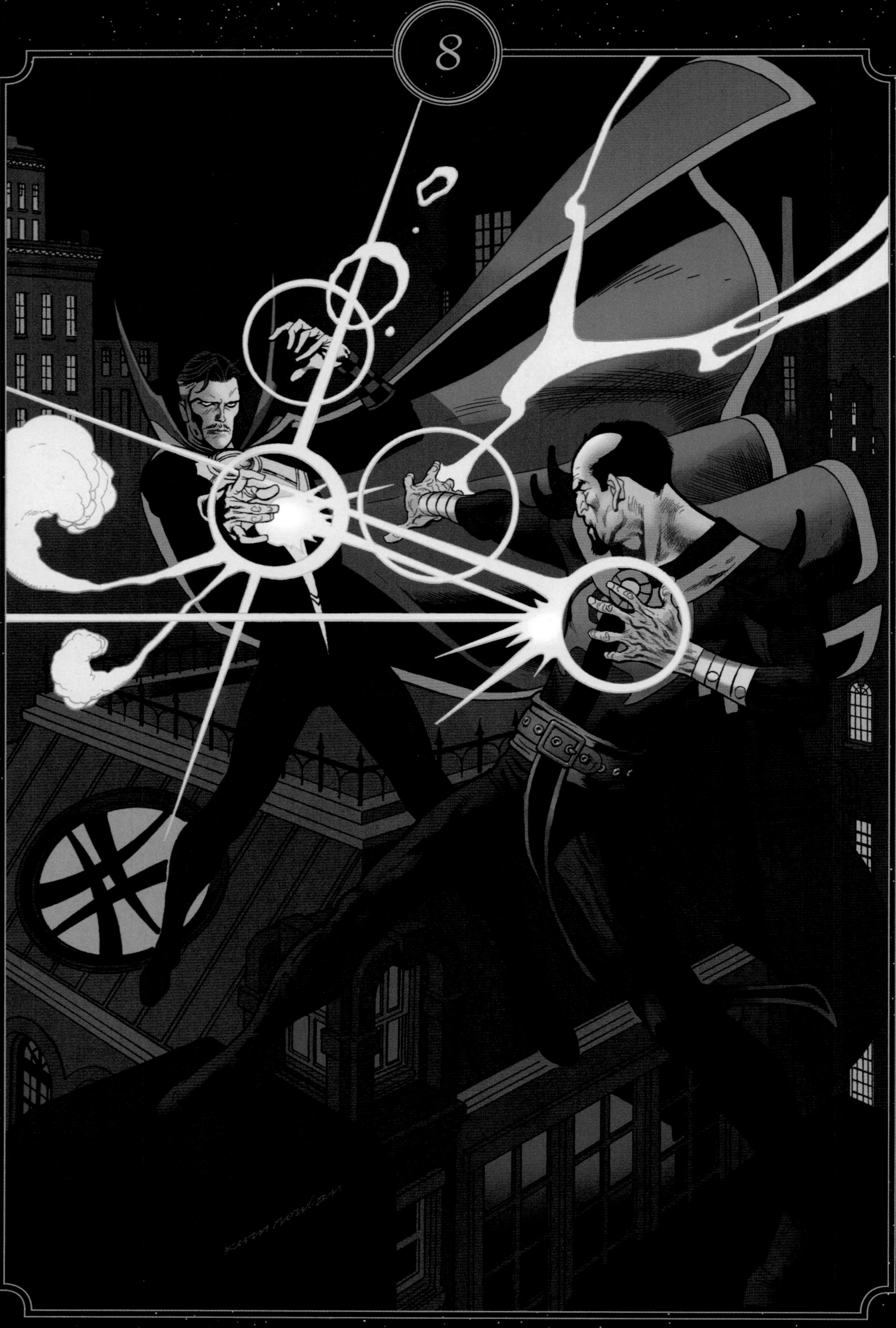
8

The Price

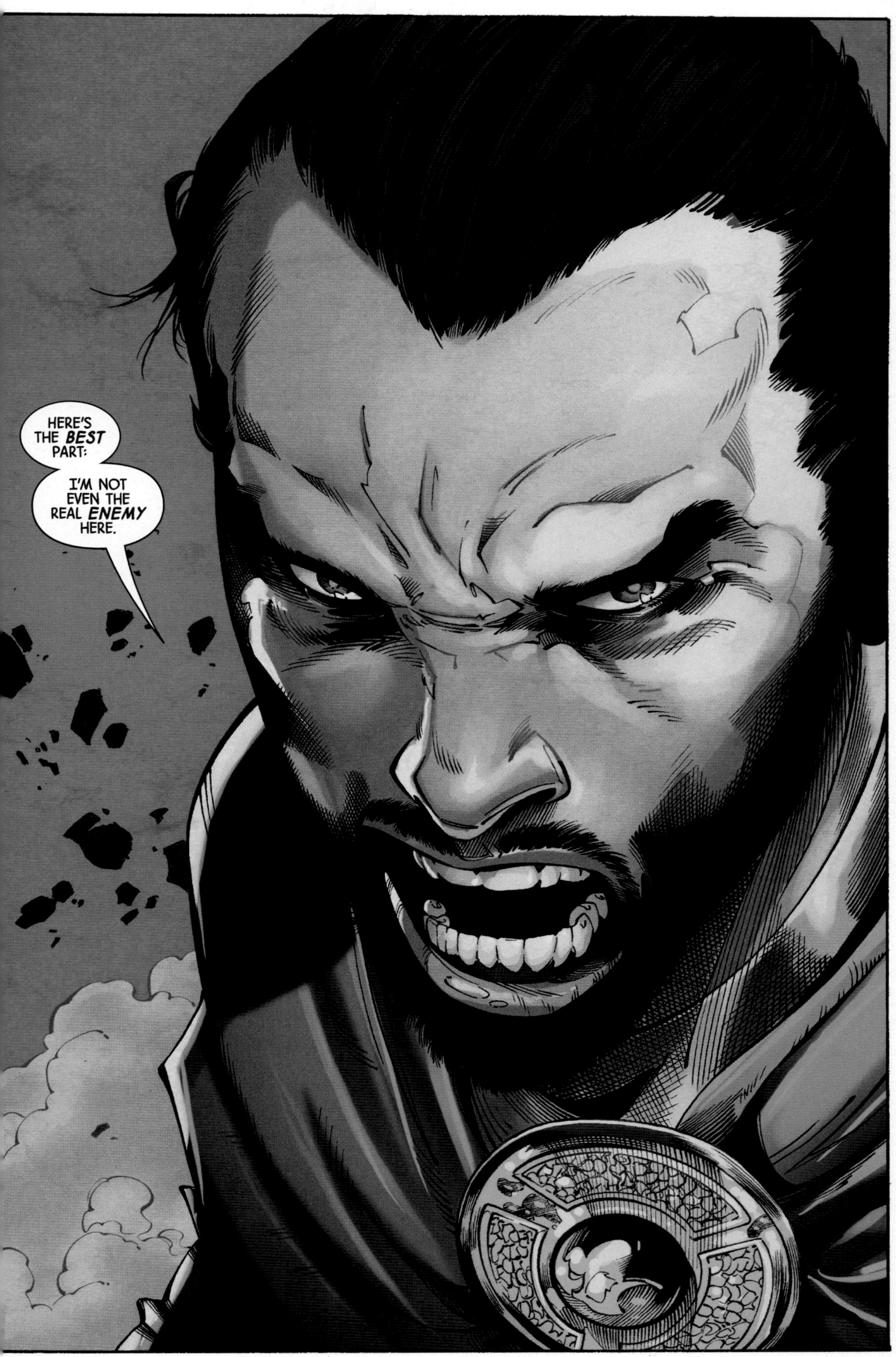

HERE'S THE *BEST* PART:
I'M NOT EVEN THE REAL *ENEMY* HERE.

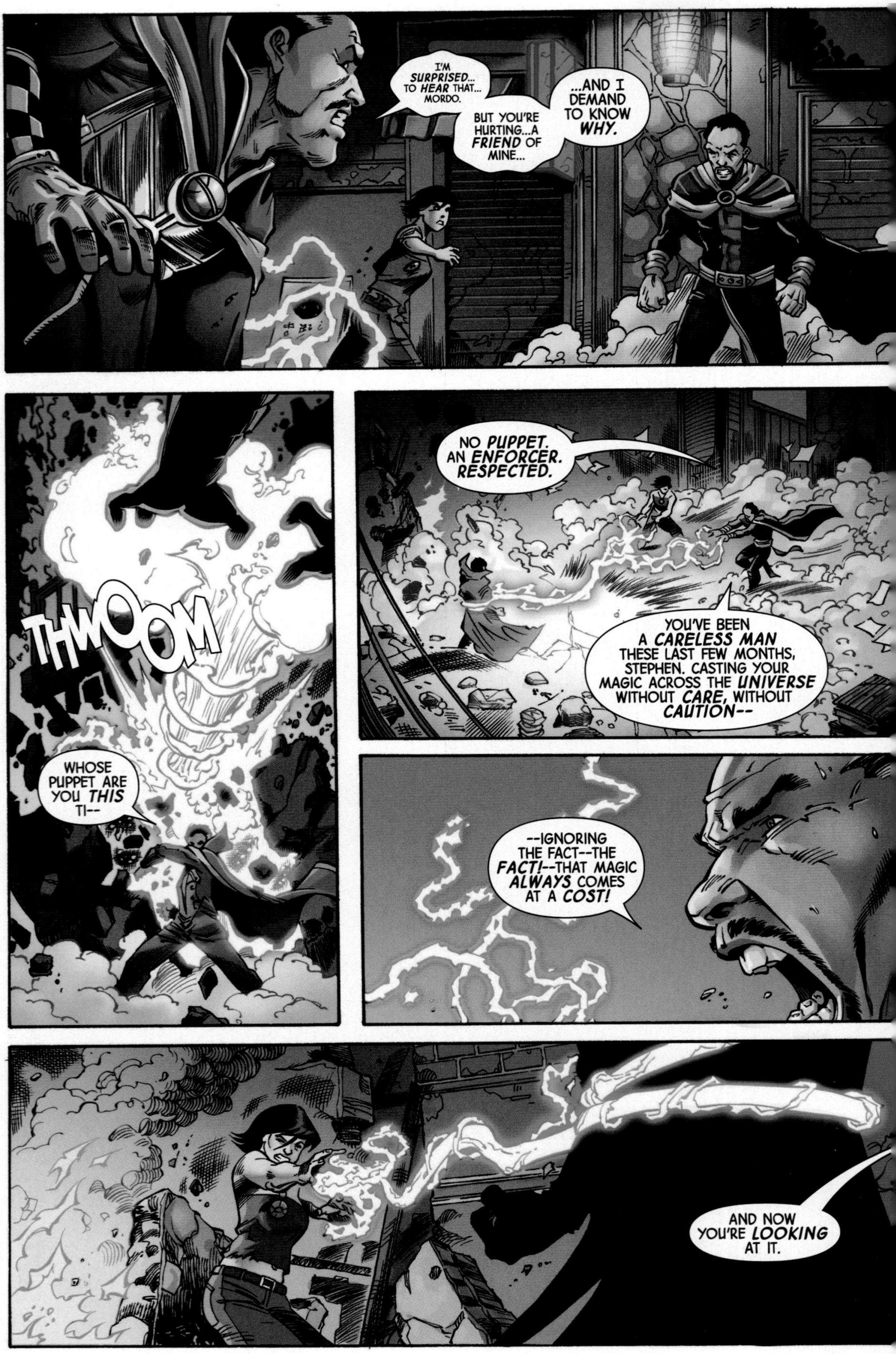
I'M SURPRISED... TO HEAR THAT... MORDO.
BUT YOU'RE HURTING...A FRIEND OF MINE...
...AND I DEMAND TO KNOW WHY.
THWOOM
WHOSE PUPPET ARE YOU THIS TI--
NO PUPPET. AN ENFORCER. RESPECTED.
YOU'VE BEEN A CARELESS MAN THESE LAST FEW MONTHS, STEPHEN. CASTING YOUR MAGIC ACROSS THE UNIVERSE WITHOUT CARE, WITHOUT CAUTION--
--IGNORING THE FACT--THE FACT!--THAT MAGIC ALWAYS COMES AT A COST!
AND NOW YOU'RE LOOKING AT IT.

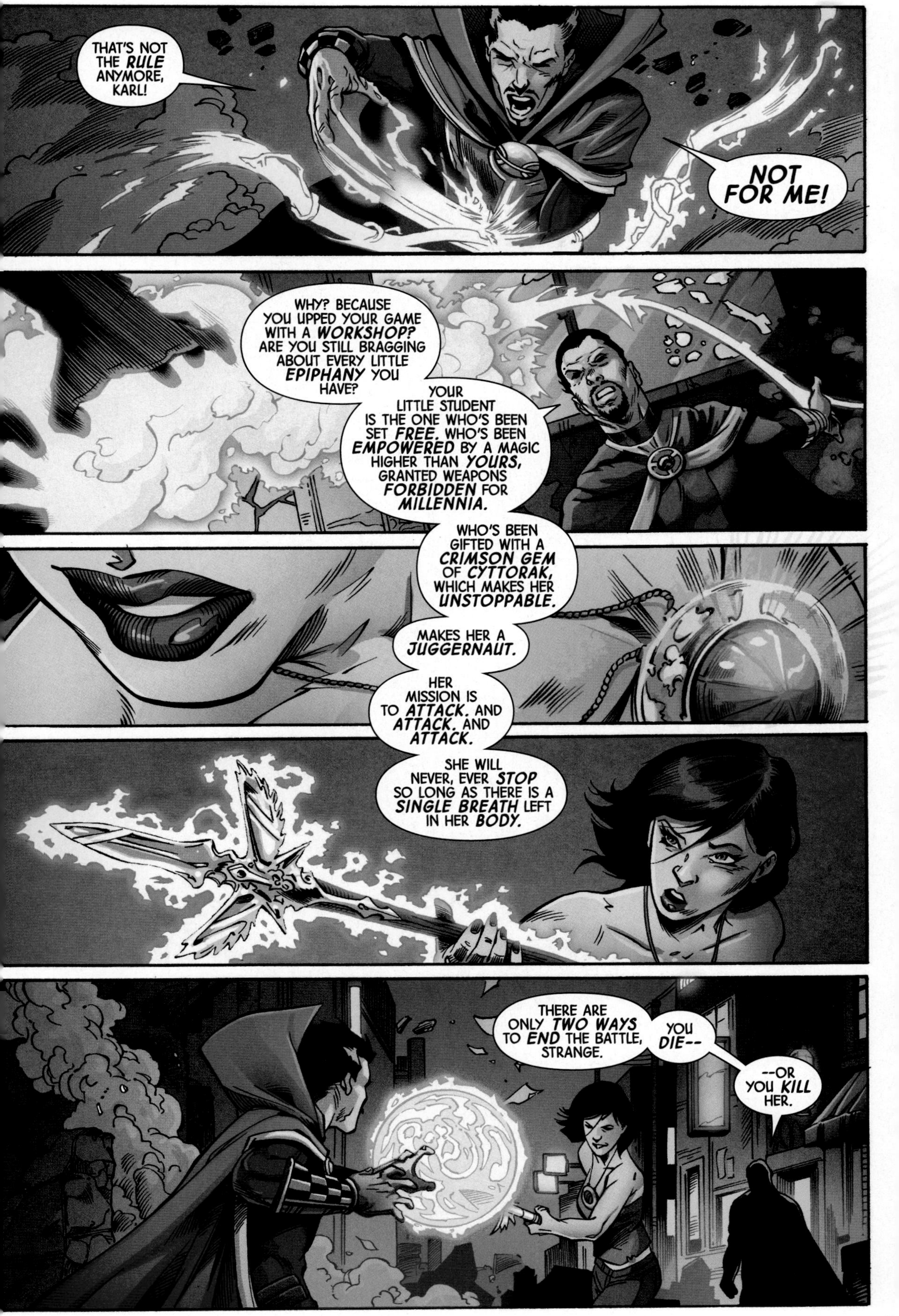

THAT'S NOT THE RULE ANYMORE, KARL!
NOT FOR ME!
WHY? BECAUSE YOU UPPED YOUR GAME WITH A WORKSHOP? ARE YOU STILL BRAGGING ABOUT EVERY LITTLE EPIPHANY YOU HAVE?
YOUR LITTLE STUDENT IS THE ONE WHO'S BEEN SET FREE. WHO'S BEEN EMPOWERED BY A MAGIC HIGHER THAN YOURS, GRANTED WEAPONS FORBIDDEN FOR MILLENNIA.
WHO'S BEEN GIFTED WITH A CRIMSON GEM OF CYTTORAK, WHICH MAKES HER UNSTOPPABLE.
MAKES HER A JUGGERNAUT.
HER MISSION IS TO ATTACK. AND ATTACK. AND ATTACK.
SHE WILL NEVER, EVER STOP SO LONG AS THERE IS A SINGLE BREATH LEFT IN HER BODY.
THERE ARE ONLY TWO WAYS TO END THE BATTLE, STRANGE.
YOU DIE--
--OR YOU KILL HER.

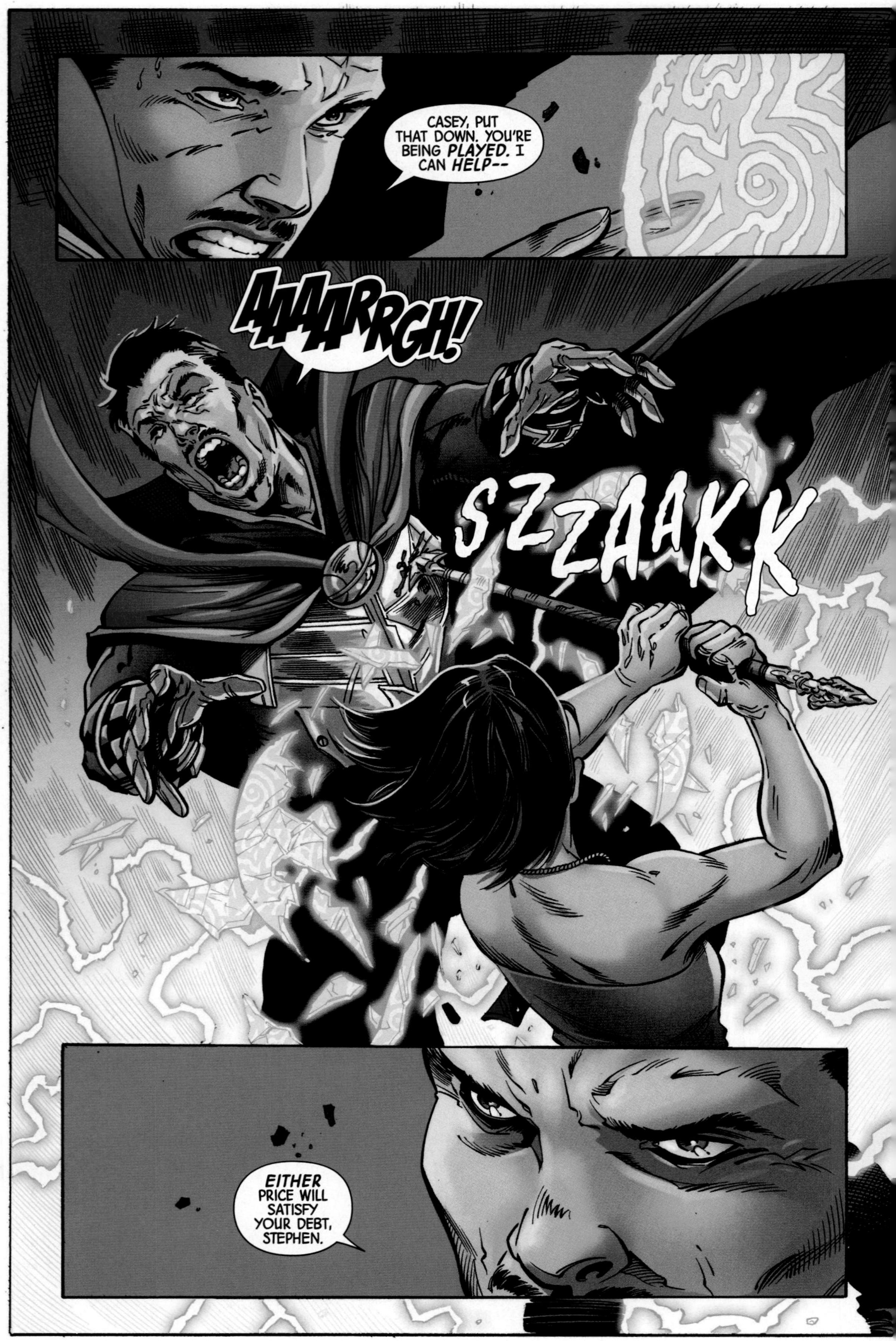
CASEY, PUT THAT DOWN. YOU'RE BEING PLAYED. I CAN HELP--
AAAARRGH!
SZZAAKK
EITHER PRICE WILL SATISFY YOUR DEBT, STEPHEN.

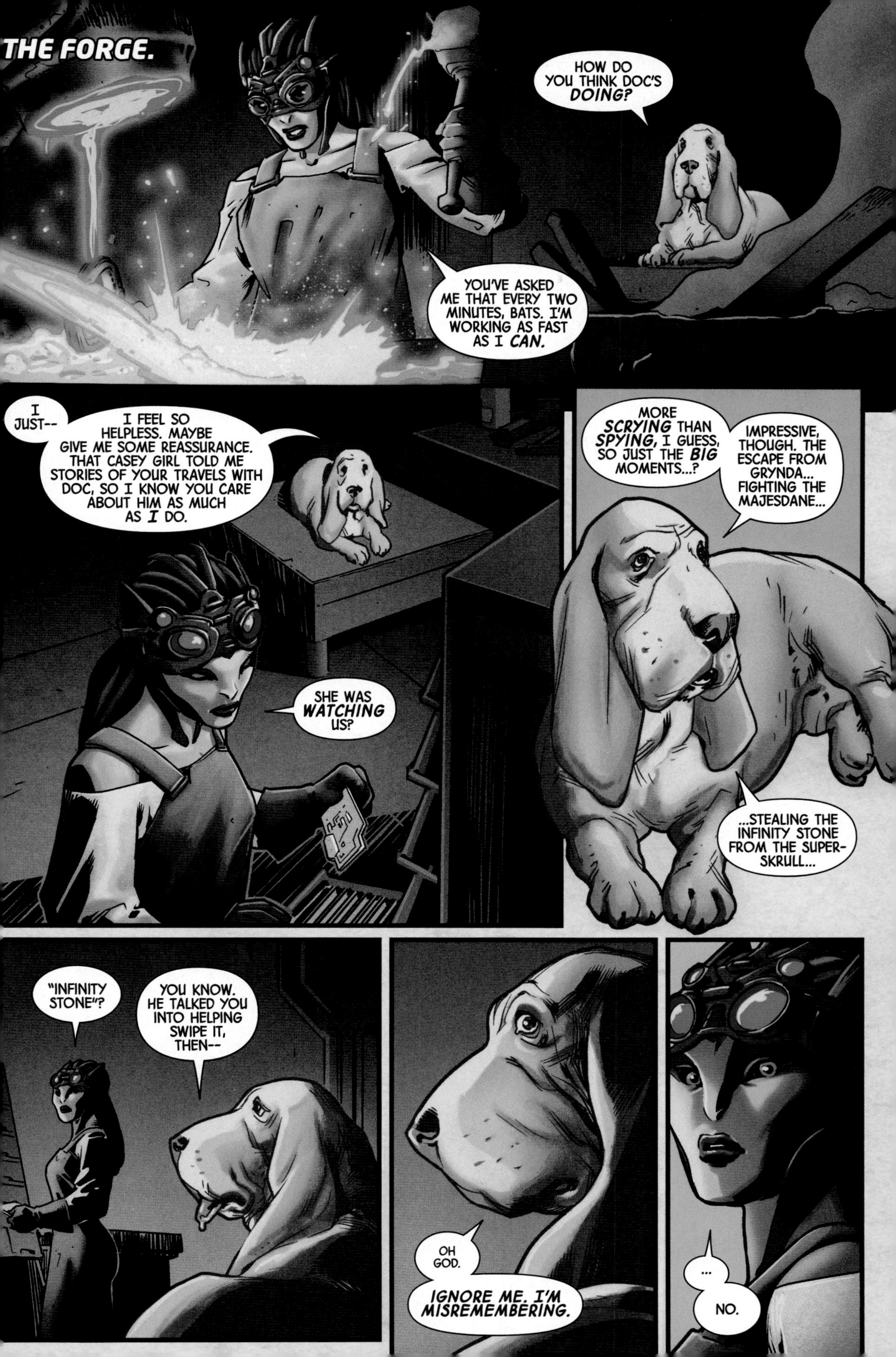
THE FORGE.
HOW DO YOU THINK DOC'S DOING?
YOU'VE ASKED ME THAT EVERY TWO MINUTES, BATS. I'M WORKING AS FAST AS I CAN.
I JUST--
I FEEL SO HELPLESS. MAYBE GIVE ME SOME REASSURANCE. THAT CASEY GIRL TOLD ME STORIES OF YOUR TRAVELS WITH DOC, SO I KNOW YOU CARE ABOUT HIM AS MUCH AS I DO.
SHE WAS WATCHING US?
MORE SCRYING THAN SPYING, I GUESS, SO JUST THE BIG MOMENTS...?
IMPRESSIVE, THOUGH. THE ESCAPE FROM GRYNDA... FIGHTING THE MAJESDANE...
...STEALING THE INFINITY STONE FROM THE SUPER-SKRULL...
"INFINITY STONE"?
YOU KNOW. HE TALKED YOU INTO HELPING SWIPE IT, THEN--
OH GOD.
IGNORE ME. I'M MISREMEMBERING.
...
NO.

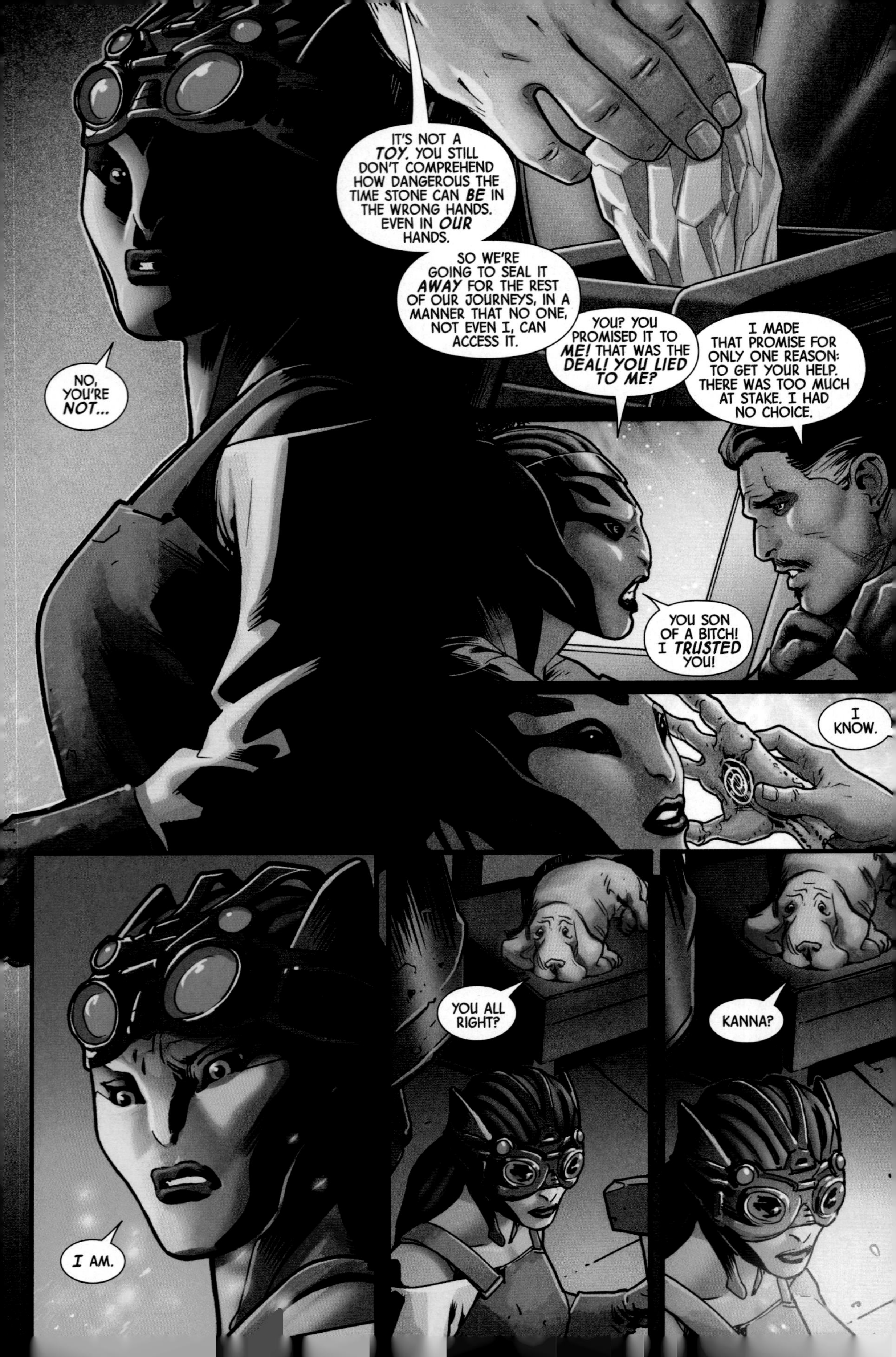
IT'S NOT A TOY. YOU STILL DON'T COMPREHEND HOW DANGEROUS THE TIME STONE CAN BE IN THE WRONG HANDS. EVEN IN OUR HANDS.
SO WE'RE GOING TO SEAL IT AWAY FOR THE REST OF OUR JOURNEYS, IN A MANNER THAT NO ONE, NOT EVEN I, CAN ACCESS IT.
NO, YOU'RE NOT...
YOU? YOU PROMISED IT TO ME! THAT WAS THE DEAL! YOU LIED TO ME?
I MADE THAT PROMISE FOR ONLY ONE REASON: TO GET YOUR HELP. THERE WAS TOO MUCH AT STAKE. I HAD NO CHOICE.
YOU SON OF A BITCH! I TRUSTED YOU!
I KNOW.
I AM.
YOU ALL RIGHT?
KANNA?

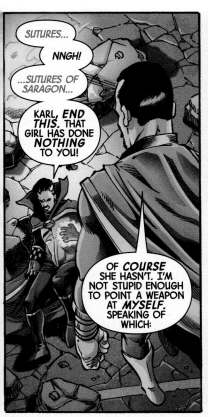

SUTURES...

NNGH!

...SUTURES OF SARAGON...

KARL, *END THIS.* THAT GIRL HAS DONE *NOTHING* TO YOU!

OF *COURSE* SHE HASN'T. I'M NOT STUPID ENOUGH TO POINT A WEAPON AT *MYSELF.* SPEAKING OF WHICH:

INCOMING.

NO!

STOP.

KSSSH

CASEY, NO!

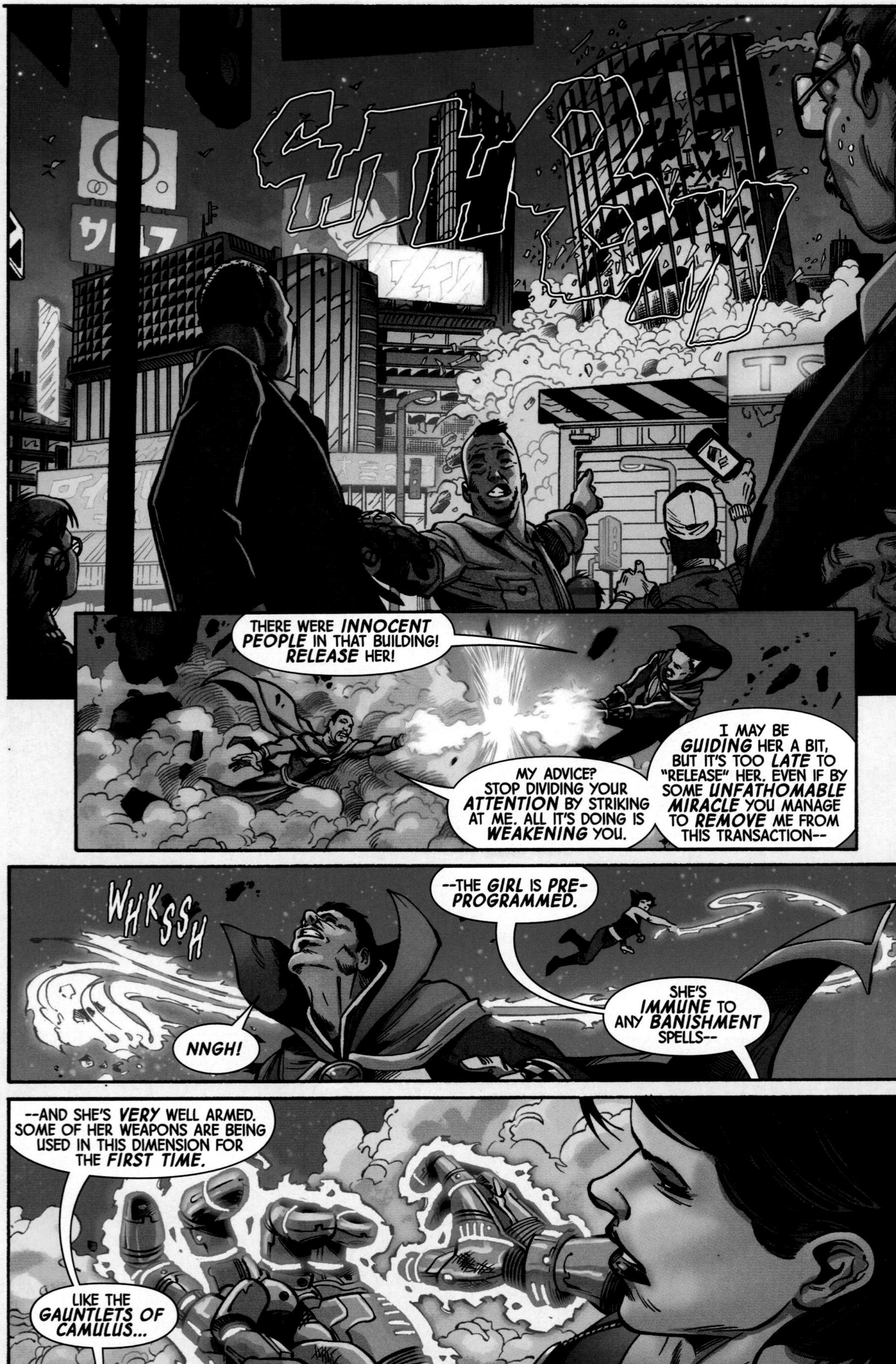

THERE WERE INNOCENT PEOPLE IN THAT BUILDING! RELEASE HER!
MY ADVICE? STOP DIVIDING YOUR ATTENTION BY STRIKING AT ME. ALL IT'S DOING IS WEAKENING YOU.
I MAY BE GUIDING HER A BIT, BUT IT'S TOO LATE TO "RELEASE" HER. EVEN IF BY SOME UNFATHOMABLE MIRACLE YOU MANAGE TO REMOVE ME FROM THIS TRANSACTION--
WHKSSH
--THE GIRL IS PRE-PROGRAMMED.
NNGH!
SHE'S IMMUNE TO ANY BANISHMENT SPELLS--
--AND SHE'S VERY WELL ARMED. SOME OF HER WEAPONS ARE BEING USED IN THIS DIMENSION FOR THE FIRST TIME.
LIKE THE GAUNTLETS OF CAMULUS...

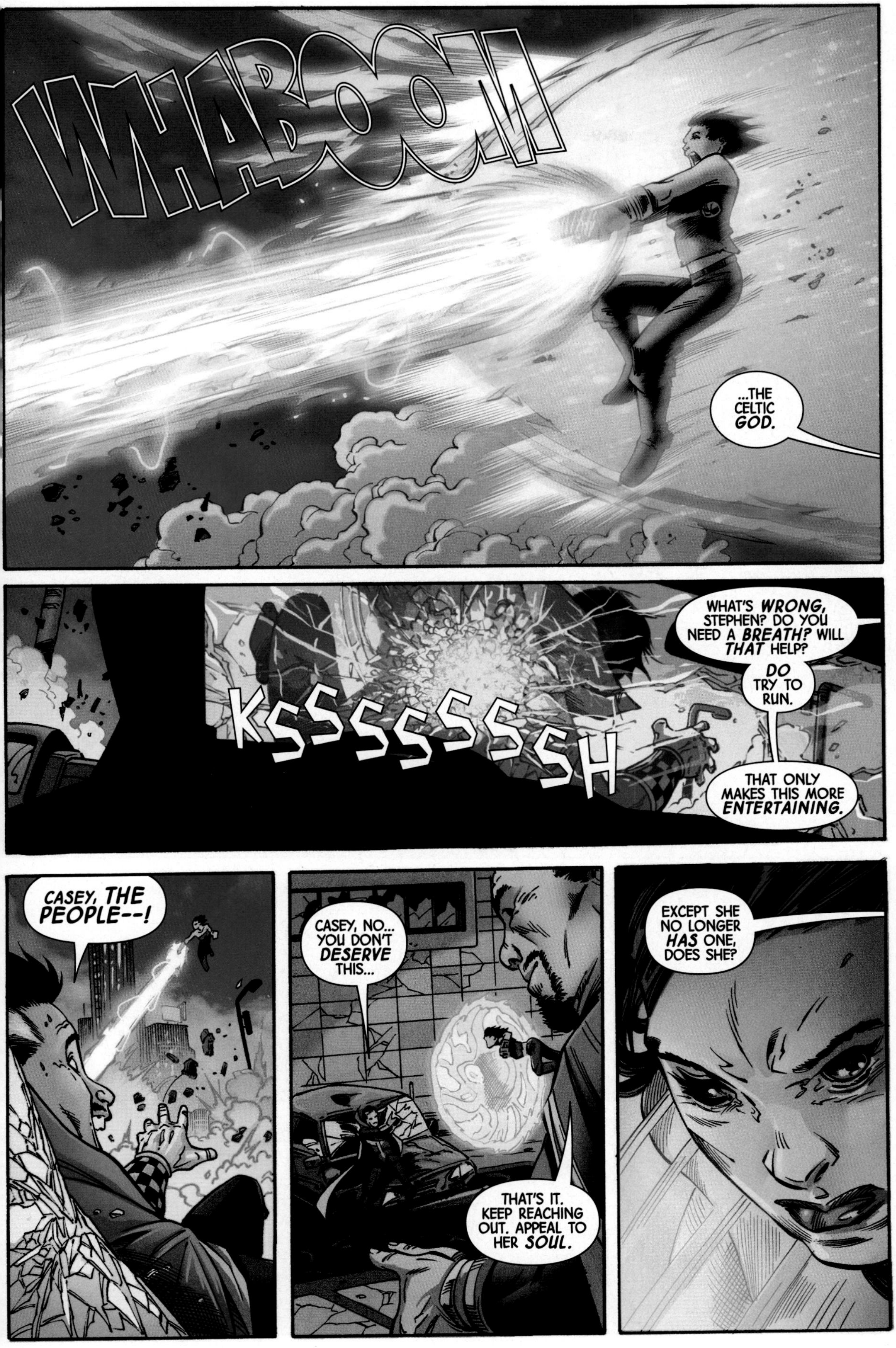
WHABOOM
...THE CELTIC GOD.
WHAT'S WRONG, STEPHEN? DO YOU NEED A BREATH? WILL THAT HELP?
DO TRY TO RUN.
KSSSSSSSH
THAT ONLY MAKES THIS MORE ENTERTAINING.
CASEY, THE PEOPLE--!
CASEY, NO... YOU DON'T DESERVE THIS...
THAT'S IT. KEEP REACHING OUT. APPEAL TO HER SOUL.
EXCEPT SHE NO LONGER HAS ONE, DOES SHE?

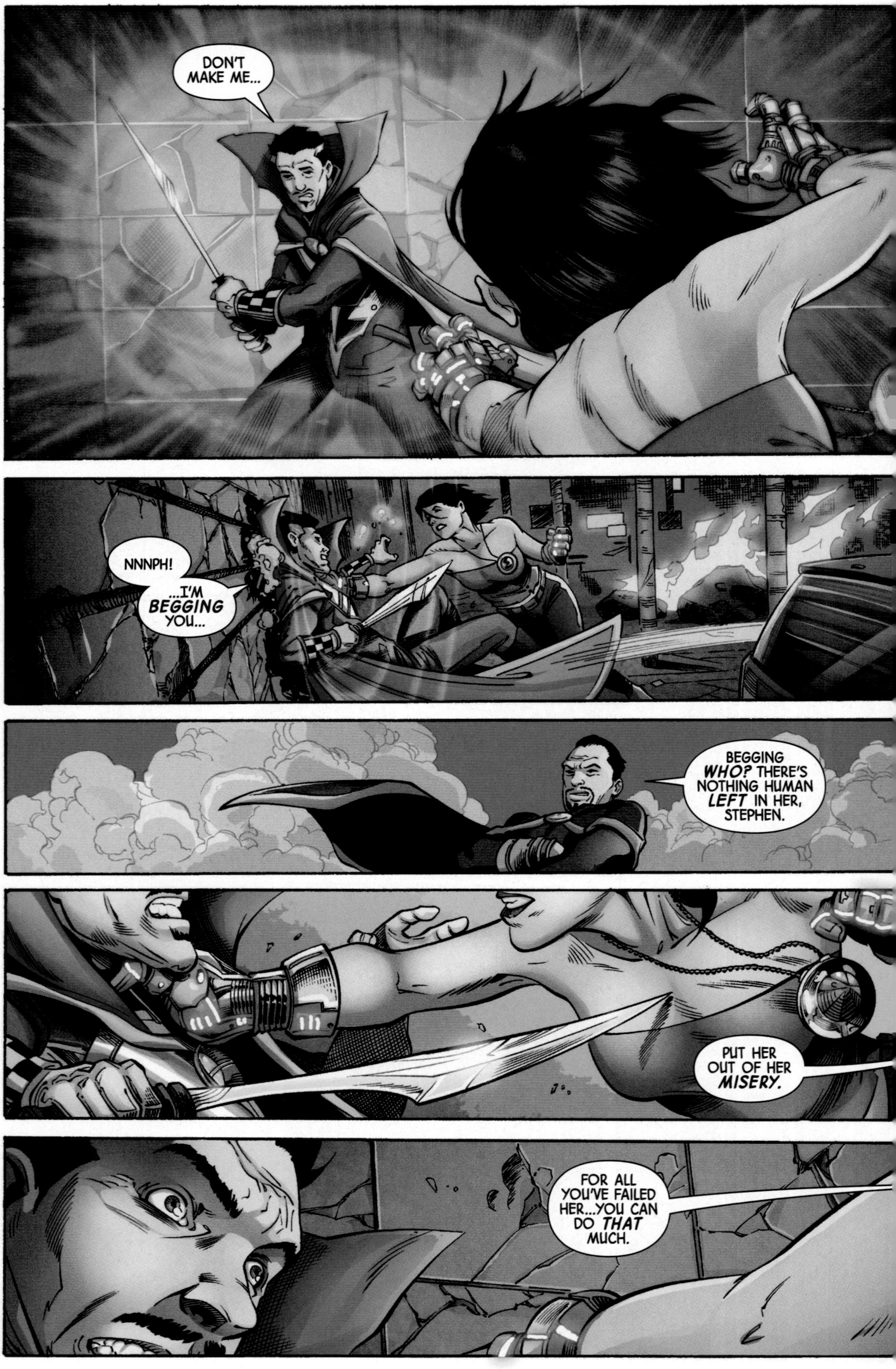
DON'T MAKE ME...
NNNPH!
...I'M BEGGING YOU...
BEGGING WHO? THERE'S NOTHING HUMAN LEFT IN HER, STEPHEN.
PUT HER OUT OF HER MISERY.
FOR ALL YOU'VE FAILED HER...YOU CAN DO THAT MUCH.

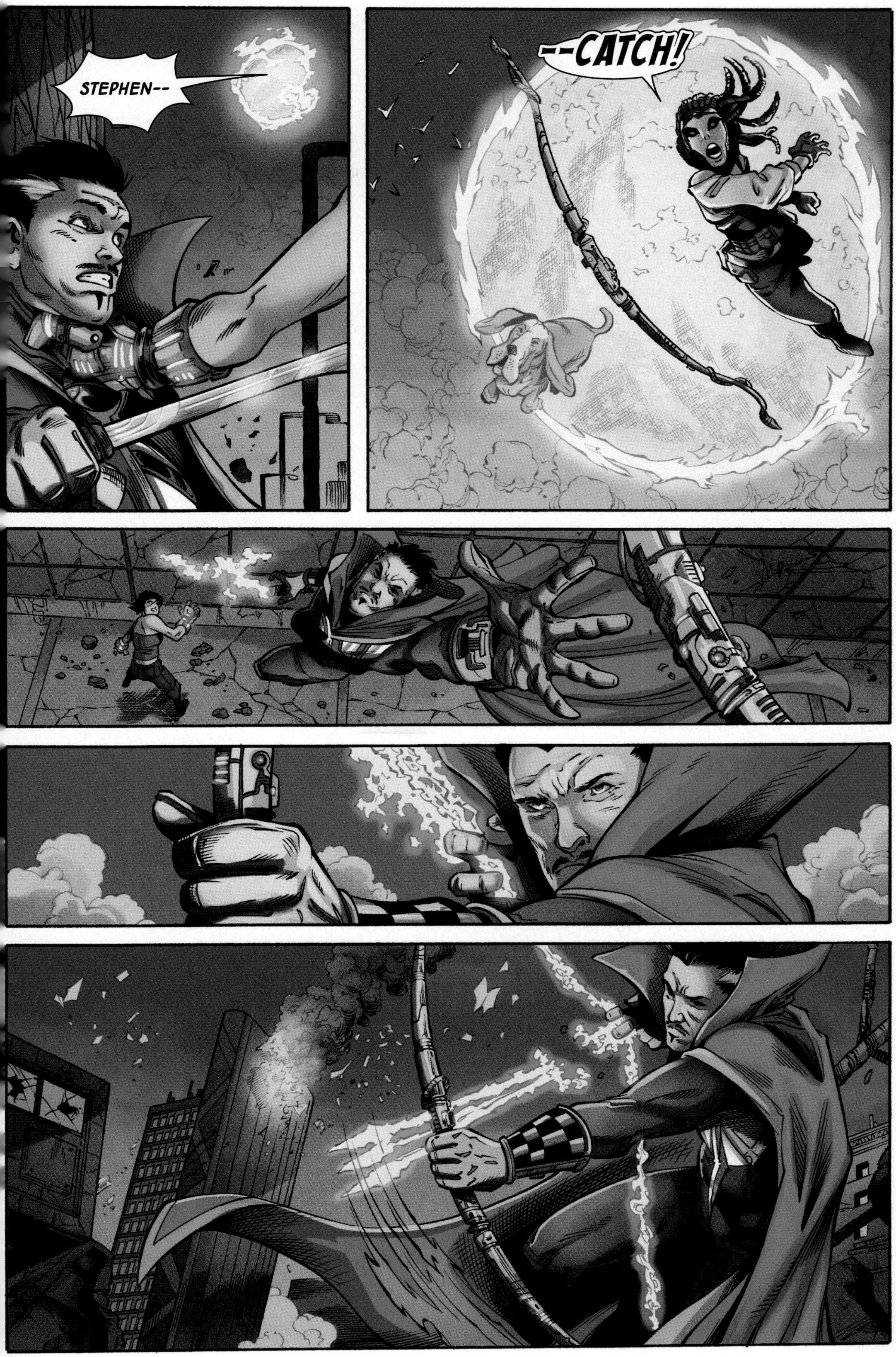
STEPHEN--
--CATCH!

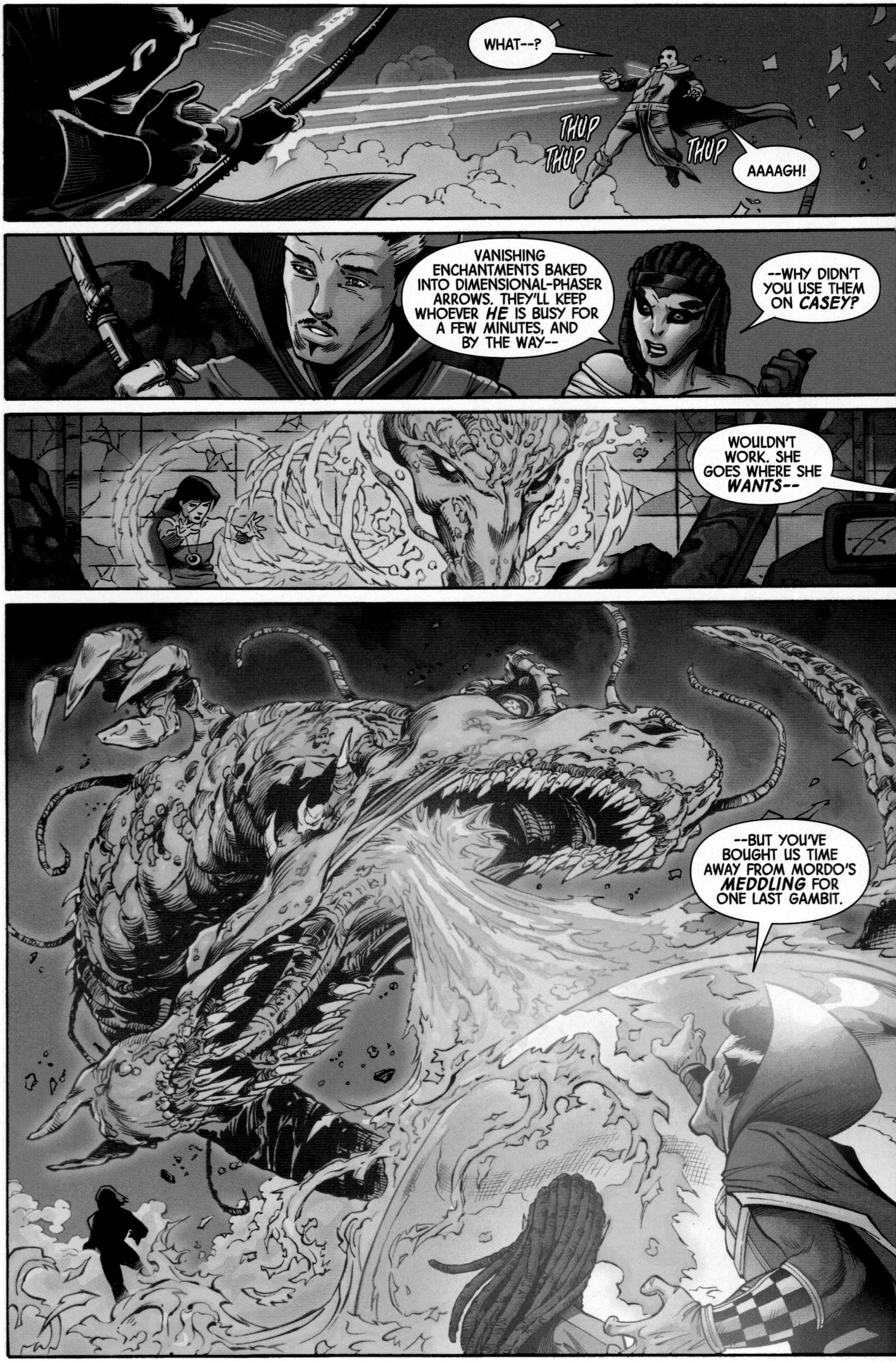

WHAT--?
THUP THUP
THUP
AAAAGH!
VANISHING ENCHANTMENTS BAKED INTO DIMENSIONAL-PHASER ARROWS. THEY'LL KEEP WHOEVER HE IS BUSY FOR A FEW MINUTES, AND BY THE WAY--
--WHY DIDN'T YOU USE THEM ON CASEY?
WOULDN'T WORK. SHE GOES WHERE SHE WANTS--
--BUT YOU'VE BOUGHT US TIME AWAY FROM MORDO'S MEDDLING FOR ONE LAST GAMBIT.

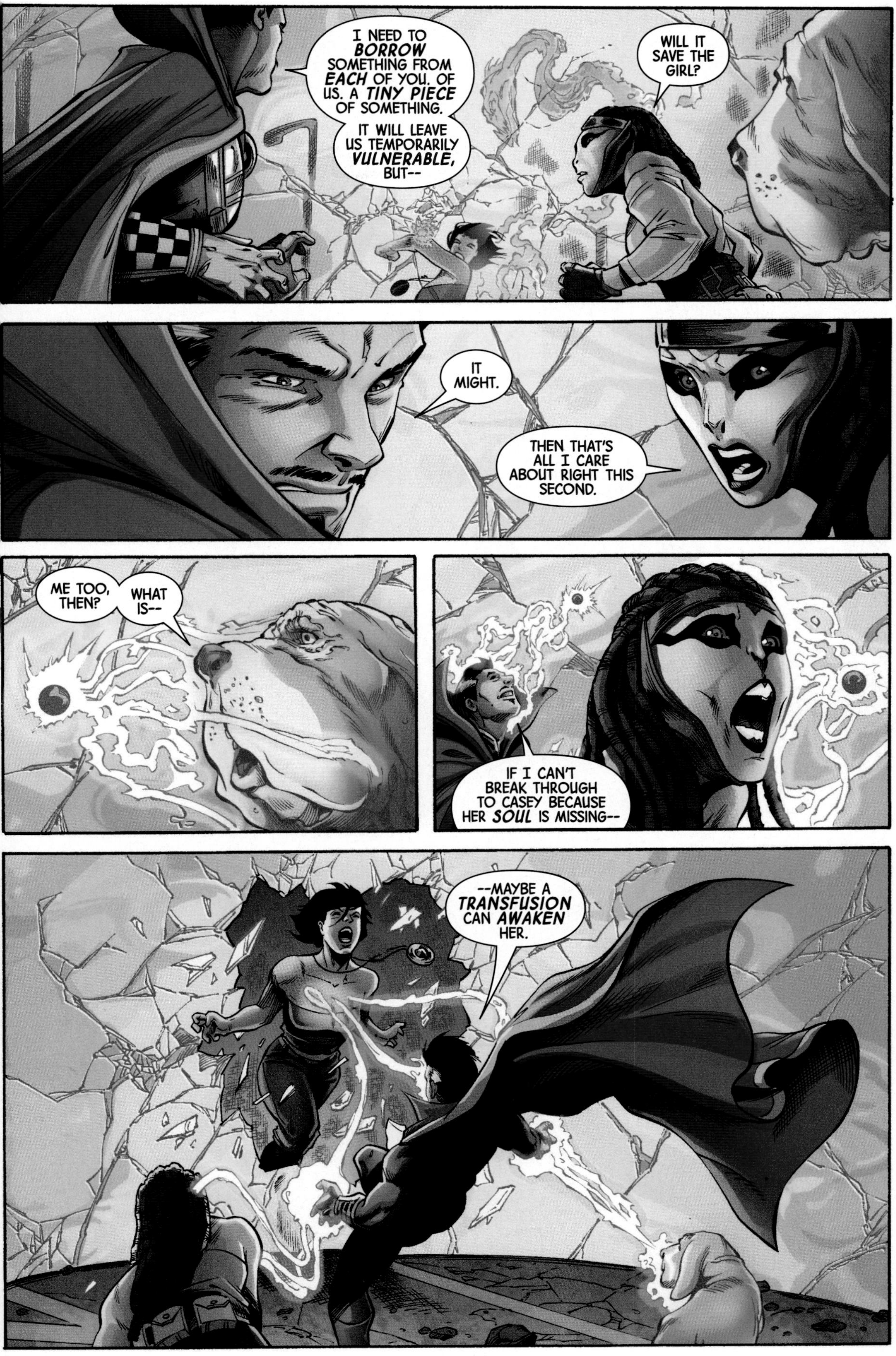
I NEED TO *BORROW* SOMETHING FROM *EACH* OF YOU. OF US. A *TINY PIECE* OF SOMETHING.
IT WILL LEAVE US TEMPORARILY *VULNERABLE,* BUT--
WILL IT SAVE THE GIRL?
IT MIGHT.
THEN THAT'S ALL I CARE ABOUT RIGHT THIS SECOND.
ME TOO, THEN?
WHAT IS--
IF I CAN'T BREAK THROUGH TO CASEY BECAUSE HER *SOUL* IS MISSING--
--MAYBE A *TRANSFUSION* CAN *AWAKEN* HER.

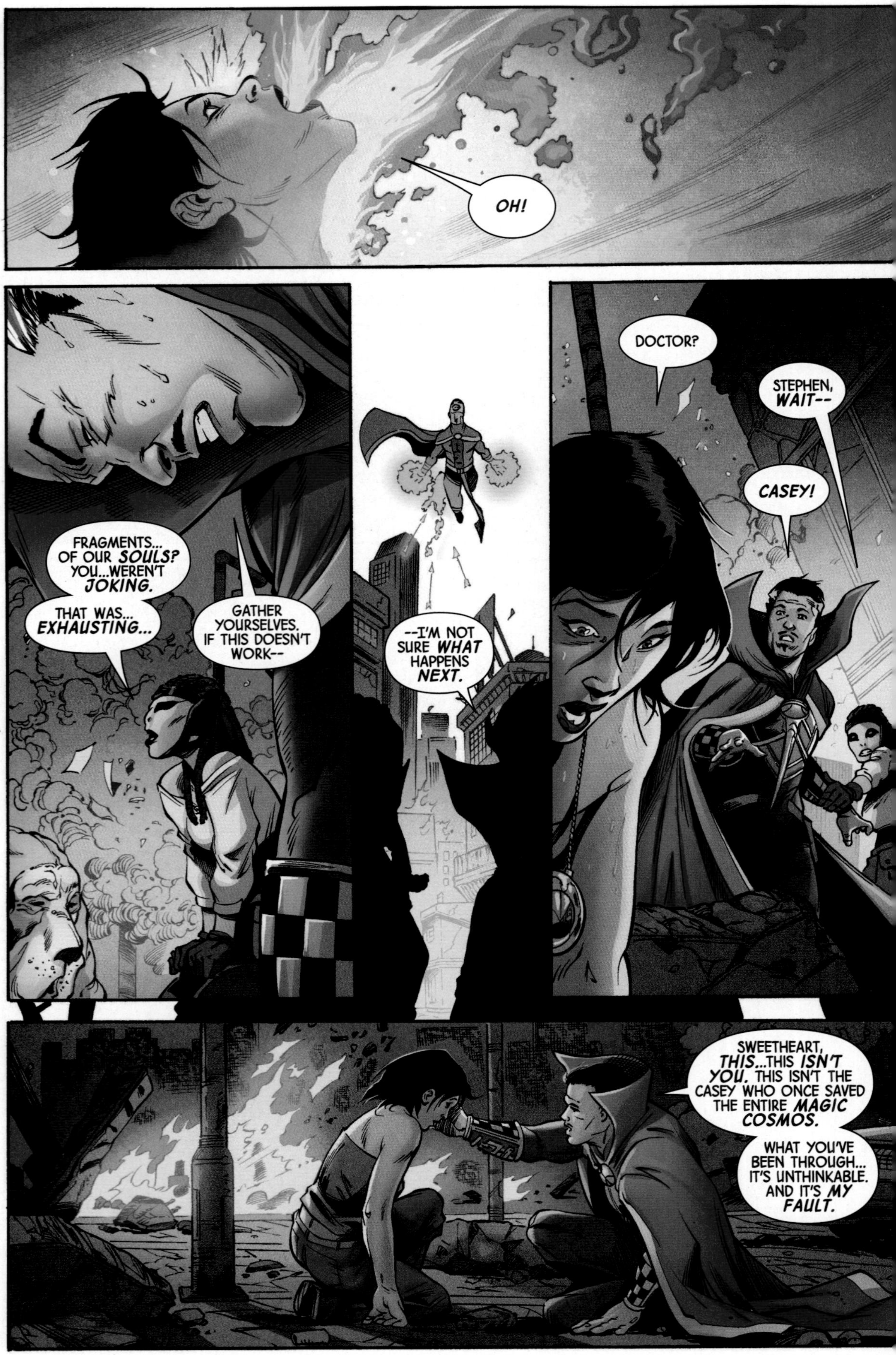
OH!
FRAGMENTS... OF OUR SOULS? YOU...WEREN'T JOKING.
THAT WAS... EXHAUSTING...
GATHER YOURSELVES. IF THIS DOESN'T WORK--
--I'M NOT SURE WHAT HAPPENS NEXT.
DOCTOR?
STEPHEN, WAIT--
CASEY!
SWEETHEART, THIS...THIS ISN'T YOU. THIS ISN'T THE CASEY WHO ONCE SAVED THE ENTIRE MAGIC COSMOS.
WHAT YOU'VE BEEN THROUGH... IT'S UNTHINKABLE. AND IT'S MY FAULT.

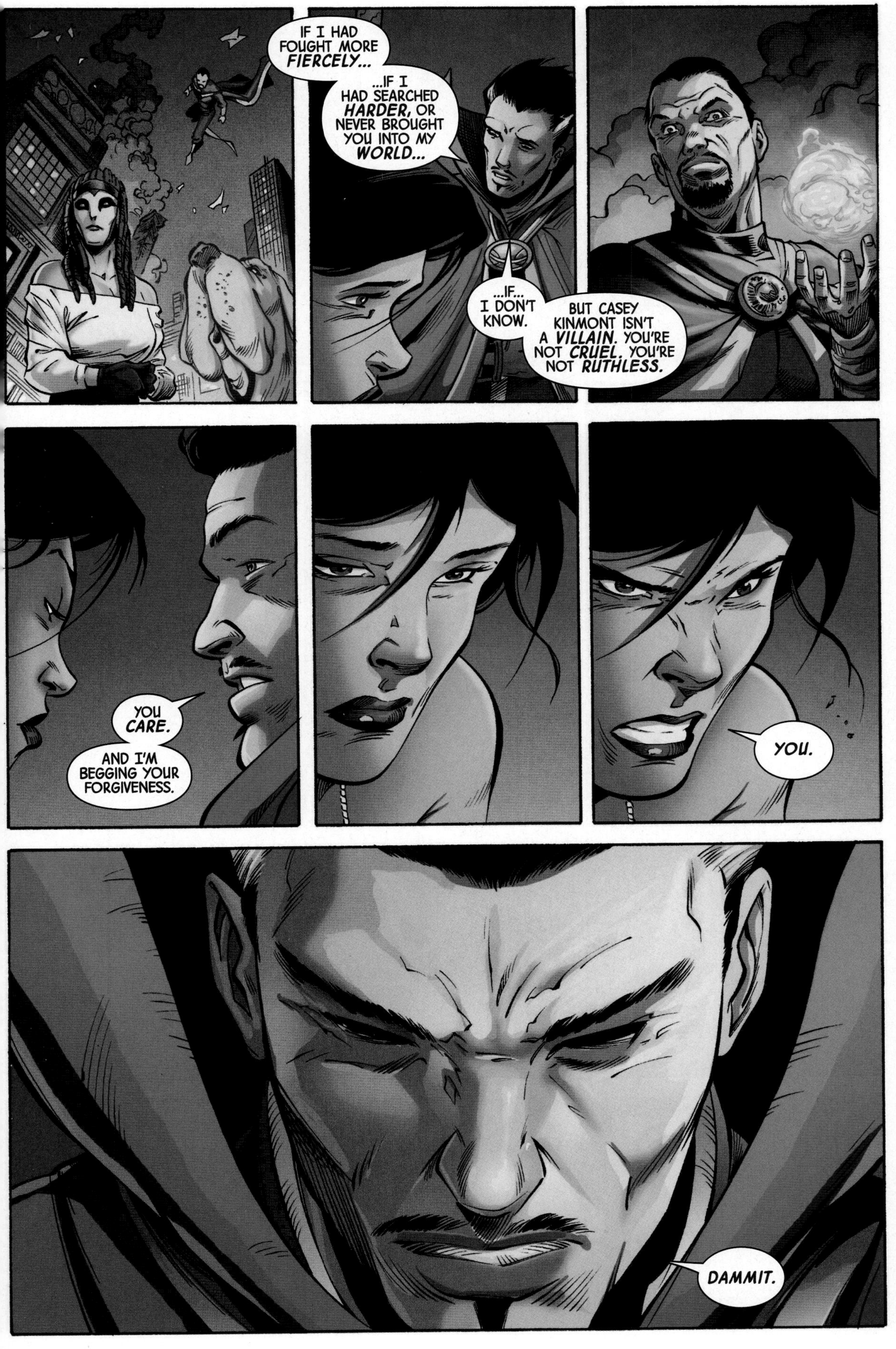
IF I HAD FOUGHT MORE FIERCELY...
...IF I HAD SEARCHED HARDER, OR NEVER BROUGHT YOU INTO MY WORLD...
...IF... I DON'T KNOW.
BUT CASEY KINMONT ISN'T A VILLAIN. YOU'RE NOT CRUEL. YOU'RE NOT RUTHLESS.
YOU CARE.
AND I'M BEGGING YOUR FORGIVENESS.
YOU.
DAMMIT.

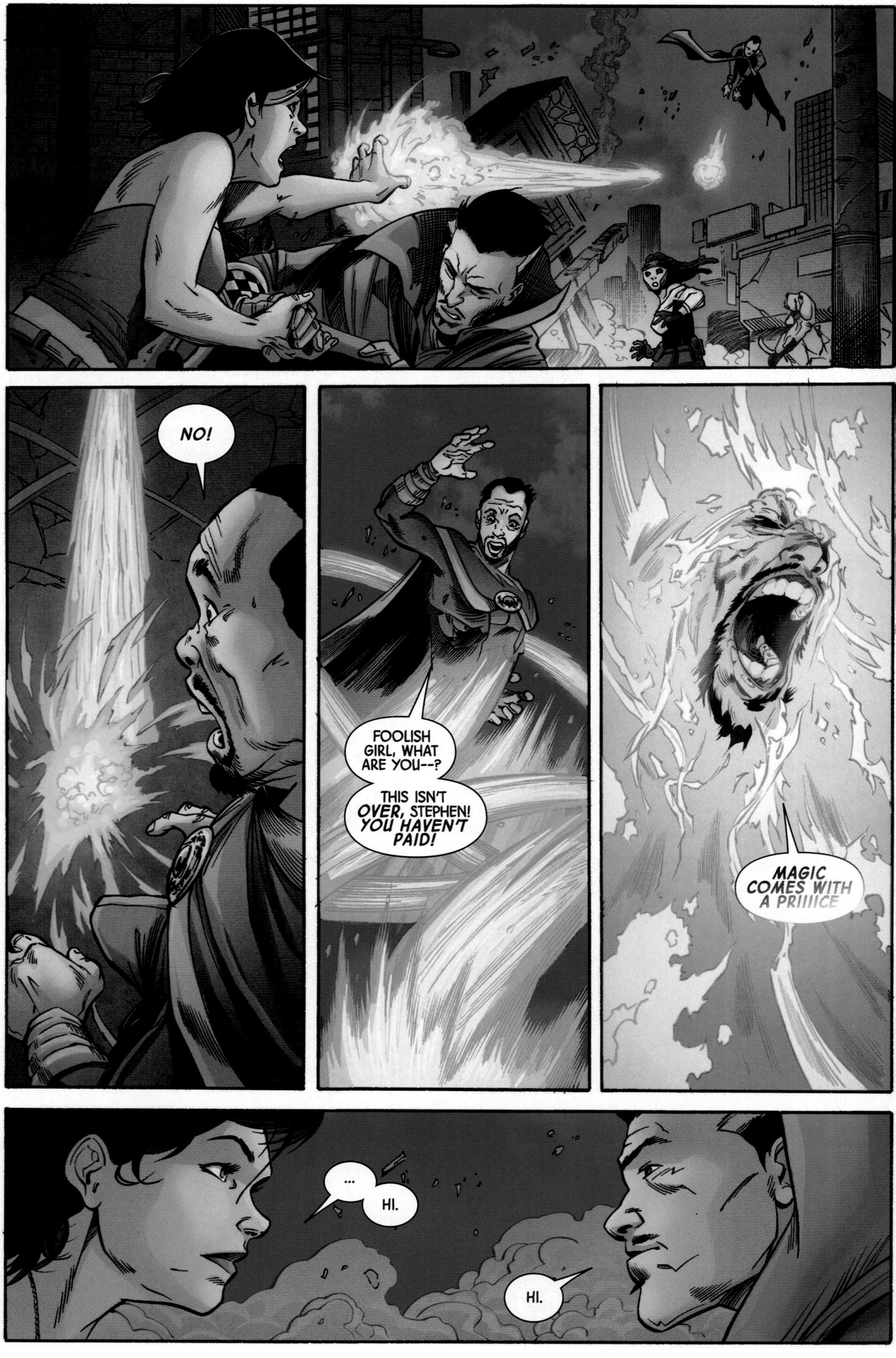
NO!
FOOLISH GIRL, WHAT ARE YOU--?
THIS ISN'T *OVER*, STEPHEN! *YOU HAVEN'T PAID!*
MAGIC COMES WITH A PRIIIICE
...
HI.
HI.

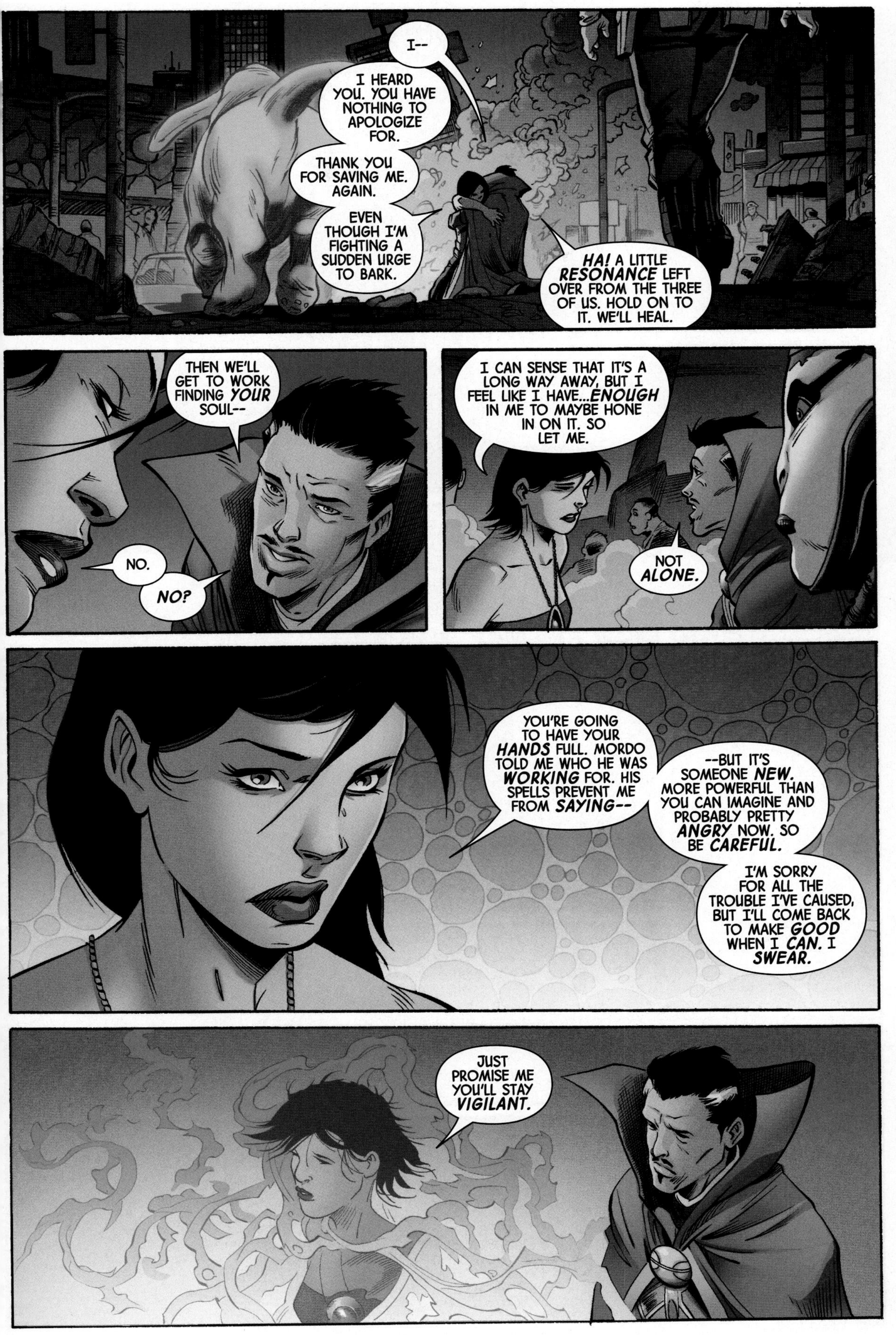
I--
I HEARD YOU. YOU HAVE NOTHING TO APOLOGIZE FOR.
THANK YOU FOR SAVING ME. AGAIN.
EVEN THOUGH I'M FIGHTING A SUDDEN URGE TO BARK.
HA! A LITTLE RESONANCE LEFT OVER FROM THE THREE OF US. HOLD ON TO IT. WE'LL HEAL.
THEN WE'LL GET TO WORK FINDING YOUR SOUL--
NO.
NO?
I CAN SENSE THAT IT'S A LONG WAY AWAY, BUT I FEEL LIKE I HAVE...ENOUGH IN ME TO MAYBE HONE IN ON IT. SO LET ME.
NOT ALONE.
YOU'RE GOING TO HAVE YOUR HANDS FULL. MORDO TOLD ME WHO HE WAS WORKING FOR. HIS SPELLS PREVENT ME FROM SAYING--
--BUT IT'S SOMEONE NEW. MORE POWERFUL THAN YOU CAN IMAGINE AND PROBABLY PRETTY ANGRY NOW. SO BE CAREFUL.
I'M SORRY FOR ALL THE TROUBLE I'VE CAUSED, BUT I'LL COME BACK TO MAKE GOOD WHEN I CAN. I SWEAR.
JUST PROMISE ME YOU'LL STAY VIGILANT.

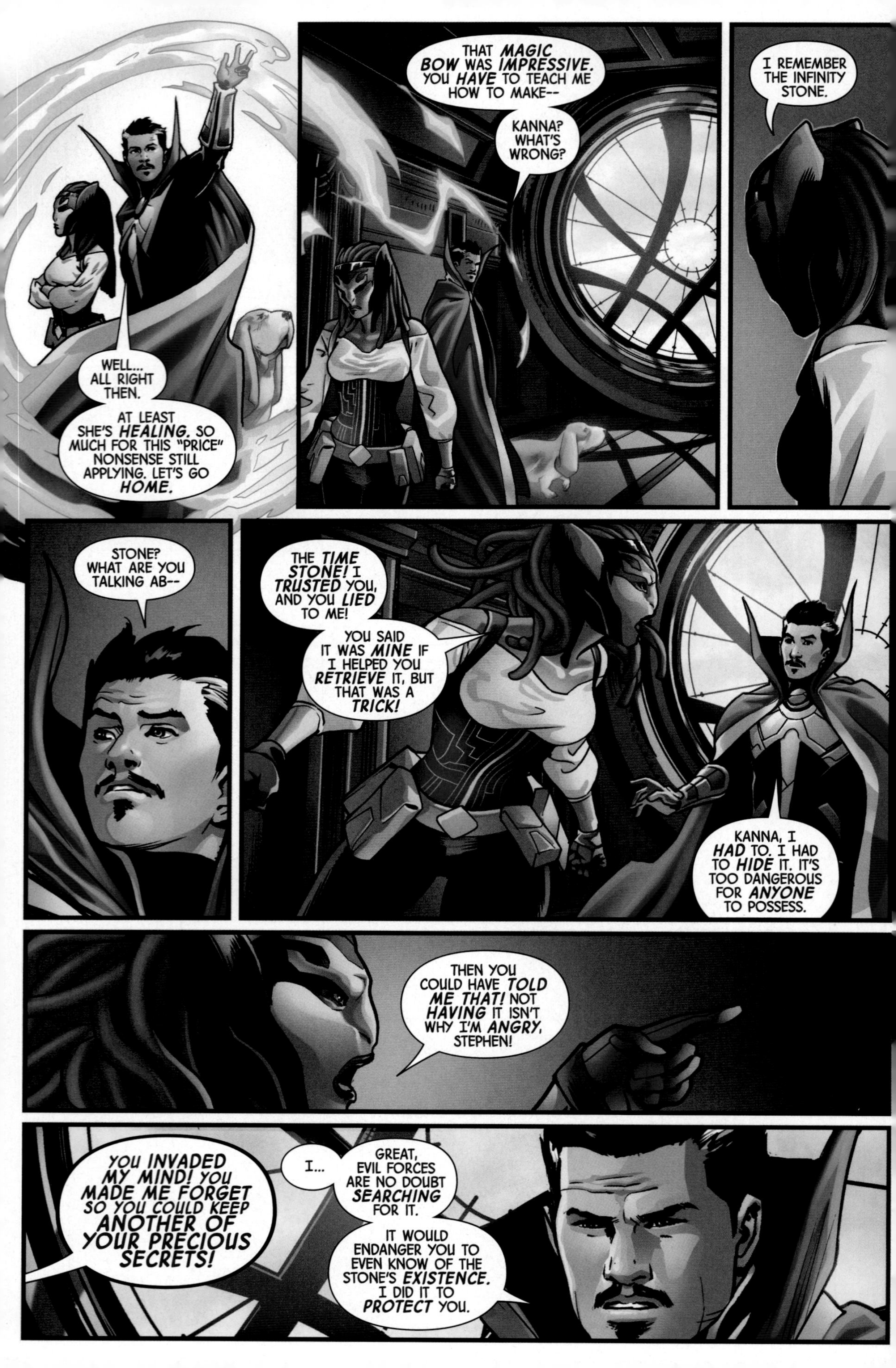
WELL... ALL RIGHT THEN.
AT LEAST SHE'S HEALING. SO MUCH FOR THIS "PRICE" NONSENSE STILL APPLYING. LET'S GO HOME.
THAT MAGIC BOW WAS IMPRESSIVE. YOU HAVE TO TEACH ME HOW TO MAKE--
KANNA? WHAT'S WRONG?
I REMEMBER THE INFINITY STONE.
STONE? WHAT ARE YOU TALKING AB--
THE TIME STONE! I TRUSTED YOU, AND YOU LIED TO ME!
YOU SAID IT WAS MINE IF I HELPED YOU RETRIEVE IT, BUT THAT WAS A TRICK!
KANNA, I HAD TO. I HAD TO HIDE IT. IT'S TOO DANGEROUS FOR ANYONE TO POSSESS.
THEN YOU COULD HAVE TOLD ME THAT! NOT HAVING IT ISN'T WHY I'M ANGRY, STEPHEN!
YOU INVADED MY MIND! YOU MADE ME FORGET SO YOU COULD KEEP ANOTHER OF YOUR PRECIOUS SECRETS!
I...
GREAT, EVIL FORCES ARE NO DOUBT SEARCHING FOR IT.
IT WOULD ENDANGER YOU TO EVEN KNOW OF THE STONE'S EXISTENCE. I DID IT TO PROTECT YOU.

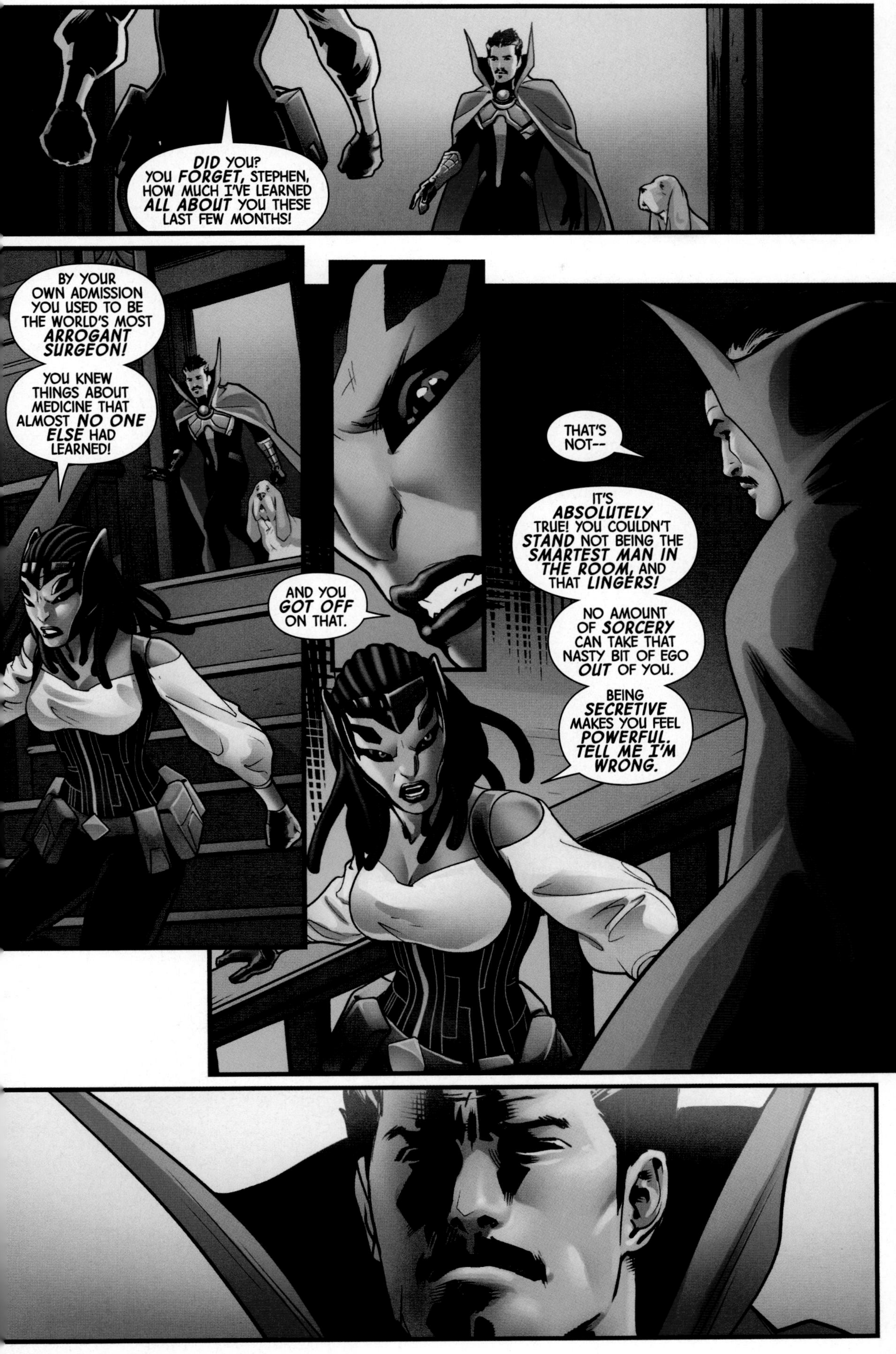
DID YOU? YOU FORGET, STEPHEN, HOW MUCH I'VE LEARNED ALL ABOUT YOU THESE LAST FEW MONTHS!
BY YOUR OWN ADMISSION YOU USED TO BE THE WORLD'S MOST ARROGANT SURGEON!
YOU KNEW THINGS ABOUT MEDICINE THAT ALMOST NO ONE ELSE HAD LEARNED!
AND YOU GOT OFF ON THAT.
THAT'S NOT--
IT'S ABSOLUTELY TRUE! YOU COULDN'T STAND NOT BEING THE SMARTEST MAN IN THE ROOM, AND THAT LINGERS!
NO AMOUNT OF SORCERY CAN TAKE THAT NASTY BIT OF EGO OUT OF YOU.
BEING SECRETIVE MAKES YOU FEEL POWERFUL. TELL ME I'M WRONG.

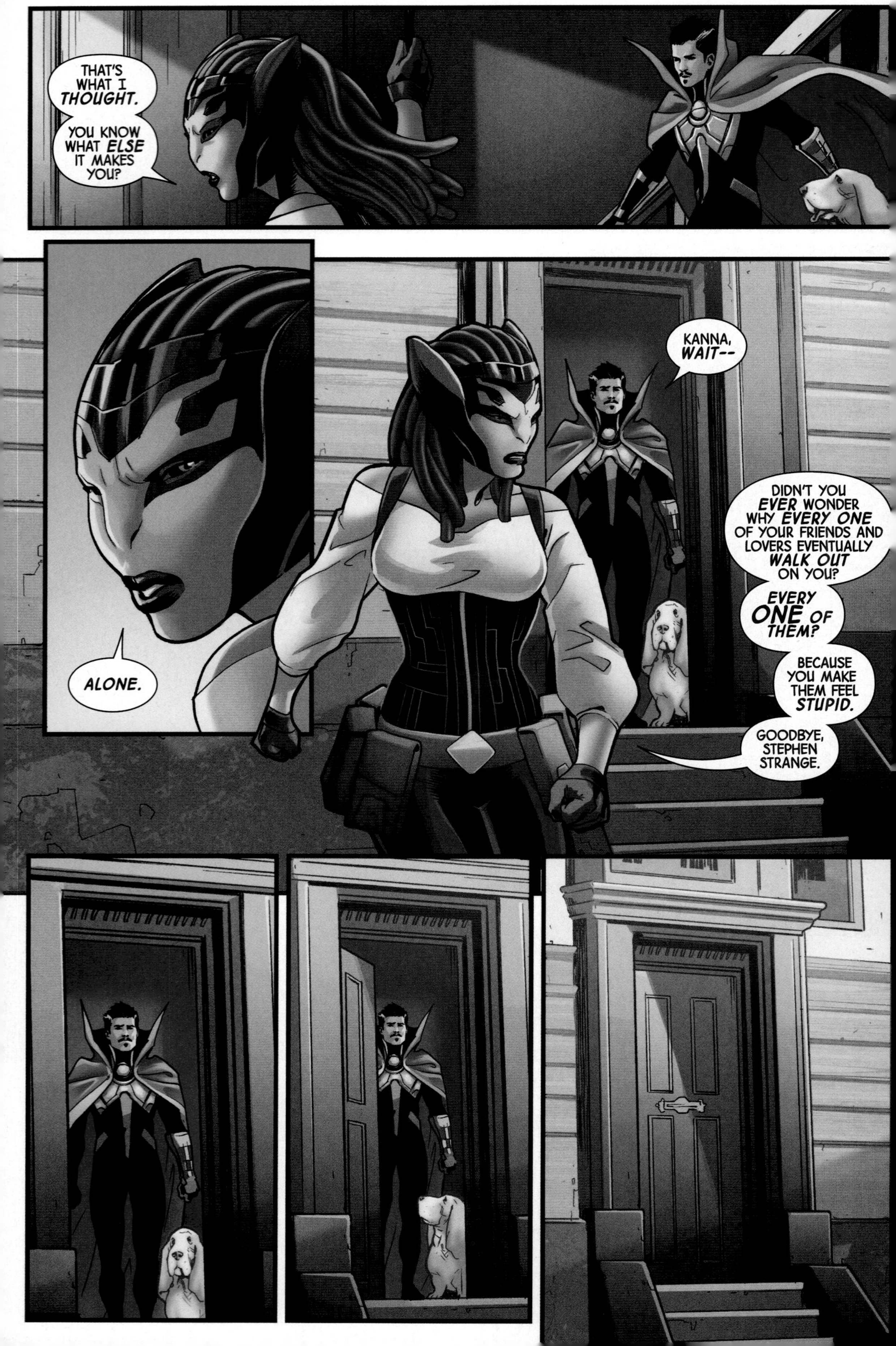
THAT'S WHAT I *THOUGHT*.
YOU KNOW WHAT *ELSE* IT MAKES YOU?
ALONE.
KANNA, *WAIT--*
DIDN'T YOU *EVER* WONDER WHY *EVERY ONE* OF YOUR FRIENDS AND LOVERS EVENTUALLY *WALK OUT* ON YOU?
EVERY ONE OF THEM?
BECAUSE YOU MAKE THEM FEEL *STUPID*.
GOODBYE, STEPHEN STRANGE.

9

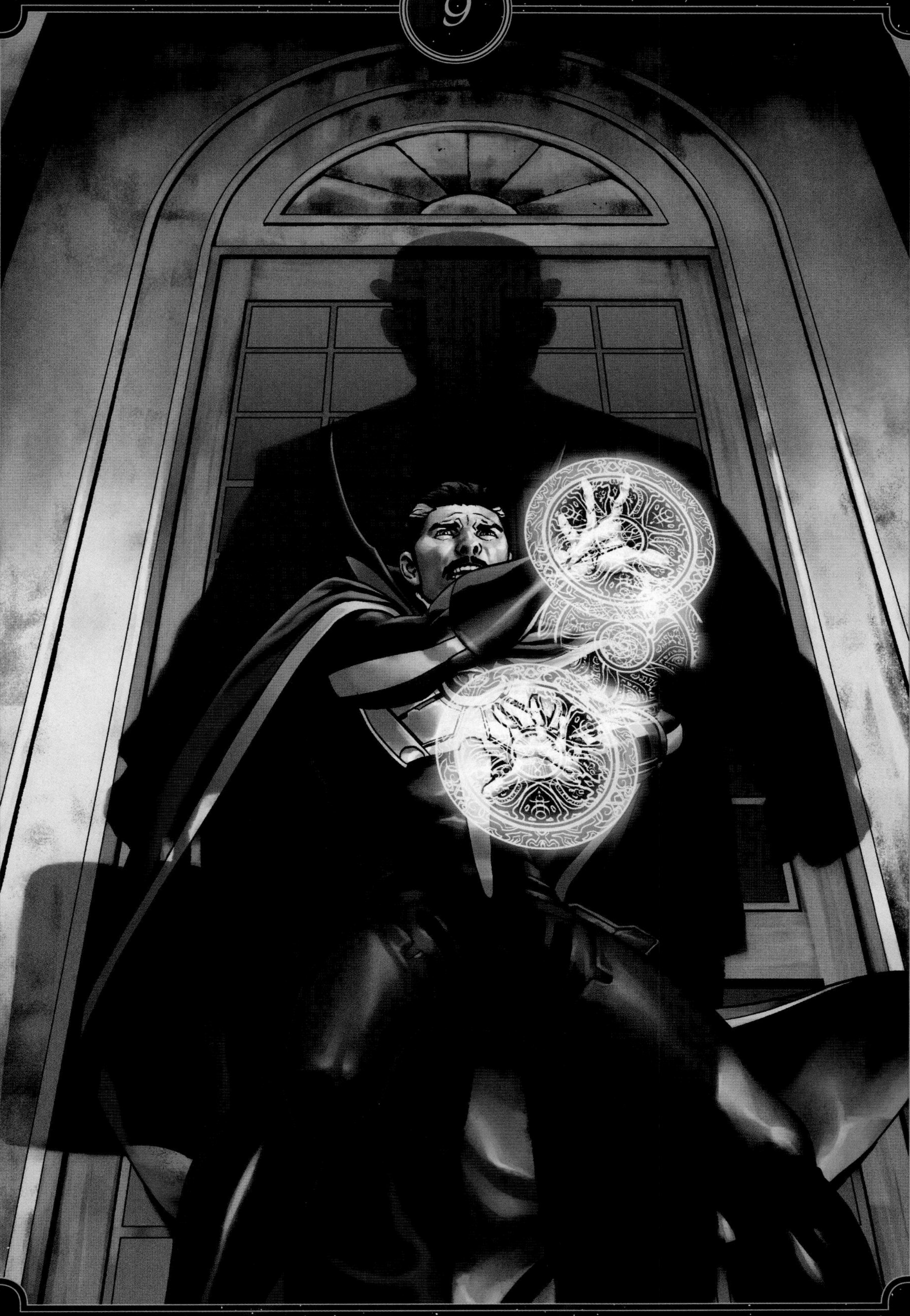

Bleecker

COMING SOON

THE NEW

BLEECKER STREET!

SHOPPING! APARTMENTS! SUITES

Phone **FALSTON REALTY**
at (212) 555-0162

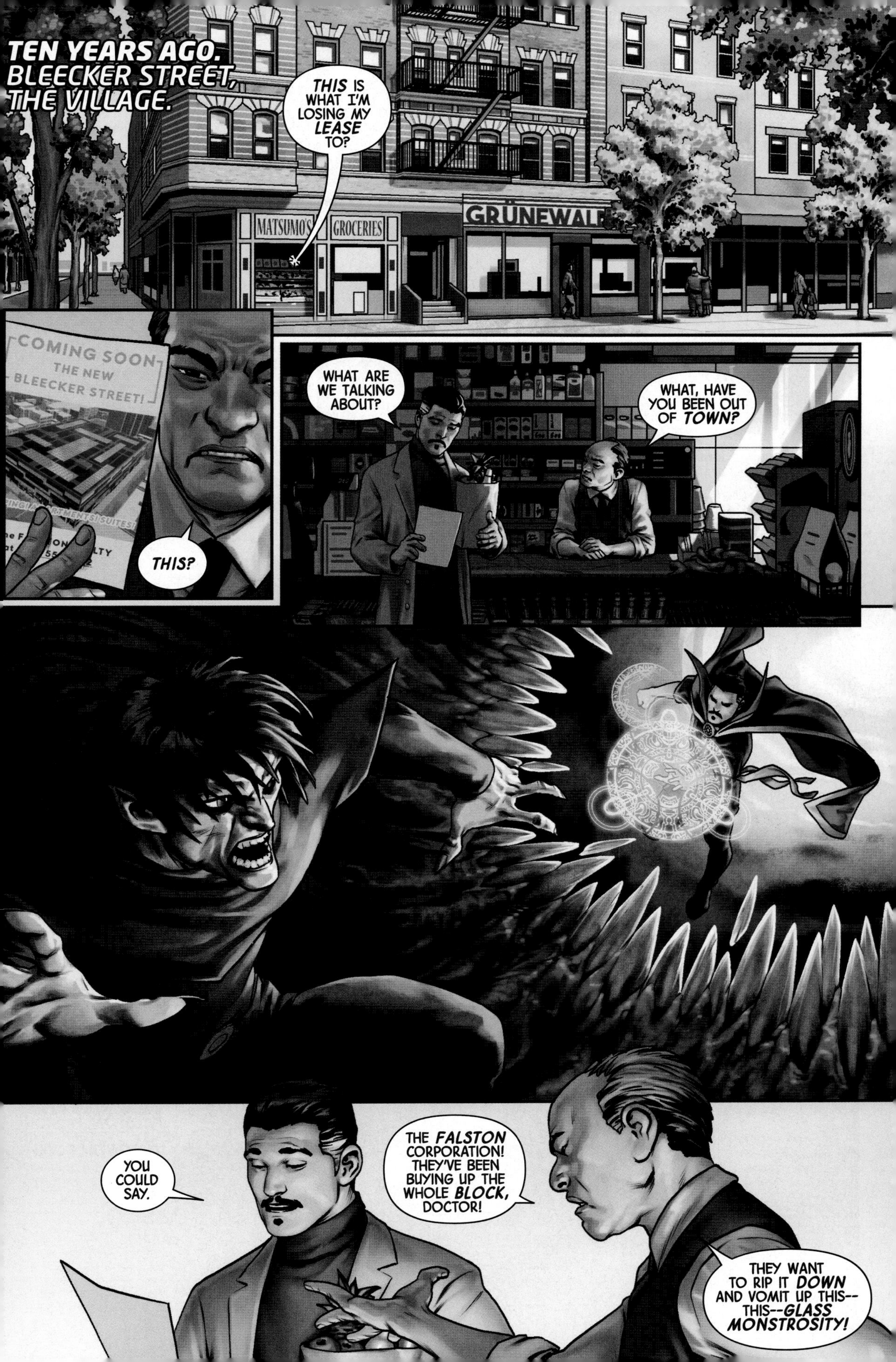
TEN YEARS AGO. BLEECKER STREET, THE VILLAGE.
THIS IS WHAT I'M LOSING MY LEASE TO?
MATSUMO'S GROCERIES
GRÜNEWAL
COMING SOON THE NEW BLEECKER STREET!
THIS?
WHAT ARE WE TALKING ABOUT?
WHAT, HAVE YOU BEEN OUT OF TOWN?
YOU COULD SAY.
THE FALSTON CORPORATION! THEY'VE BEEN BUYING UP THE WHOLE BLOCK, DOCTOR!
THEY WANT TO RIP IT DOWN AND VOMIT UP THIS--THIS--GLASS MONSTROSITY!

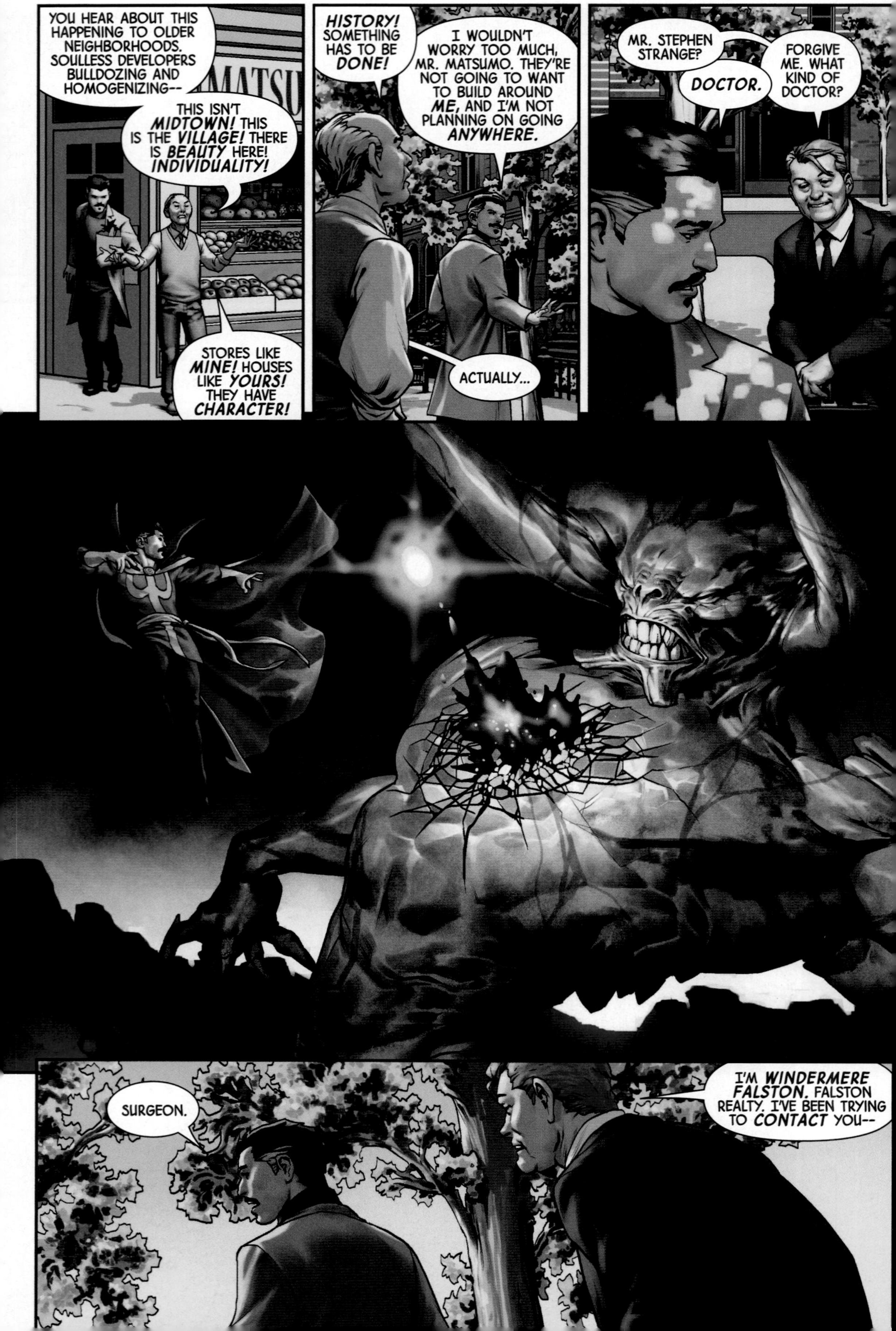

YOU HEAR ABOUT THIS HAPPENING TO OLDER NEIGHBORHOODS. SOULLESS DEVELOPERS BULLDOZING AND HOMOGENIZING--
THIS ISN'T MIDTOWN! THIS IS THE VILLAGE! THERE IS BEAUTY HERE! INDIVIDUALITY!
STORES LIKE MINE! HOUSES LIKE YOURS! THEY HAVE CHARACTER!
HISTORY! SOMETHING HAS TO BE DONE!
I WOULDN'T WORRY TOO MUCH, MR. MATSUMO. THEY'RE NOT GOING TO WANT TO BUILD AROUND ME, AND I'M NOT PLANNING ON GOING ANYWHERE.
ACTUALLY...
MR. STEPHEN STRANGE?
DOCTOR.
FORGIVE ME. WHAT KIND OF DOCTOR?
SURGEON.
I'M WINDERMERE FALSTON. FALSTON REALTY. I'VE BEEN TRYING TO CONTACT YOU--

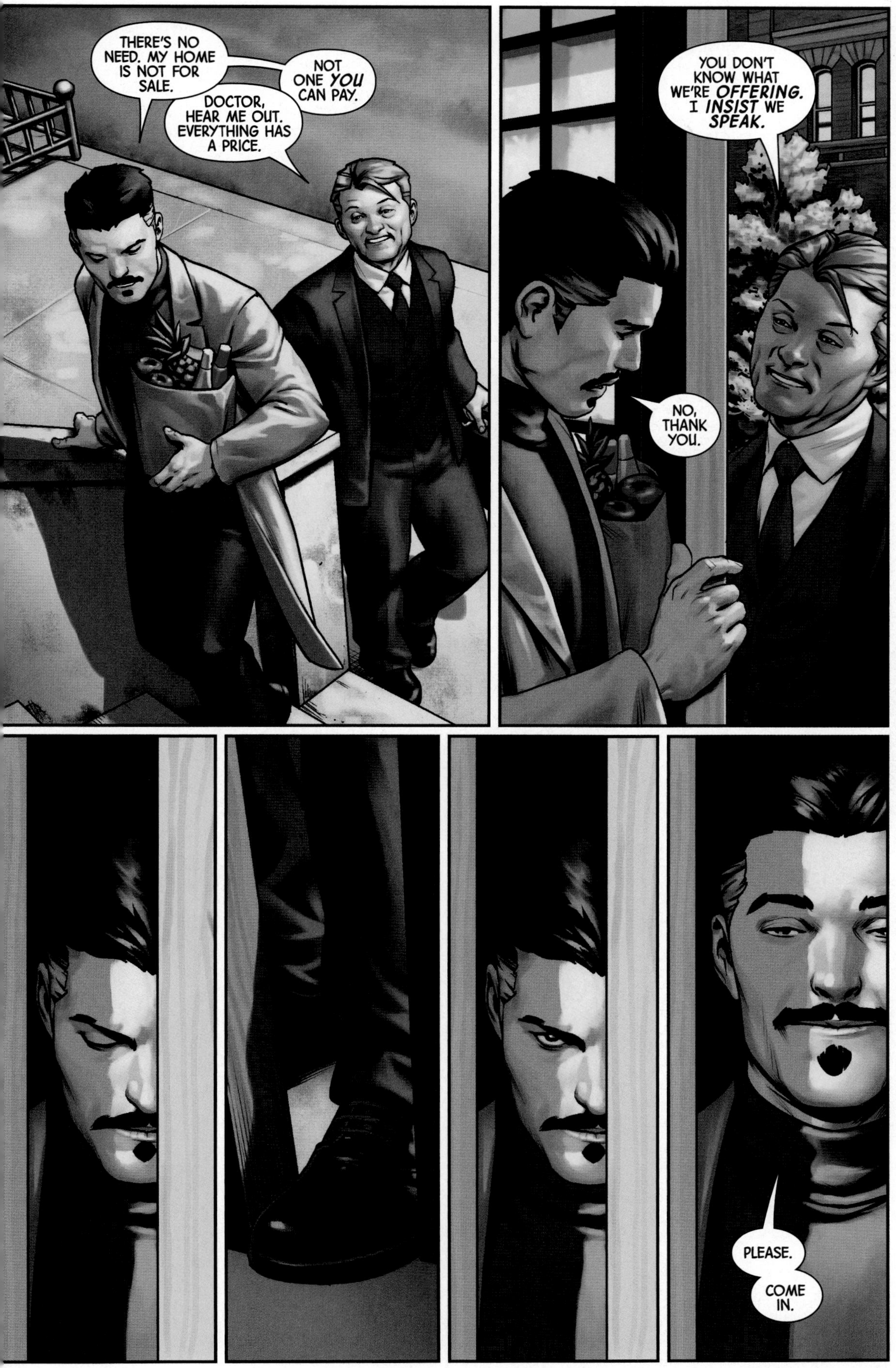
THERE'S NO NEED. MY HOME IS NOT FOR SALE.
NOT ONE YOU CAN PAY.
DOCTOR, HEAR ME OUT. EVERYTHING HAS A PRICE.
YOU DON'T KNOW WHAT WE'RE OFFERING. I INSIST WE SPEAK.
NO, THANK YOU.
PLEASE.
COME IN.

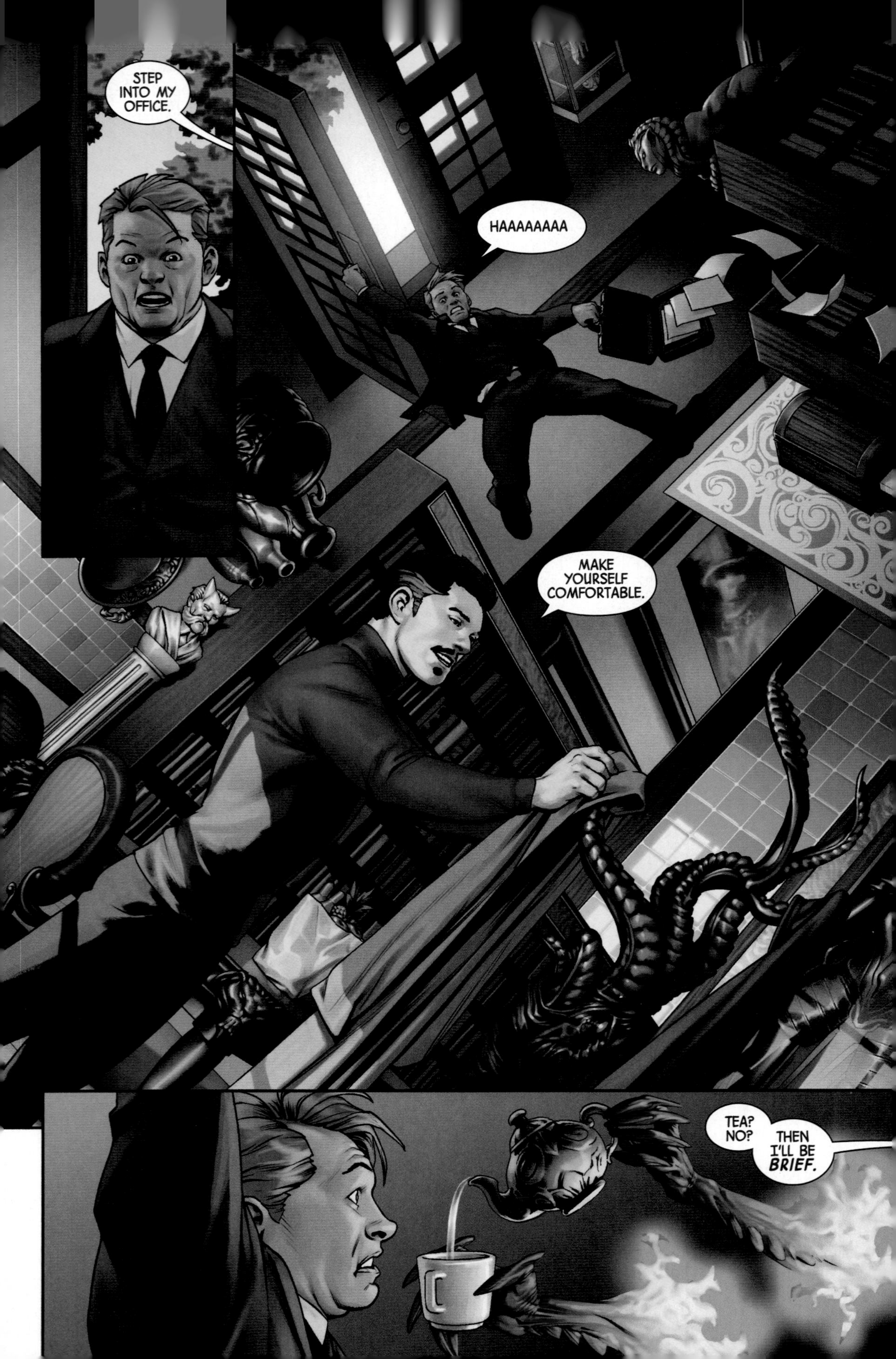
STEP INTO MY OFFICE.
HAAAAAAAA
MAKE YOURSELF COMFORTABLE.
TEA? NO?
THEN I'LL BE *BRIEF.*

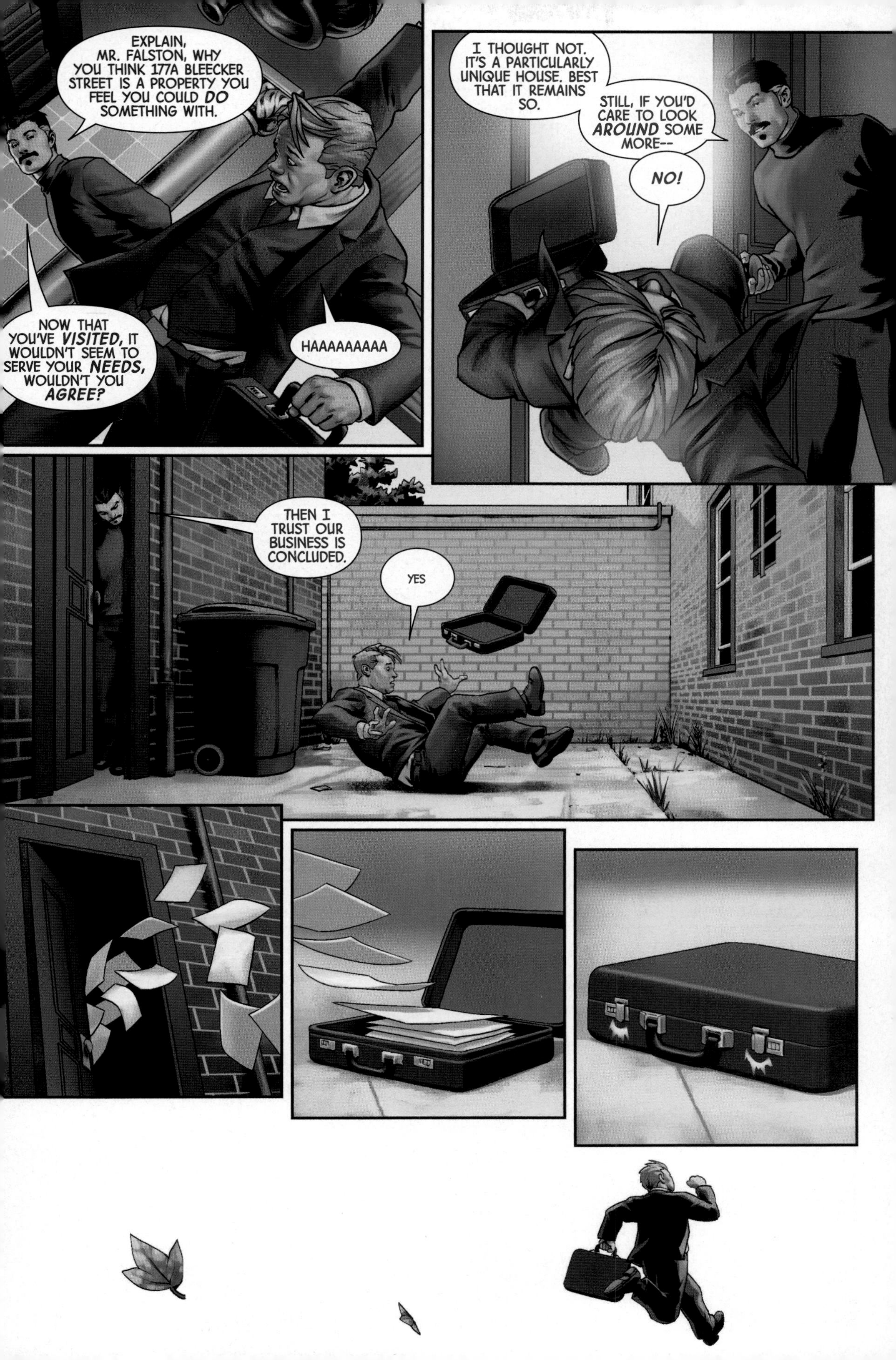
EXPLAIN, MR. FALSTON, WHY YOU THINK 177A BLEECKER STREET IS A PROPERTY YOU FEEL YOU COULD DO SOMETHING WITH.
NOW THAT YOU'VE VISITED, IT WOULDN'T SEEM TO SERVE YOUR NEEDS, WOULDN'T YOU AGREE?
HAAAAAAAAA
I THOUGHT NOT. IT'S A PARTICULARLY UNIQUE HOUSE. BEST THAT IT REMAINS SO.
STILL, IF YOU'D CARE TO LOOK AROUND SOME MORE--
NO!
THEN I TRUST OUR BUSINESS IS CONCLUDED.
YES

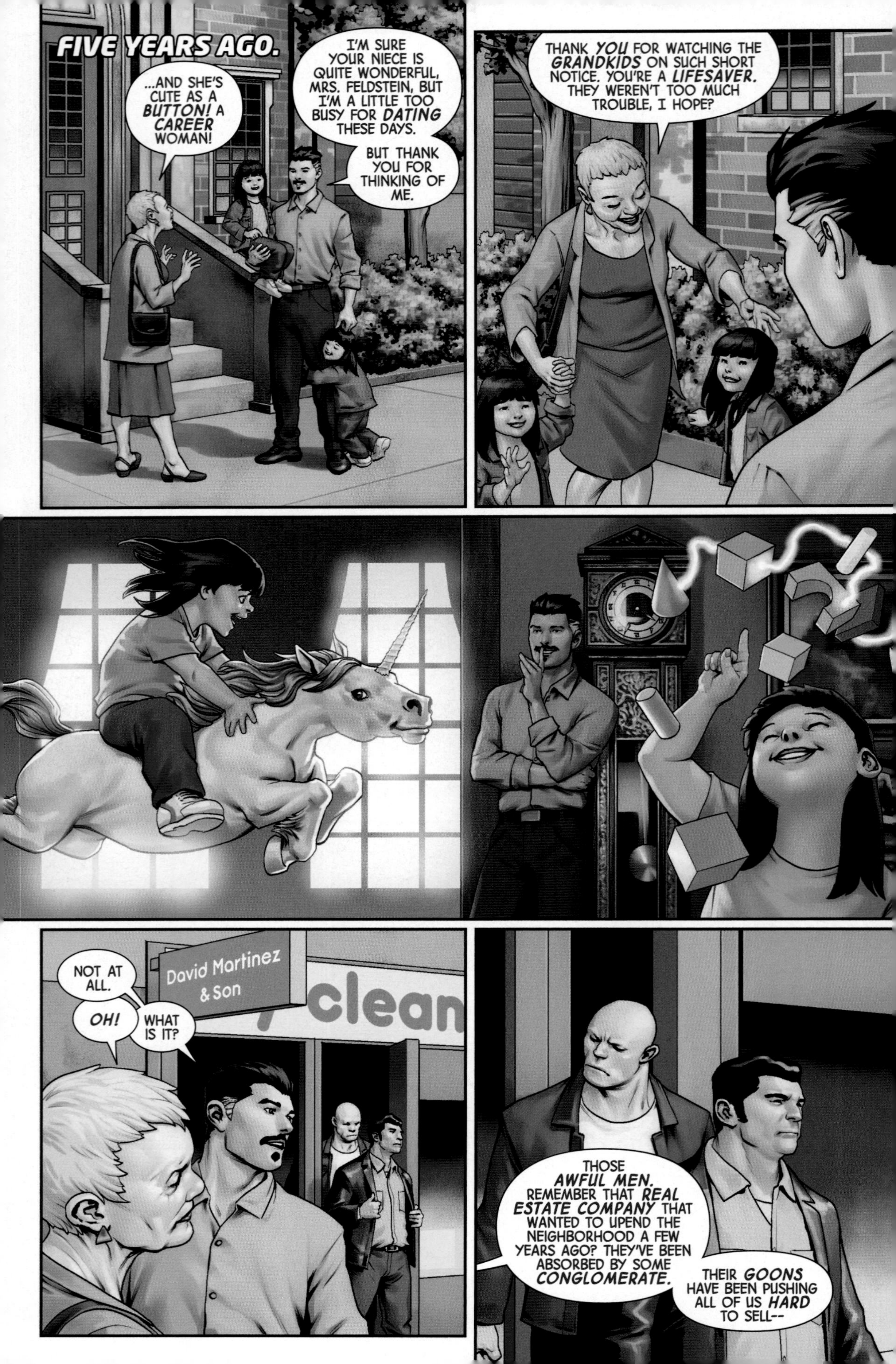
FIVE YEARS AGO.
...AND SHE'S CUTE AS A BUTTON! A CAREER WOMAN!
I'M SURE YOUR NIECE IS QUITE WONDERFUL, MRS. FELDSTEIN, BUT I'M A LITTLE TOO BUSY FOR DATING THESE DAYS.
BUT THANK YOU FOR THINKING OF ME.
THANK YOU FOR WATCHING THE GRANDKIDS ON SUCH SHORT NOTICE. YOU'RE A LIFESAVER. THEY WEREN'T TOO MUCH TROUBLE, I HOPE?
NOT AT ALL.
OH!
WHAT IS IT?
David Martinez & Son
clean
THOSE AWFUL MEN. REMEMBER THAT REAL ESTATE COMPANY THAT WANTED TO UPEND THE NEIGHBORHOOD A FEW YEARS AGO? THEY'VE BEEN ABSORBED BY SOME CONGLOMERATE.
THEIR GOONS HAVE BEEN PUSHING ALL OF US HARD TO SELL--

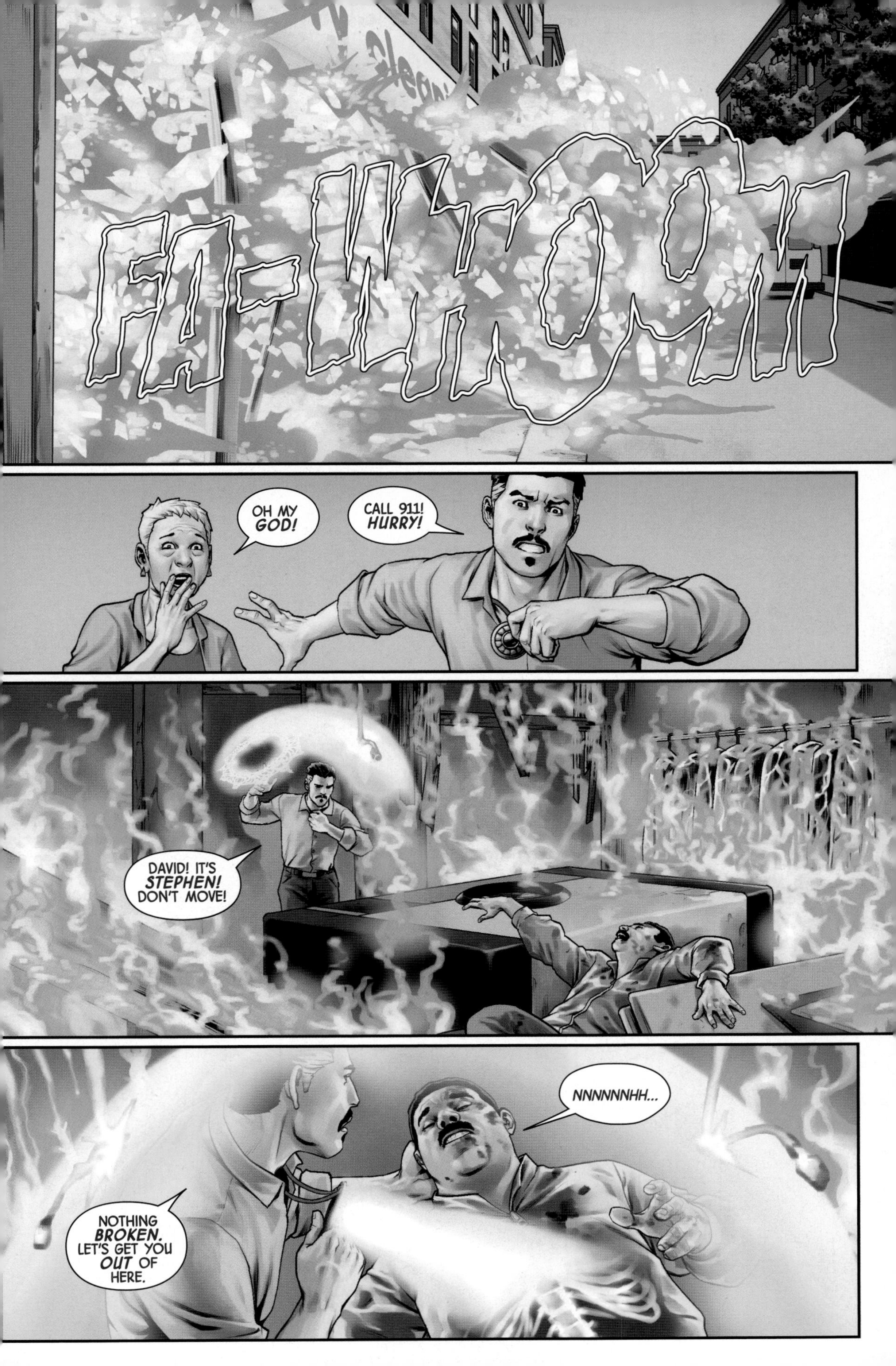
KA-WHOOOM
OH MY GOD!
CALL 911! HURRY!
DAVID! IT'S STEPHEN! DON'T MOVE!
NNNNNNHH...
NOTHING BROKEN. LET'S GET YOU OUT OF HERE.

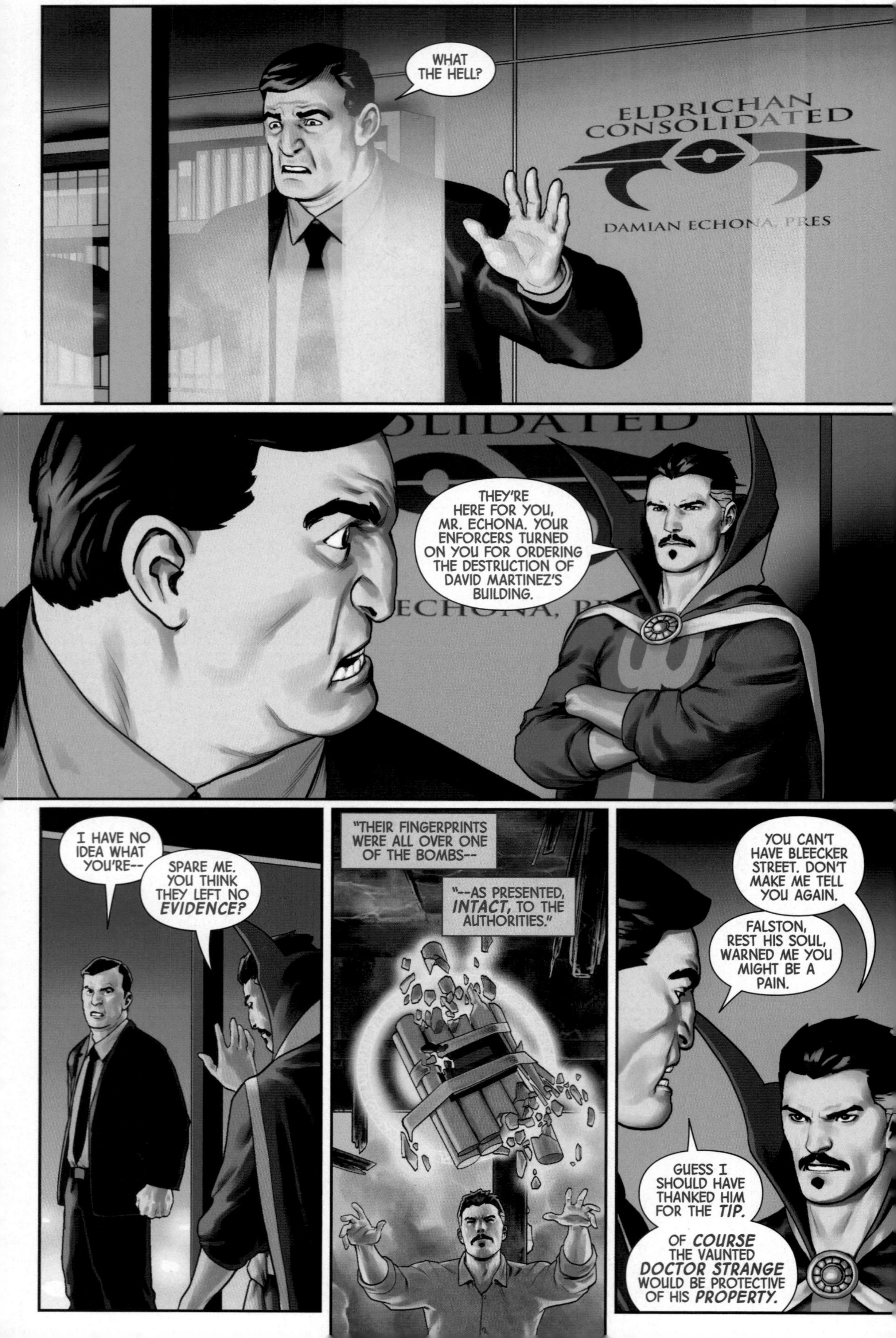
WHAT THE HELL?
ELDRICHAN CONSOLIDATED
DAMIAN ECHONA, PRES
THEY'RE HERE FOR YOU, MR. ECHONA. YOUR ENFORCERS TURNED ON YOU FOR ORDERING THE DESTRUCTION OF DAVID MARTINEZ'S BUILDING.
I HAVE NO IDEA WHAT YOU'RE--
SPARE ME. YOU THINK THEY LEFT NO EVIDENCE?
"THEIR FINGERPRINTS WERE ALL OVER ONE OF THE BOMBS--
"--AS PRESENTED, INTACT, TO THE AUTHORITIES."
YOU CAN'T HAVE BLEECKER STREET. DON'T MAKE ME TELL YOU AGAIN.
FALSTON, REST HIS SOUL, WARNED ME YOU MIGHT BE A PAIN.
GUESS I SHOULD HAVE THANKED HIM FOR THE TIP.
OF COURSE THE VAUNTED DOCTOR STRANGE WOULD BE PROTECTIVE OF HIS PROPERTY.

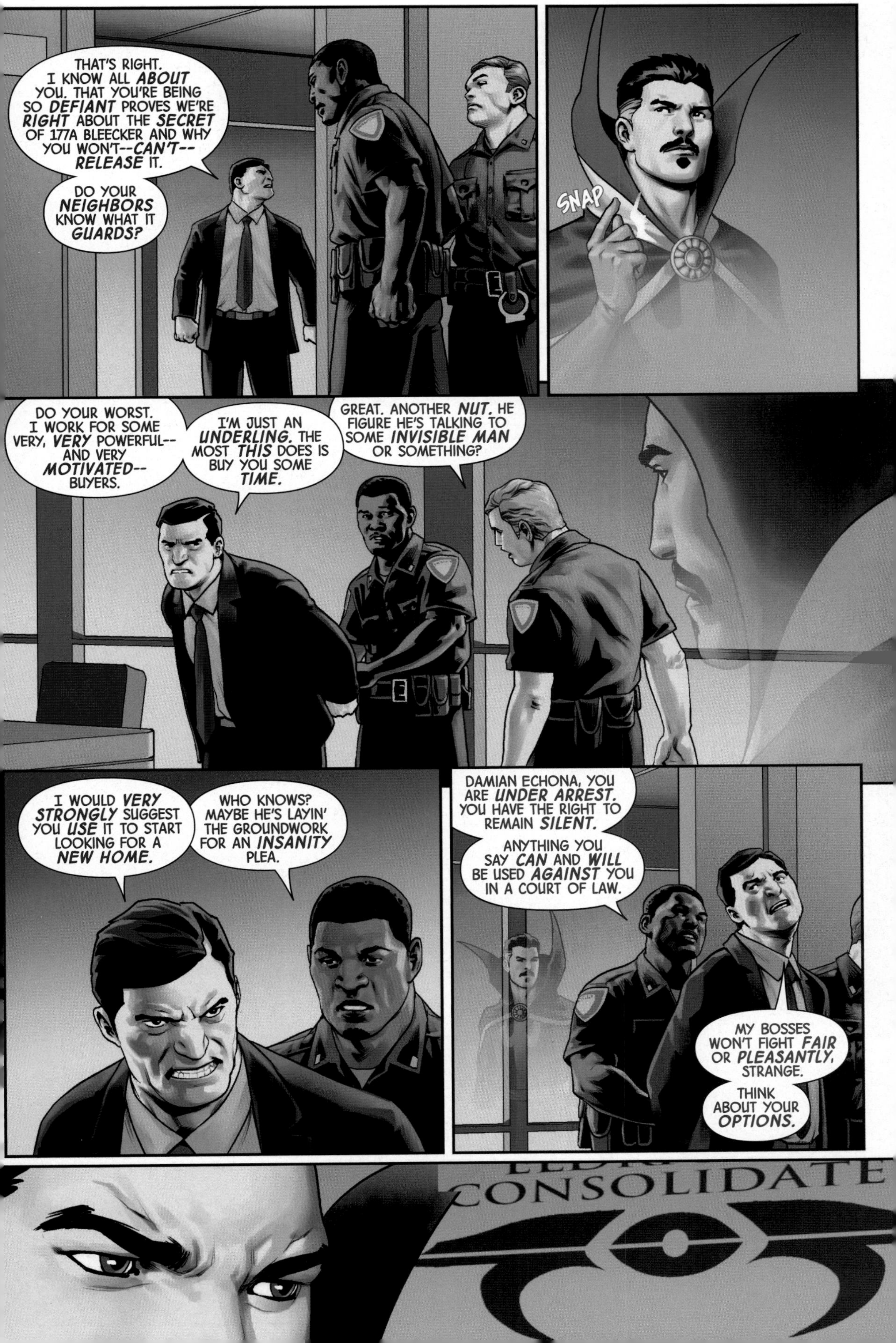
THAT'S RIGHT. I KNOW ALL ABOUT YOU. THAT YOU'RE BEING SO DEFIANT PROVES WE'RE RIGHT ABOUT THE SECRET OF 177A BLEECKER AND WHY YOU WON'T--CAN'T--RELEASE IT.
DO YOUR NEIGHBORS KNOW WHAT IT GUARDS?
SNAP
DO YOUR WORST. I WORK FOR SOME VERY, VERY POWERFUL-- AND VERY MOTIVATED-- BUYERS.
I'M JUST AN UNDERLING. THE MOST THIS DOES IS BUY YOU SOME TIME.
GREAT. ANOTHER NUT. HE FIGURE HE'S TALKING TO SOME INVISIBLE MAN OR SOMETHING?
I WOULD VERY STRONGLY SUGGEST YOU USE IT TO START LOOKING FOR A NEW HOME.
WHO KNOWS? MAYBE HE'S LAYIN' THE GROUNDWORK FOR AN INSANITY PLEA.
DAMIAN ECHONA, YOU ARE UNDER ARREST. YOU HAVE THE RIGHT TO REMAIN SILENT.
ANYTHING YOU SAY CAN AND WILL BE USED AGAINST YOU IN A COURT OF LAW.
MY BOSSES WON'T FIGHT FAIR OR PLEASANTLY, STRANGE.
THINK ABOUT YOUR OPTIONS.
CONSOLIDATE

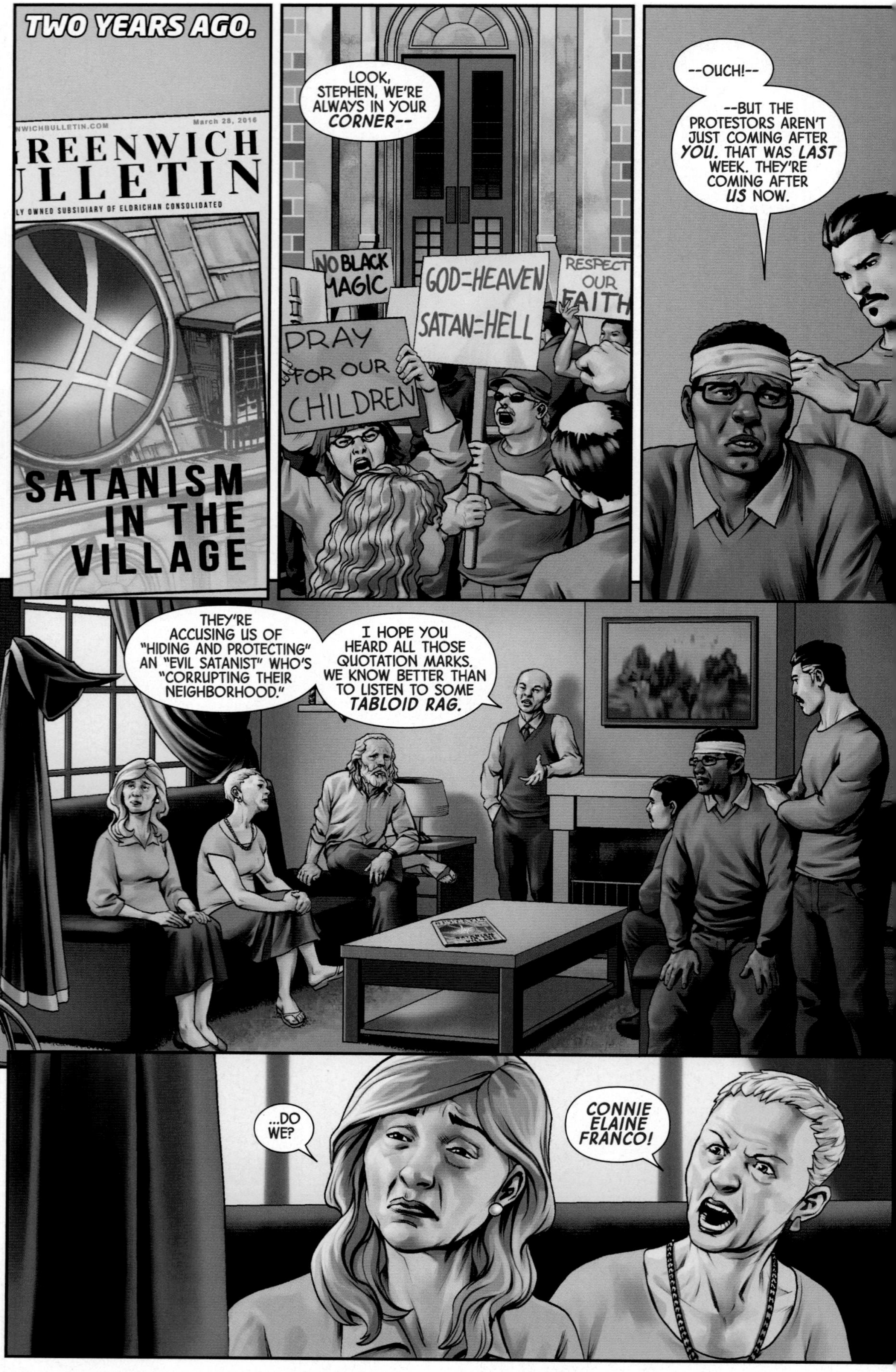
TWO YEARS AGO.
NWICHBULLETIN.COM
March 28, 2016
REENWICH
ULLETIN
LY OWNED SUBSIDIARY OF ELDRICHAN CONSOLIDATED
SATANISM IN THE VILLAGE
LOOK, STEPHEN, WE'RE ALWAYS IN YOUR CORNER--
NO BLACK MAGIC
GOD=HEAVEN SATAN=HELL
RESPECT OUR FAITH
PRAY FOR OUR CHILDREN
--OUCH!--
--BUT THE PROTESTORS AREN'T JUST COMING AFTER YOU. THAT WAS LAST WEEK. THEY'RE COMING AFTER US NOW.
THEY'RE ACCUSING US OF "HIDING AND PROTECTING" AN "EVIL SATANIST" WHO'S "CORRUPTING THEIR NEIGHBORHOOD."
I HOPE YOU HEARD ALL THOSE QUOTATION MARKS. WE KNOW BETTER THAN TO LISTEN TO SOME TABLOID RAG.
...DO WE?
CONNIE ELAINE FRANCO!

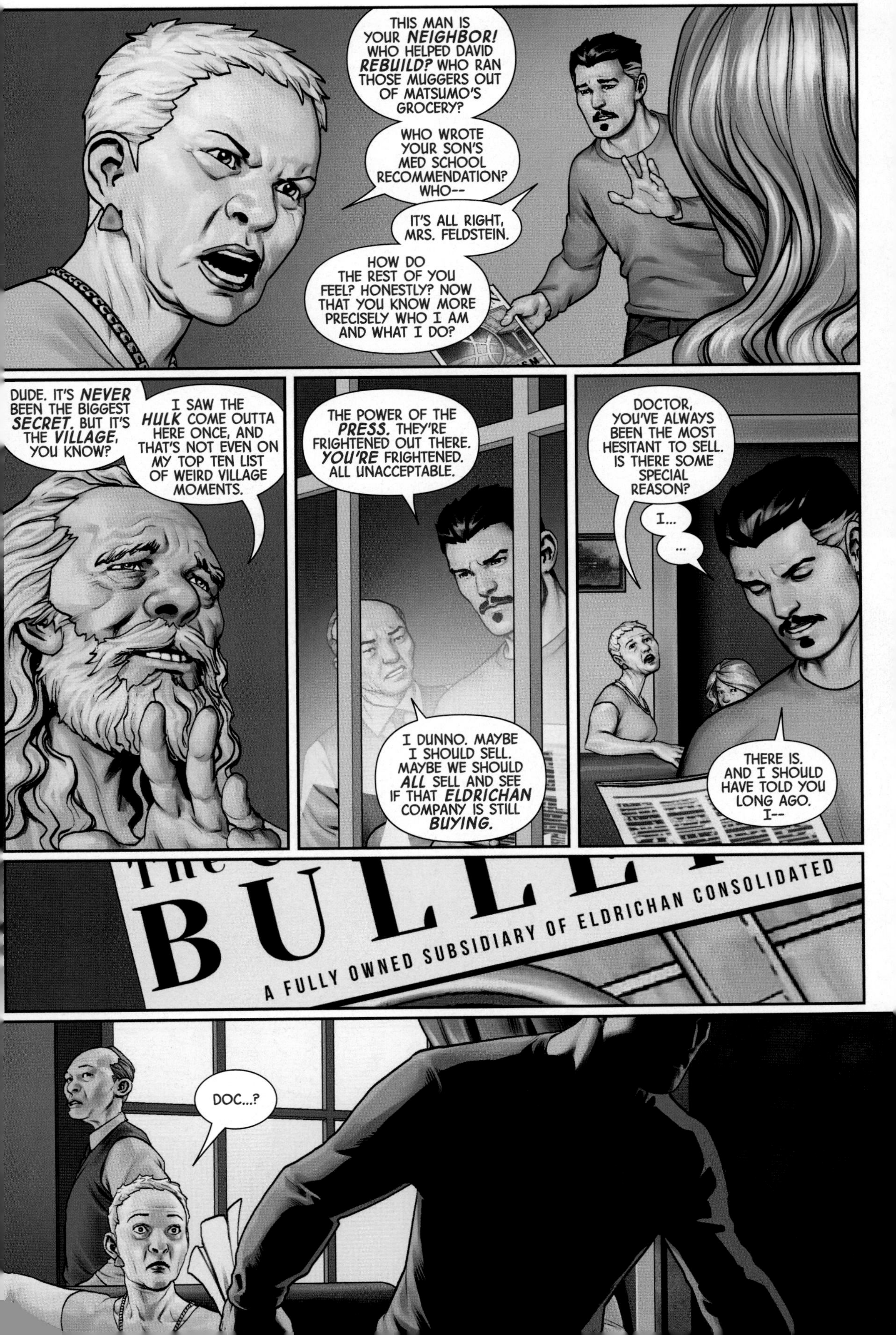
THIS MAN IS YOUR NEIGHBOR! WHO HELPED DAVID REBUILD? WHO RAN THOSE MUGGERS OUT OF MATSUMO'S GROCERY?
WHO WROTE YOUR SON'S MED SCHOOL RECOMMENDATION? WHO--
IT'S ALL RIGHT, MRS. FELDSTEIN.
HOW DO THE REST OF YOU FEEL? HONESTLY? NOW THAT YOU KNOW MORE PRECISELY WHO I AM AND WHAT I DO?
DUDE. IT'S NEVER BEEN THE BIGGEST SECRET. BUT IT'S THE VILLAGE, YOU KNOW?
I SAW THE HULK COME OUTTA HERE ONCE, AND THAT'S NOT EVEN ON MY TOP TEN LIST OF WEIRD VILLAGE MOMENTS.
THE POWER OF THE PRESS. THEY'RE FRIGHTENED OUT THERE. YOU'RE FRIGHTENED. ALL UNACCEPTABLE.
I DUNNO. MAYBE I SHOULD SELL. MAYBE WE SHOULD ALL SELL AND SEE IF THAT ELDRICHAN COMPANY IS STILL BUYING.
DOCTOR, YOU'VE ALWAYS BEEN THE MOST HESITANT TO SELL. IS THERE SOME SPECIAL REASON?
I...
...
THERE IS. AND I SHOULD HAVE TOLD YOU LONG AGO. I--
BULL
A FULLY OWNED SUBSIDIARY OF ELDRICHAN CONSOLIDATED
DOC...?

I SEE I'M MOVING AWAY FROM THE *MIDDLE MANAGERS.* THIS TIME, I'M DEALING WITH THE C.E.O.

WHAT A VERY CLEVER END RUN. I'M ACTUALLY IMPRESSED.

YOU WANT ME *OUT*, SO YOU'VE STOKED A CROWD TO DO YOUR STRONG-ARMING FOR YOU. THAT'S A HELL OF A LIBEL CAMPAIGN YOU'RE RUNNING.

JACKSON, DRAFT A REAL ESTATE CONTRACT FOR THIS MAN.

LIBEL? THE PUBLIC HAS A RIGHT TO *KNOW* WHAT EVIL LURKS AMONGST THEM, DOCTOR.

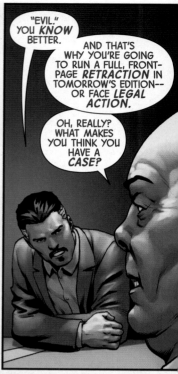

"EVIL." YOU *KNOW* BETTER.

AND THAT'S WHY YOU'RE GOING TO RUN A FULL, FRONT-PAGE *RETRACTION* IN TOMORROW'S EDITION-- OR FACE *LEGAL ACTION.*

OH, REALLY? WHAT MAKES YOU THINK YOU HAVE A *CASE?*

I'LL LET MY *LAWYER* EXPLAIN.

BULLE[T]

A FULLY OWNED SUBSIDIARY OF ELDRICHAN CONSOLIDATED

WE WERE WRONG

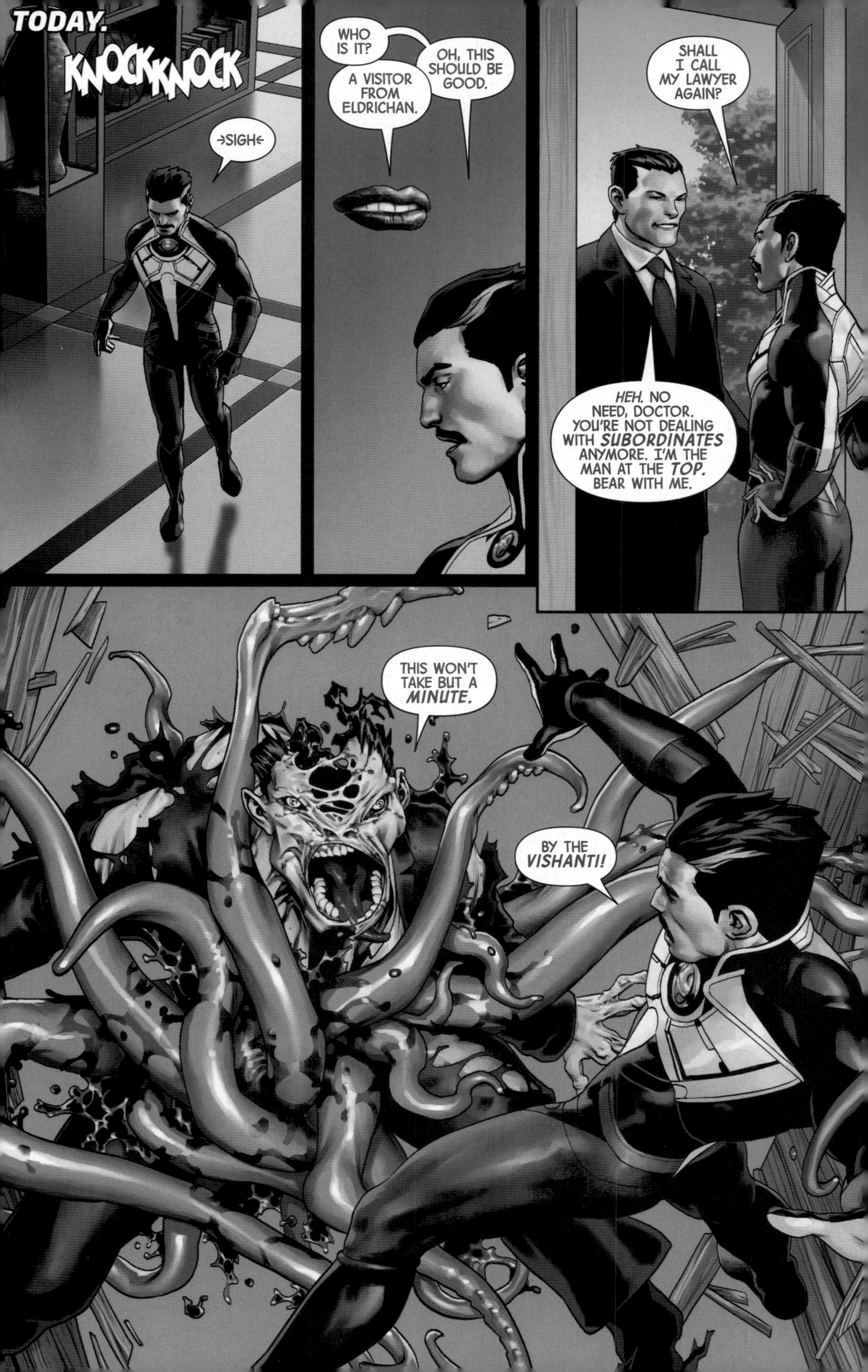
TODAY.
KNOCKKNOCK
SIGH
WHO IS IT?
A VISITOR FROM ELDRICHAN.
OH, THIS SHOULD BE GOOD.
SHALL I CALL MY LAWYER AGAIN?
HEH. NO NEED, DOCTOR. YOU'RE NOT DEALING WITH SUBORDINATES ANYMORE. I'M THE MAN AT THE TOP. BEAR WITH ME.
THIS WON'T TAKE BUT A MINUTE.
BY THE VISHANTI!

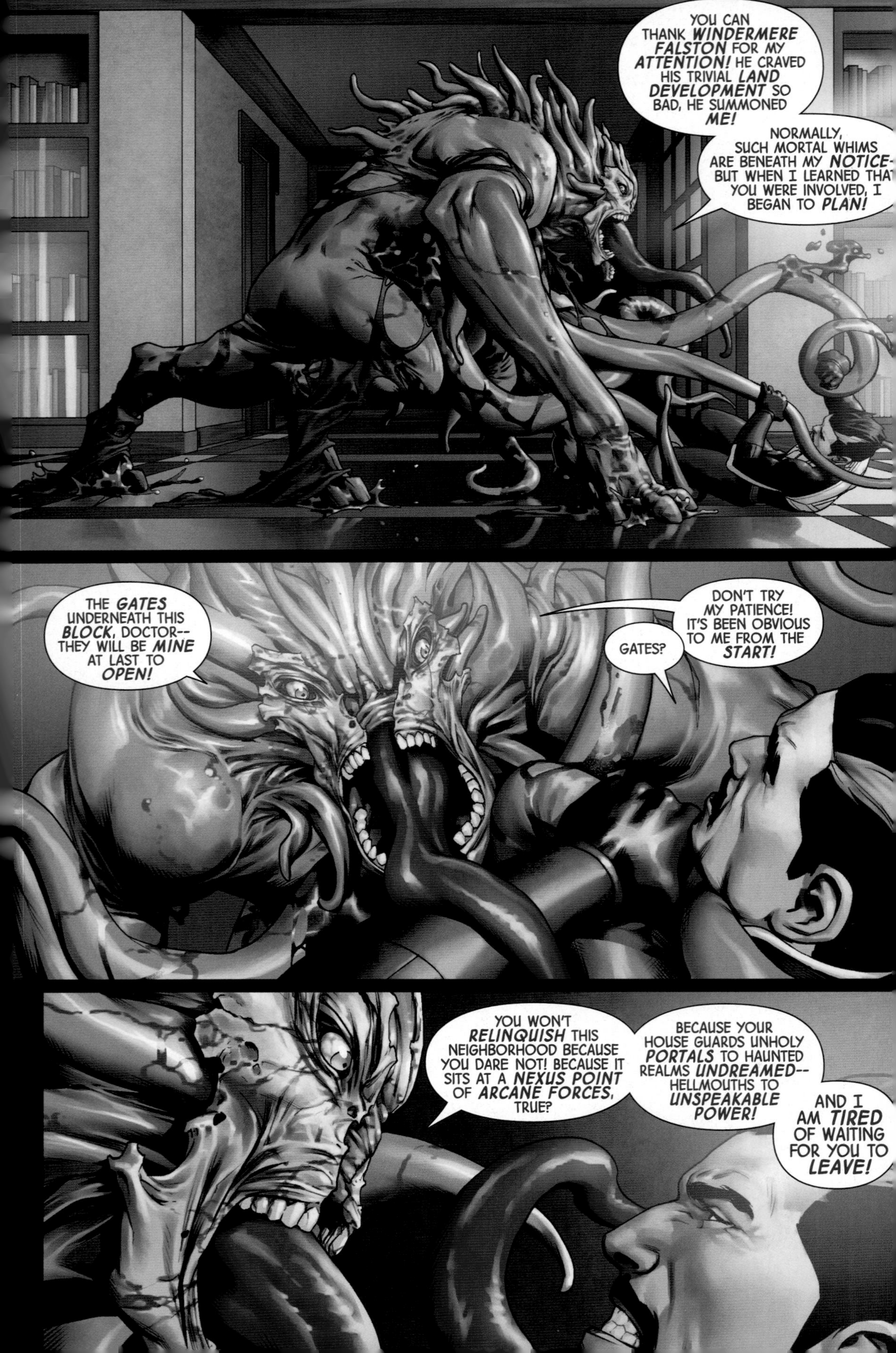
YOU CAN THANK WINDERMERE FALSTON FOR MY ATTENTION! HE CRAVED HIS TRIVIAL LAND DEVELOPMENT SO BAD, HE SUMMONED ME!
NORMALLY, SUCH MORTAL WHIMS ARE BENEATH MY NOTICE-- BUT WHEN I LEARNED THAT YOU WERE INVOLVED, I BEGAN TO PLAN!
THE GATES UNDERNEATH THIS BLOCK, DOCTOR-- THEY WILL BE MINE AT LAST TO OPEN!
GATES?
DON'T TRY MY PATIENCE! IT'S BEEN OBVIOUS TO ME FROM THE START!
YOU WON'T RELINQUISH THIS NEIGHBORHOOD BECAUSE YOU DARE NOT! BECAUSE IT SITS AT A NEXUS POINT OF ARCANE FORCES, TRUE?
BECAUSE YOUR HOUSE GUARDS UNHOLY PORTALS TO HAUNTED REALMS UNDREAMED-- HELLMOUTHS TO UNSPEAKABLE POWER!
AND I AM TIRED OF WAITING FOR YOU TO LEAVE!

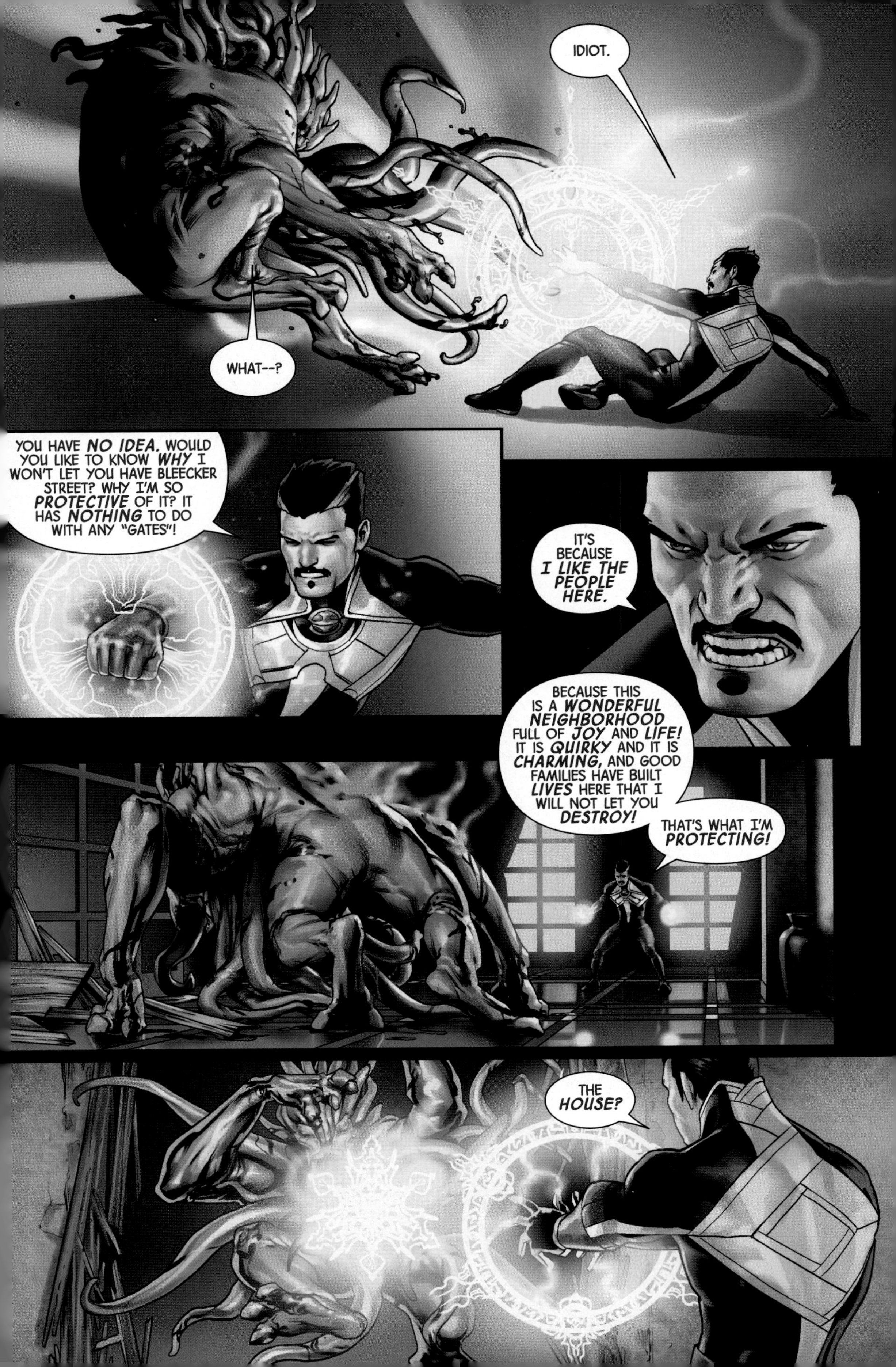
IDIOT.
WHAT--?
YOU HAVE NO IDEA. WOULD YOU LIKE TO KNOW WHY I WON'T LET YOU HAVE BLEECKER STREET? WHY I'M SO PROTECTIVE OF IT? IT HAS NOTHING TO DO WITH ANY "GATES"!
IT'S BECAUSE I LIKE THE PEOPLE HERE.
BECAUSE THIS IS A WONDERFUL NEIGHBORHOOD FULL OF JOY AND LIFE! IT IS QUIRKY AND IT IS CHARMING, AND GOOD FAMILIES HAVE BUILT LIVES HERE THAT I WILL NOT LET YOU DESTROY!
THAT'S WHAT I'M PROTECTING!
THE HOUSE?

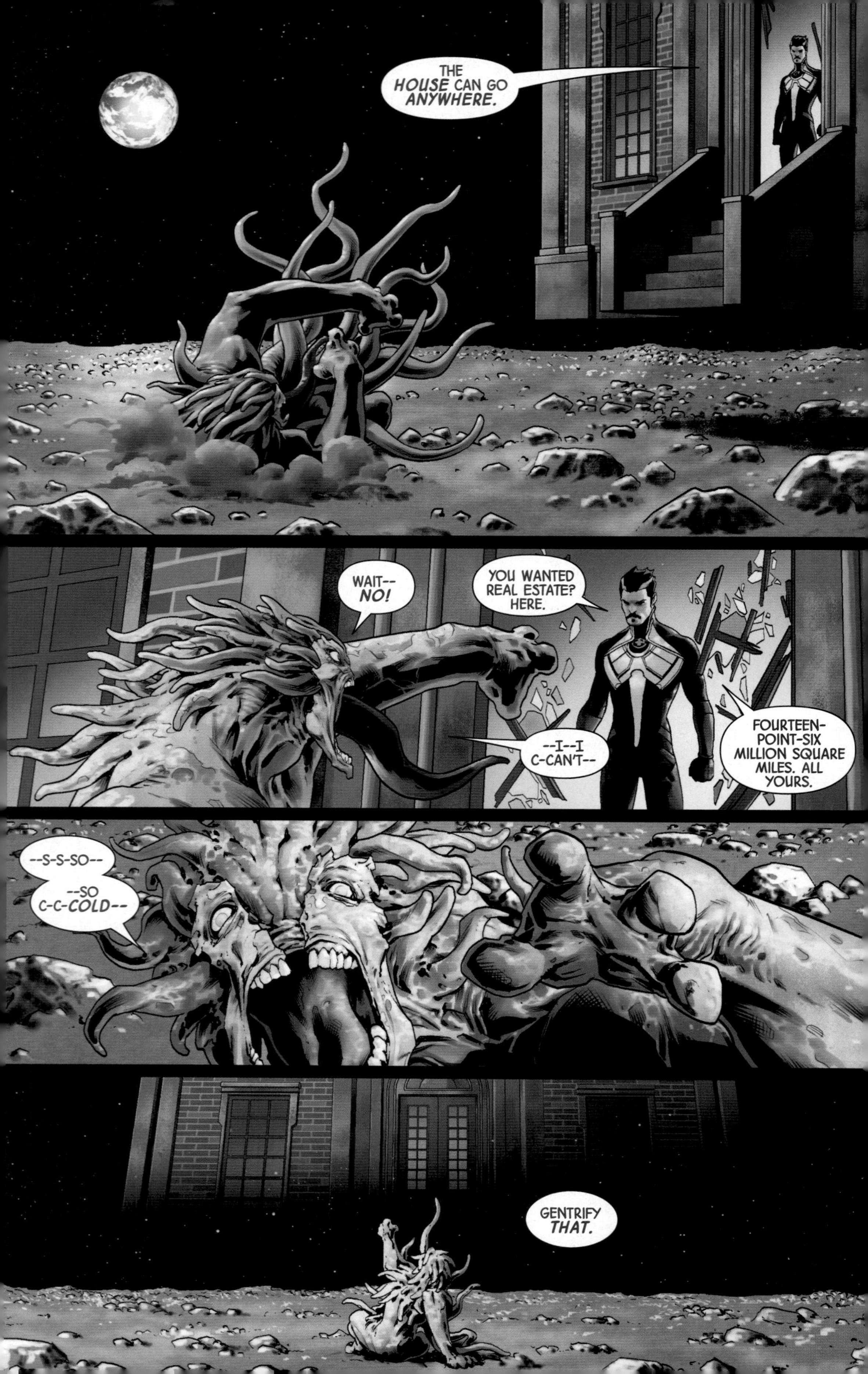
THE HOUSE CAN GO ANYWHERE.
WAIT-- NO!
YOU WANTED REAL ESTATE? HERE.
--I--I C-CAN'T--
FOURTEEN-POINT-SIX MILLION SQUARE MILES. ALL YOURS.
--S-S-SO--
--SO C-C-COLD--
GENTRIFY THAT.

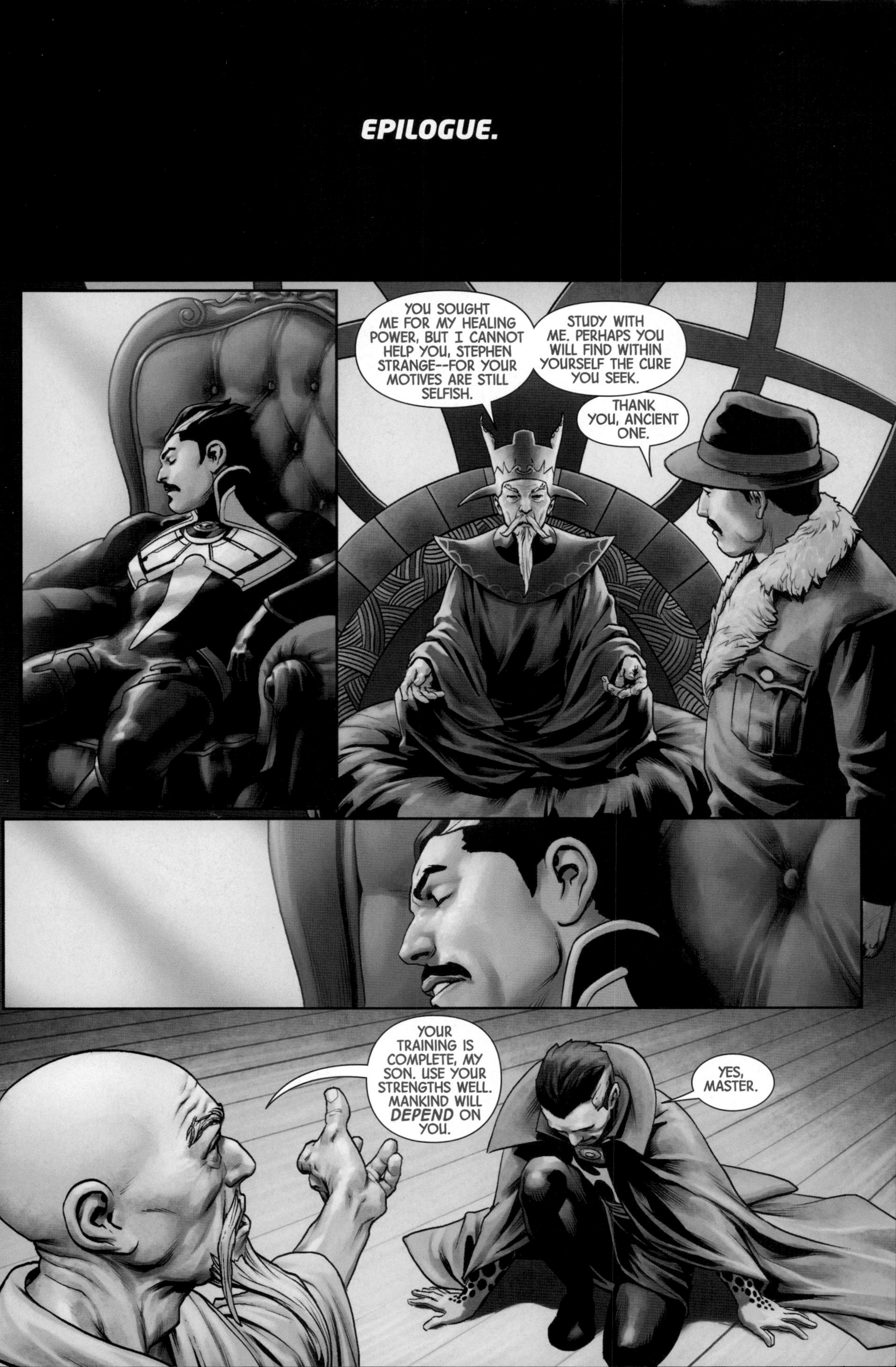
EPILOGUE.
YOU SOUGHT ME FOR MY HEALING POWER, BUT I CANNOT HELP YOU, STEPHEN STRANGE--FOR YOUR MOTIVES ARE STILL SELFISH.
STUDY WITH ME. PERHAPS YOU WILL FIND WITHIN YOURSELF THE CURE YOU SEEK.
THANK YOU, ANCIENT ONE.
YOUR TRAINING IS COMPLETE, MY SON. USE YOUR STRENGTHS WELL. MANKIND WILL DEPEND ON YOU.
YES, MASTER.

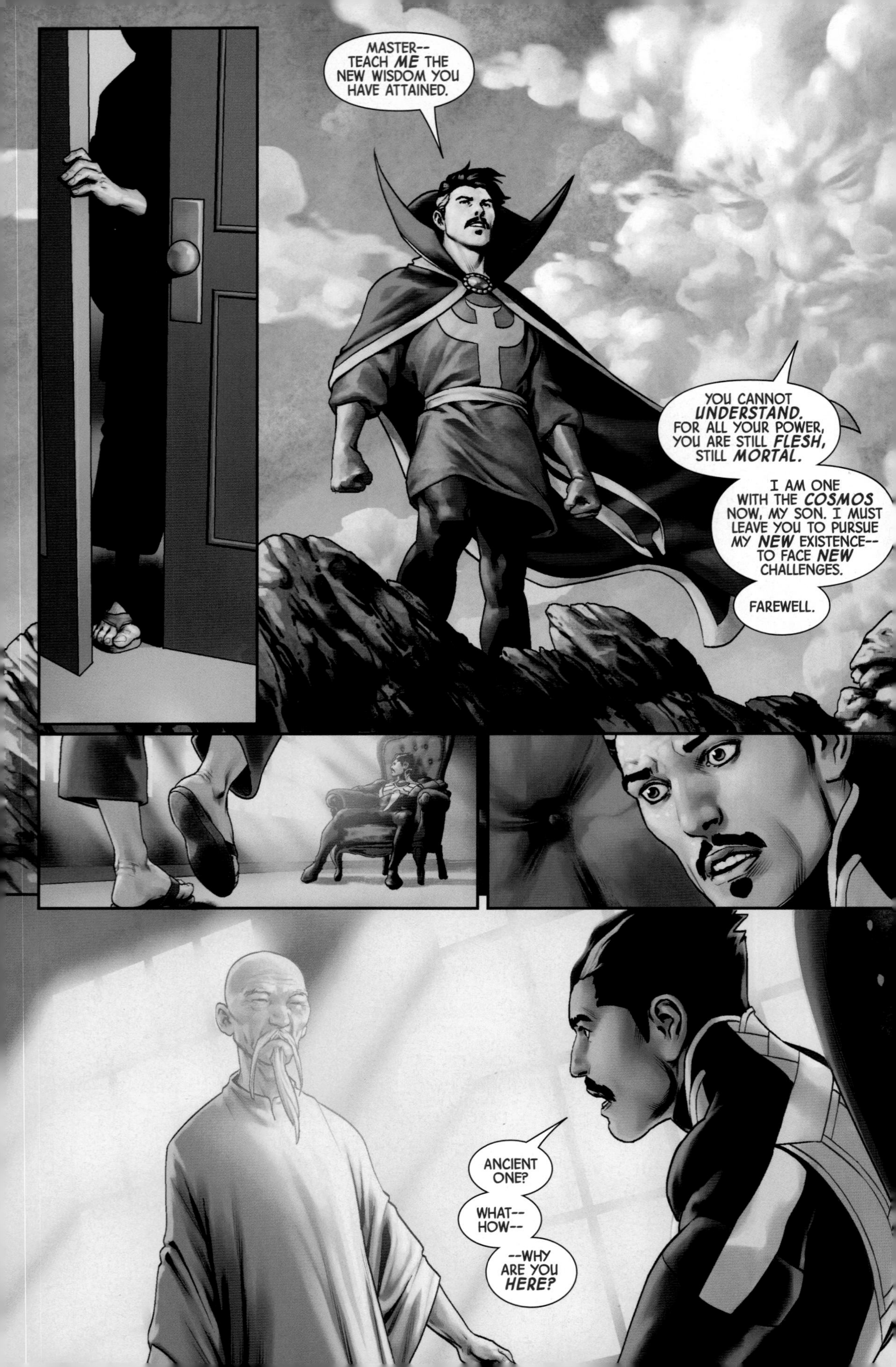
MASTER-- TEACH *ME* THE NEW WISDOM YOU HAVE ATTAINED.
YOU CANNOT *UNDERSTAND.* FOR ALL YOUR POWER, YOU ARE STILL *FLESH,* STILL *MORTAL.*
I AM ONE WITH THE *COSMOS* NOW, MY SON. I MUST LEAVE YOU TO PURSUE MY *NEW* EXISTENCE-- TO FACE *NEW* CHALLENGES.
FAREWELL.
ANCIENT ONE?
WHAT-- HOW--
--WHY ARE YOU *HERE?*

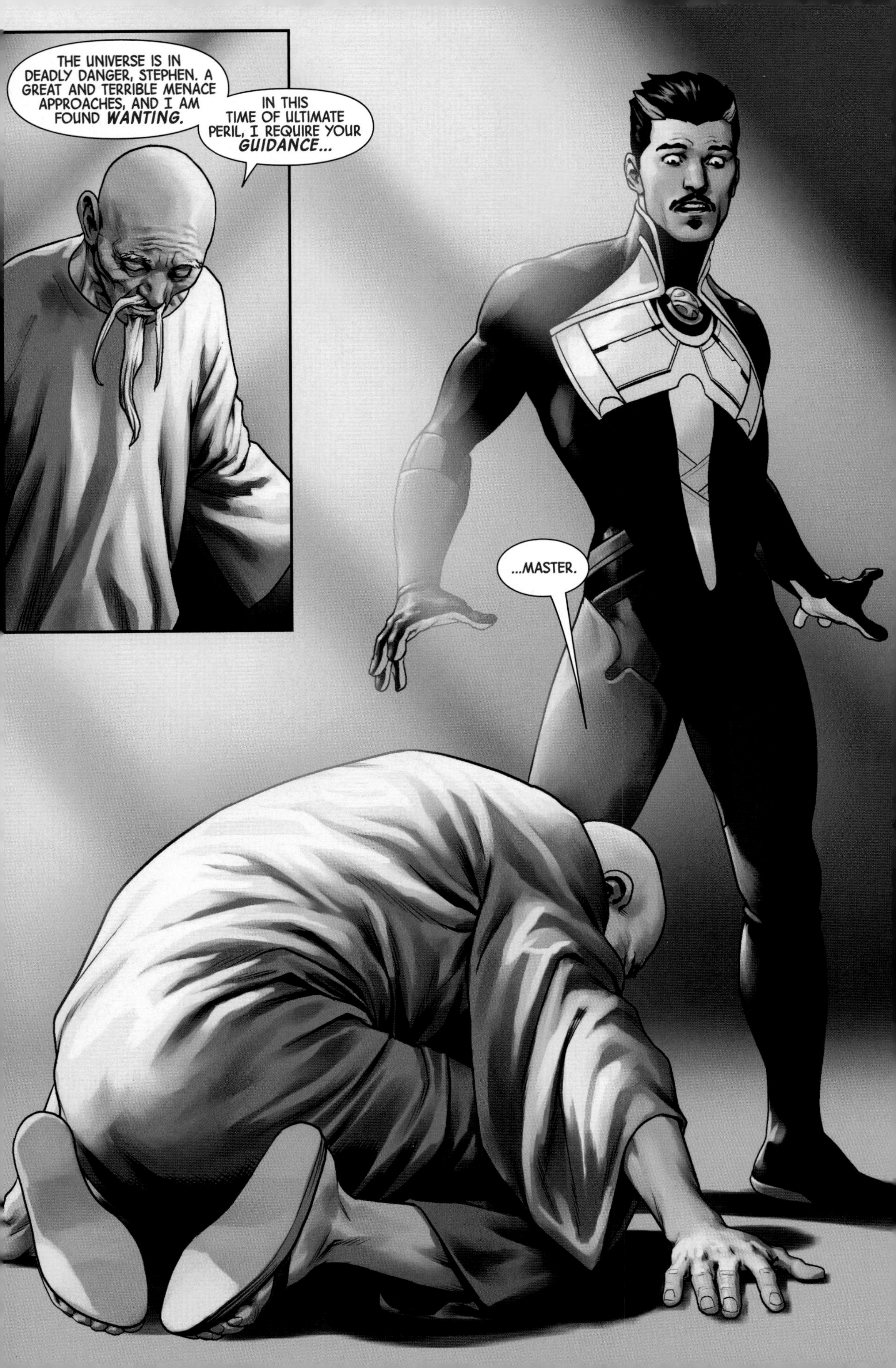
THE UNIVERSE IS IN DEADLY DANGER, STEPHEN. A GREAT AND TERRIBLE MENACE APPROACHES, AND I AM FOUND WANTING.
IN THIS TIME OF ULTIMATE PERIL, I REQUIRE YOUR GUIDANCE...
...MASTER.

10

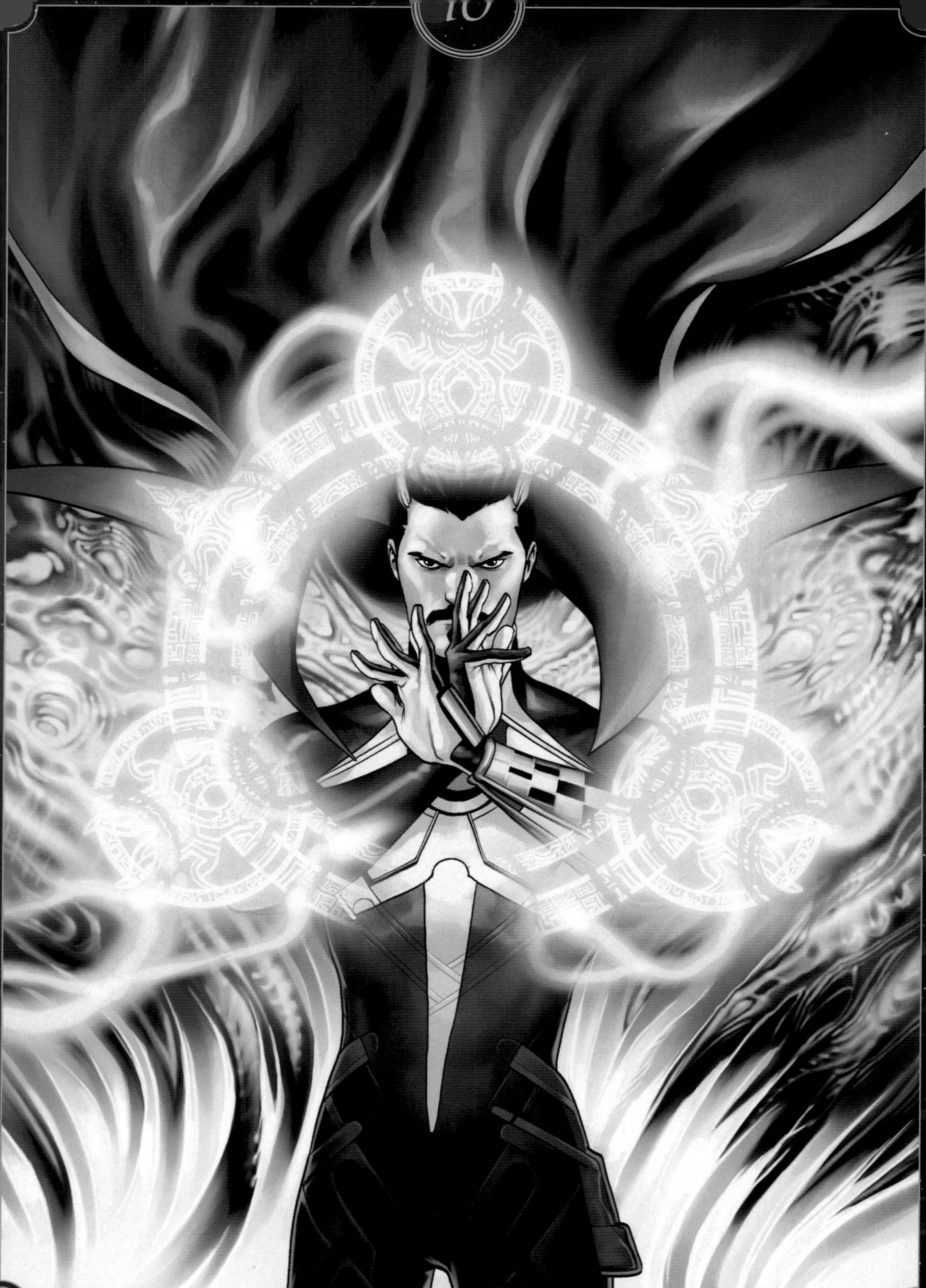

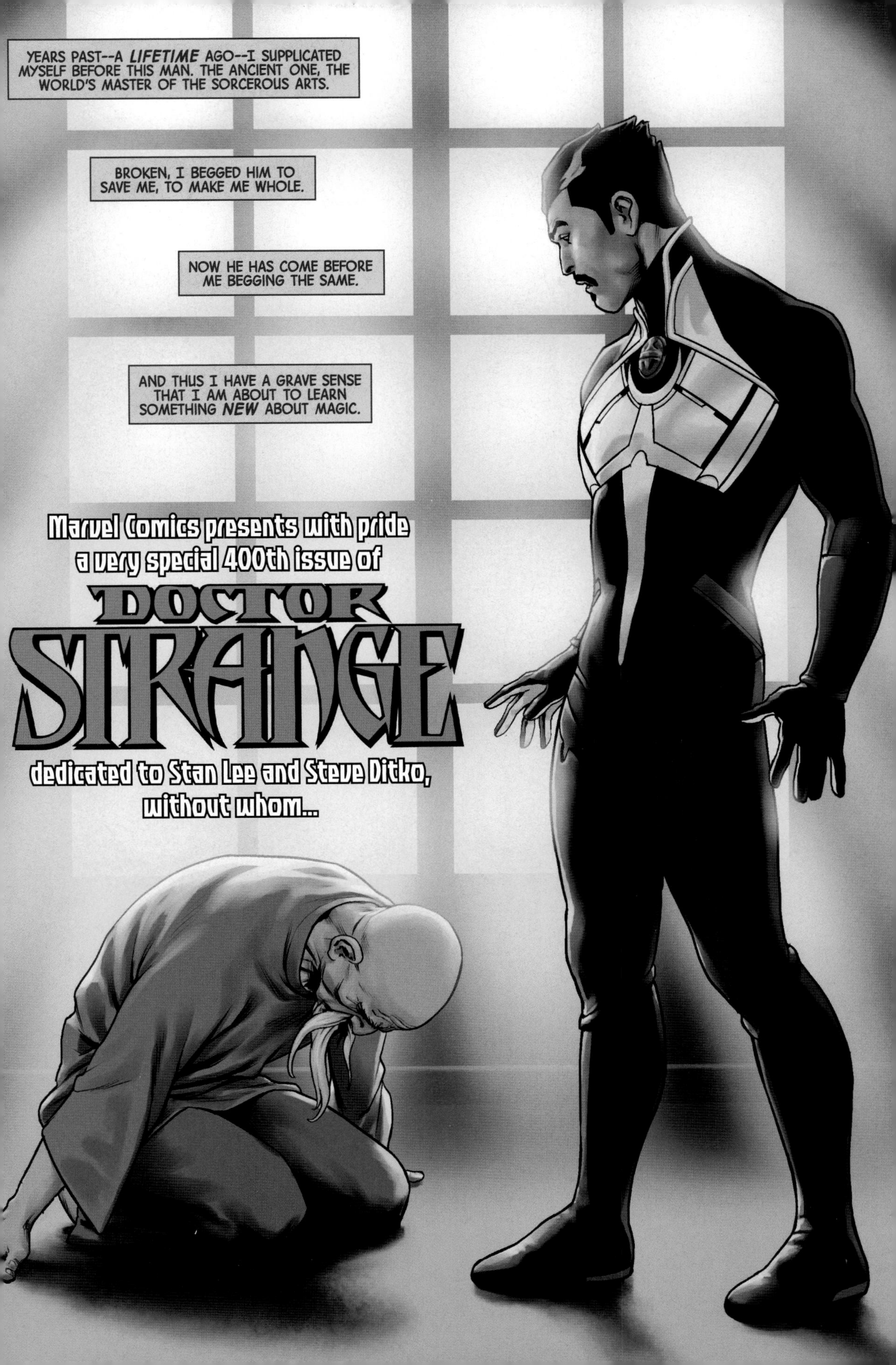
YEARS PAST--A *LIFETIME* AGO--I SUPPLICATED MYSELF BEFORE THIS MAN. THE ANCIENT ONE, THE WORLD'S MASTER OF THE SORCEROUS ARTS.
BROKEN, I BEGGED HIM TO SAVE ME, TO MAKE ME WHOLE.
NOW HE HAS COME BEFORE ME BEGGING THE SAME.
AND THUS I HAVE A GRAVE SENSE THAT I AM ABOUT TO LEARN SOMETHING *NEW* ABOUT MAGIC.
Marvel Comics presents with pride a very special 400th issue of
DOCTOR STRANGE
dedicated to Stan Lee and Steve Ditko, without whom...

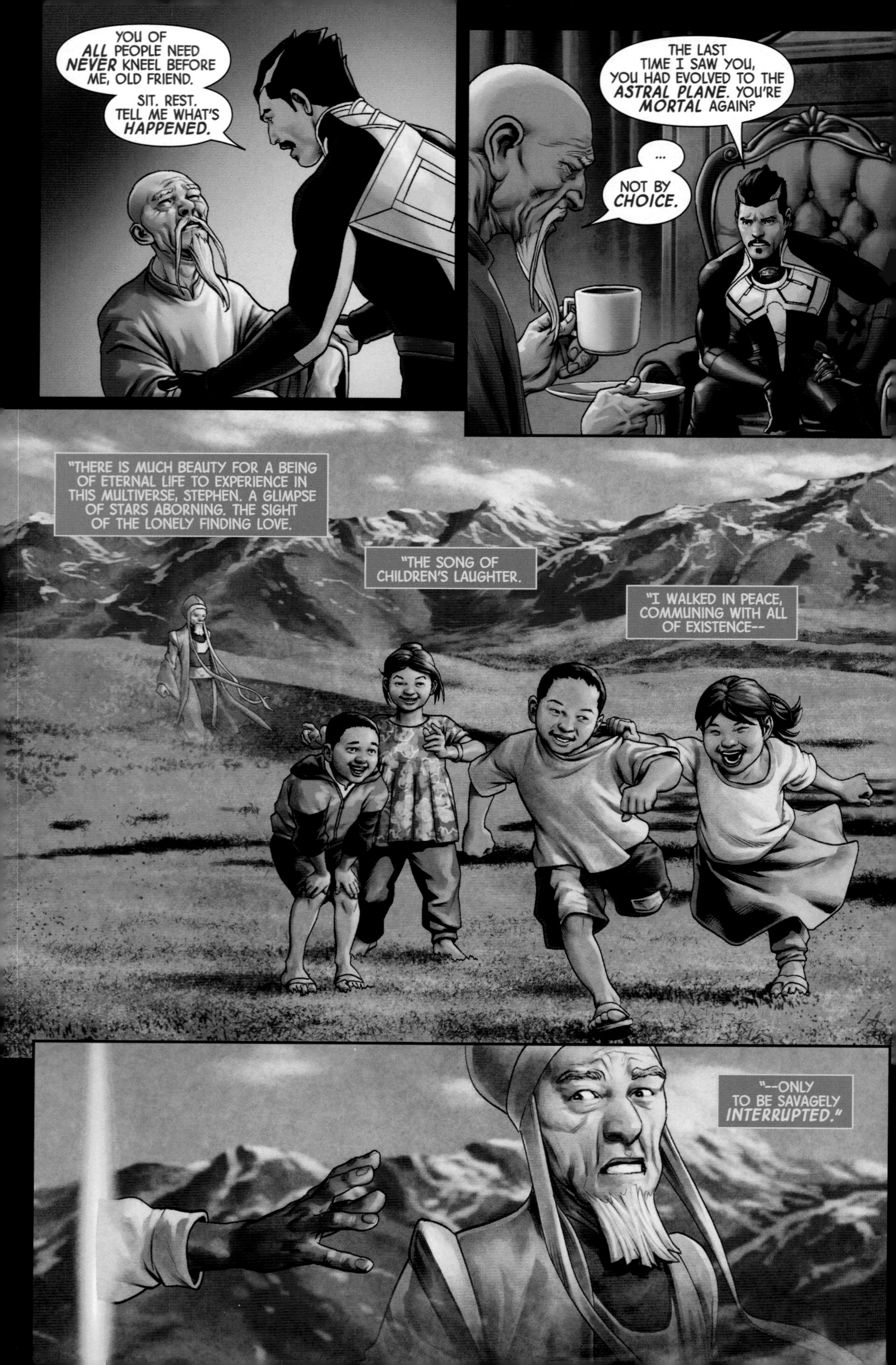
YOU OF ALL PEOPLE NEED NEVER KNEEL BEFORE ME, OLD FRIEND.
SIT. REST. TELL ME WHAT'S HAPPENED.
THE LAST TIME I SAW YOU, YOU HAD EVOLVED TO THE ASTRAL PLANE. YOU'RE MORTAL AGAIN?
...
NOT BY CHOICE.
"THERE IS MUCH BEAUTY FOR A BEING OF ETERNAL LIFE TO EXPERIENCE IN THIS MULTIVERSE, STEPHEN. A GLIMPSE OF STARS ABORNING. THE SIGHT OF THE LONELY FINDING LOVE.
"THE SONG OF CHILDREN'S LAUGHTER.
"I WALKED IN PEACE, COMMUNING WITH ALL OF EXISTENCE--
"--ONLY TO BE SAVAGELY INTERRUPTED."

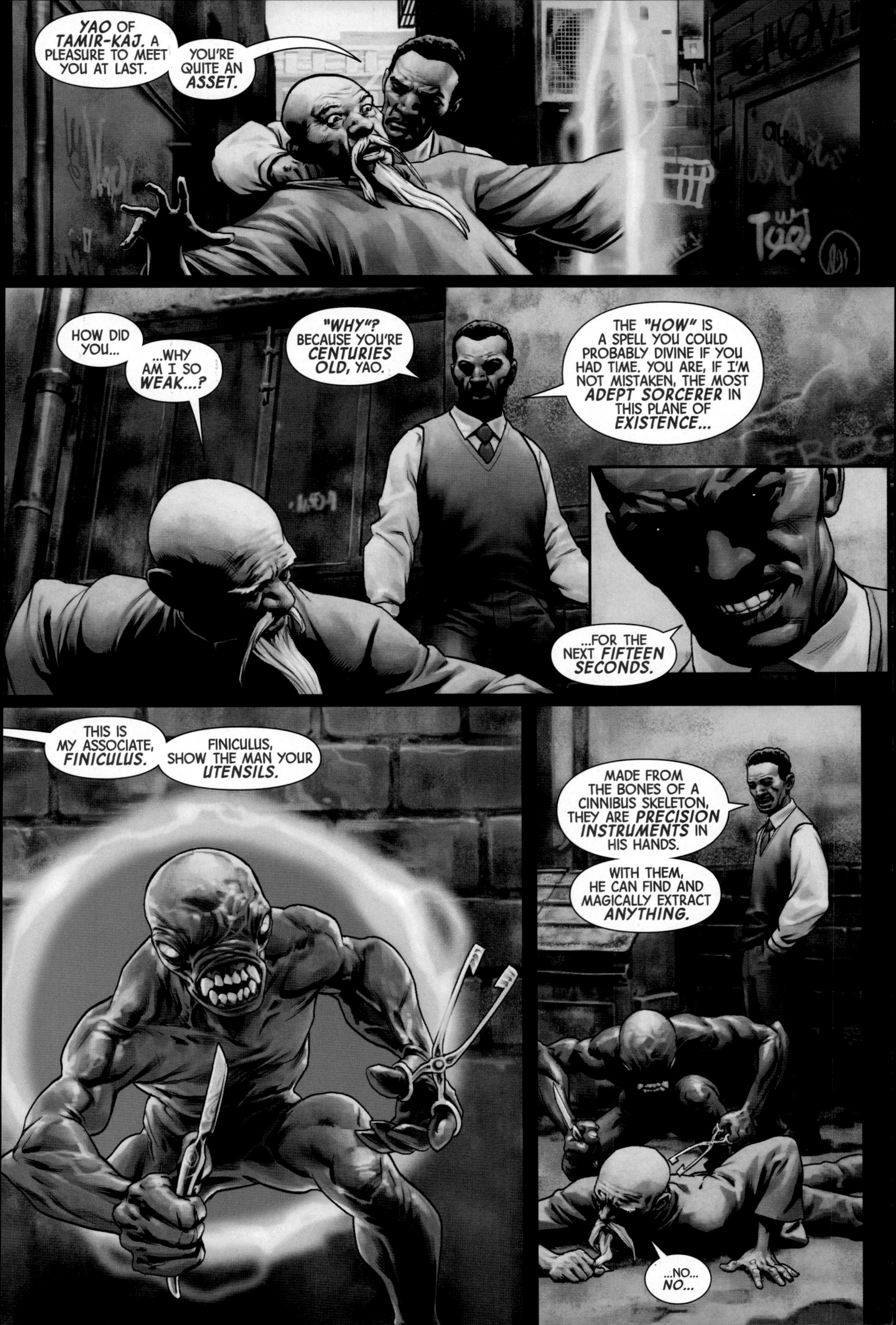
YAO OF TAMIR-KAJ. A PLEASURE TO MEET YOU AT LAST.
YOU'RE QUITE AN ASSET.
HOW DID YOU...
...WHY AM I SO WEAK...?
"WHY"? BECAUSE YOU'RE CENTURIES OLD, YAO.
THE "HOW" IS A SPELL YOU COULD PROBABLY DIVINE IF YOU HAD TIME. YOU ARE, IF I'M NOT MISTAKEN, THE MOST ADEPT SORCERER IN THIS PLANE OF EXISTENCE...
...FOR THE NEXT FIFTEEN SECONDS.
THIS IS MY ASSOCIATE, FINICULUS.
FINICULUS, SHOW THE MAN YOUR UTENSILS.
MADE FROM THE BONES OF A CINNIBUS SKELETON, THEY ARE PRECISION INSTRUMENTS IN HIS HANDS.
WITH THEM, HE CAN FIND AND MAGICALLY EXTRACT ANYTHING.
...NO... NO...

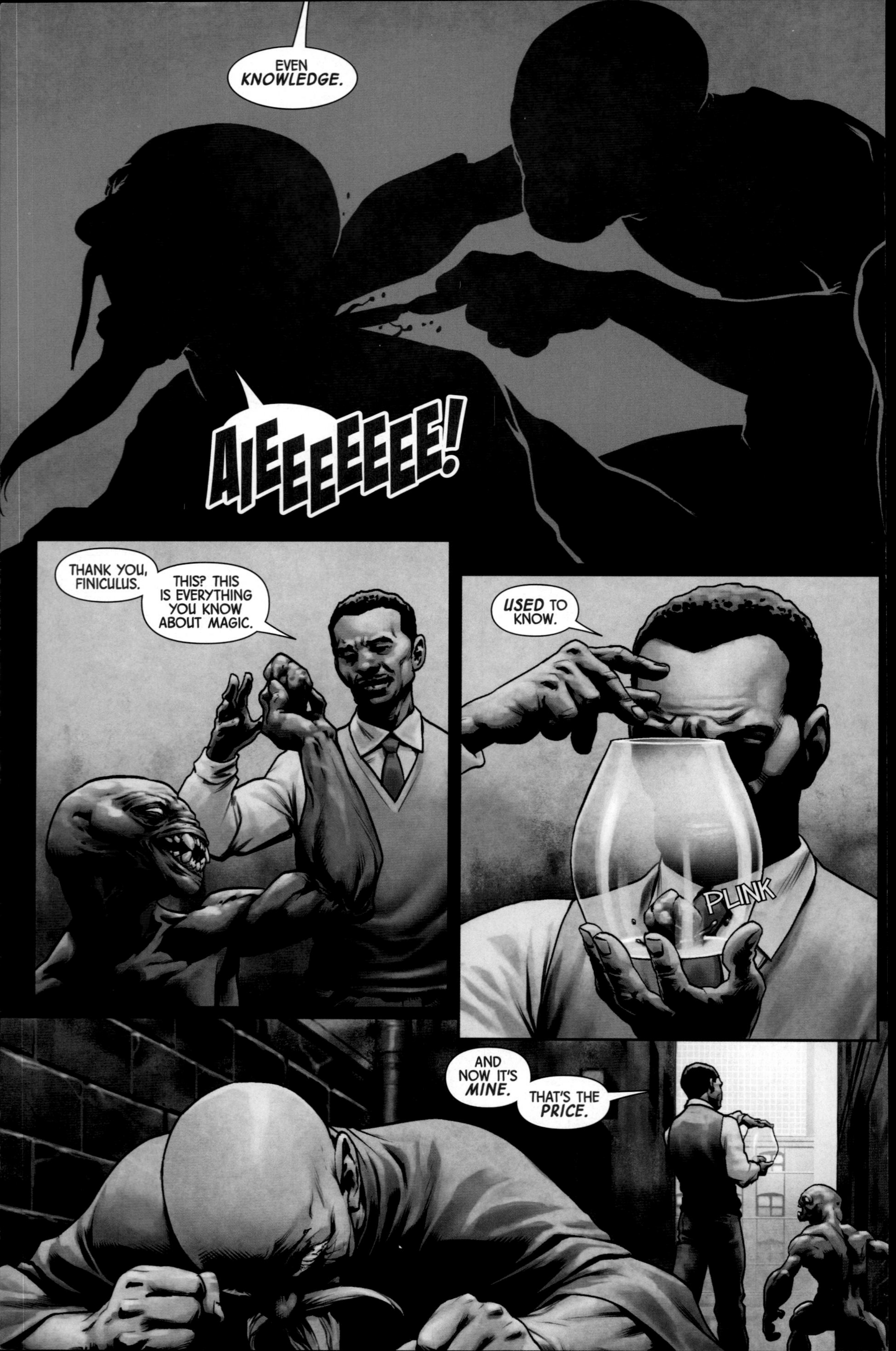

EVEN KNOWLEDGE.
AIEEEEEEE!
THANK YOU, FINICULUS.
THIS? THIS IS EVERYTHING YOU KNOW ABOUT MAGIC.
USED TO KNOW.
PLINK
AND NOW IT'S MINE.
THAT'S THE PRICE.

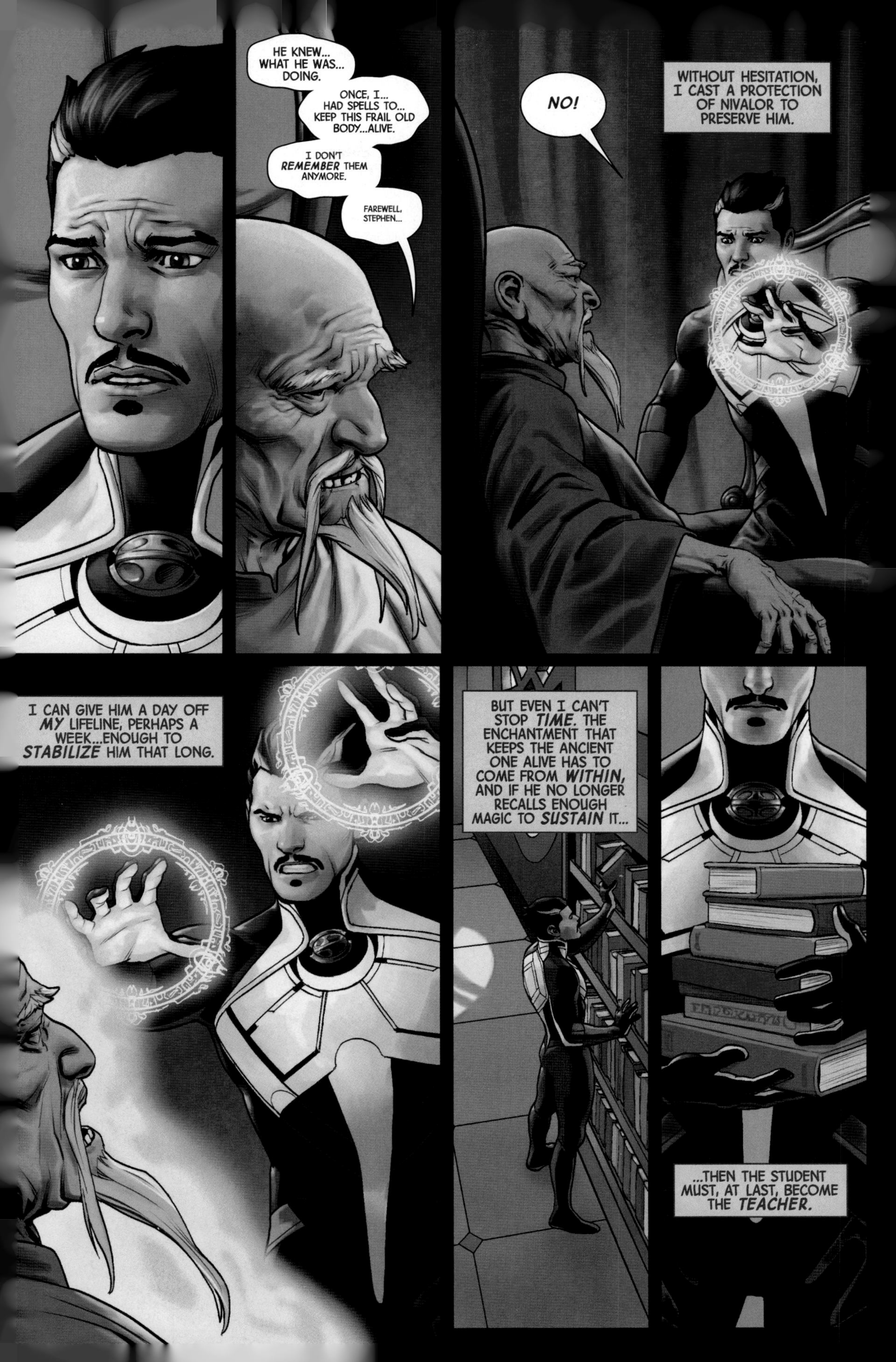
HE KNEW... WHAT HE WAS... DOING.
ONCE, I... HAD SPELLS TO... KEEP THIS FRAIL OLD BODY...ALIVE.
I DON'T REMEMBER THEM ANYMORE.
FAREWELL, STEPHEN...
NO!
WITHOUT HESITATION, I CAST A PROTECTION OF NIVALOR TO PRESERVE HIM.
I CAN GIVE HIM A DAY OFF MY LIFELINE, PERHAPS A WEEK...ENOUGH TO STABILIZE HIM THAT LONG.
BUT EVEN I CAN'T STOP TIME. THE ENCHANTMENT THAT KEEPS THE ANCIENT ONE ALIVE HAS TO COME FROM WITHIN, AND IF HE NO LONGER RECALLS ENOUGH MAGIC TO SUSTAIN IT...
...THEN THE STUDENT MUST, AT LAST, BECOME THE TEACHER.

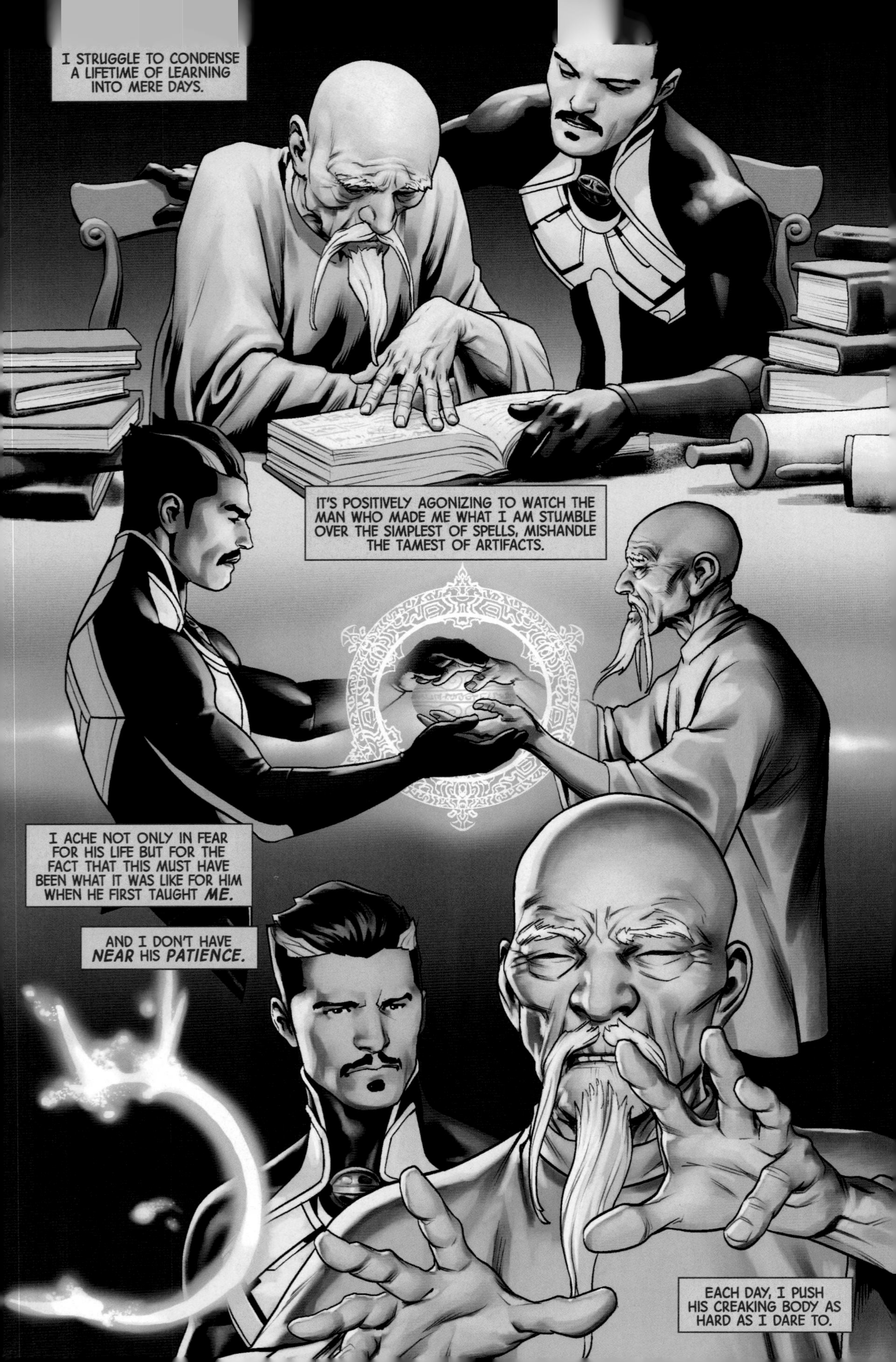
I STRUGGLE TO CONDENSE A LIFETIME OF LEARNING INTO MERE DAYS.
IT'S POSITIVELY AGONIZING TO WATCH THE MAN WHO MADE ME WHAT I AM STUMBLE OVER THE SIMPLEST OF SPELLS, MISHANDLE THE TAMEST OF ARTIFACTS.
I ACHE NOT ONLY IN FEAR FOR HIS LIFE BUT FOR THE FACT THAT THIS MUST HAVE BEEN WHAT IT WAS LIKE FOR HIM WHEN HE FIRST TAUGHT *ME.*
AND I DON'T HAVE *NEAR* HIS *PATIENCE.*
EACH DAY, I PUSH HIS CREAKING BODY AS HARD AS I DARE TO.

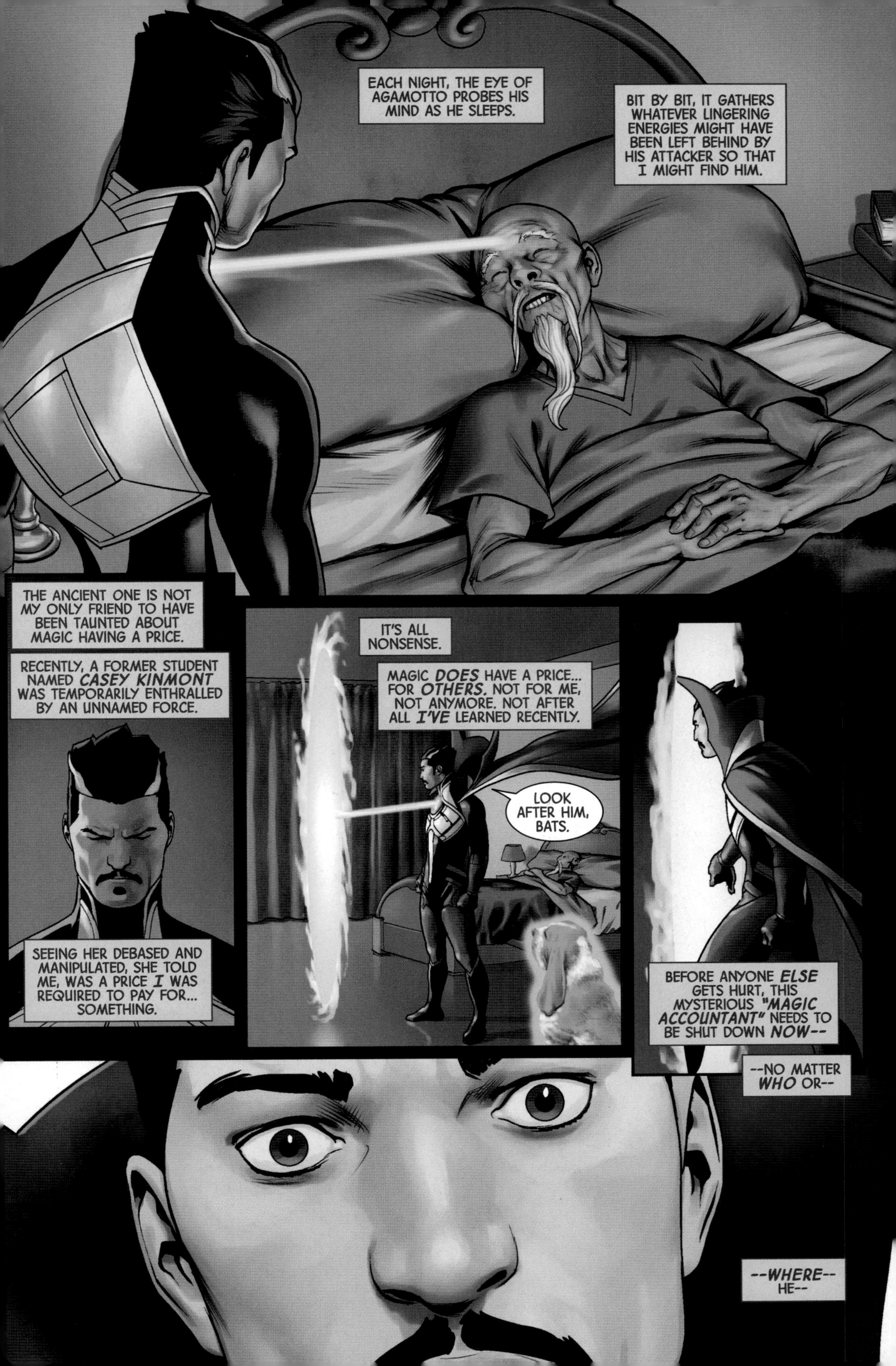
EACH NIGHT, THE EYE OF AGAMOTTO PROBES HIS MIND AS HE SLEEPS.
BIT BY BIT, IT GATHERS WHATEVER LINGERING ENERGIES MIGHT HAVE BEEN LEFT BEHIND BY HIS ATTACKER SO THAT I MIGHT FIND HIM.
THE ANCIENT ONE IS NOT MY ONLY FRIEND TO HAVE BEEN TAUNTED ABOUT MAGIC HAVING A PRICE.
RECENTLY, A FORMER STUDENT NAMED CASEY KINMONT WAS TEMPORARILY ENTHRALLED BY AN UNNAMED FORCE.
SEEING HER DEBASED AND MANIPULATED, SHE TOLD ME, WAS A PRICE I WAS REQUIRED TO PAY FOR... SOMETHING.
IT'S ALL NONSENSE.
MAGIC DOES HAVE A PRICE... FOR OTHERS. NOT FOR ME, NOT ANYMORE. NOT AFTER ALL I'VE LEARNED RECENTLY.
LOOK AFTER HIM, BATS.
BEFORE ANYONE ELSE GETS HURT, THIS MYSTERIOUS "MAGIC ACCOUNTANT" NEEDS TO BE SHUT DOWN NOW--
--NO MATTER WHO OR--
--WHERE-- HE--

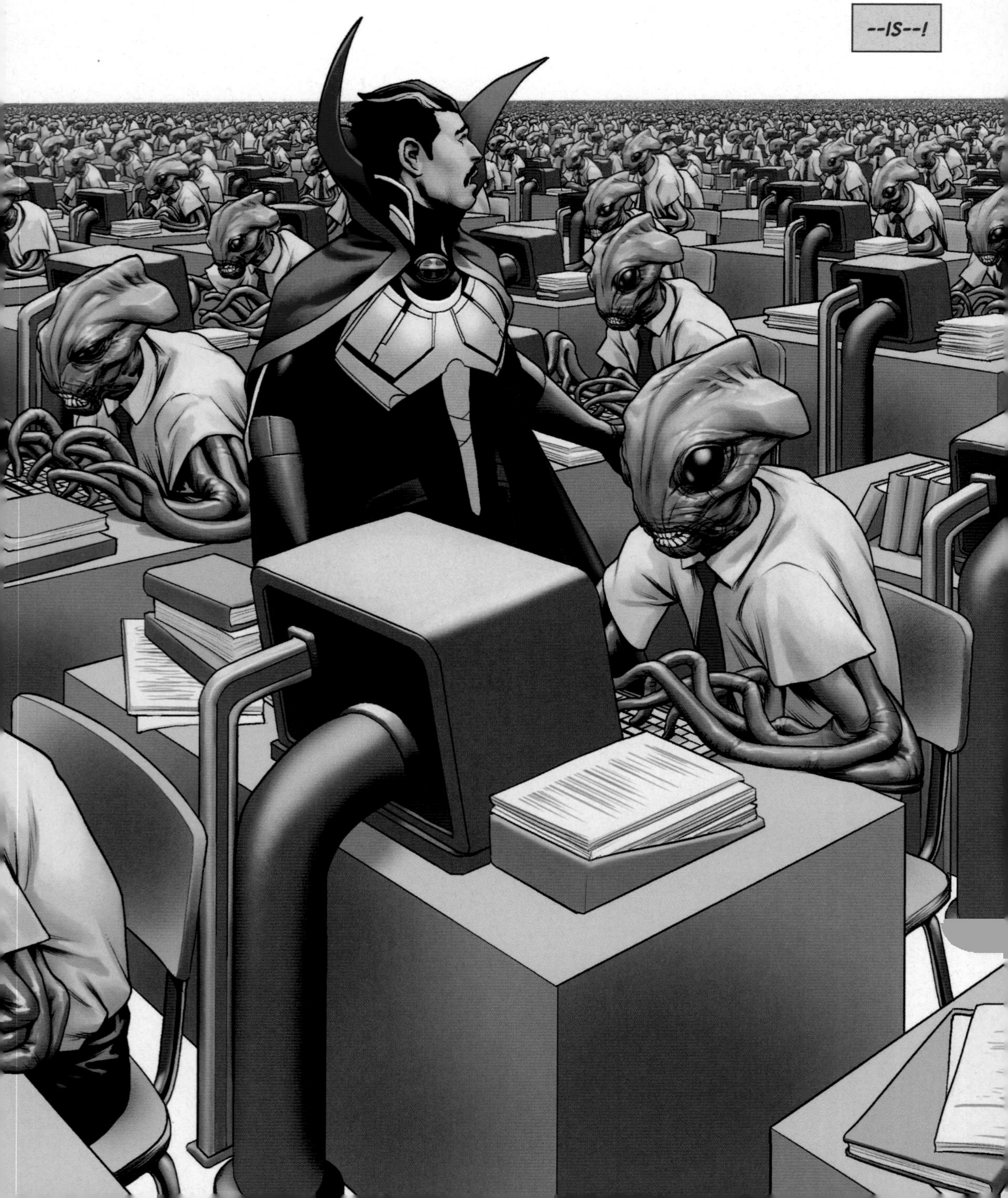
--IS--!

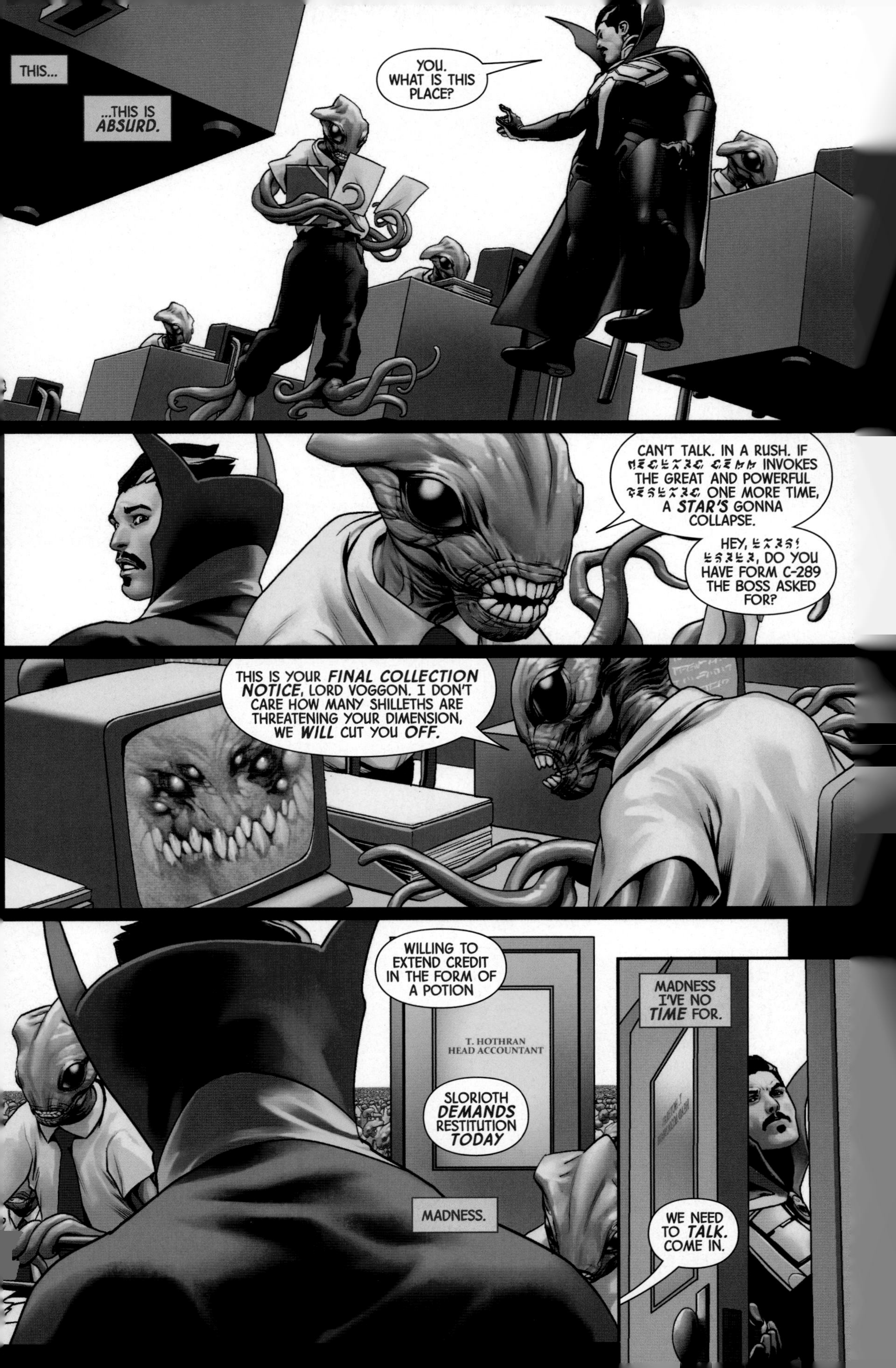
THIS...
...THIS IS ABSURD.
YOU. WHAT IS THIS PLACE?
CAN'T TALK. IN A RUSH. IF INVOKES THE GREAT AND POWERFUL ONE MORE TIME, A STAR'S GONNA COLLAPSE.
HEY, ! , DO YOU HAVE FORM C-289 THE BOSS ASKED FOR?
THIS IS YOUR FINAL COLLECTION NOTICE, LORD VOGGON. I DON'T CARE HOW MANY SHILLETHS ARE THREATENING YOUR DIMENSION, WE WILL CUT YOU OFF.
WILLING TO EXTEND CREDIT IN THE FORM OF A POTION
T. HOTHRAN HEAD ACCOUNTANT
SLORIOTH DEMANDS RESTITUTION TODAY
MADNESS.
MADNESS I'VE NO TIME FOR.
WE NEED TO TALK. COME IN.

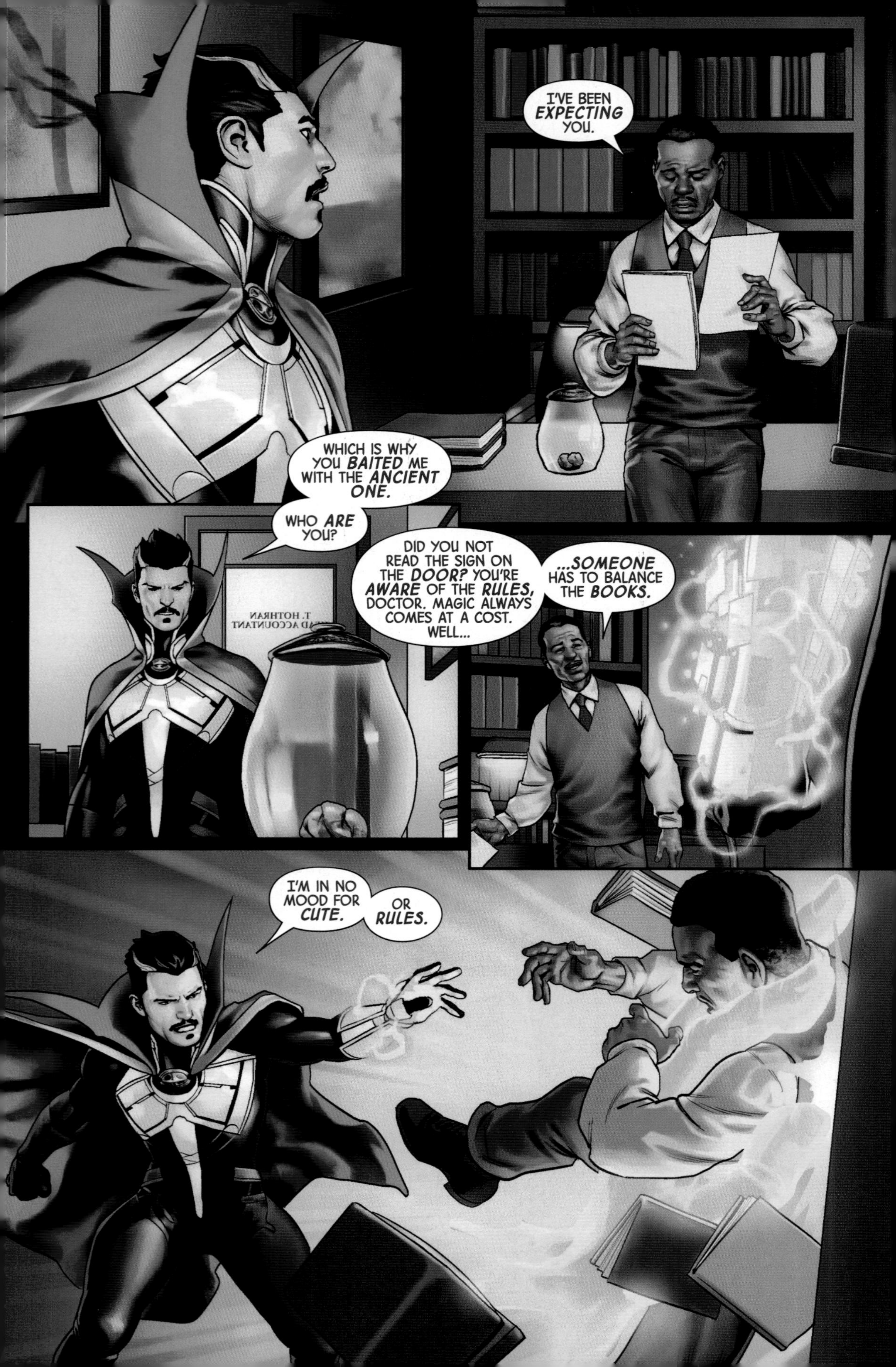

I'VE BEEN EXPECTING YOU.
WHICH IS WHY YOU BAITED ME WITH THE ANCIENT ONE.
WHO ARE YOU?
DID YOU NOT READ THE SIGN ON THE DOOR? YOU'RE AWARE OF THE RULES, DOCTOR. MAGIC ALWAYS COMES AT A COST. WELL...
...SOMEONE HAS TO BALANCE THE BOOKS.
I'M IN NO MOOD FOR CUTE.
OR RULES.

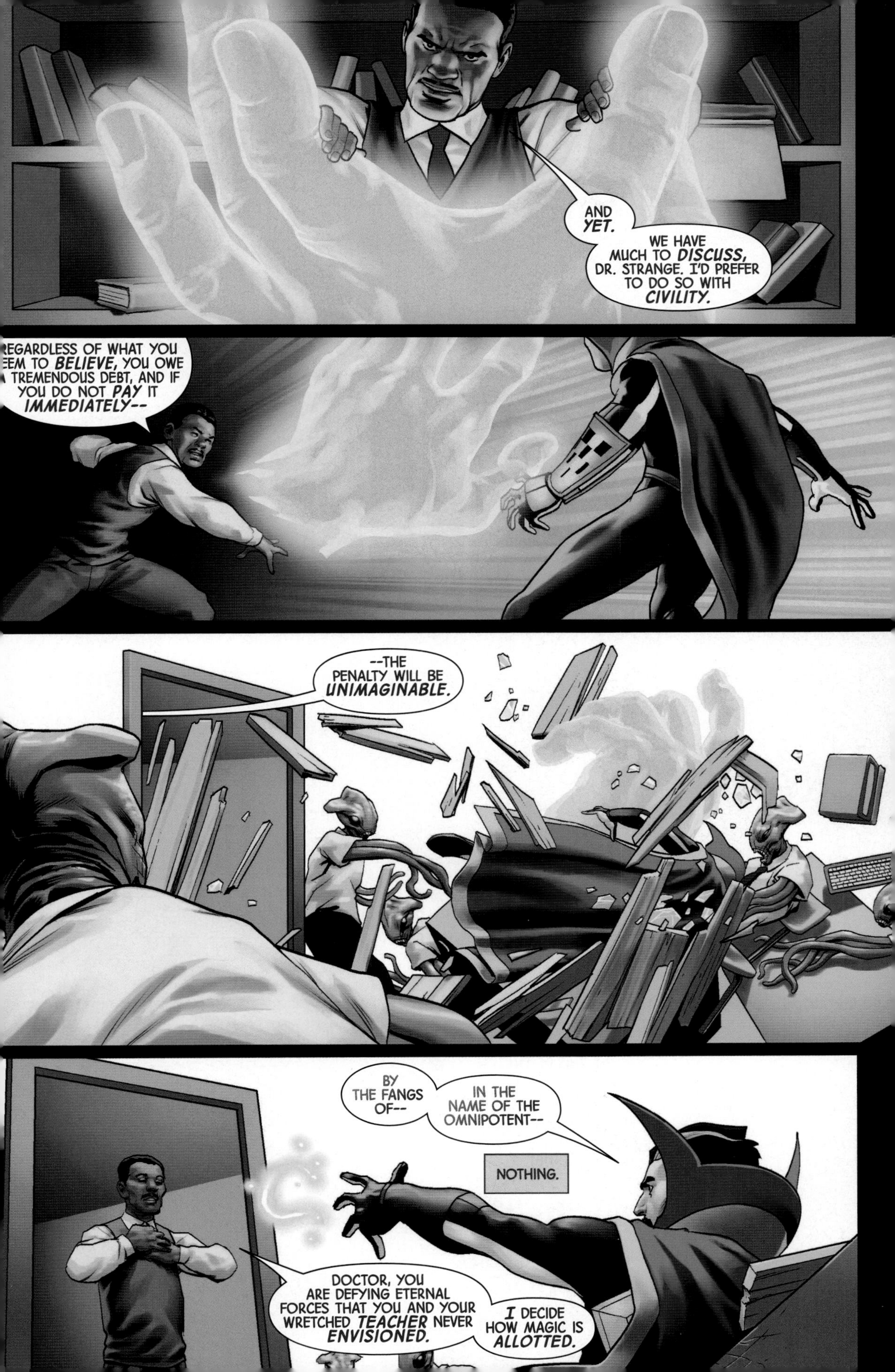
AND YET.
WE HAVE MUCH TO DISCUSS, DR. STRANGE. I'D PREFER TO DO SO WITH CIVILITY.
REGARDLESS OF WHAT YOU SEEM TO BELIEVE, YOU OWE A TREMENDOUS DEBT, AND IF YOU DO NOT PAY IT IMMEDIATELY--
--THE PENALTY WILL BE UNIMAGINABLE.
BY THE FANGS OF--
IN THE NAME OF THE OMNIPOTENT--
NOTHING.
DOCTOR, YOU ARE DEFYING ETERNAL FORCES THAT YOU AND YOUR WRETCHED TEACHER NEVER ENVISIONED.
I DECIDE HOW MAGIC IS ALLOTTED.

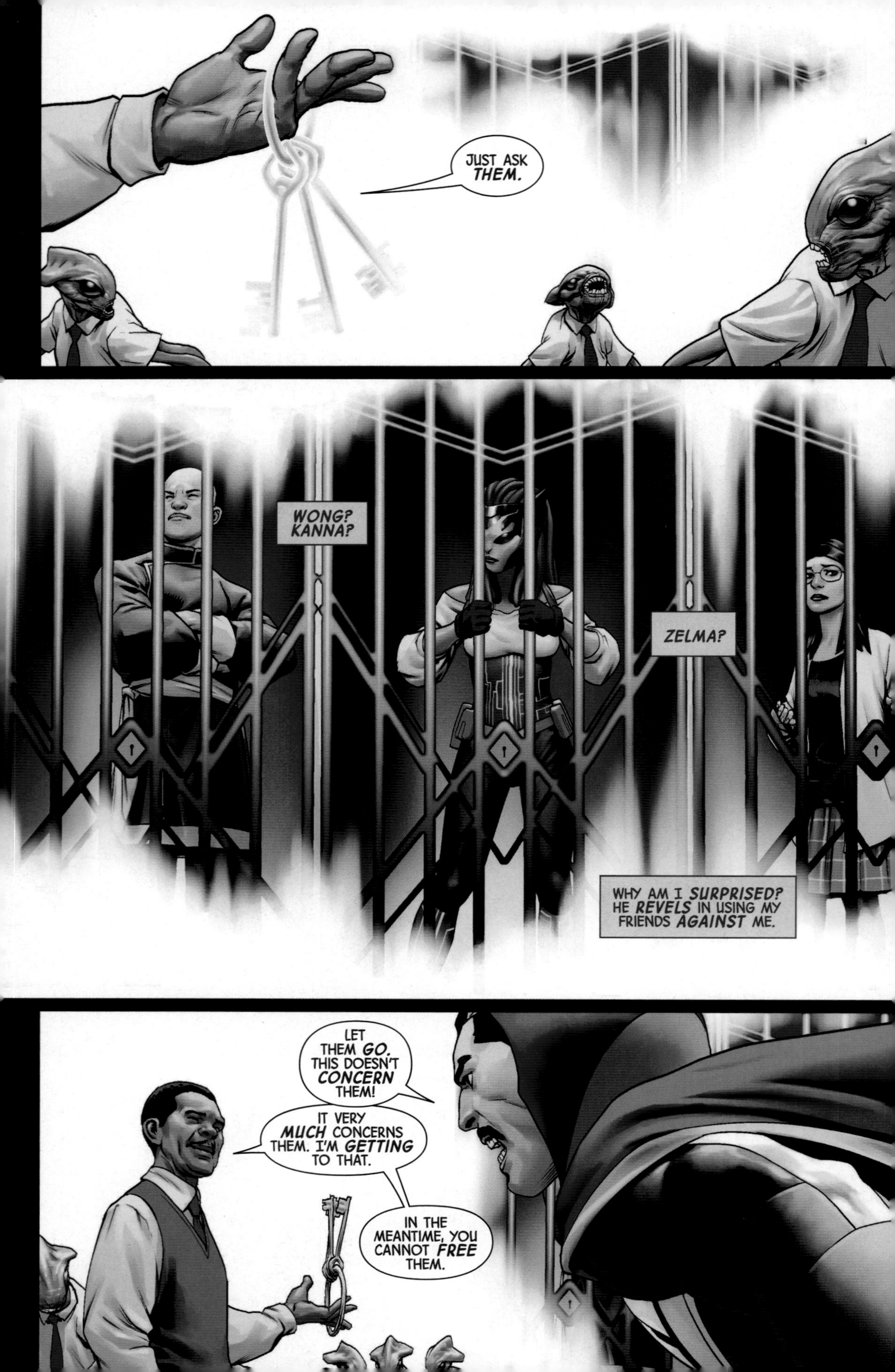
JUST ASK THEM.
WONG? KANNA?
ZELMA?
WHY AM I SURPRISED? HE REVELS IN USING MY FRIENDS AGAINST ME.
LET THEM GO. THIS DOESN'T CONCERN THEM!
IT VERY MUCH CONCERNS THEM. I'M GETTING TO THAT.
IN THE MEANTIME, YOU CANNOT FREE THEM.

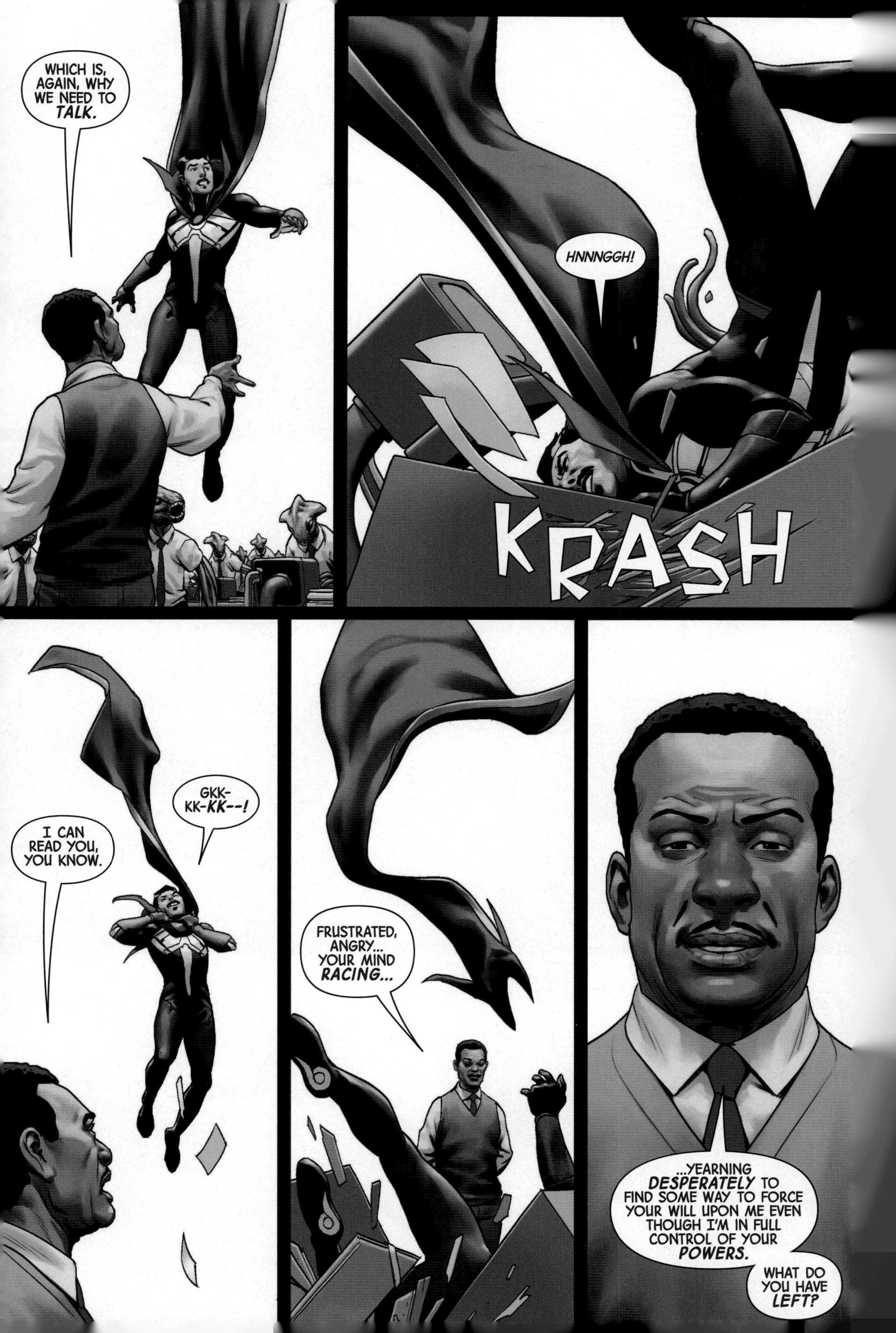
WHICH IS, AGAIN, WHY WE NEED TO *TALK.*
HNNNGGH!
KRASH
GKK-KK-*KK*--!
I CAN READ YOU, YOU KNOW.
FRUSTRATED, ANGRY... YOUR MIND *RACING...*
...YEARNING *DESPERATELY* TO FIND SOME WAY TO FORCE YOUR WILL UPON ME EVEN THOUGH I'M IN FULL CONTROL OF YOUR *POWERS.*
WHAT DO YOU HAVE *LEFT?*

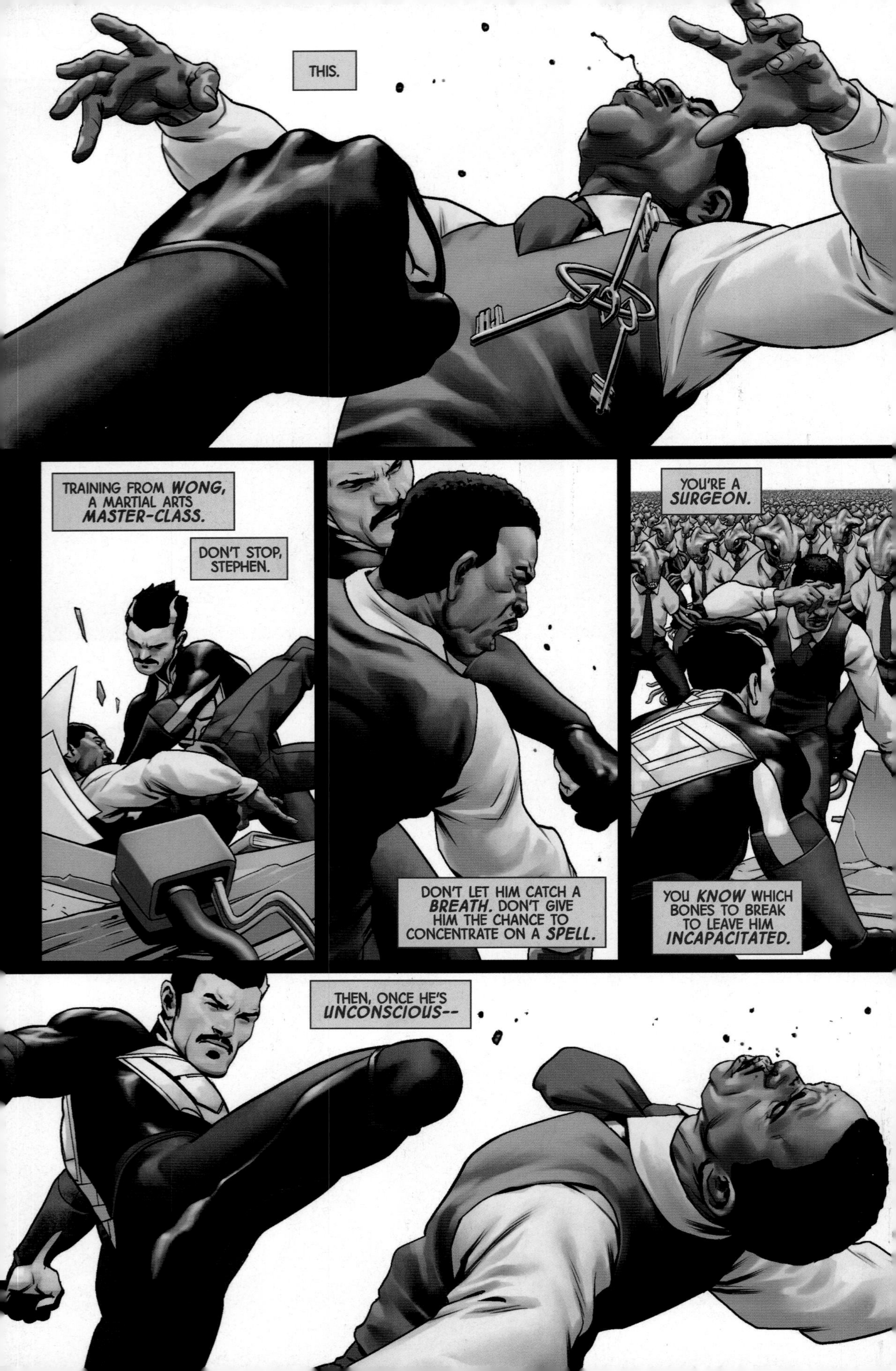
THIS.
TRAINING FROM WONG, A MARTIAL ARTS MASTER-CLASS.
DON'T STOP, STEPHEN.
DON'T LET HIM CATCH A BREATH. DON'T GIVE HIM THE CHANCE TO CONCENTRATE ON A SPELL.
YOU'RE A SURGEON.
YOU KNOW WHICH BONES TO BREAK TO LEAVE HIM INCAPACITATED.
THEN, ONCE HE'S UNCONSCIOUS--

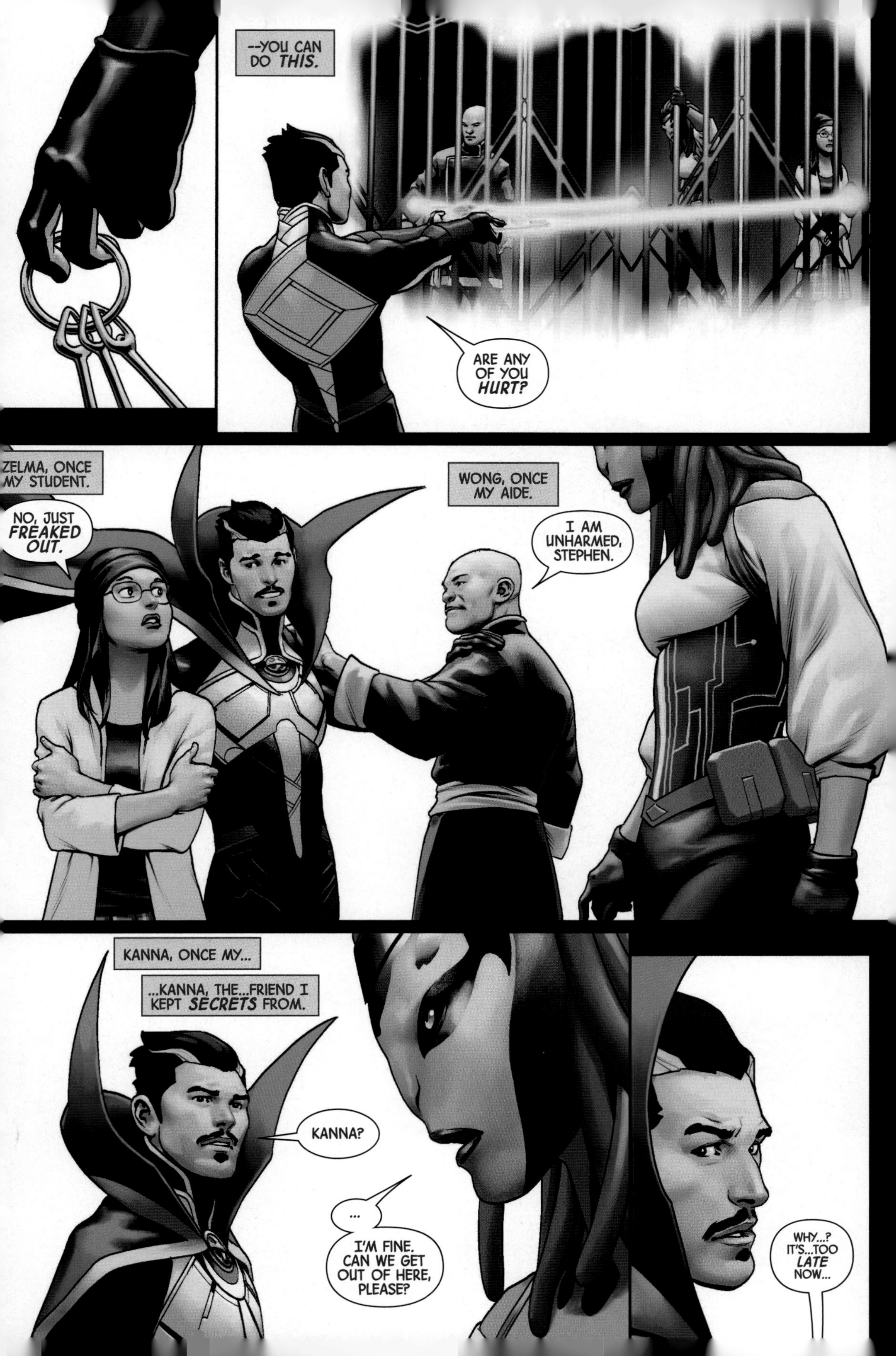
--YOU CAN DO THIS.
ARE ANY OF YOU HURT?
ZELMA, ONCE MY STUDENT.
NO, JUST FREAKED OUT.
WONG, ONCE MY AIDE.
I AM UNHARMED, STEPHEN.
KANNA, ONCE MY...
...KANNA, THE...FRIEND I KEPT SECRETS FROM.
KANNA?
...
I'M FINE. CAN WE GET OUT OF HERE, PLEASE?
WHY...? IT'S...TOO LATE NOW...

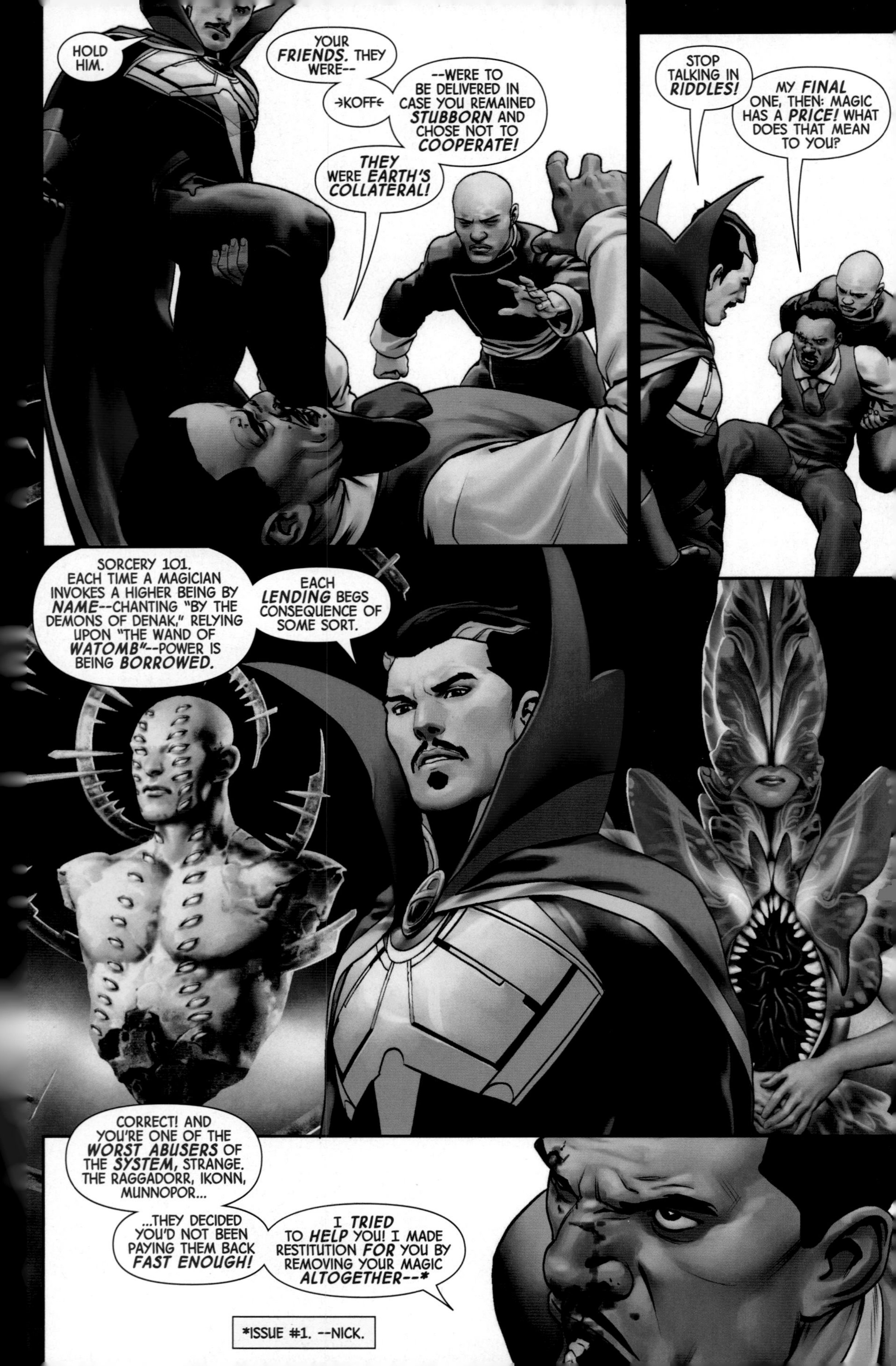
HOLD HIM.
YOUR FRIENDS. THEY WERE--
»KOFF«
--WERE TO BE DELIVERED IN CASE YOU REMAINED STUBBORN AND CHOSE NOT TO COOPERATE!
THEY WERE EARTH'S COLLATERAL!
STOP TALKING IN RIDDLES!
MY FINAL ONE, THEN: MAGIC HAS A PRICE! WHAT DOES THAT MEAN TO YOU?
SORCERY 101. EACH TIME A MAGICIAN INVOKES A HIGHER BEING BY NAME--CHANTING "BY THE DEMONS OF DENAK," RELYING UPON "THE WAND OF WATOMB"--POWER IS BEING BORROWED.
EACH LENDING BEGS CONSEQUENCE OF SOME SORT.
CORRECT! AND YOU'RE ONE OF THE WORST ABUSERS OF THE SYSTEM, STRANGE. THE RAGGADORR, IKONN, MUNNOPOR...
...THEY DECIDED YOU'D NOT BEEN PAYING THEM BACK FAST ENOUGH!
I TRIED TO HELP YOU! I MADE RESTITUTION FOR YOU BY REMOVING YOUR MAGIC ALTOGETHER--*
*ISSUE #1. --NICK.

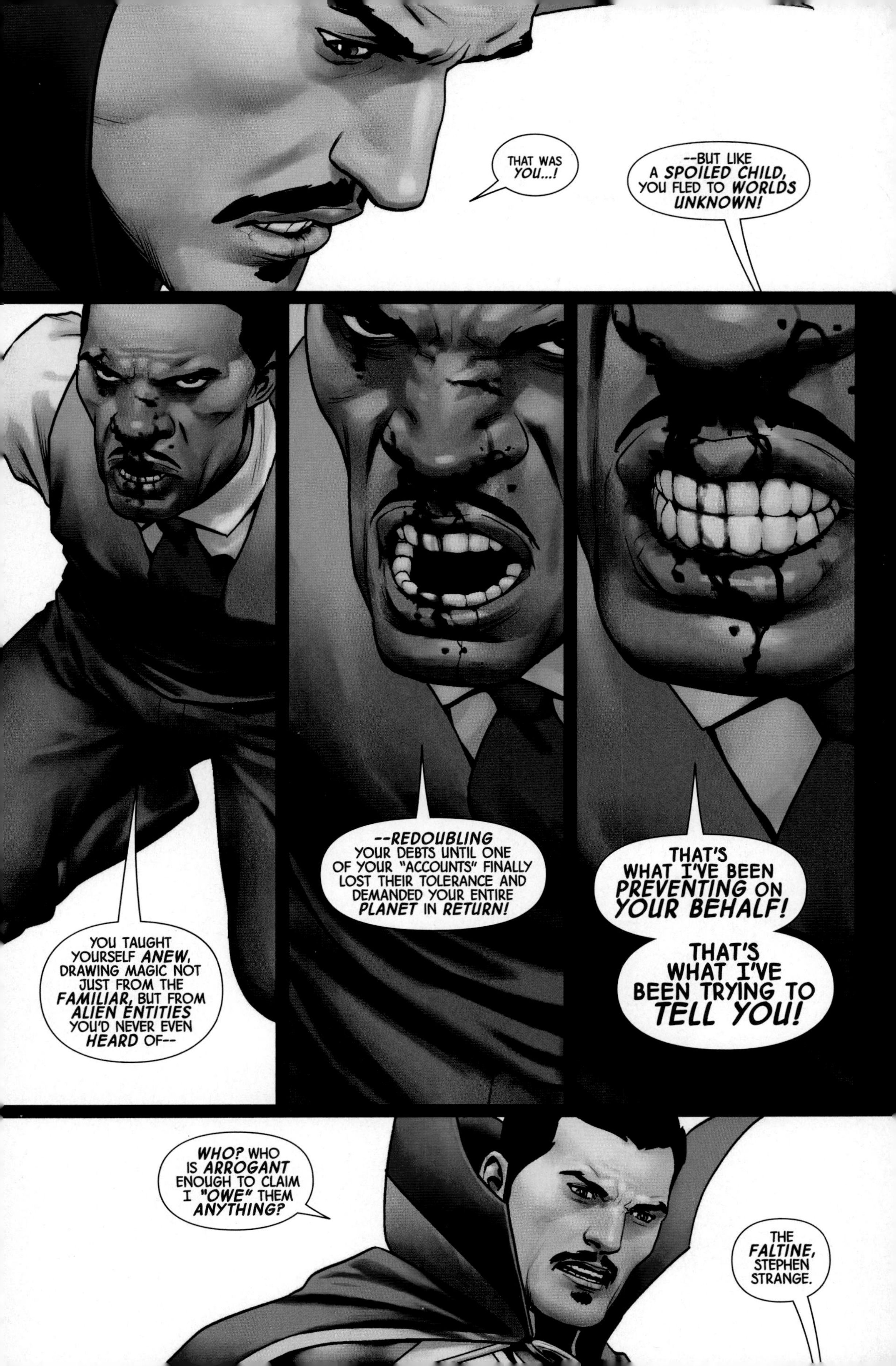
THAT WAS YOU...!
--BUT LIKE A SPOILED CHILD, YOU FLED TO WORLDS UNKNOWN!
YOU TAUGHT YOURSELF ANEW, DRAWING MAGIC NOT JUST FROM THE FAMILIAR, BUT FROM ALIEN ENTITIES YOU'D NEVER EVEN HEARD OF--
--REDOUBLING YOUR DEBTS UNTIL ONE OF YOUR "ACCOUNTS" FINALLY LOST THEIR TOLERANCE AND DEMANDED YOUR ENTIRE PLANET IN RETURN!
THAT'S WHAT I'VE BEEN PREVENTING ON YOUR BEHALF!
THAT'S WHAT I'VE BEEN TRYING TO TELL YOU!
WHO? WHO IS ARROGANT ENOUGH TO CLAIM I "OWE" THEM ANYTHING?
THE FALTINE, STEPHEN STRANGE.

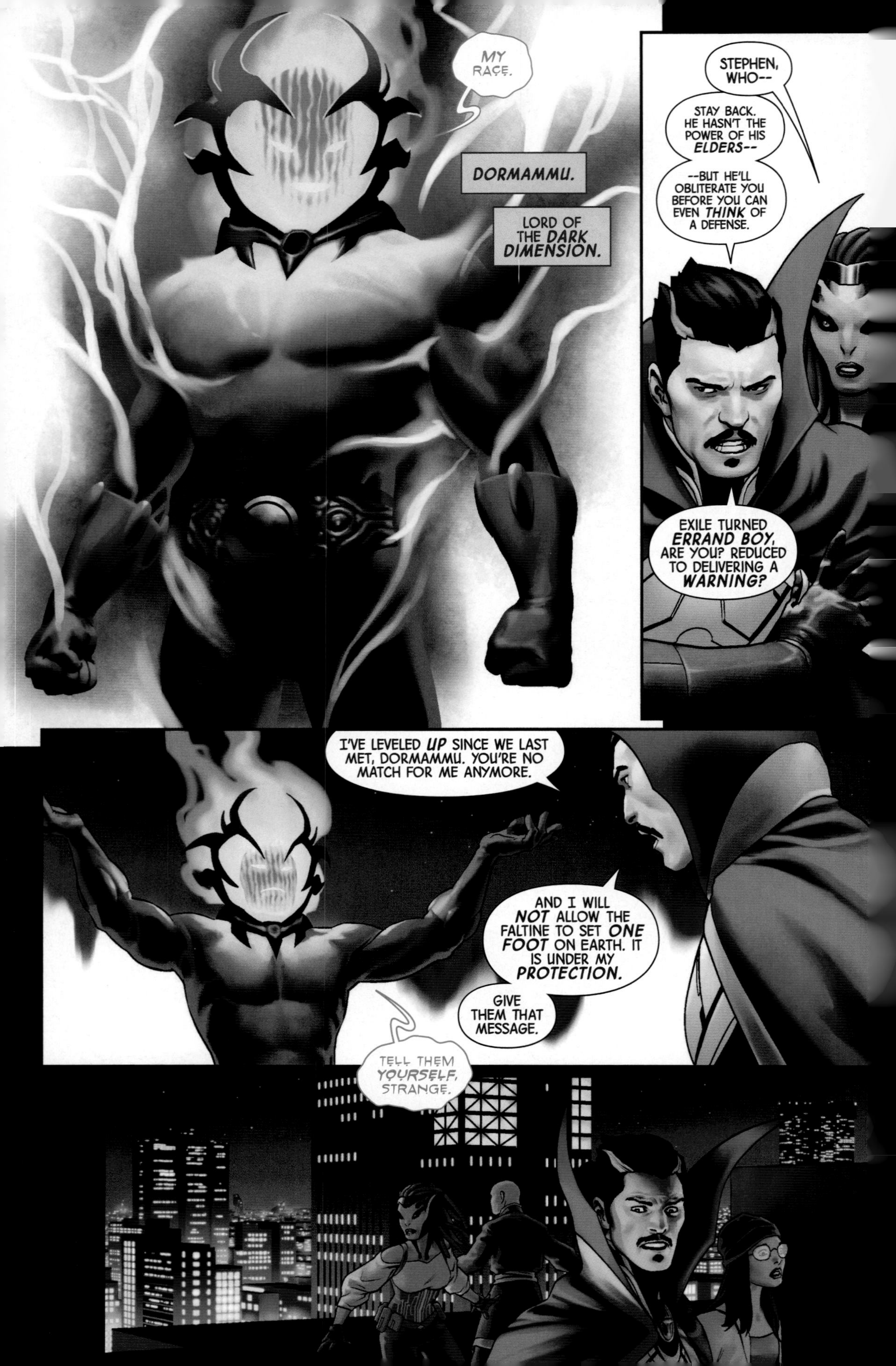
MY RACE.
DORMAMMU.
LORD OF THE DARK DIMENSION.
STEPHEN, WHO--
STAY BACK. HE HASN'T THE POWER OF HIS ELDERS--
--BUT HE'LL OBLITERATE YOU BEFORE YOU CAN EVEN THINK OF A DEFENSE.
EXILE TURNED ERRAND BOY, ARE YOU? REDUCED TO DELIVERING A WARNING?
I'VE LEVELED UP SINCE WE LAST MET, DORMAMMU. YOU'RE NO MATCH FOR ME ANYMORE.
AND I WILL NOT ALLOW THE FALTINE TO SET ONE FOOT ON EARTH. IT IS UNDER MY PROTECTION.
GIVE THEM THAT MESSAGE.
TELL THEM YOURSELF, STRANGE.

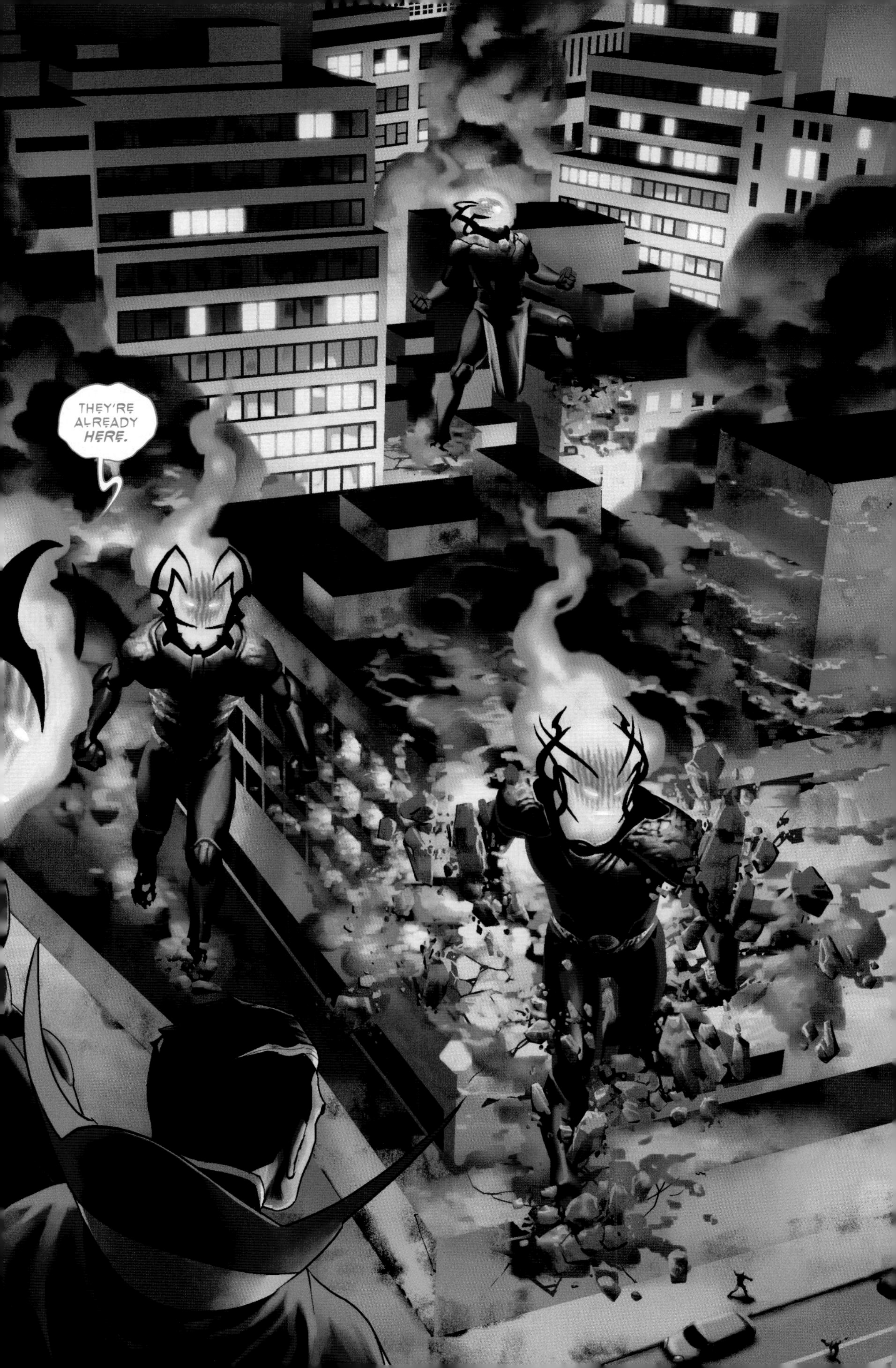
THEY'RE ALREADY *HERE.*

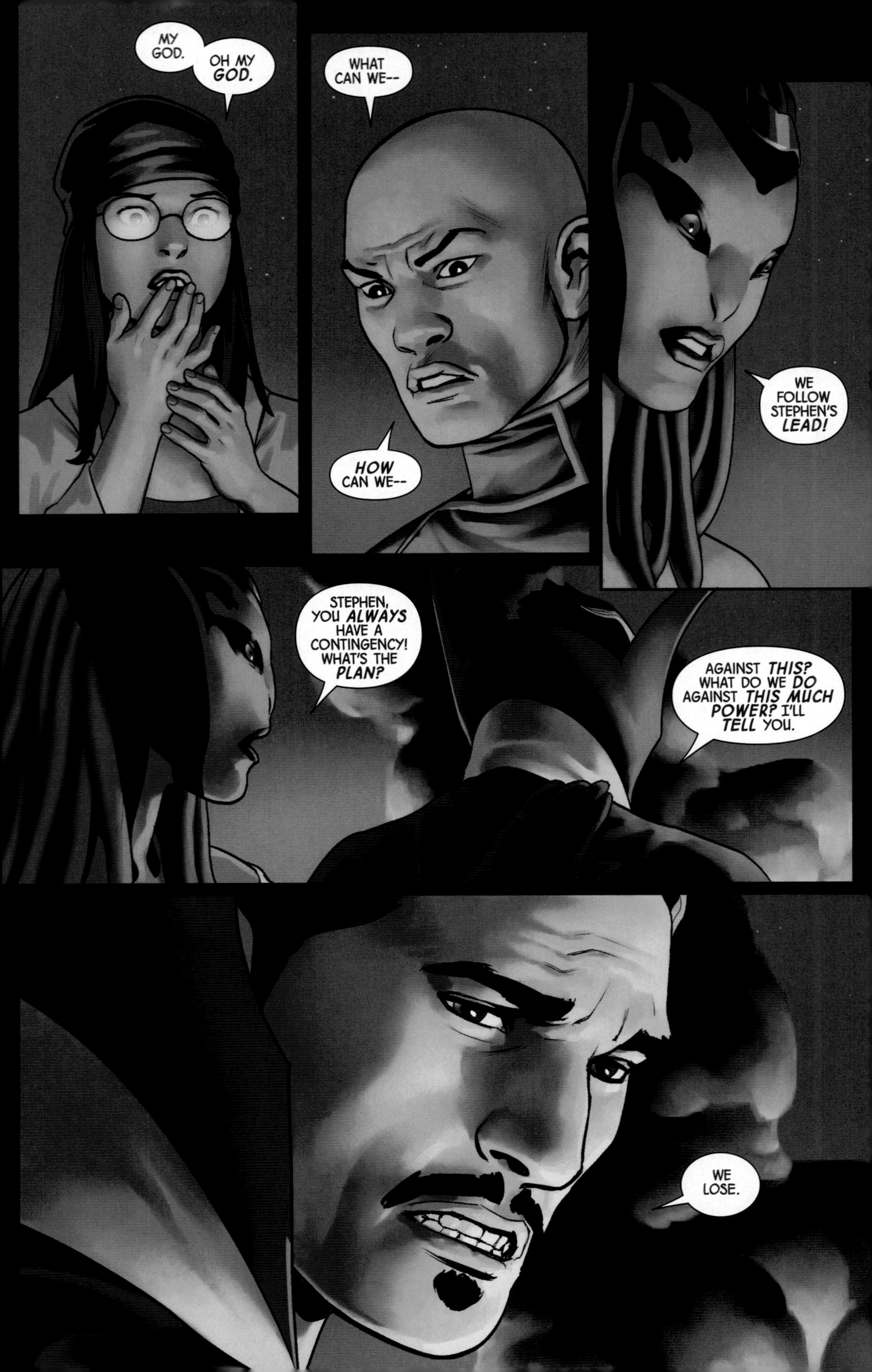
MY GOD.
OH MY GOD.
WHAT CAN WE--
HOW CAN WE--
WE FOLLOW STEPHEN'S LEAD!
STEPHEN, YOU ALWAYS HAVE A CONTINGENCY! WHAT'S THE PLAN?
AGAINST THIS? WHAT DO WE DO AGAINST THIS MUCH POWER? I'LL TELL YOU.
WE LOSE.

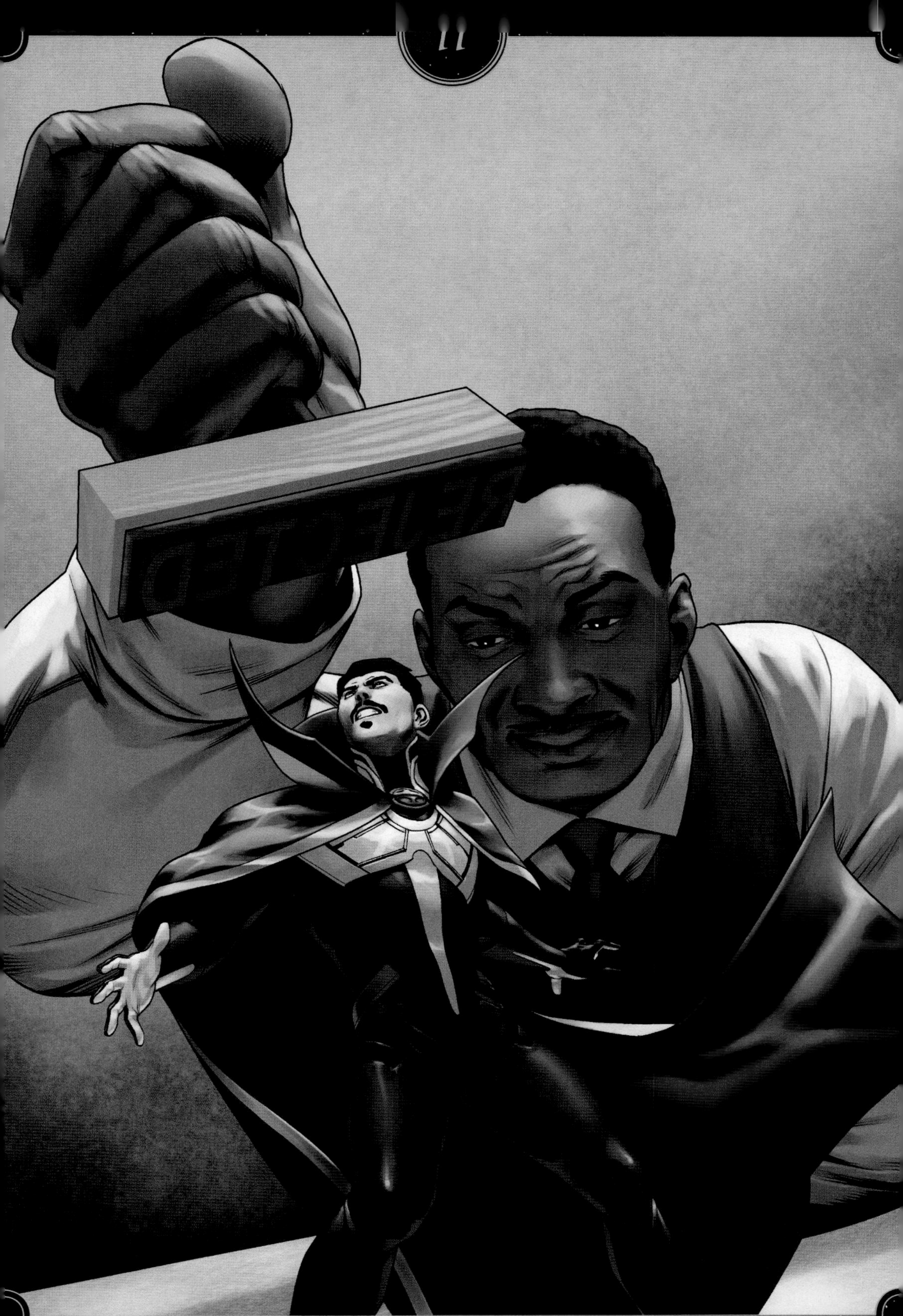

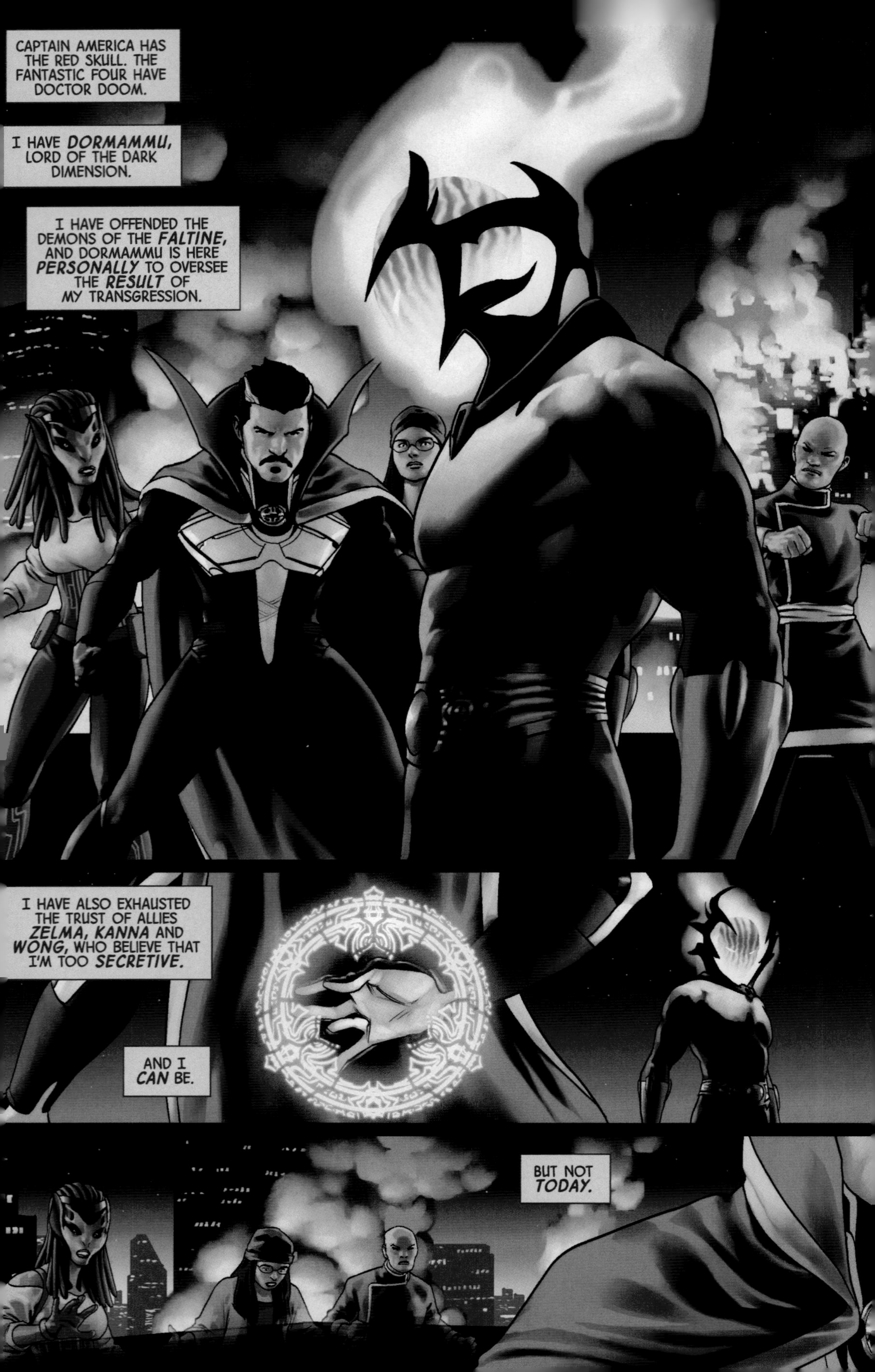
CAPTAIN AMERICA HAS THE RED SKULL. THE FANTASTIC FOUR HAVE DOCTOR DOOM.
I HAVE DORMAMMU, LORD OF THE DARK DIMENSION.
I HAVE OFFENDED THE DEMONS OF THE FALTINE, AND DORMAMMU IS HERE PERSONALLY TO OVERSEE THE RESULT OF MY TRANSGRESSION.
I HAVE ALSO EXHAUSTED THE TRUST OF ALLIES ZELMA, KANNA AND WONG, WHO BELIEVE THAT I'M TOO SECRETIVE.
AND I CAN BE.
BUT NOT TODAY.

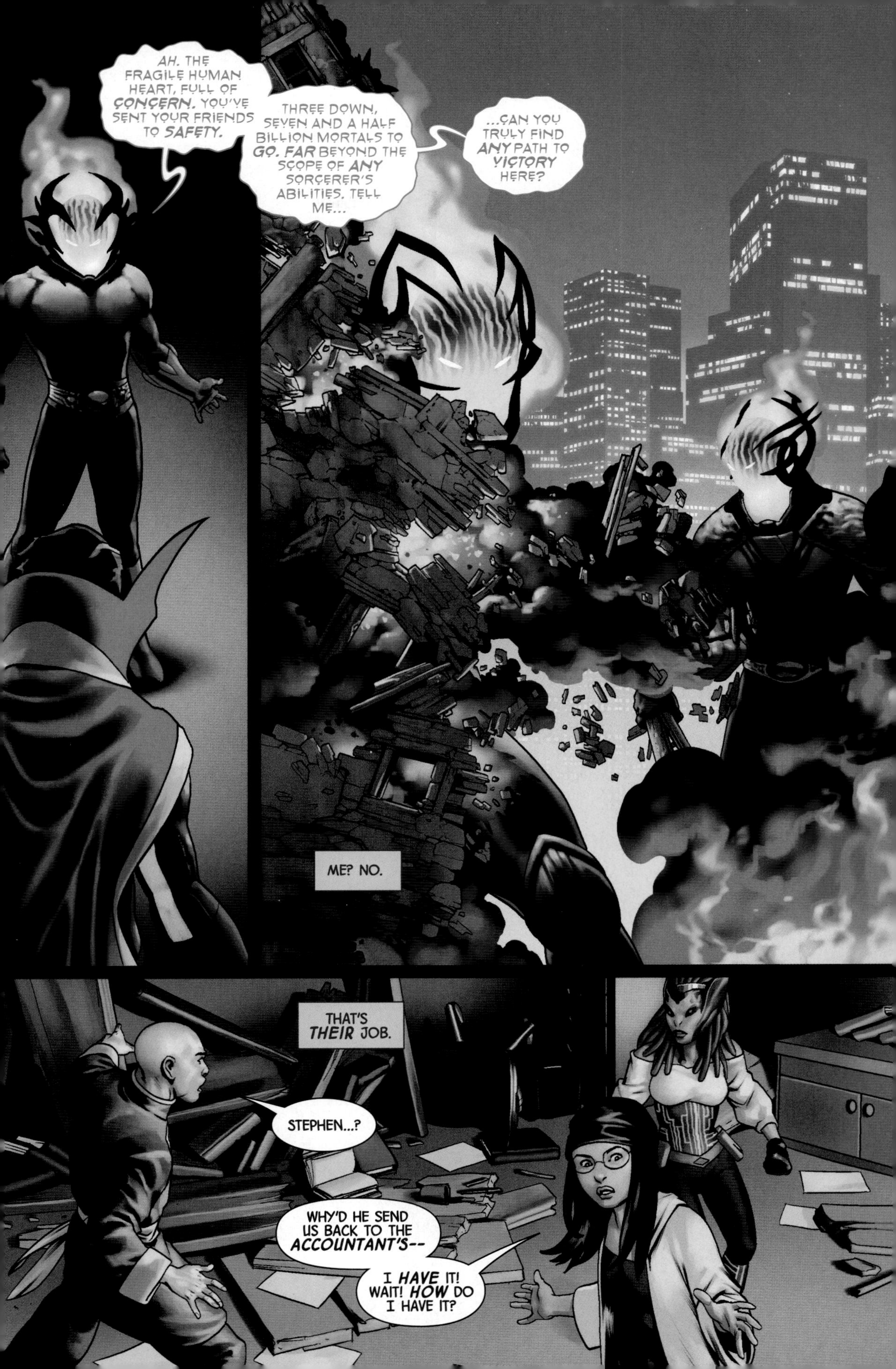
AH. THE FRAGILE HUMAN HEART, FULL OF CONCERN. YOU'VE SENT YOUR FRIENDS TO SAFETY.
THREE DOWN, SEVEN AND A HALF BILLION MORTALS TO GO. FAR BEYOND THE SCOPE OF ANY SORCERER'S ABILITIES. TELL ME...
...CAN YOU TRULY FIND ANY PATH TO VICTORY HERE?
ME? NO.
THAT'S THEIR JOB.
STEPHEN...?
WHY'D HE SEND US BACK TO THE ACCOUNTANT'S--
I HAVE IT! WAIT! HOW DO I HAVE IT?

BECAUSE HE ZAPPED IT INTO OUR *HEADS.* IS THAT *NORMALLY* HOW HE COMMUNICATES HIS SECRET PLANS?

I WOULDN'T KNOW.

FIGURES.

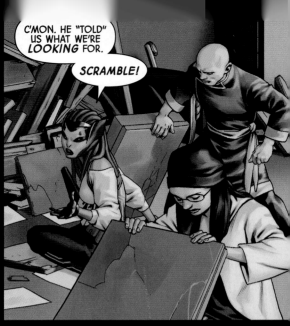

C'MON. HE "TOLD" US WHAT WE'RE *LOOKING* FOR.

SCRAMBLE!

A MOMENT AGO, I BRAGGED THAT DORMAMMU WAS NO *MATCH* FOR ME ANYMORE.

THE TRUTH IS THAT I CAN'T BE CERTAIN, BUT THE SEED'S BEEN PLANTED IN HIS BRAIN. OTHERWISE, HE'D STRIKE WITHOUT *HESITATION.*

SO WE CIRCLE ONE ANOTHER LIKE TWO GUNSLINGERS WAITING FOR ONE ANOTHER TO *FLINCH.* I HAVE TO KEEP HIM DISTRACTED. I HAVE TO BUY *TIME.*

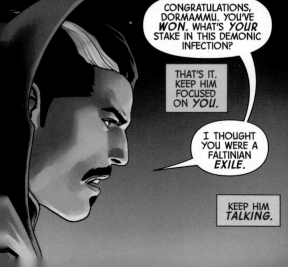

CONGRATULATIONS, DORMAMMU. YOU'VE *WON.* WHAT'S *YOUR* STAKE IN THIS DEMONIC INFECTION?

THAT'S IT. KEEP HIM FOCUSED ON *YOU.*

I THOUGHT YOU WERE A FALTINIAN *EXILE.*

KEEP HIM *TALKING.*

THE FALTINE *ENVY* ME...

...HE LIED.

THEY HAVE FOR *MILLENNIA.*

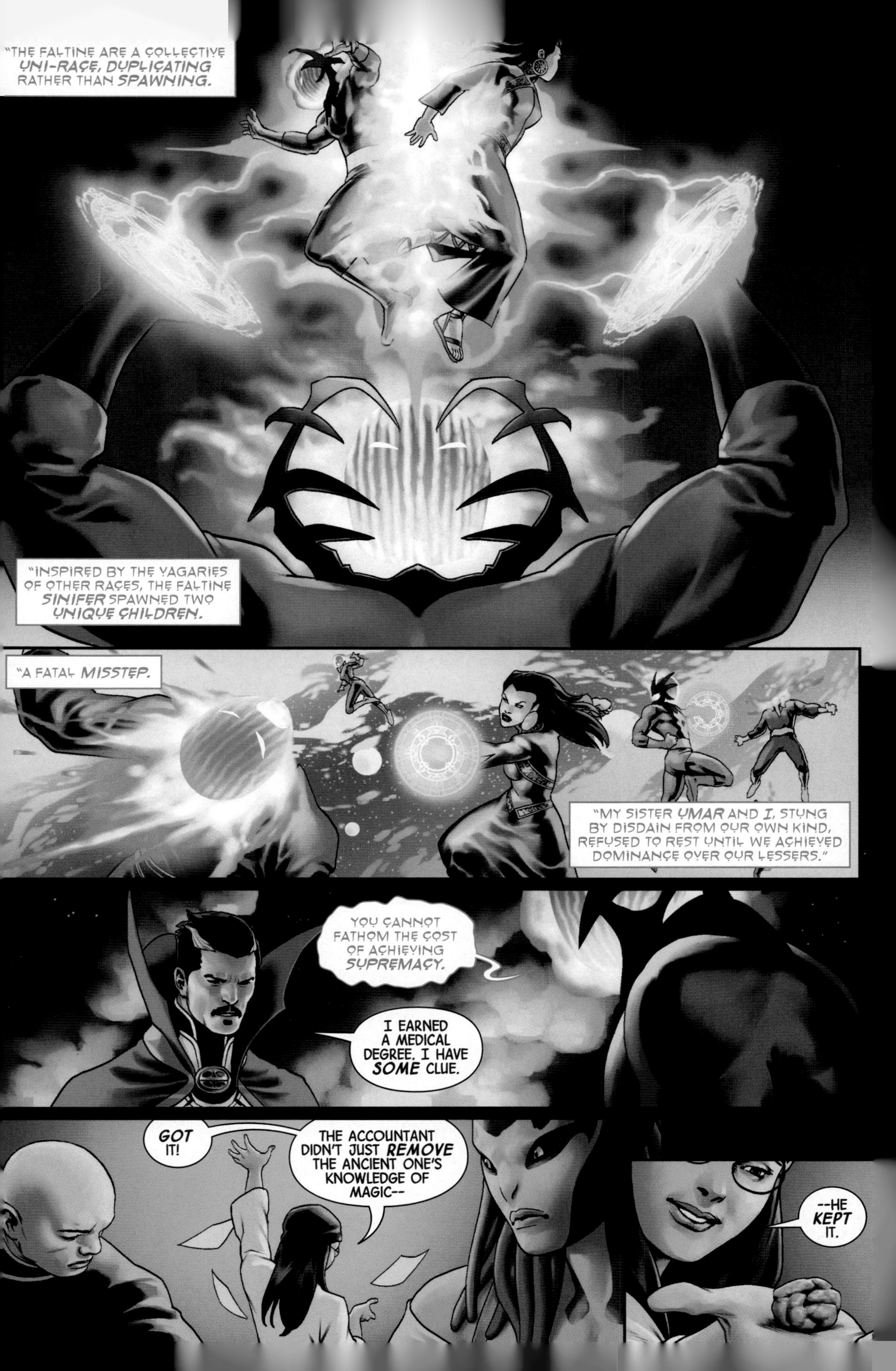
"THE FALTINE ARE A COLLECTIVE UNI-RACE, DUPLICATING RATHER THAN SPAWNING.
"INSPIRED BY THE VAGARIES OF OTHER RACES, THE FALTINE SINIFER SPAWNED TWO UNIQUE CHILDREN.
"A FATAL MISSTEP.
"MY SISTER UMAR AND I, STUNG BY DISDAIN FROM OUR OWN KIND, REFUSED TO REST UNTIL WE ACHIEVED DOMINANCE OVER OUR LESSERS."
YOU CANNOT FATHOM THE COST OF ACHIEVING SUPREMACY.
I EARNED A MEDICAL DEGREE. I HAVE SOME CLUE.
GOT IT!
THE ACCOUNTANT DIDN'T JUST REMOVE THE ANCIENT ONE'S KNOWLEDGE OF MAGIC--
--HE KEPT IT.

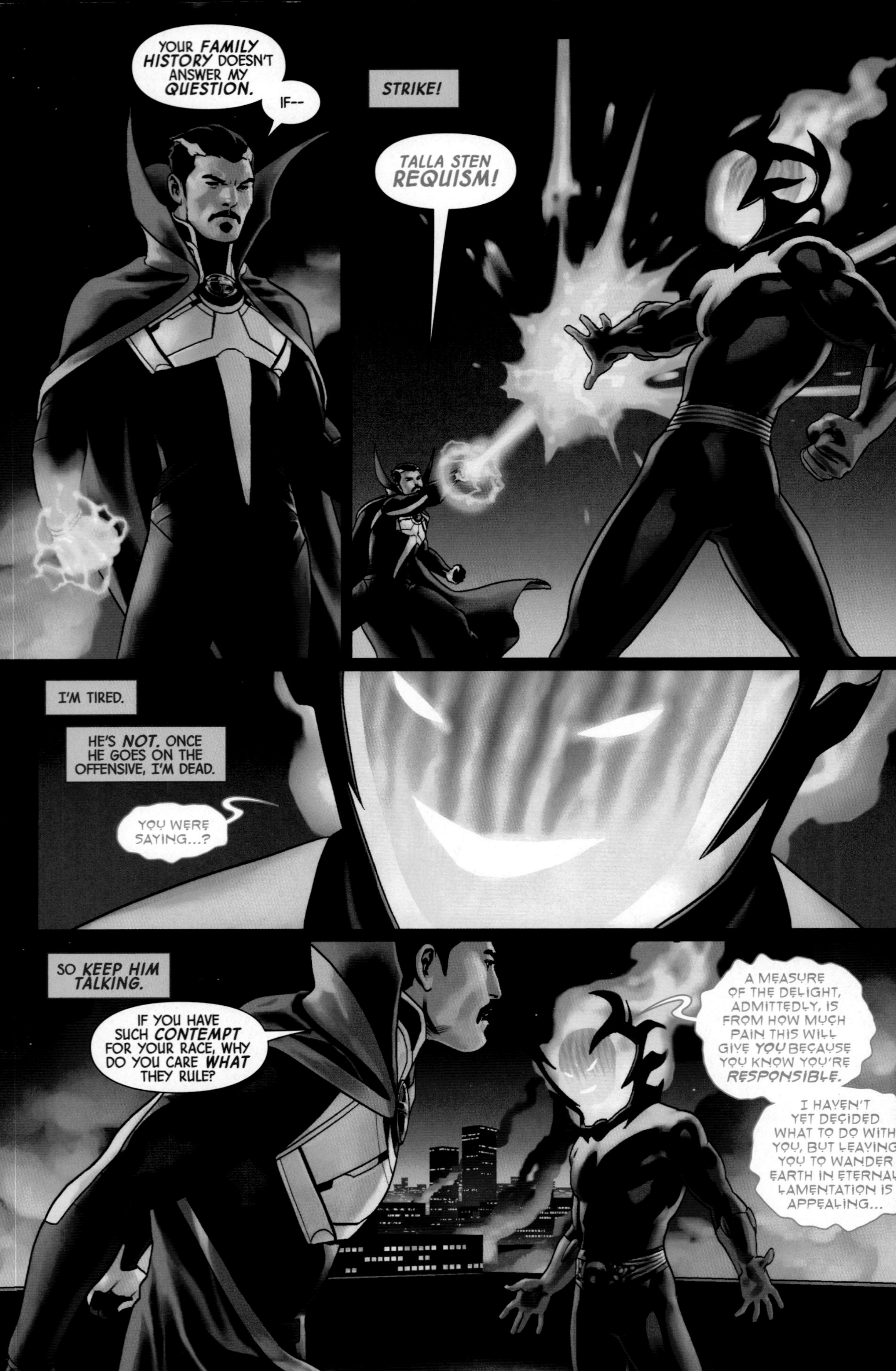
YOUR FAMILY HISTORY DOESN'T ANSWER MY QUESTION.
IF--
STRIKE!
TALLA STEN REQUISM!
I'M TIRED.
HE'S NOT. ONCE HE GOES ON THE OFFENSIVE, I'M DEAD.
YOU WERE SAYING...?
SO KEEP HIM TALKING.
IF YOU HAVE SUCH CONTEMPT FOR YOUR RACE, WHY DO YOU CARE WHAT THEY RULE?
A MEASURE OF THE DELIGHT, ADMITTEDLY, IS FROM HOW MUCH PAIN THIS WILL GIVE YOU BECAUSE YOU KNOW YOU'RE RESPONSIBLE.
I HAVEN'T YET DECIDED WHAT TO DO WITH YOU, BUT LEAVING YOU TO WANDER EARTH IN ETERNAL LAMENTATION IS APPEALING...

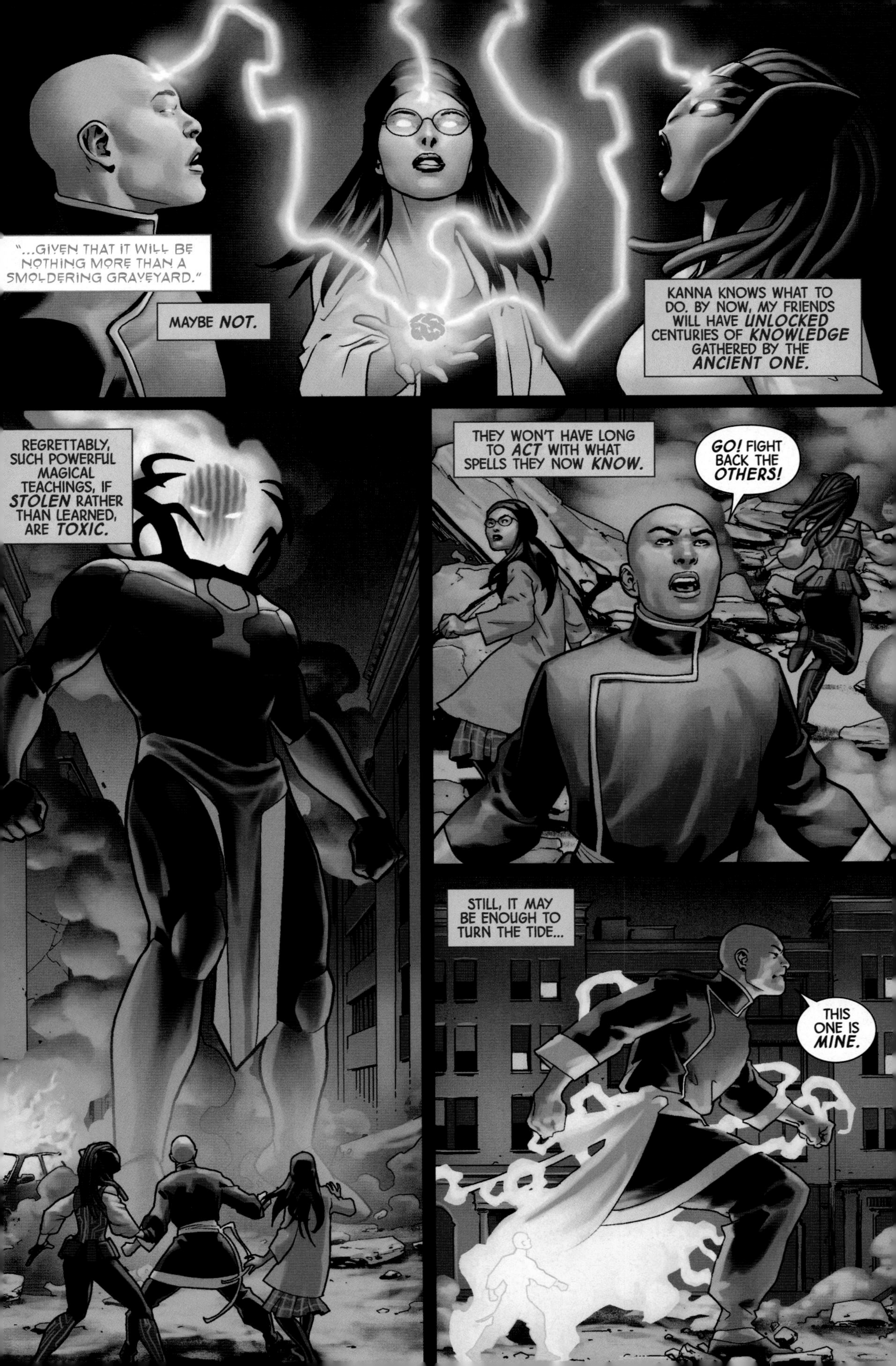
"...GIVEN THAT IT WILL BE NOTHING MORE THAN A SMOLDERING GRAVEYARD."
MAYBE NOT.
KANNA KNOWS WHAT TO DO. BY NOW, MY FRIENDS WILL HAVE UNLOCKED CENTURIES OF KNOWLEDGE GATHERED BY THE ANCIENT ONE.
REGRETTABLY, SUCH POWERFUL MAGICAL TEACHINGS, IF STOLEN RATHER THAN LEARNED, ARE TOXIC.
THEY WON'T HAVE LONG TO ACT WITH WHAT SPELLS THEY NOW KNOW.
GO! FIGHT BACK THE OTHERS!
STILL, IT MAY BE ENOUGH TO TURN THE TIDE...
THIS ONE IS MINE.

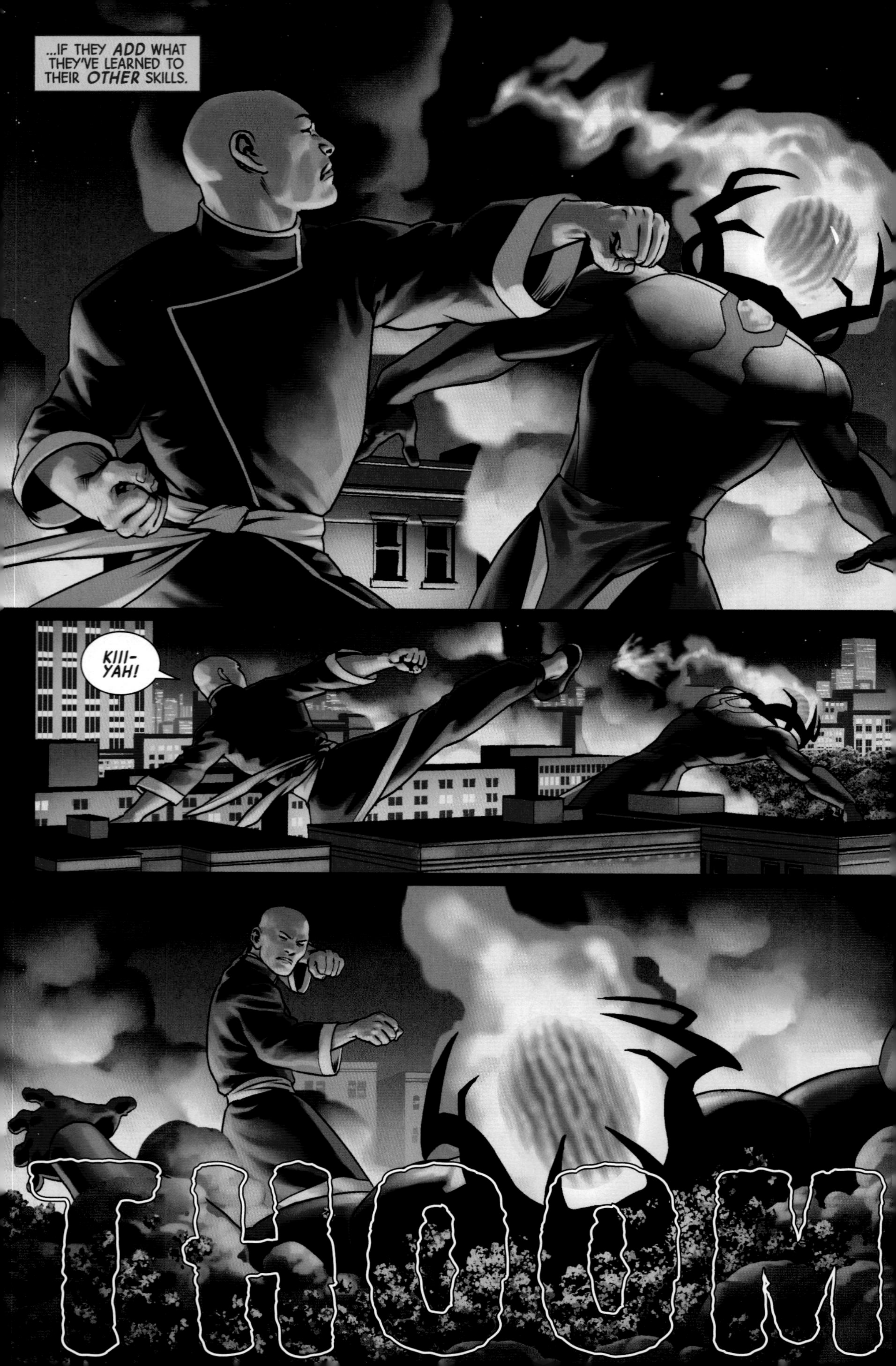
...IF THEY ADD WHAT THEY'VE LEARNED TO THEIR OTHER SKILLS.
KIII-YAH!
THOOM

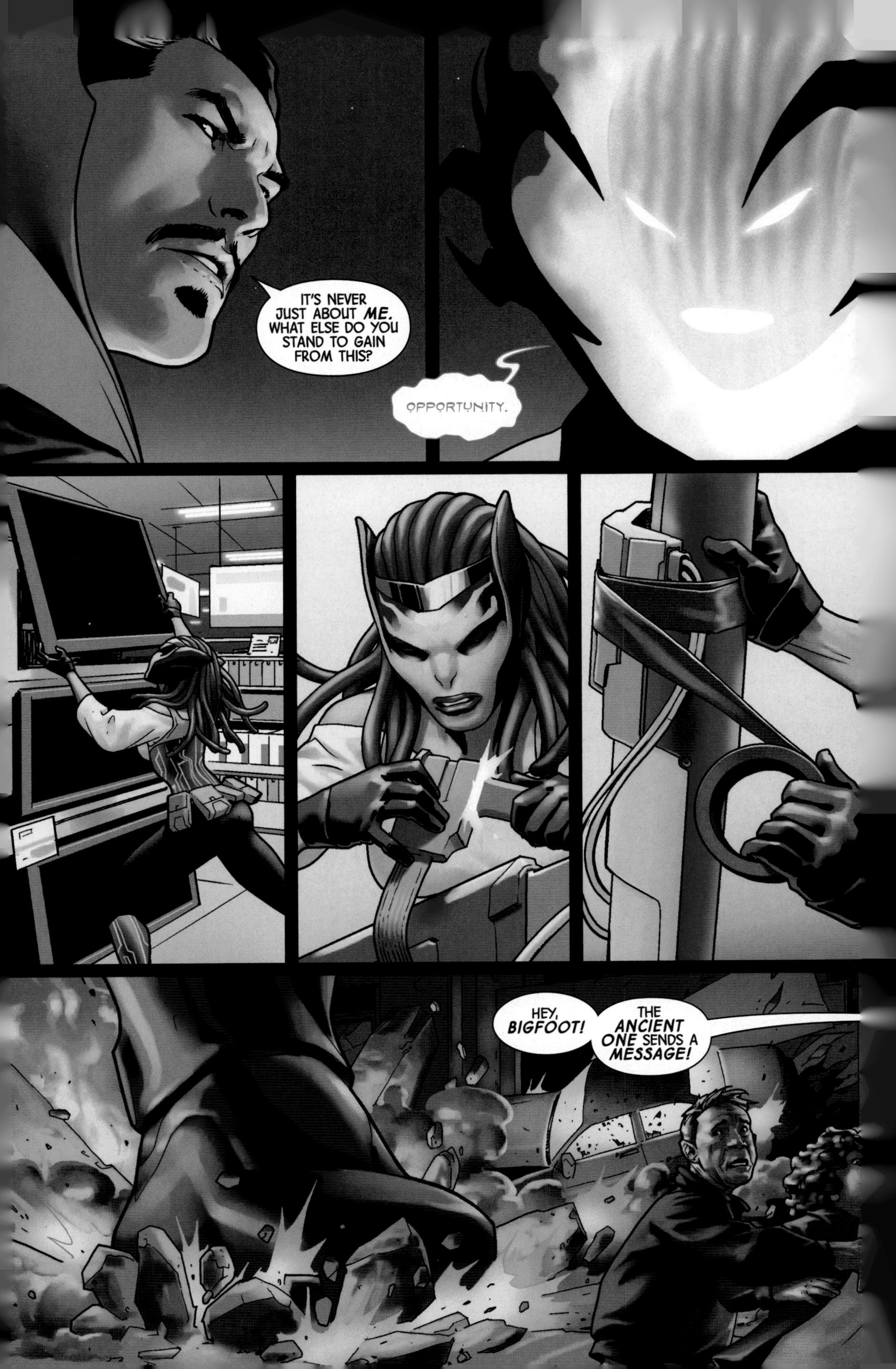
IT'S NEVER JUST ABOUT ME. WHAT ELSE DO YOU STAND TO GAIN FROM THIS?
OPPORTUNITY.
HEY, BIGFOOT!
THE ANCIENT ONE SENDS A MESSAGE!

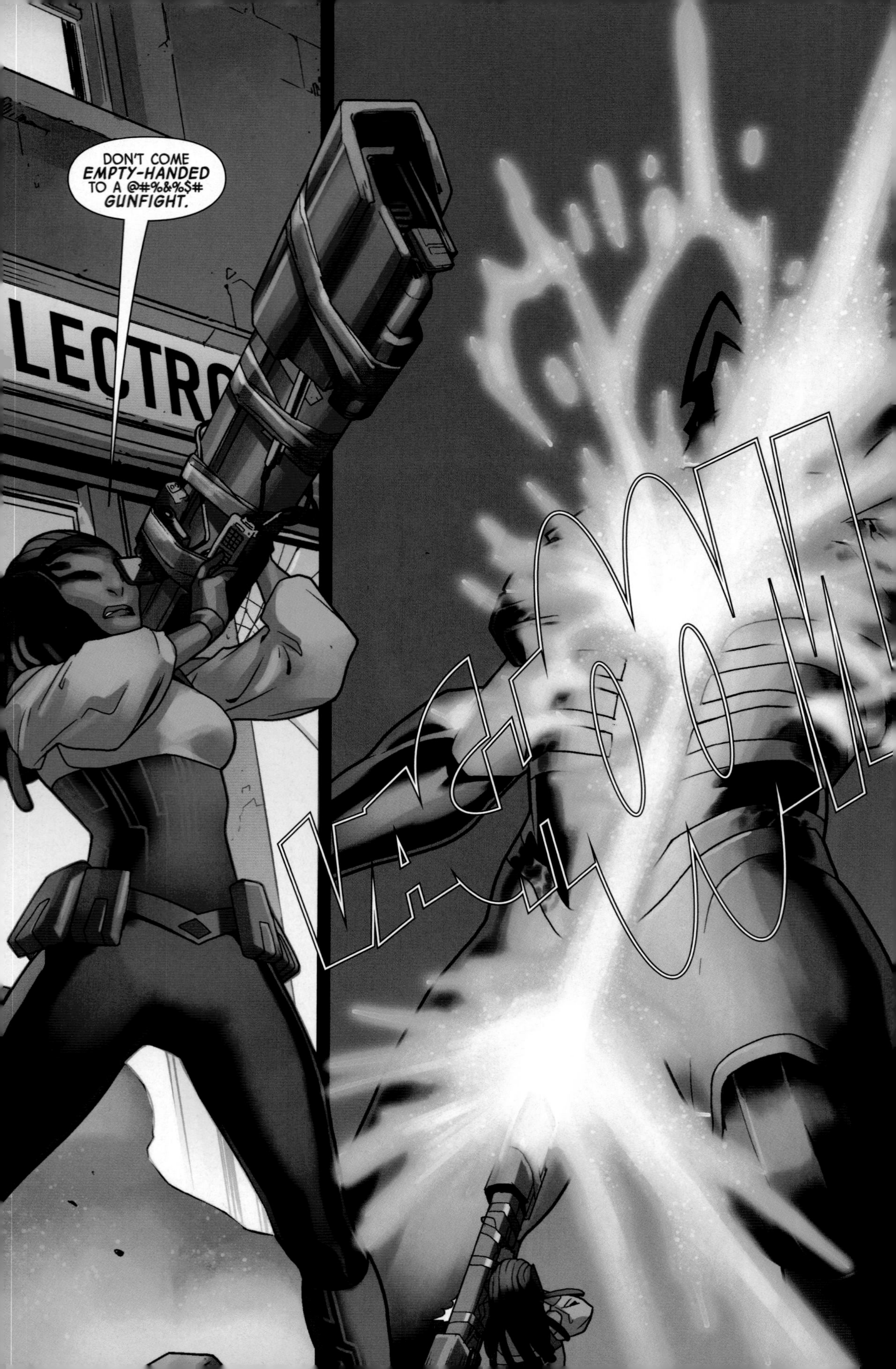
DON'T COME EMPTY-HANDED TO A @#%&%$# GUNFIGHT.
LECTRO
VRA-BOOM!

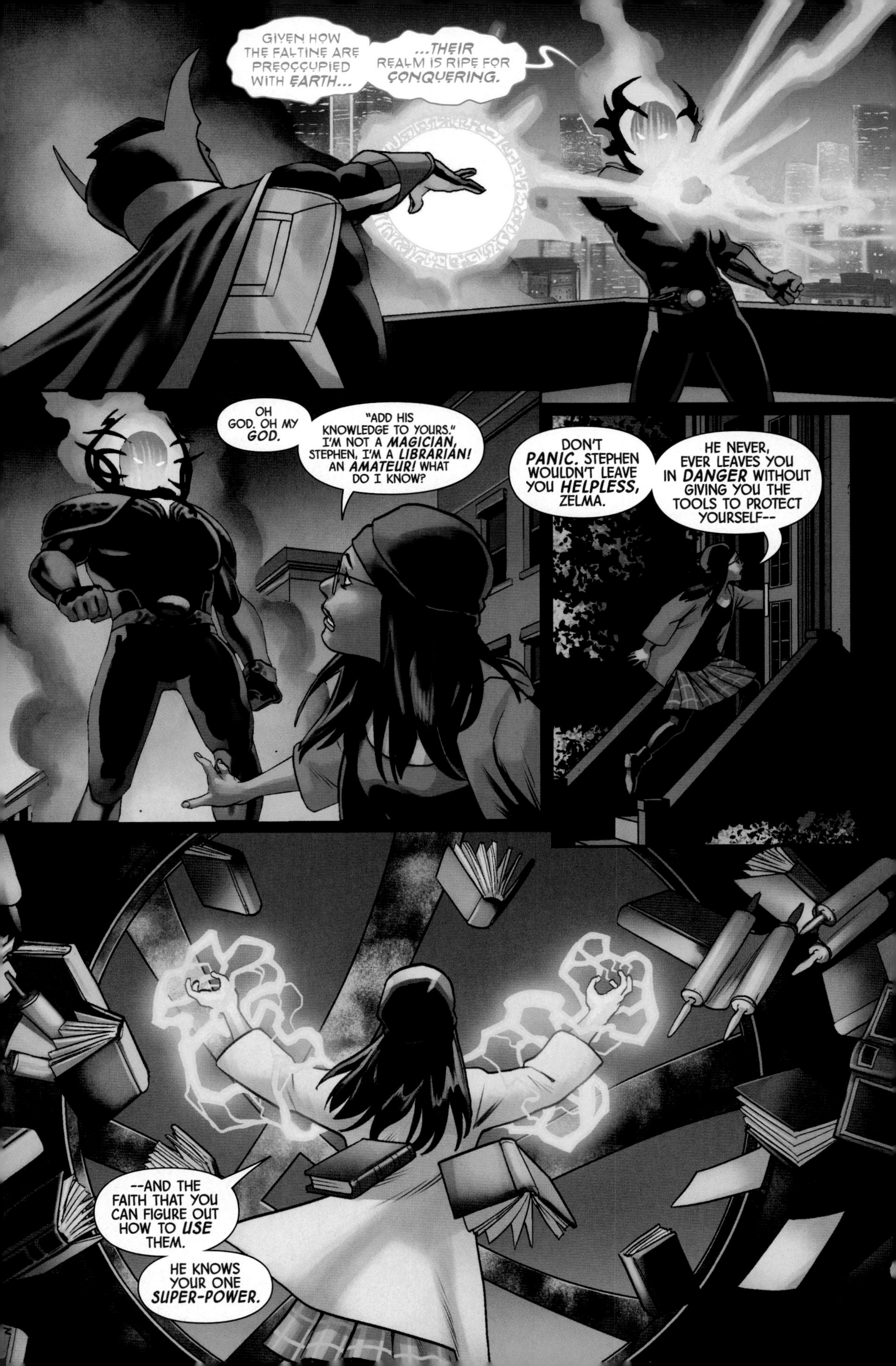
GIVEN HOW THE FALTINE ARE PREOCCUPIED WITH EARTH...
...THEIR REALM IS RIPE FOR CONQUERING.
OH GOD. OH MY GOD.
"ADD HIS KNOWLEDGE TO YOURS." I'M NOT A MAGICIAN, STEPHEN, I'M A LIBRARIAN! AN AMATEUR! WHAT DO I KNOW?
DON'T PANIC. STEPHEN WOULDN'T LEAVE YOU HELPLESS, ZELMA.
HE NEVER, EVER LEAVES YOU IN DANGER WITHOUT GIVING YOU THE TOOLS TO PROTECT YOURSELF--
--AND THE FAITH THAT YOU CAN FIGURE OUT HOW TO USE THEM.
HE KNOWS YOUR ONE SUPER-POWER.

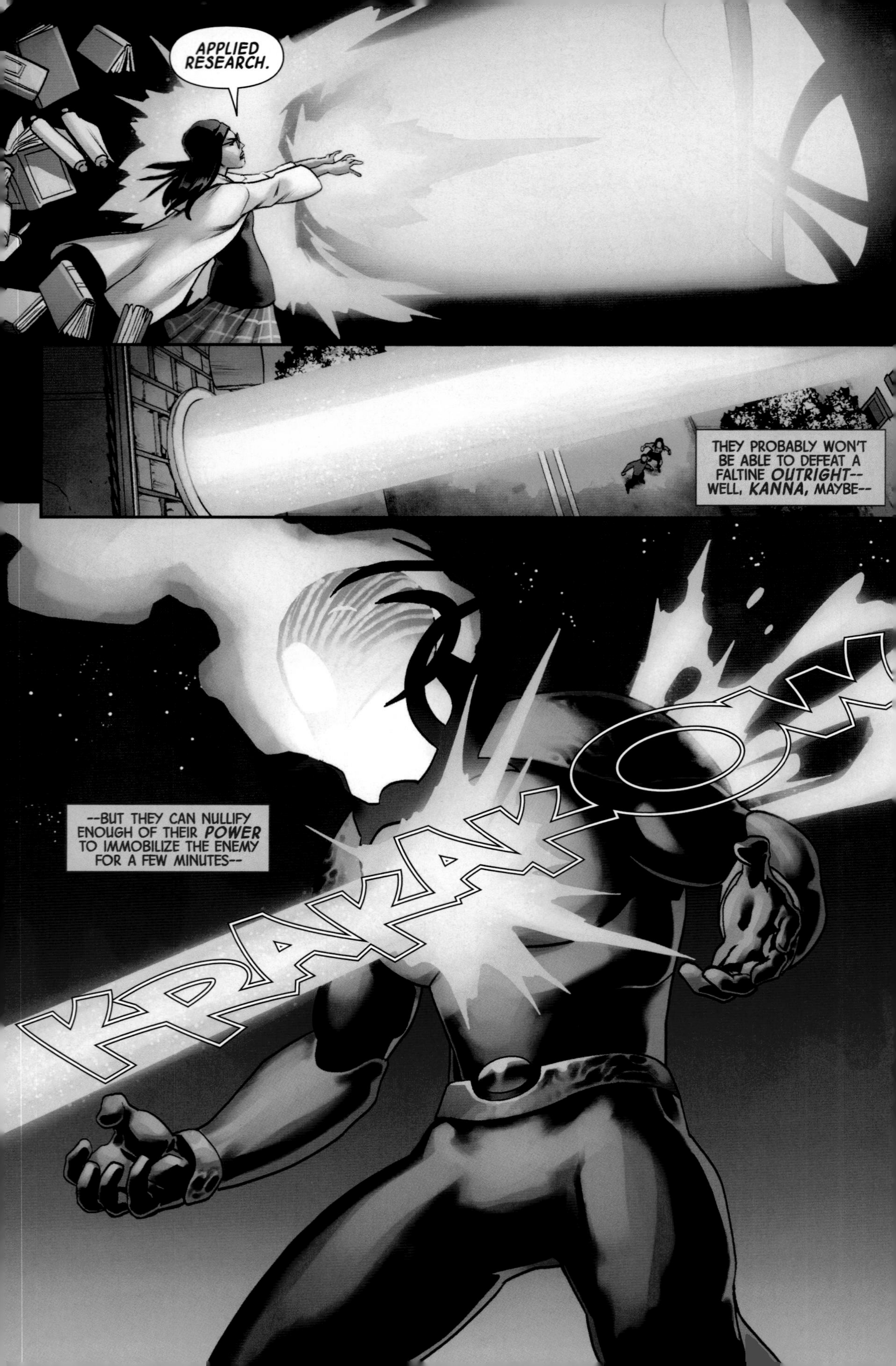
APPLIED RESEARCH.
THEY PROBABLY WON'T BE ABLE TO DEFEAT A FALTINE OUTRIGHT--WELL, KANNA, MAYBE--
--BUT THEY CAN NULLIFY ENOUGH OF THEIR POWER TO IMMOBILIZE THE ENEMY FOR A FEW MINUTES--
KRAKAKOOM

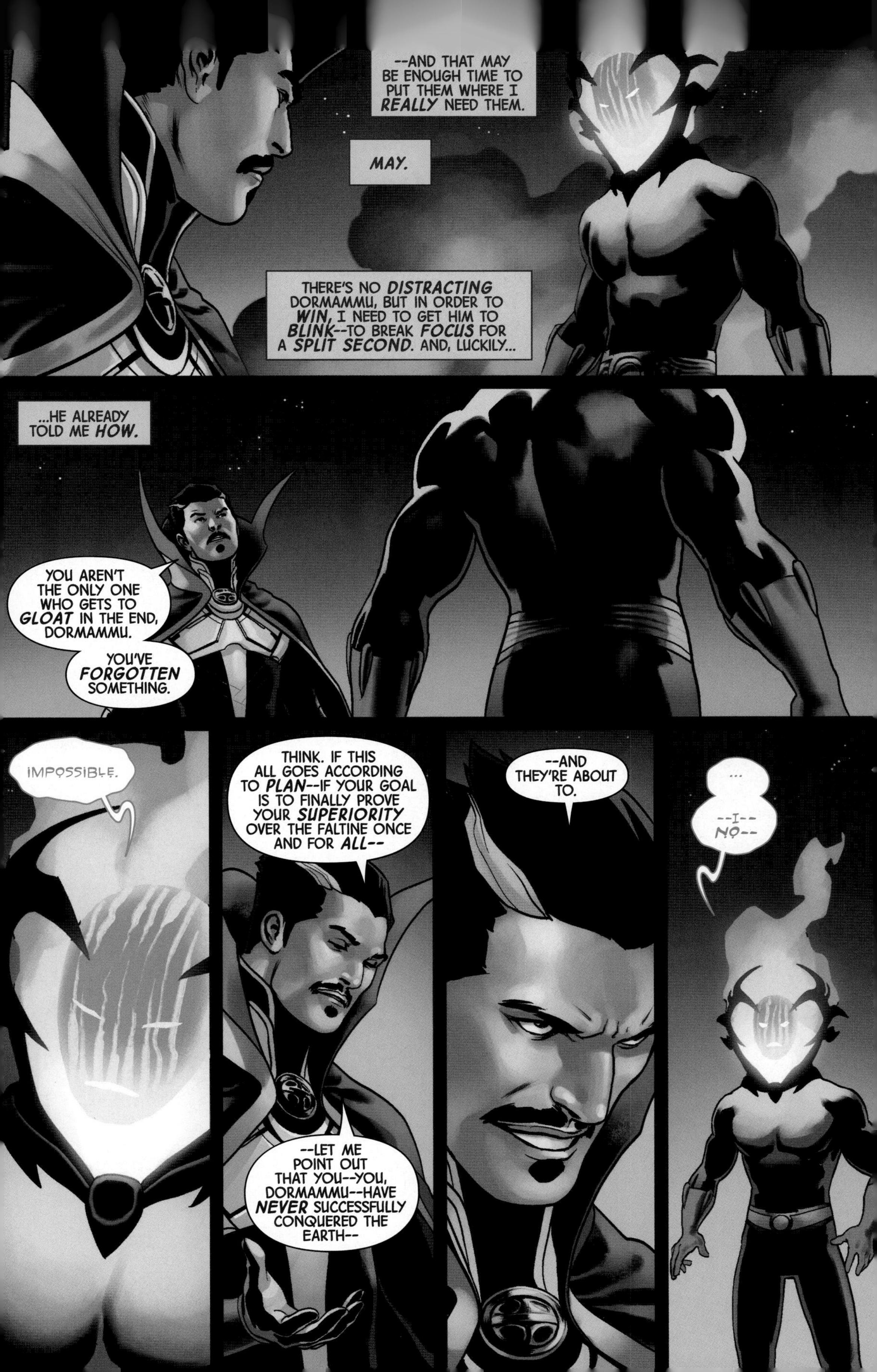
--AND THAT MAY BE ENOUGH TIME TO PUT THEM WHERE I REALLY NEED THEM.
MAY.
THERE'S NO DISTRACTING DORMAMMU, BUT IN ORDER TO WIN, I NEED TO GET HIM TO BLINK--TO BREAK FOCUS FOR A SPLIT SECOND. AND, LUCKILY...
...HE ALREADY TOLD ME HOW.
YOU AREN'T THE ONLY ONE WHO GETS TO GLOAT IN THE END, DORMAMMU.
YOU'VE FORGOTTEN SOMETHING.
IMPOSSIBLE.
THINK. IF THIS ALL GOES ACCORDING TO PLAN--IF YOUR GOAL IS TO FINALLY PROVE YOUR SUPERIORITY OVER THE FALTINE ONCE AND FOR ALL--
--LET ME POINT OUT THAT YOU--YOU, DORMAMMU--HAVE NEVER SUCCESSFULLY CONQUERED THE EARTH--
--AND THEY'RE ABOUT TO.
...
--I--
NO--

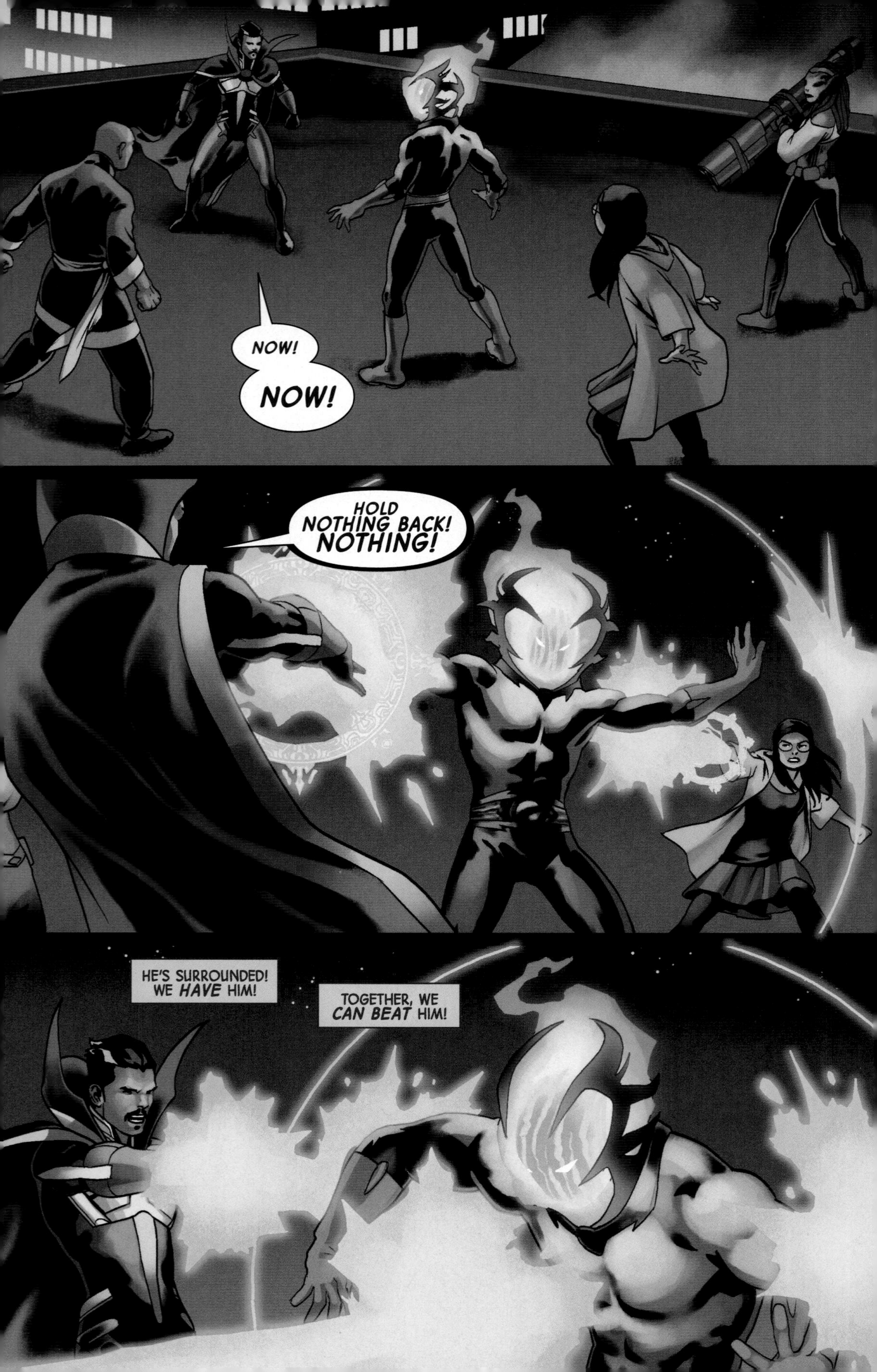
NOW!
NOW!
HOLD NOTHING BACK! NOTHING!
HE'S SURROUNDED! WE HAVE HIM!
TOGETHER, WE CAN BEAT HIM!

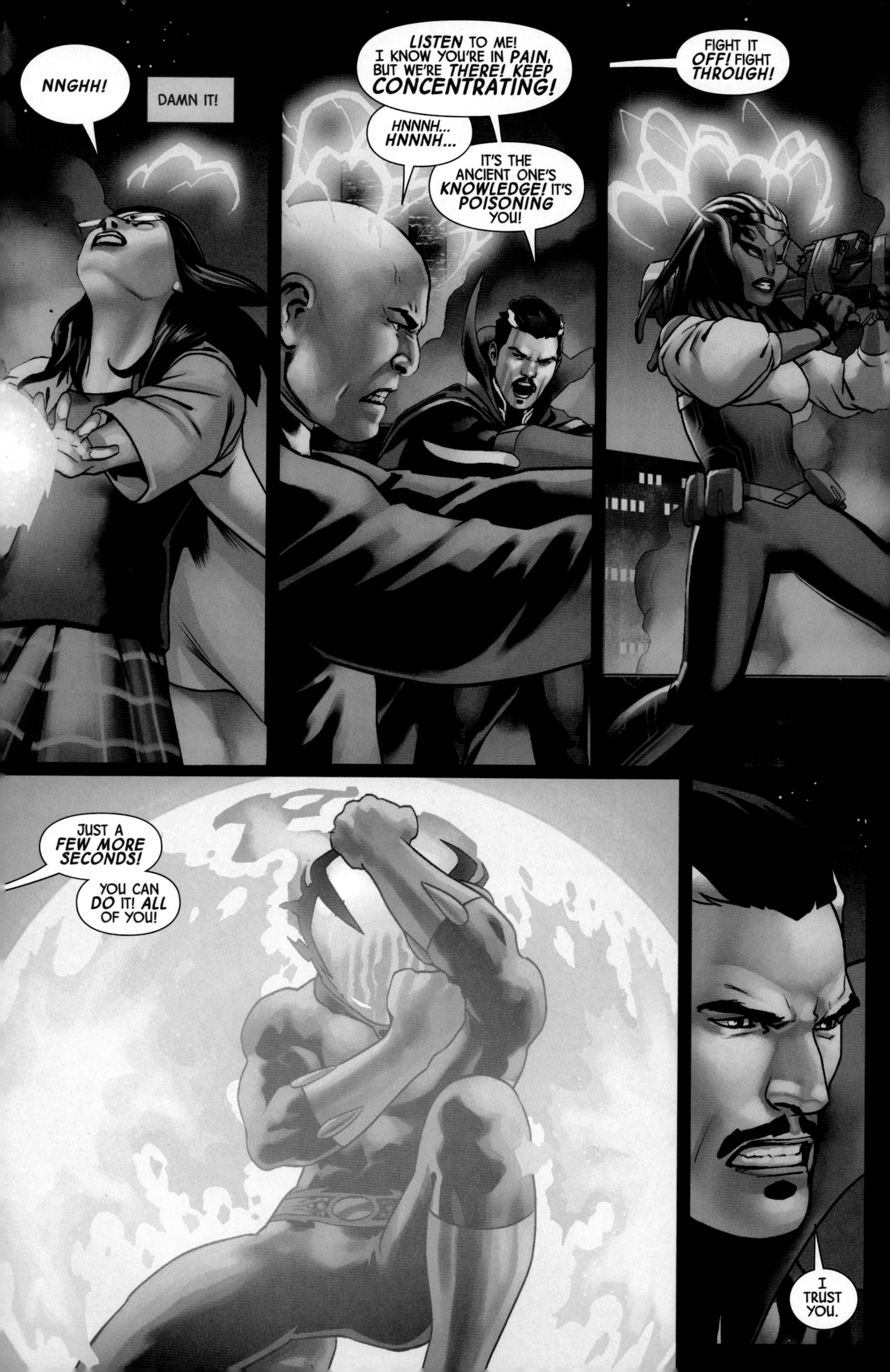
NNGHH!
DAMN IT!
LISTEN TO ME! I KNOW YOU'RE IN PAIN, BUT WE'RE THERE! KEEP CONCENTRATING!
HNNNH... HNNNH...
IT'S THE ANCIENT ONE'S KNOWLEDGE! IT'S POISONING YOU!
FIGHT IT OFF! FIGHT THROUGH!
JUST A FEW MORE SECONDS!
YOU CAN DO IT! ALL OF YOU!
I TRUST YOU.

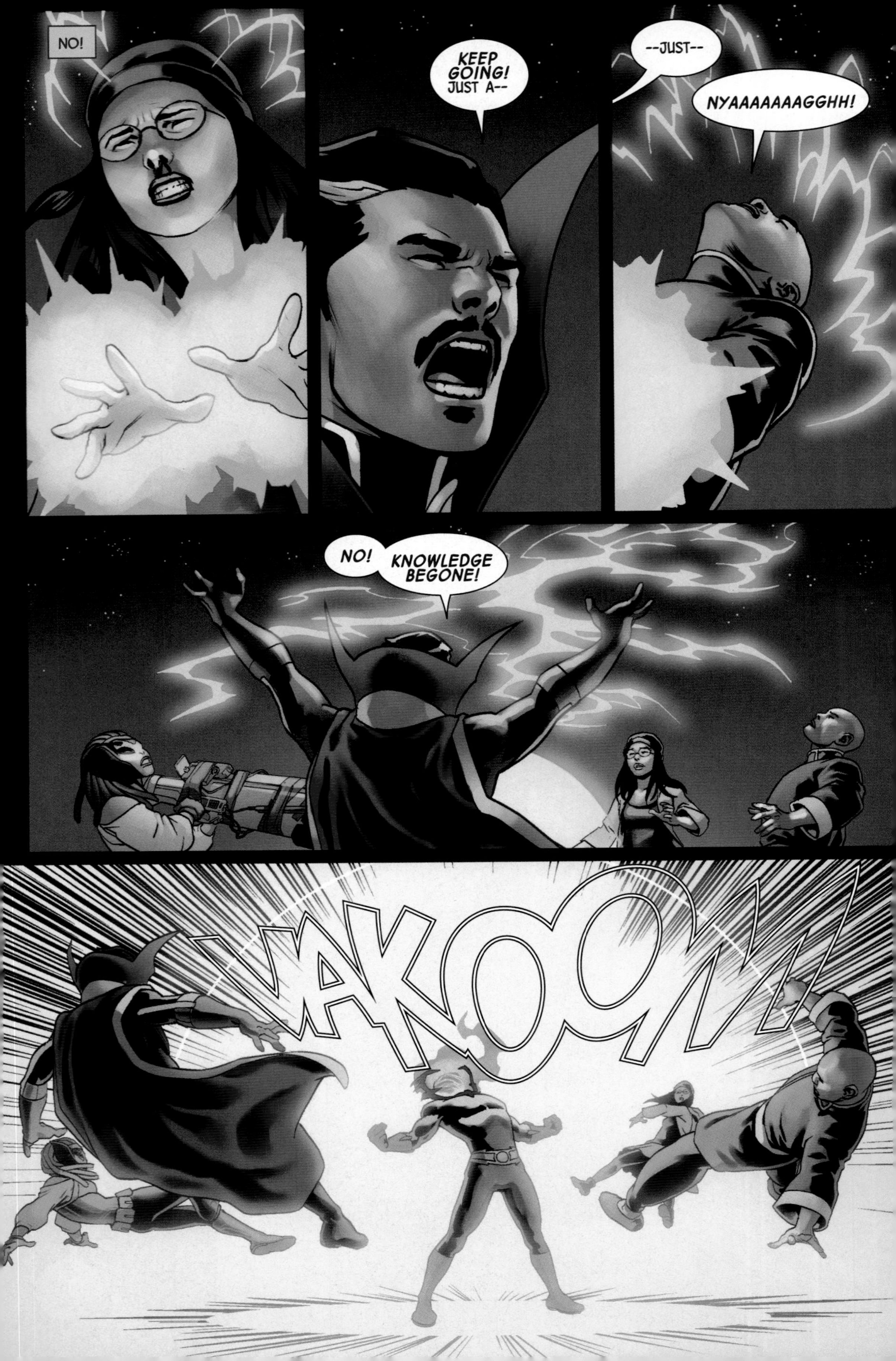
NO!
KEEP GOING! JUST A--
--JUST--
NYAAAAAAAGGHH!
NO!
KNOWLEDGE BEGONE!
VAKOOM

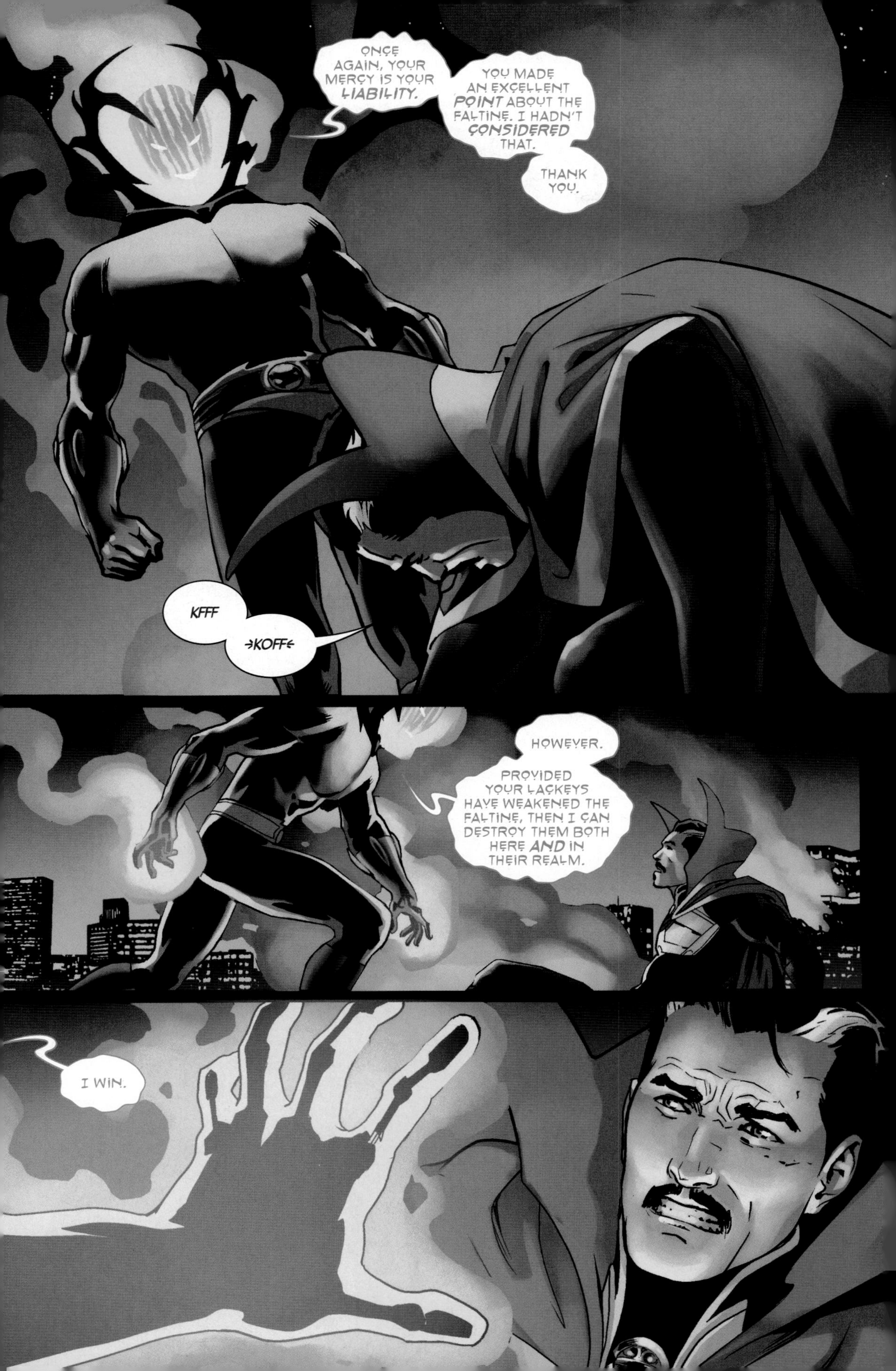
ONCE AGAIN, YOUR MERCY IS YOUR LIABILITY.
YOU MADE AN EXCELLENT POINT ABOUT THE FALTINE. I HADN'T CONSIDERED THAT.
THANK YOU.
KFFF
KOFF
HOWEVER.
PROVIDED YOUR LACKEYS HAVE WEAKENED THE FALTINE, THEN I CAN DESTROY THEM BOTH HERE AND IN THEIR REALM.
I WIN.

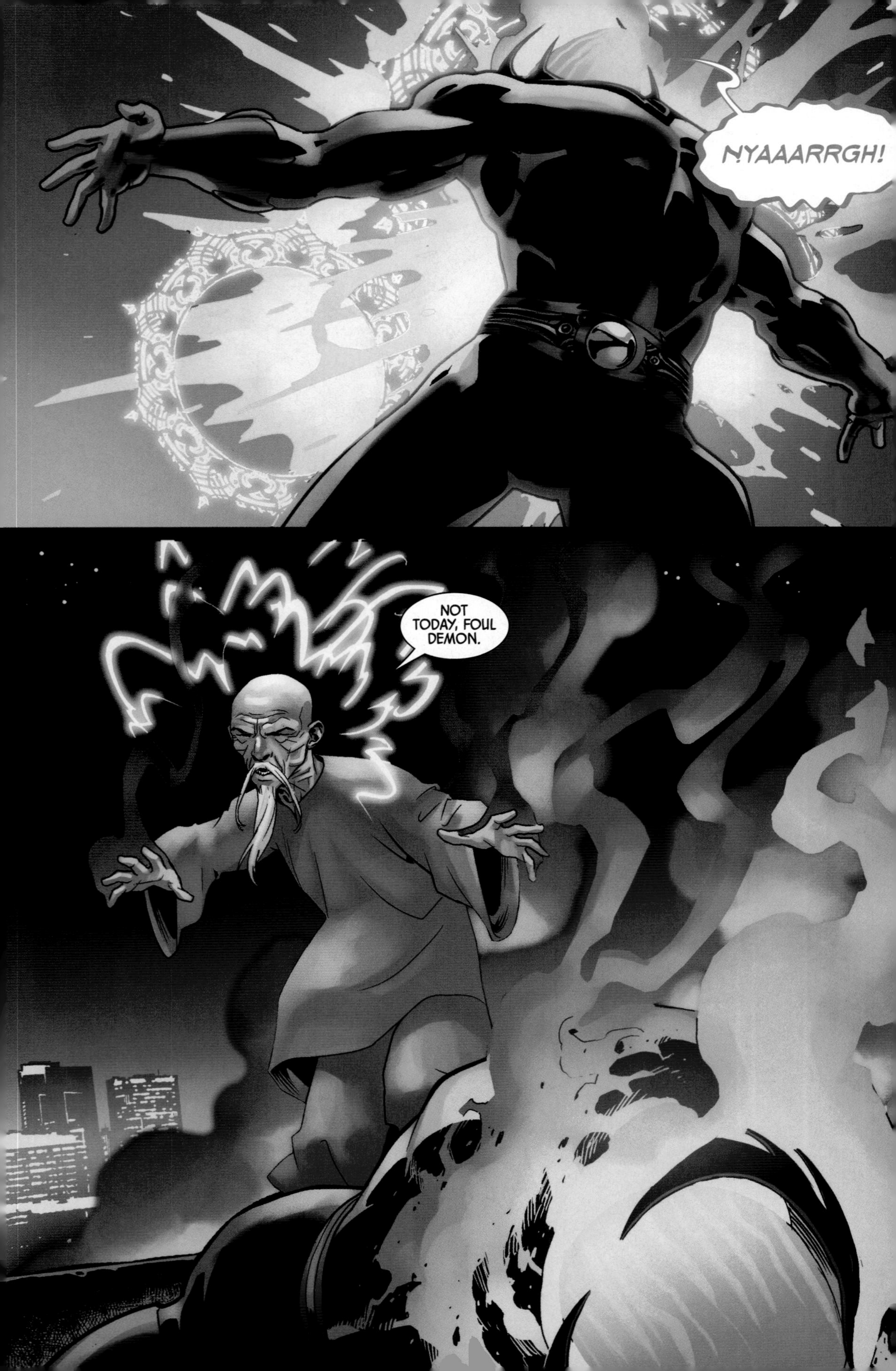
N!YAAARRGH!
NOT TODAY, FOUL DEMON.

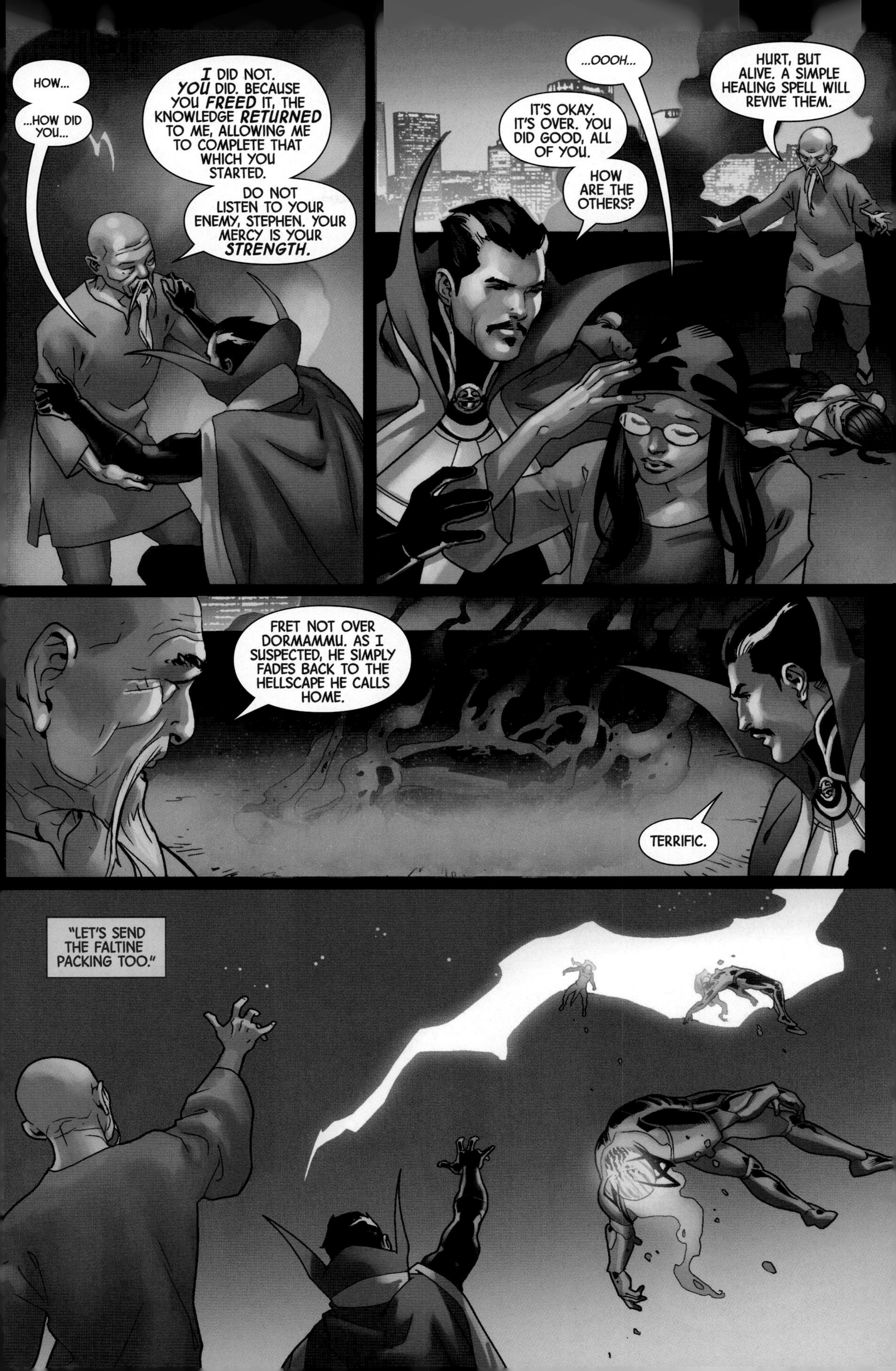
HOW...
...HOW DID YOU...
I DID NOT. YOU DID. BECAUSE YOU FREED IT, THE KNOWLEDGE RETURNED TO ME, ALLOWING ME TO COMPLETE THAT WHICH YOU STARTED.
DO NOT LISTEN TO YOUR ENEMY, STEPHEN. YOUR MERCY IS YOUR STRENGTH.
...OOOH...
IT'S OKAY. IT'S OVER. YOU DID GOOD, ALL OF YOU.
HOW ARE THE OTHERS?
HURT, BUT ALIVE. A SIMPLE HEALING SPELL WILL REVIVE THEM.
FRET NOT OVER DORMAMMU. AS I SUSPECTED, HE SIMPLY FADES BACK TO THE HELLSCAPE HE CALLS HOME.
TERRIFIC.
"LET'S SEND THE FALTINE PACKING TOO."

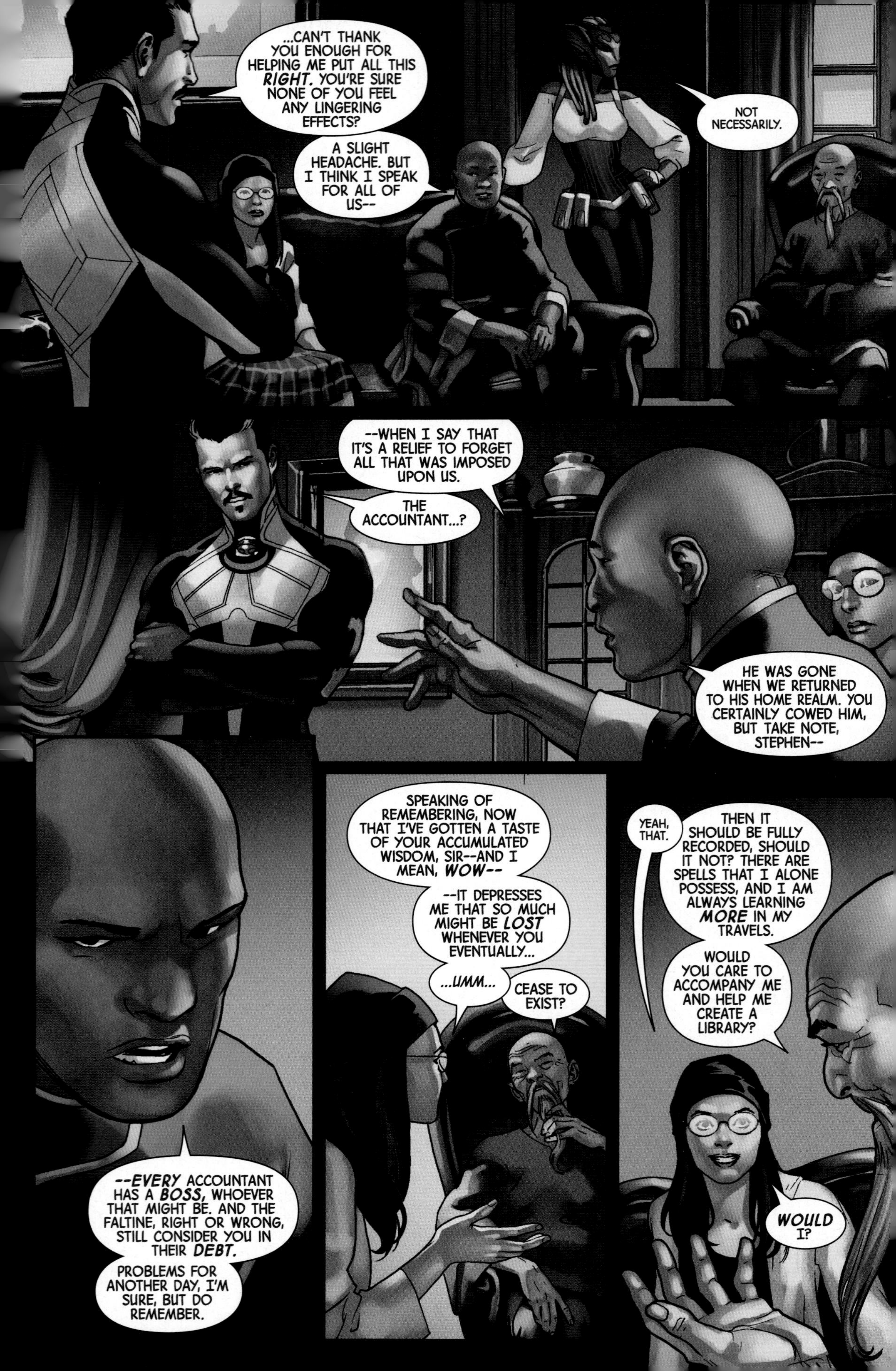
...CAN'T THANK YOU ENOUGH FOR HELPING ME PUT ALL THIS RIGHT. YOU'RE SURE NONE OF YOU FEEL ANY LINGERING EFFECTS?
A SLIGHT HEADACHE. BUT I THINK I SPEAK FOR ALL OF US--
NOT NECESSARILY.
--WHEN I SAY THAT IT'S A RELIEF TO FORGET ALL THAT WAS IMPOSED UPON US.
THE ACCOUNTANT...?
HE WAS GONE WHEN WE RETURNED TO HIS HOME REALM. YOU CERTAINLY COWED HIM, BUT TAKE NOTE, STEPHEN--
--EVERY ACCOUNTANT HAS A BOSS, WHOEVER THAT MIGHT BE. AND THE FALTINE, RIGHT OR WRONG, STILL CONSIDER YOU IN THEIR DEBT.
PROBLEMS FOR ANOTHER DAY, I'M SURE, BUT DO REMEMBER.
SPEAKING OF REMEMBERING, NOW THAT I'VE GOTTEN A TASTE OF YOUR ACCUMULATED WISDOM, SIR--AND I MEAN, WOW--
--IT DEPRESSES ME THAT SO MUCH MIGHT BE LOST WHENEVER YOU EVENTUALLY...
...UMM...
CEASE TO EXIST?
YEAH, THAT.
THEN IT SHOULD BE FULLY RECORDED, SHOULD IT NOT? THERE ARE SPELLS THAT I ALONE POSSESS, AND I AM ALWAYS LEARNING MORE IN MY TRAVELS.
WOULD YOU CARE TO ACCOMPANY ME AND HELP ME CREATE A LIBRARY?
WOULD I?

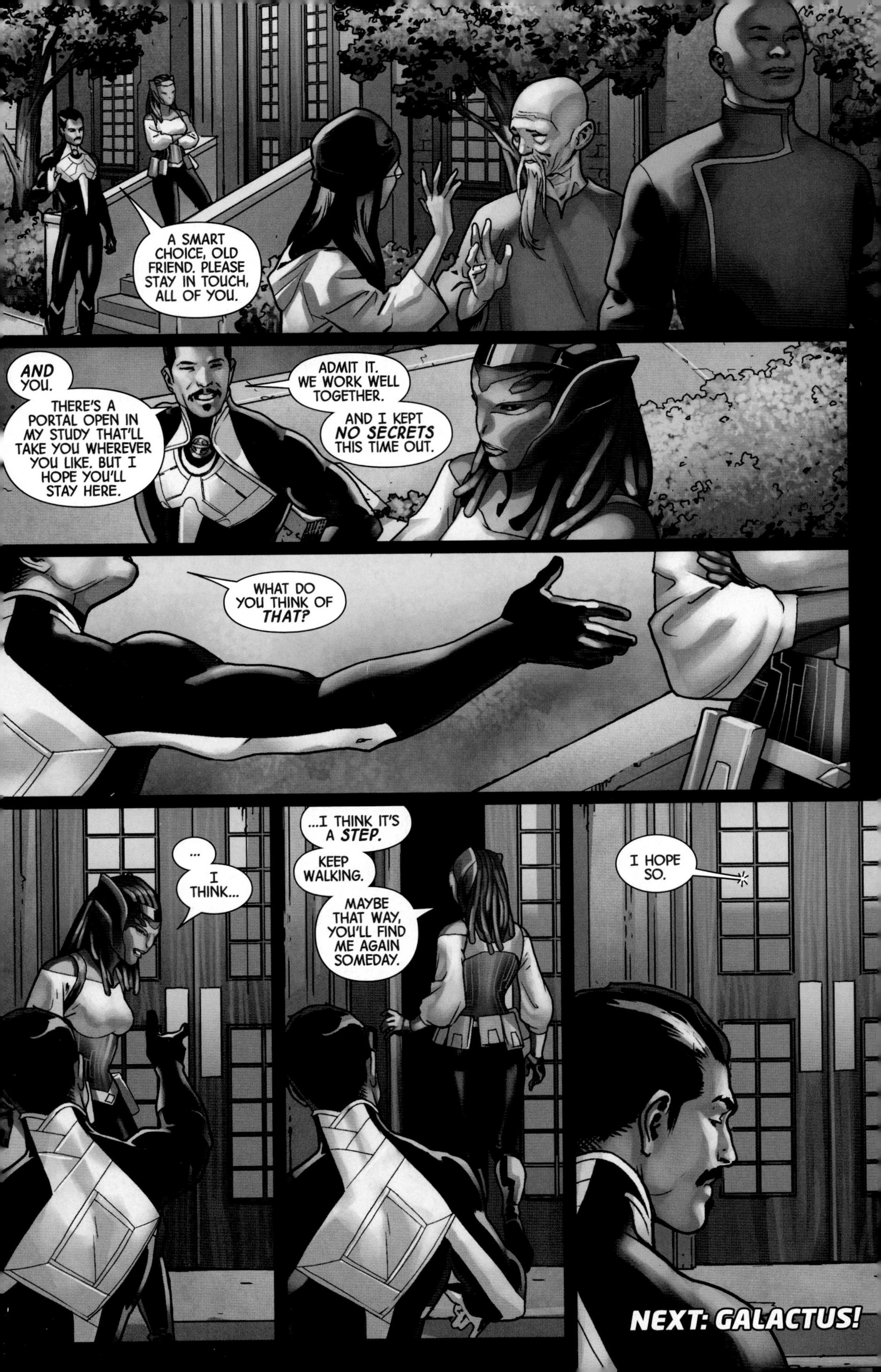
A SMART CHOICE, OLD FRIEND. PLEASE STAY IN TOUCH, ALL OF YOU.
AND YOU.
THERE'S A PORTAL OPEN IN MY STUDY THAT'LL TAKE YOU WHEREVER YOU LIKE. BUT I HOPE YOU'LL STAY HERE.
ADMIT IT. WE WORK WELL TOGETHER.
AND I KEPT NO SECRETS THIS TIME OUT.
WHAT DO YOU THINK OF THAT?
... I THINK...
...I THINK IT'S A STEP.
KEEP WALKING.
MAYBE THAT WAY, YOU'LL FIND ME AGAIN SOMEDAY.
I HOPE SO.
NEXT: GALACTUS!

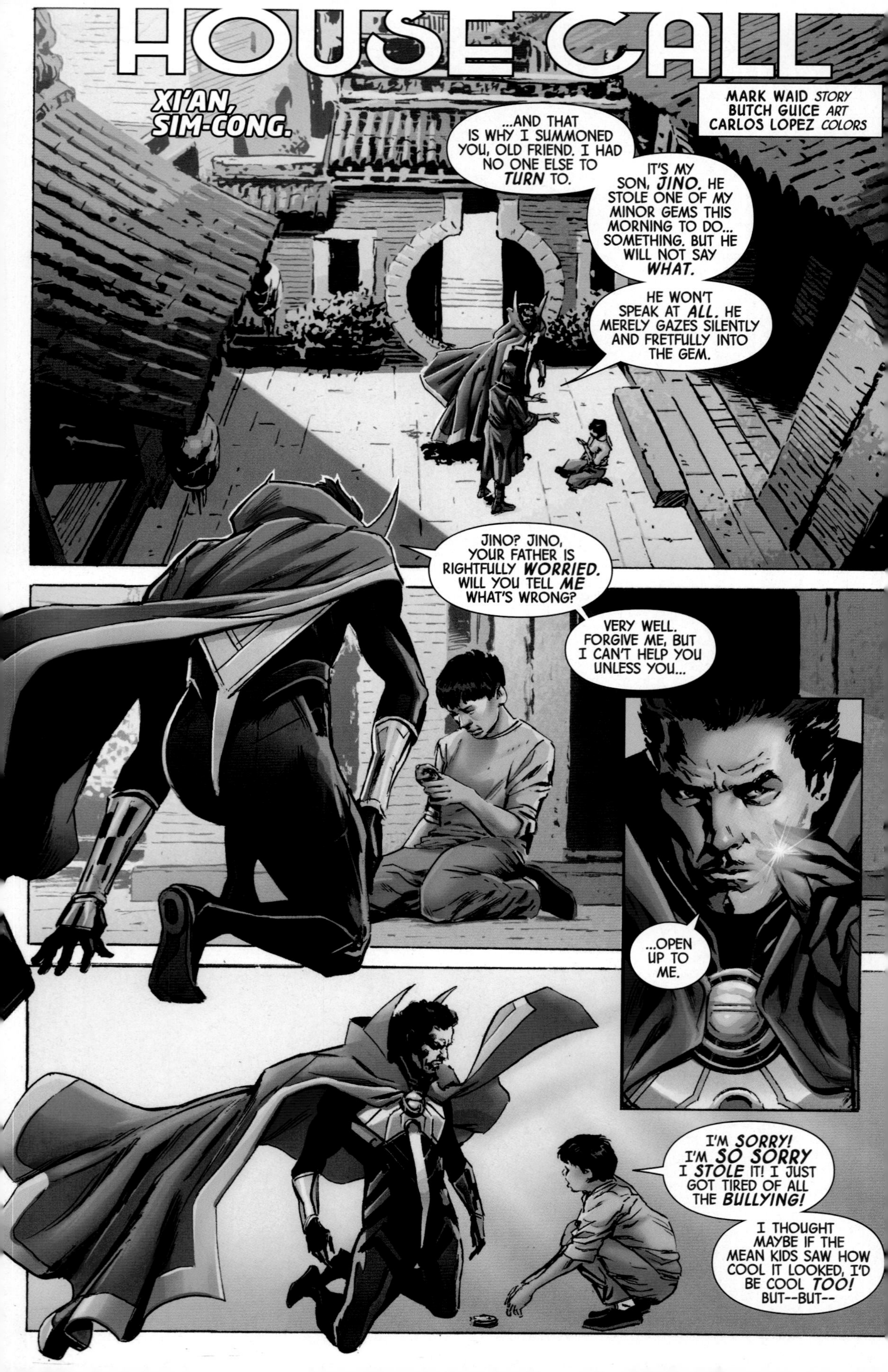
HOUSE CALL
XI'AN, SIM-CONG.
MARK WAID STORY
BUTCH GUICE ART
CARLOS LOPEZ COLORS
...AND THAT IS WHY I SUMMONED YOU, OLD FRIEND. I HAD NO ONE ELSE TO TURN TO.
IT'S MY SON, JINO. HE STOLE ONE OF MY MINOR GEMS THIS MORNING TO DO... SOMETHING. BUT HE WILL NOT SAY WHAT.
HE WON'T SPEAK AT ALL. HE MERELY GAZES SILENTLY AND FRETFULLY INTO THE GEM.
JINO? JINO, YOUR FATHER IS RIGHTFULLY WORRIED. WILL YOU TELL ME WHAT'S WRONG?
VERY WELL. FORGIVE ME, BUT I CAN'T HELP YOU UNLESS YOU...
...OPEN UP TO ME.
I'M SORRY! I'M SO SORRY I STOLE IT! I JUST GOT TIRED OF ALL THE BULLYING!
I THOUGHT MAYBE IF THE MEAN KIDS SAW HOW COOL IT LOOKED, I'D BE COOL TOO! BUT--BUT--

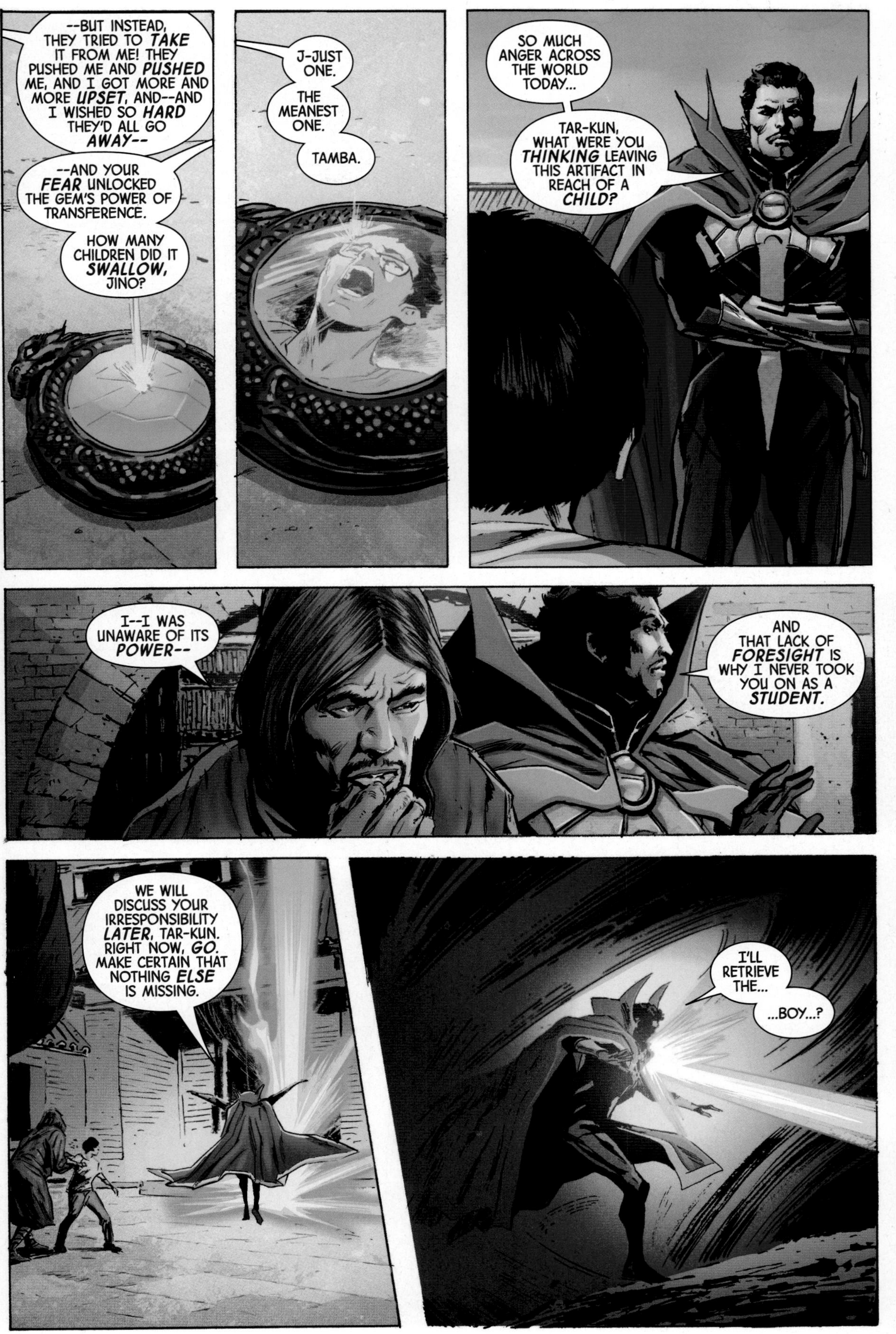
--BUT INSTEAD, THEY TRIED TO TAKE IT FROM ME! THEY PUSHED ME AND PUSHED ME, AND I GOT MORE AND MORE UPSET, AND--AND I WISHED SO HARD THEY'D ALL GO AWAY--
--AND YOUR FEAR UNLOCKED THE GEM'S POWER OF TRANSFERENCE.
HOW MANY CHILDREN DID IT SWALLOW, JINO?
J-JUST ONE.
THE MEANEST ONE.
TAMBA.
SO MUCH ANGER ACROSS THE WORLD TODAY...
TAR-KUN, WHAT WERE YOU THINKING LEAVING THIS ARTIFACT IN REACH OF A CHILD?
I--I WAS UNAWARE OF ITS POWER--
AND THAT LACK OF FORESIGHT IS WHY I NEVER TOOK YOU ON AS A STUDENT.
WE WILL DISCUSS YOUR IRRESPONSIBILITY LATER, TAR-KUN. RIGHT NOW, GO. MAKE CERTAIN THAT NOTHING ELSE IS MISSING.
I'LL RETRIEVE THE...
...BOY...?

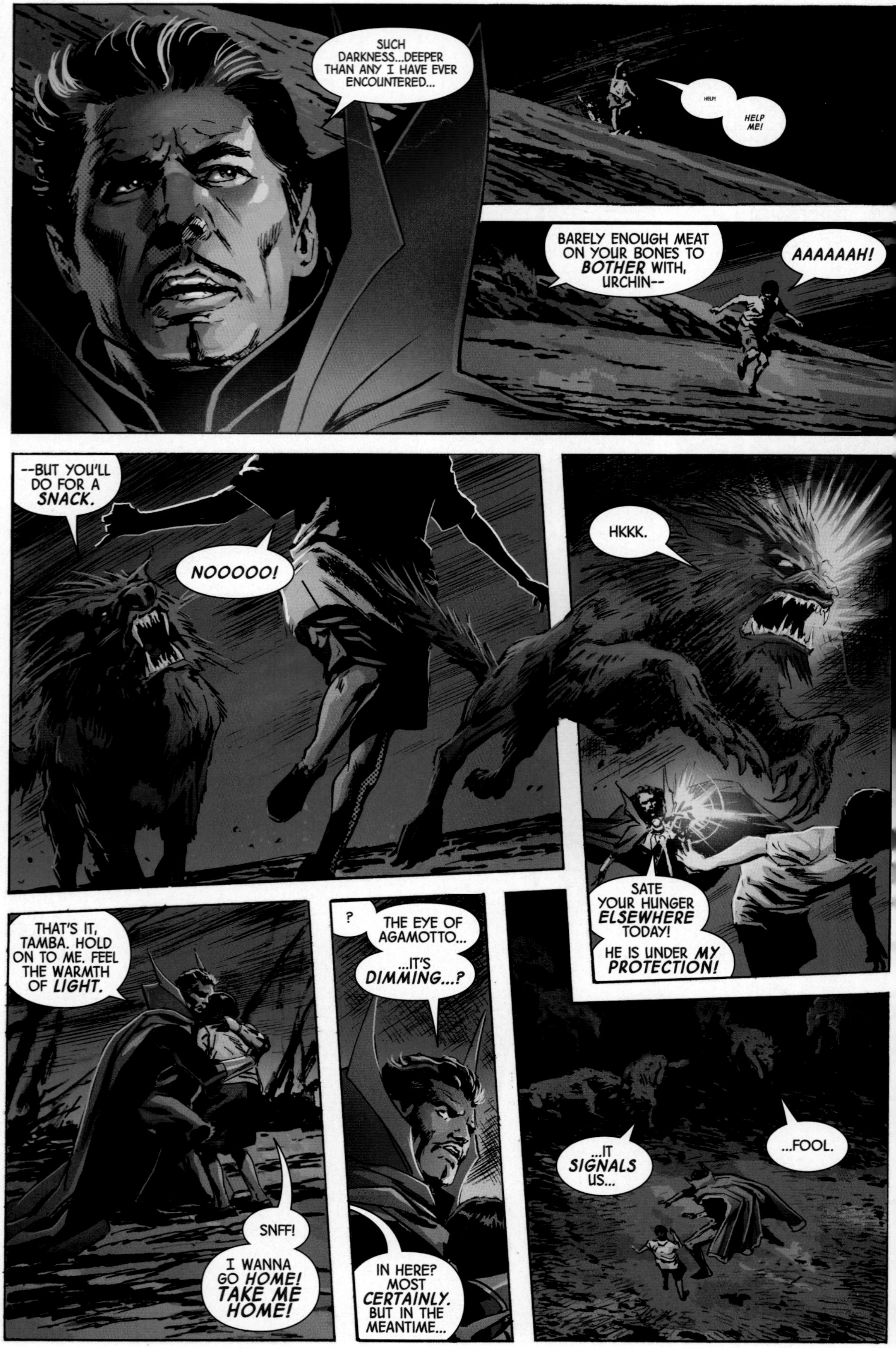
SUCH DARKNESS...DEEPER THAN ANY I HAVE EVER ENCOUNTERED...
HELP!
HELP ME!
BARELY ENOUGH MEAT ON YOUR BONES TO BOTHER WITH, URCHIN--
AAAAAAH!
--BUT YOU'LL DO FOR A SNACK.
NOOOOO!
HKKK.
SATE YOUR HUNGER ELSEWHERE TODAY!
HE IS UNDER MY PROTECTION!
THAT'S IT, TAMBA. HOLD ON TO ME. FEEL THE WARMTH OF LIGHT.
SNFF!
I WANNA GO HOME! TAKE ME HOME!
?
THE EYE OF AGAMOTTO...
...IT'S DIMMING...?
IN HERE? MOST CERTAINLY. BUT IN THE MEANTIME...
...IT SIGNALS US...
...FOOL.

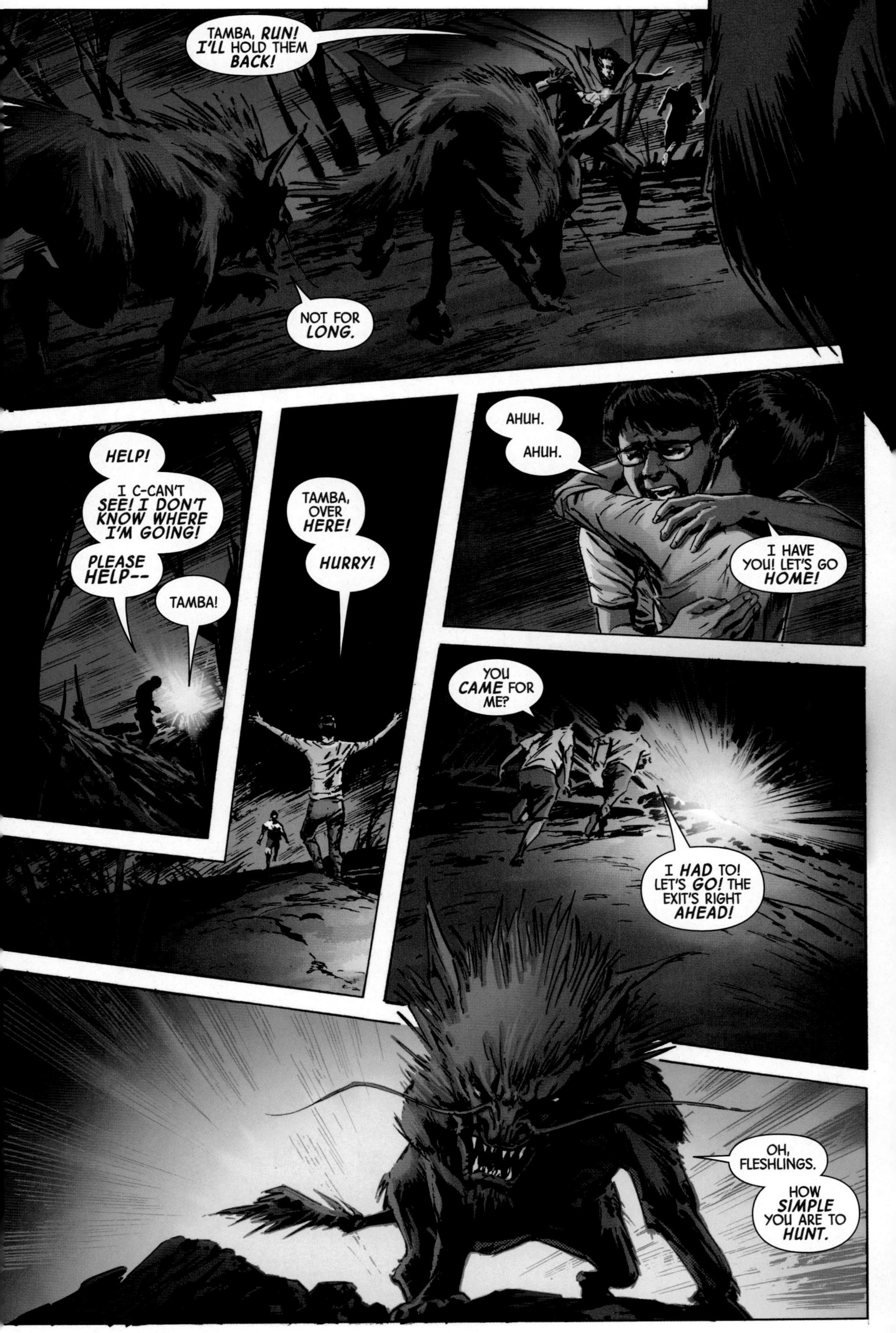
TAMBA, RUN! I'LL HOLD THEM BACK!
NOT FOR LONG.
HELP!
I C-CAN'T SEE! I DON'T KNOW WHERE I'M GOING!
PLEASE HELP--
TAMBA!
TAMBA, OVER HERE!
HURRY!
AHUH.
AHUH.
I HAVE YOU! LET'S GO HOME!
YOU CAME FOR ME?
I HAD TO! LET'S GO! THE EXIT'S RIGHT AHEAD!
OH, FLESHLINGS.
HOW SIMPLE YOU ARE TO HUNT.

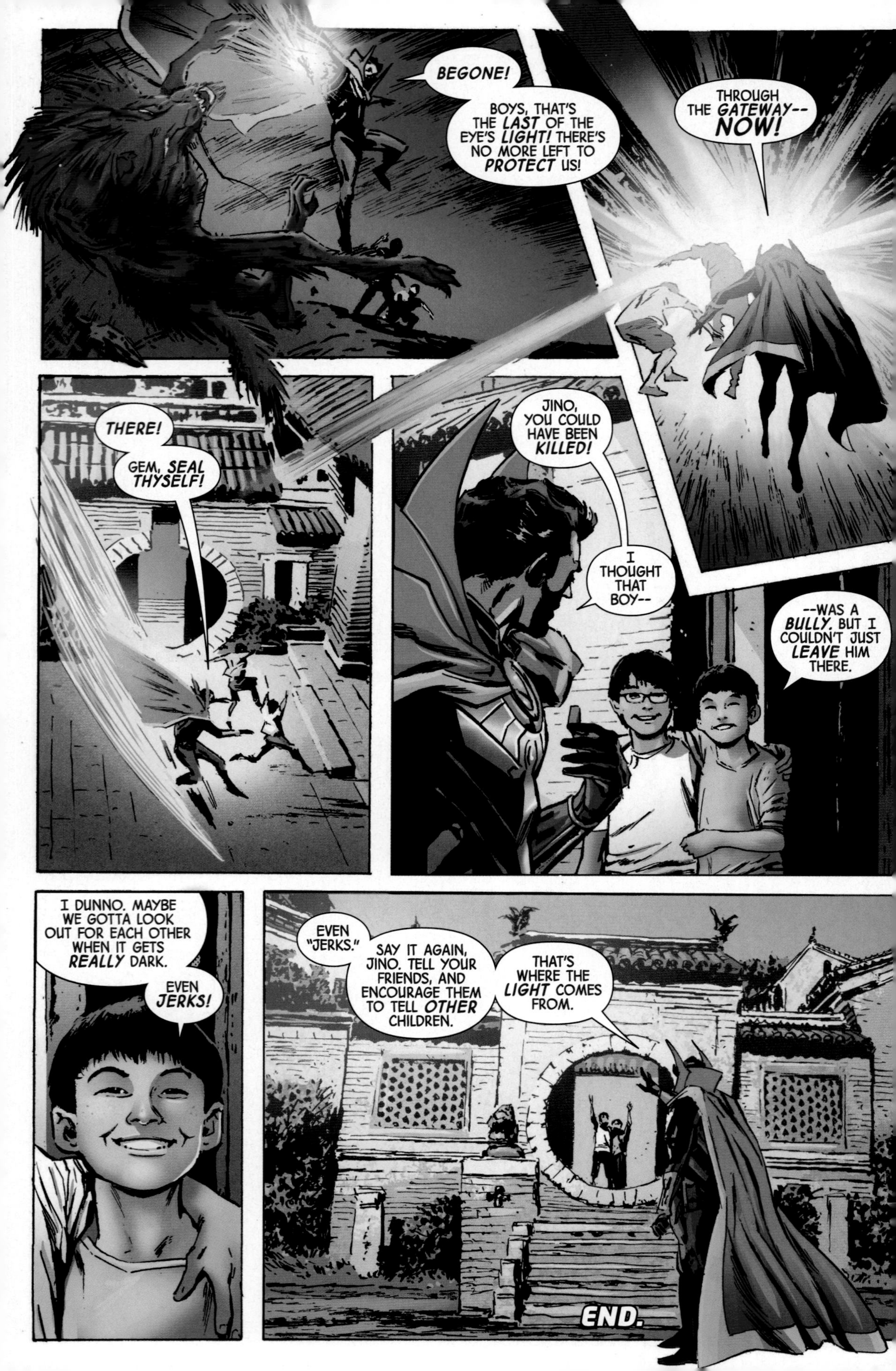
BEGONE!
BOYS, THAT'S THE LAST OF THE EYE'S LIGHT! THERE'S NO MORE LEFT TO PROTECT US!
THROUGH THE GATEWAY-- NOW!
THERE!
GEM, SEAL THYSELF!
JINO, YOU COULD HAVE BEEN KILLED!
I THOUGHT THAT BOY--
--WAS A BULLY. BUT I COULDN'T JUST LEAVE HIM THERE.
I DUNNO. MAYBE WE GOTTA LOOK OUT FOR EACH OTHER WHEN IT GETS REALLY DARK.
EVEN JERKS!
EVEN "JERKS."
SAY IT AGAIN, JINO. TELL YOUR FRIENDS, AND ENCOURAGE THEM TO TELL OTHER CHILDREN.
THAT'S WHERE THE LIGHT COMES FROM.
END.

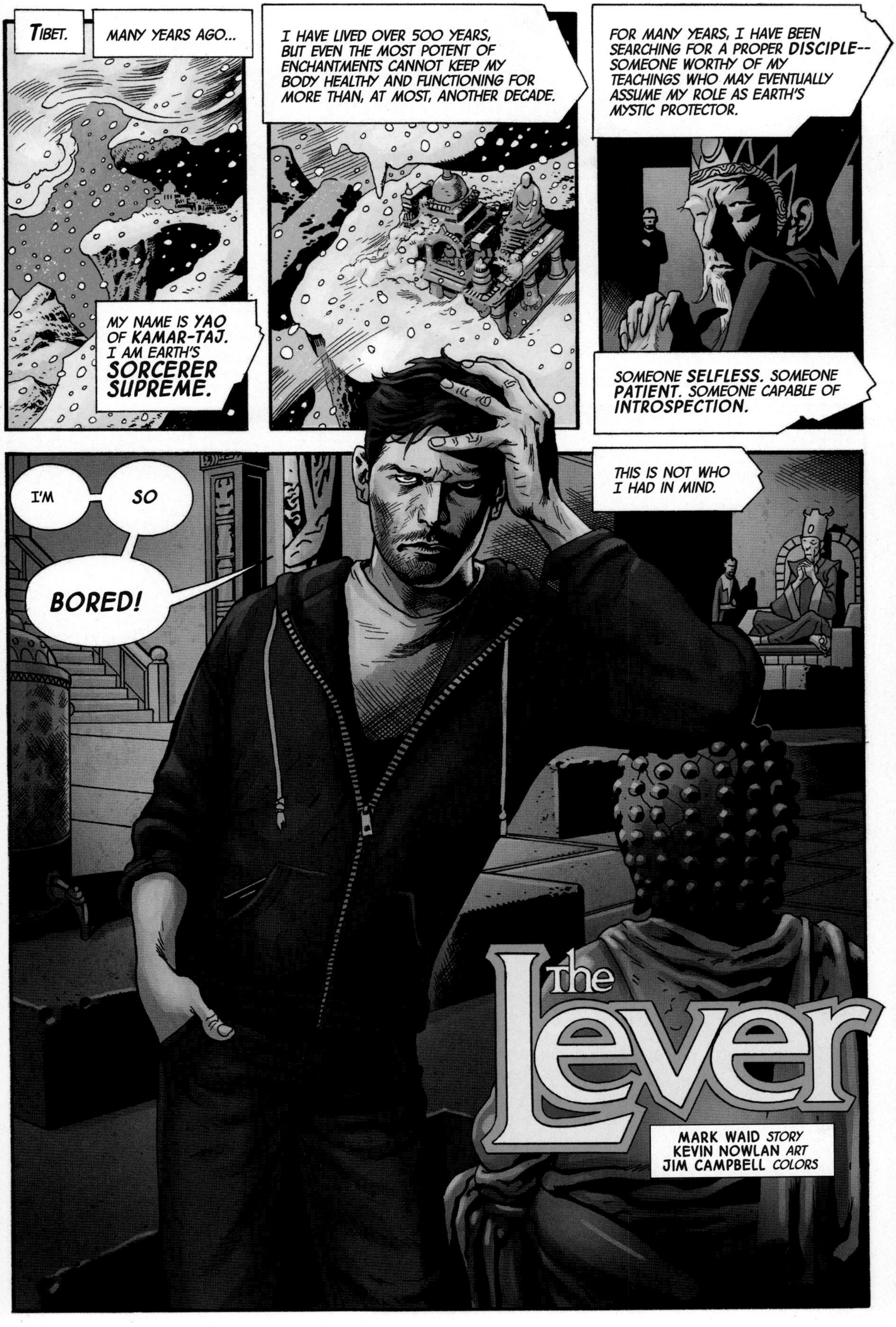
TIBET.
MANY YEARS AGO...
MY NAME IS YAO OF KAMAR-TAJ. I AM EARTH'S SORCERER SUPREME.
I HAVE LIVED OVER 500 YEARS, BUT EVEN THE MOST POTENT OF ENCHANTMENTS CANNOT KEEP MY BODY HEALTHY AND FUNCTIONING FOR MORE THAN, AT MOST, ANOTHER DECADE.
FOR MANY YEARS, I HAVE BEEN SEARCHING FOR A PROPER DISCIPLE-- SOMEONE WORTHY OF MY TEACHINGS WHO MAY EVENTUALLY ASSUME MY ROLE AS EARTH'S MYSTIC PROTECTOR.
SOMEONE SELFLESS. SOMEONE PATIENT. SOMEONE CAPABLE OF INTROSPECTION.
I'M SO BORED!
THIS IS NOT WHO I HAD IN MIND.
The Lever
MARK WAID STORY
KEVIN NOWLAN ART
JIM CAMPBELL COLORS

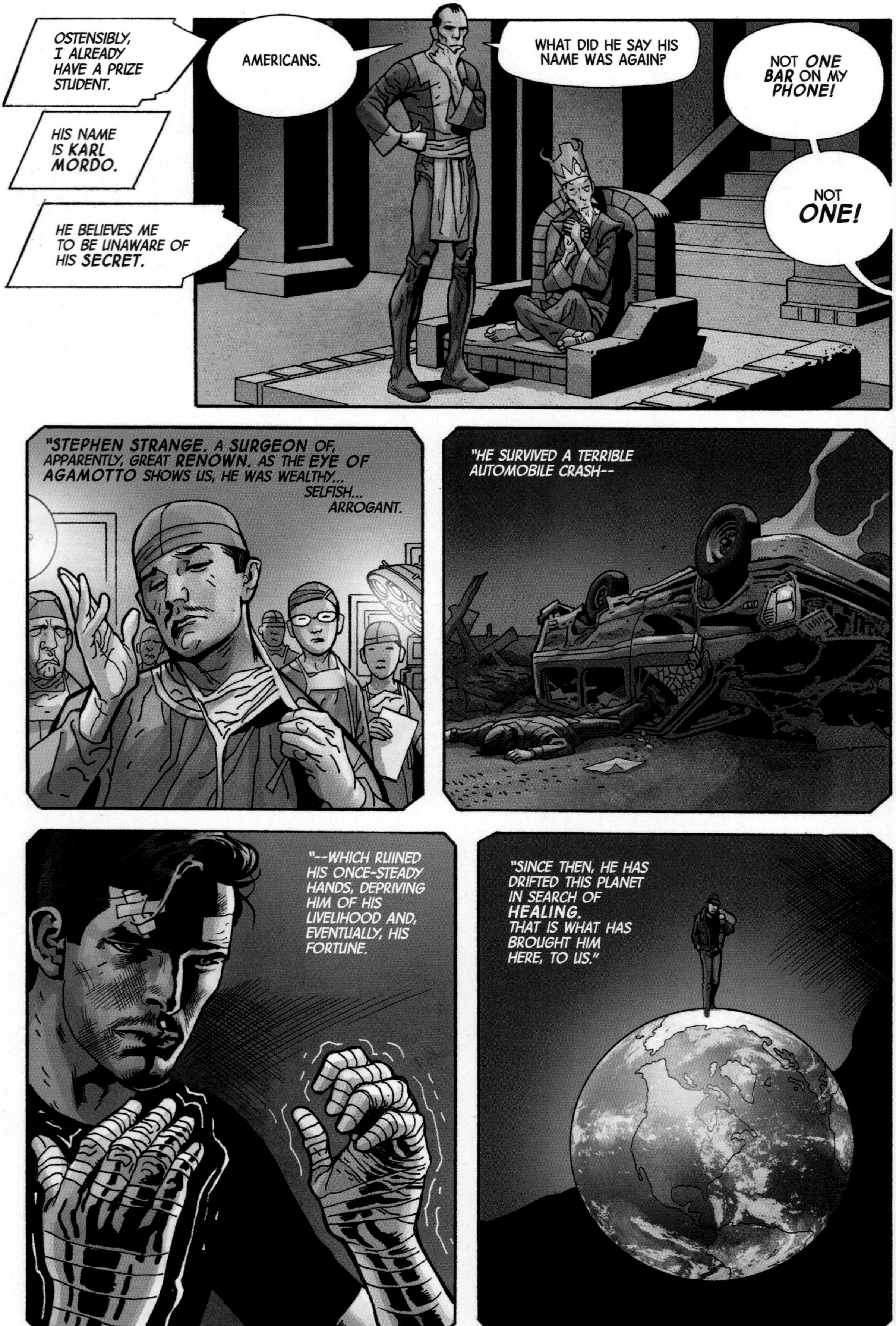
OSTENSIBLY, I ALREADY HAVE A PRIZE STUDENT.
HIS NAME IS KARL MORDO.
HE BELIEVES ME TO BE UNAWARE OF HIS SECRET.
AMERICANS.
WHAT DID HE SAY HIS NAME WAS AGAIN?
NOT ONE BAR ON MY PHONE!
NOT ONE!
"STEPHEN STRANGE. A SURGEON OF, APPARENTLY, GREAT RENOWN. AS THE EYE OF AGAMOTTO SHOWS US, HE WAS WEALTHY... SELFISH... ARROGANT.
"HE SURVIVED A TERRIBLE AUTOMOBILE CRASH--
"--WHICH RUINED HIS ONCE-STEADY HANDS, DEPRIVING HIM OF HIS LIVELIHOOD AND, EVENTUALLY, HIS FORTUNE.
"SINCE THEN, HE HAS DRIFTED THIS PLANET IN SEARCH OF HEALING. THAT IS WHAT HAS BROUGHT HIM HERE, TO US."

THAT BLIZZARD CAME OUT OF *NOWHERE!* I'LL BE STUCK HERE FOR *WEEKS!* YOU DID THAT TO *KEEP* ME HERE, DIDN'T YOU?

YOU CAN CONTROL THE *WEATHER* WITH YOUR *HOODOO!*

IF ONLY.

BUDDY, I'M *TELLING* YOU...I'VE BEEN EVERYWHERE FROM *NEW ORLEANS* TO *TIMBUKTU,* AND *EVERYONE* SAYS *YOU'RE* THE ONE WHO CAN FIX ME UP *FAST.*

GIVE ME MY *LIFE* BACK.

AS I TOLD YOU A *MOMENT* AGO, THERE IS NO "QUICK FIX" FOR YOUR CONDITION.

IT'S NOT A *CONDITION,* DAMMIT! IT'S *NERVE DAMAGE!*

I WAS NOT REFERRING TO HIS HANDS.

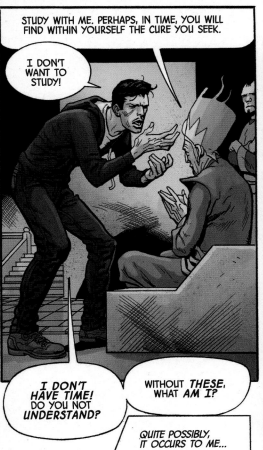

STUDY WITH ME. PERHAPS, IN TIME, YOU WILL FIND WITHIN YOURSELF THE CURE YOU SEEK.

I DON'T WANT TO STUDY!

I DON'T *HAVE TIME!* DO YOU NOT *UNDERSTAND?*

WITHOUT *THESE,* WHAT *AM* I?

QUITE POSSIBLY, IT OCCURS TO ME...

...A USEFUL *LEVER.*

KARL, PREPARE A COT FOR OUR VISITOR. HE WILL SHARE YOUR QUARTERS UNTIL... THINGS CHANGE.

HMMPH.

HIS GARMENTS *REEK.*

AGREED.

REST, STRANGER. TOMORROW BRINGS NEW LIGHT...

...AND, FOR *YOU,* NEW *PURPOSE.*

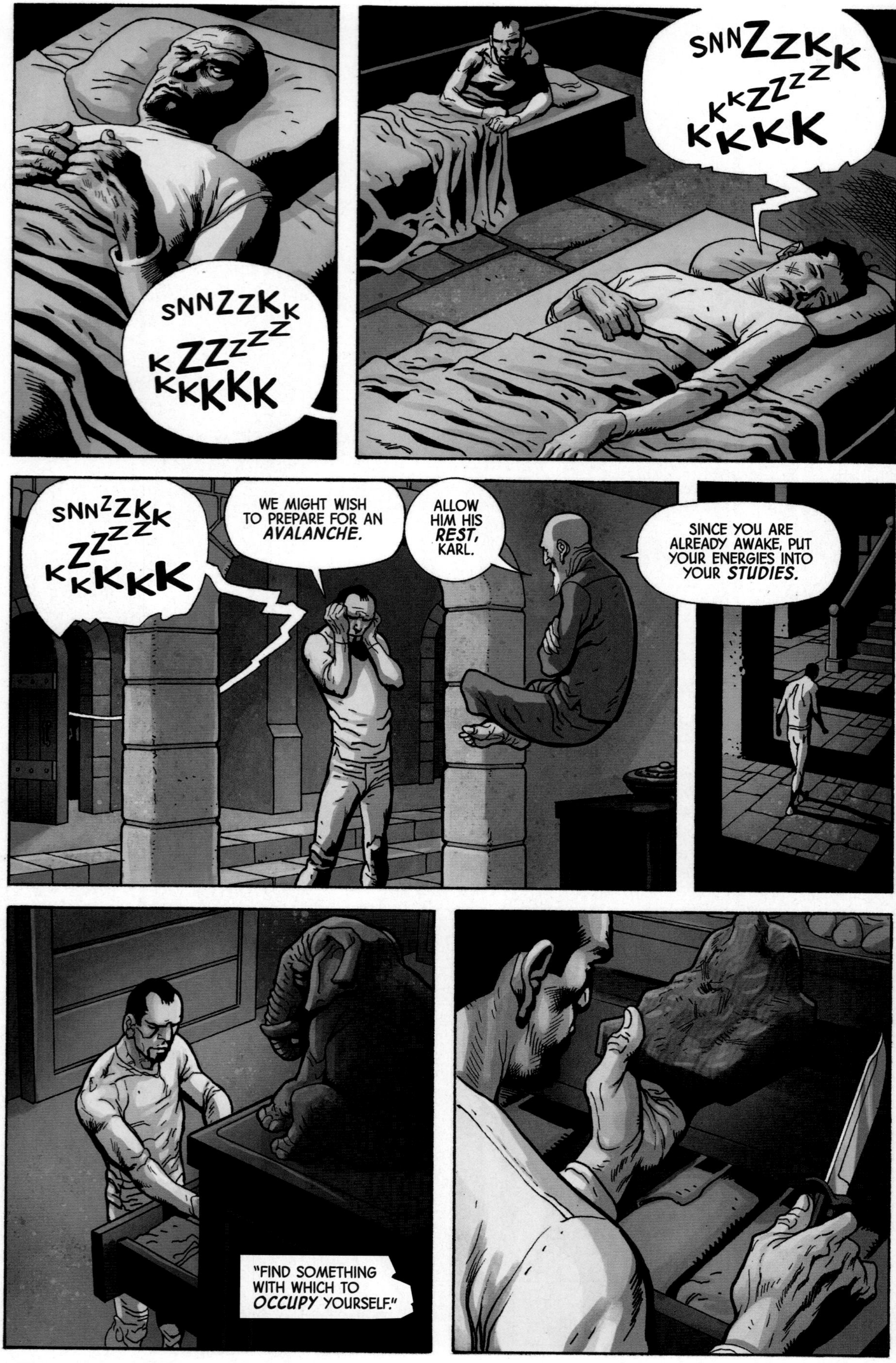
SNNZZKKK
KZZZZZ
KKKKK
SNNZZKK
KKZZZZZK
KKKK
SNNZZKK
KZZZZZ
KKKKK
WE MIGHT WISH TO PREPARE FOR AN AVALANCHE.
ALLOW HIM HIS REST, KARL.
SINCE YOU ARE ALREADY AWAKE, PUT YOUR ENERGIES INTO YOUR STUDIES.
"FIND SOMETHING WITH WHICH TO OCCUPY YOURSELF."

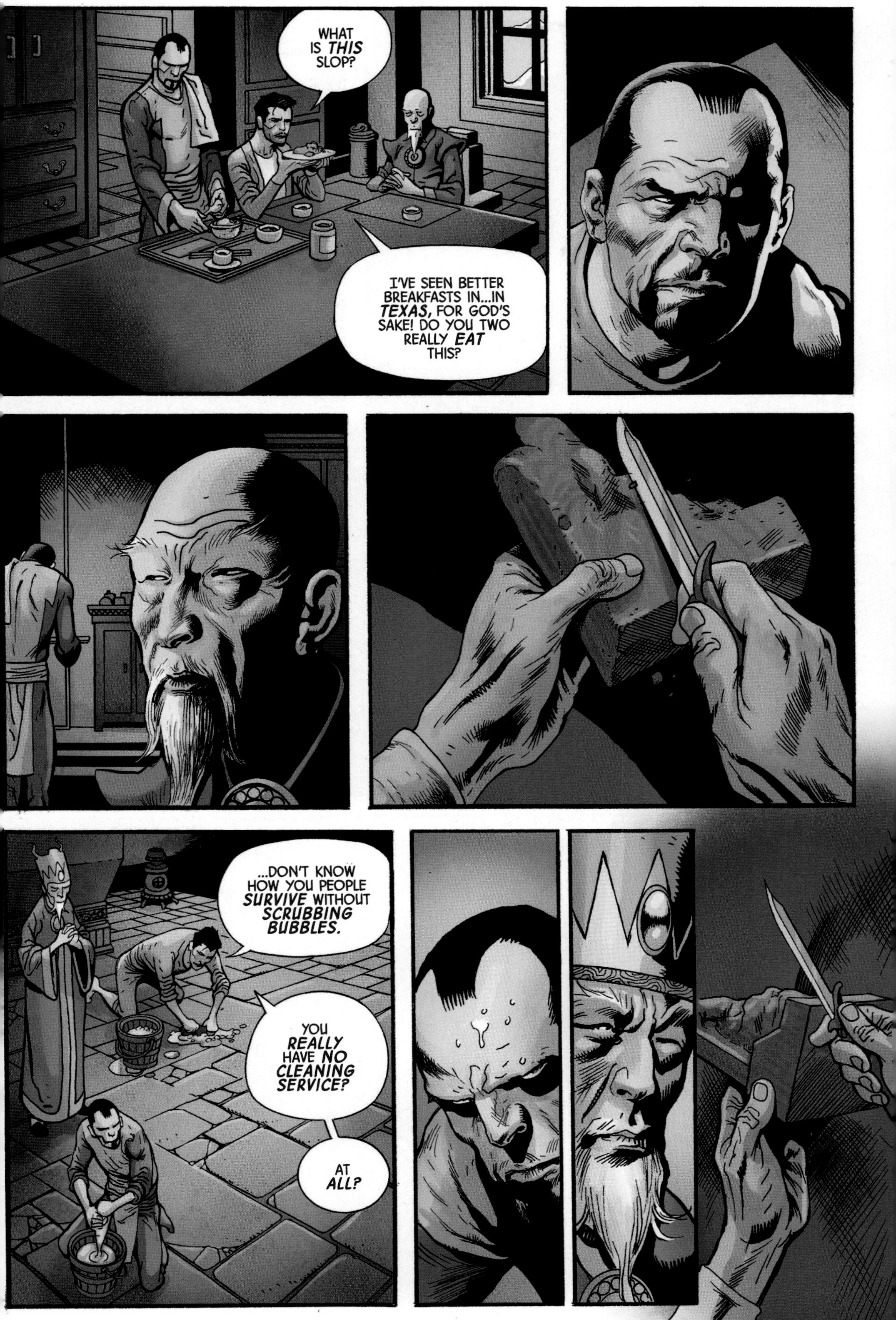
WHAT IS THIS SLOP?
I'VE SEEN BETTER BREAKFASTS IN...IN TEXAS, FOR GOD'S SAKE! DO YOU TWO REALLY EAT THIS?
...DON'T KNOW HOW YOU PEOPLE SURVIVE WITHOUT SCRUBBING BUBBLES.
YOU REALLY HAVE NO CLEANING SERVICE?
AT ALL?

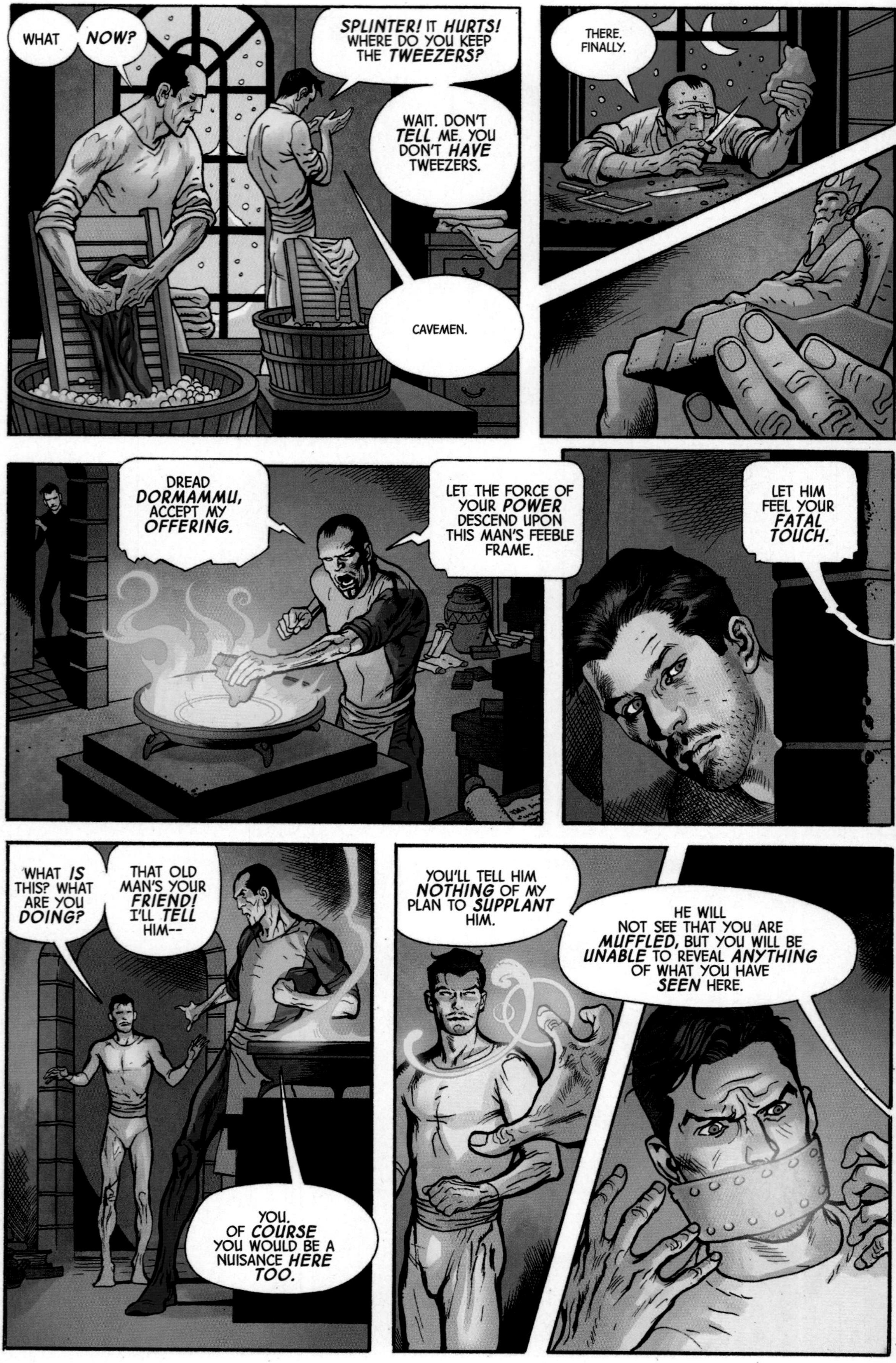
WHAT NOW?
SPLINTER! IT HURTS! WHERE DO YOU KEEP THE TWEEZERS?
WAIT. DON'T TELL ME. YOU DON'T HAVE TWEEZERS.
CAVEMEN.
THERE. FINALLY.
DREAD DORMAMMU, ACCEPT MY OFFERING.
LET THE FORCE OF YOUR POWER DESCEND UPON THIS MAN'S FEEBLE FRAME.
LET HIM FEEL YOUR FATAL TOUCH.
WHAT IS THIS? WHAT ARE YOU DOING?
THAT OLD MAN'S YOUR FRIEND! I'LL TELL HIM--
YOU. OF COURSE YOU WOULD BE A NUISANCE HERE TOO.
YOU'LL TELL HIM NOTHING OF MY PLAN TO SUPPLANT HIM.
HE WILL NOT SEE THAT YOU ARE MUFFLED, BUT YOU WILL BE UNABLE TO REVEAL ANYTHING OF WHAT YOU HAVE SEEN HERE.

"THE SPRING THAW IS *UPON* US. I CAN SOON BE RID OF YOU AT *LAST*.

"IN THE MEANTIME, THERE IS *NOTHING* YOU CAN DO TO *STOP* ME. *SAVOR* THE FACT THAT I HAVE LET YOU *LIVE*.

"I SHALL NOT BE AS *COURTEOUS* TO THE *OLD MAN*."

ANCIENT ONE, I... I REALIZE I WAS *DISMISSIVE* OF YOUR OFFER TO *HEAL* ME. RUDE. FORGIVE ME.

I *DO* WISH TO STUDY AT YOUR FEET...TO LEARN YOUR KNOWLEDGE...

...TO BECOME A *WORTHY STUDENT* OF THE MYSTIC--

ACCEPTED.

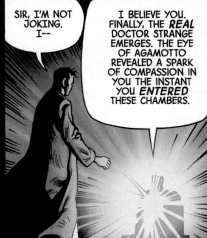

SIR, I'M NOT JOKING. I--

I BELIEVE YOU. FINALLY, THE *REAL* DOCTOR STRANGE EMERGES. THE EYE OF AGAMOTTO REVEALED A SPARK OF COMPASSION IN YOU THE INSTANT YOU *ENTERED* THESE CHAMBERS.

YOU SHALL BE MY *RIGHTFUL DISCIPLE*.

FIRST, HOWEVER, LET ME RELEASE YOU FROM MORDO'S *SPELL*.

YOU *KNEW*?

SIR, PLEASE, HEAR ME *OUT!* HE'S PLOTTING TO--

I KNOW THIS.

I HAVE BEEN AWARE OF HIS DARK MOTIVES SINCE THE DAY HE FIRST KNELT *BEFORE* ME.

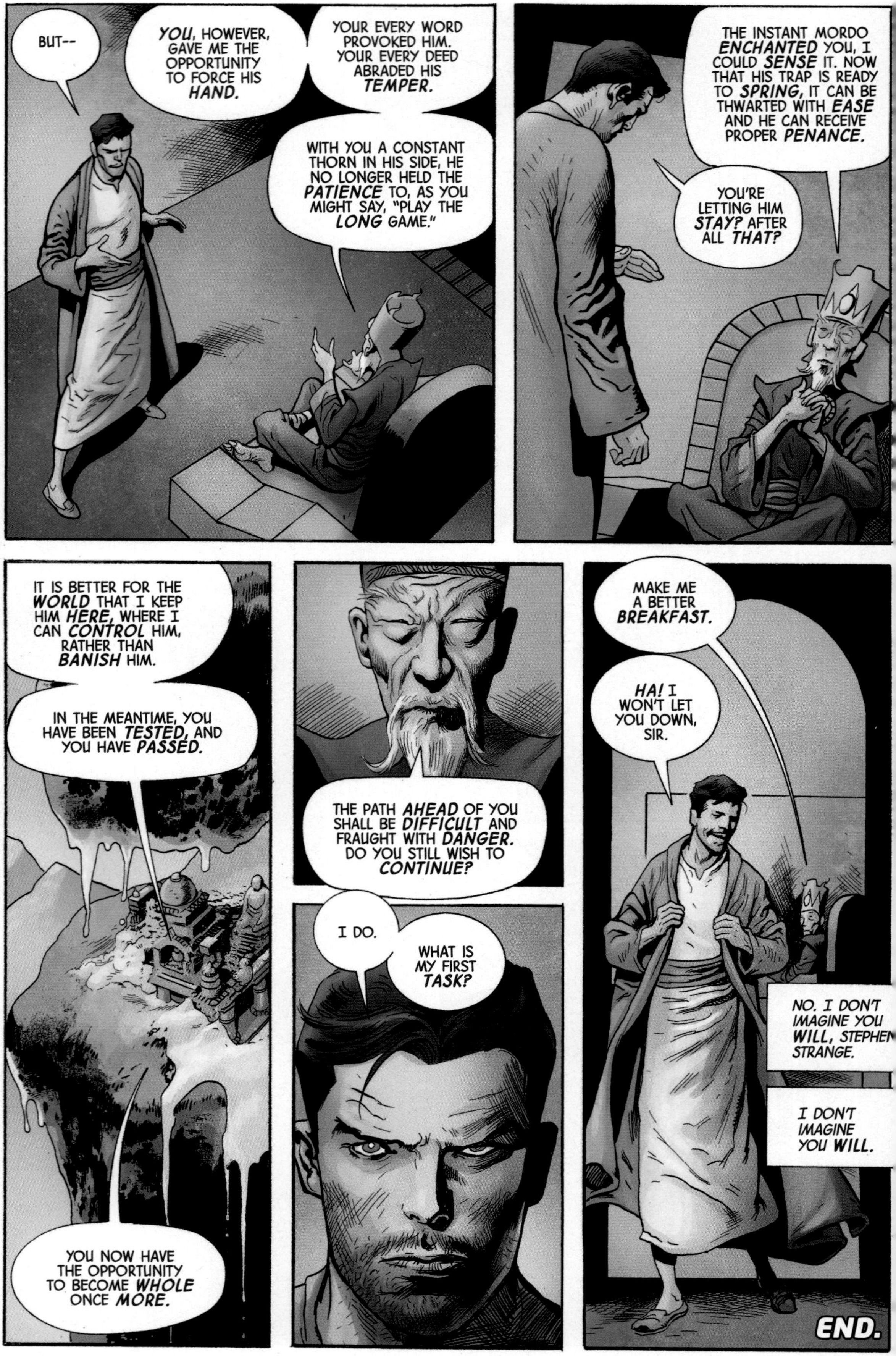
BUT--
YOU, HOWEVER, GAVE ME THE OPPORTUNITY TO FORCE HIS HAND.
YOUR EVERY WORD PROVOKED HIM. YOUR EVERY DEED ABRADED HIS TEMPER.
WITH YOU A CONSTANT THORN IN HIS SIDE, HE NO LONGER HELD THE PATIENCE TO, AS YOU MIGHT SAY, "PLAY THE LONG GAME."
THE INSTANT MORDO ENCHANTED YOU, I COULD SENSE IT. NOW THAT HIS TRAP IS READY TO SPRING, IT CAN BE THWARTED WITH EASE AND HE CAN RECEIVE PROPER PENANCE.
YOU'RE LETTING HIM STAY? AFTER ALL THAT?
IT IS BETTER FOR THE WORLD THAT I KEEP HIM HERE, WHERE I CAN CONTROL HIM, RATHER THAN BANISH HIM.
IN THE MEANTIME, YOU HAVE BEEN TESTED, AND YOU HAVE PASSED.
YOU NOW HAVE THE OPPORTUNITY TO BECOME WHOLE ONCE MORE.
THE PATH AHEAD OF YOU SHALL BE DIFFICULT AND FRAUGHT WITH DANGER. DO YOU STILL WISH TO CONTINUE?
I DO.
WHAT IS MY FIRST TASK?
MAKE ME A BETTER BREAKFAST.
HA! I WON'T LET YOU DOWN, SIR.
NO. I DON'T IMAGINE YOU WILL, STEPHEN STRANGE.
I DON'T IMAGINE YOU WILL.
END.

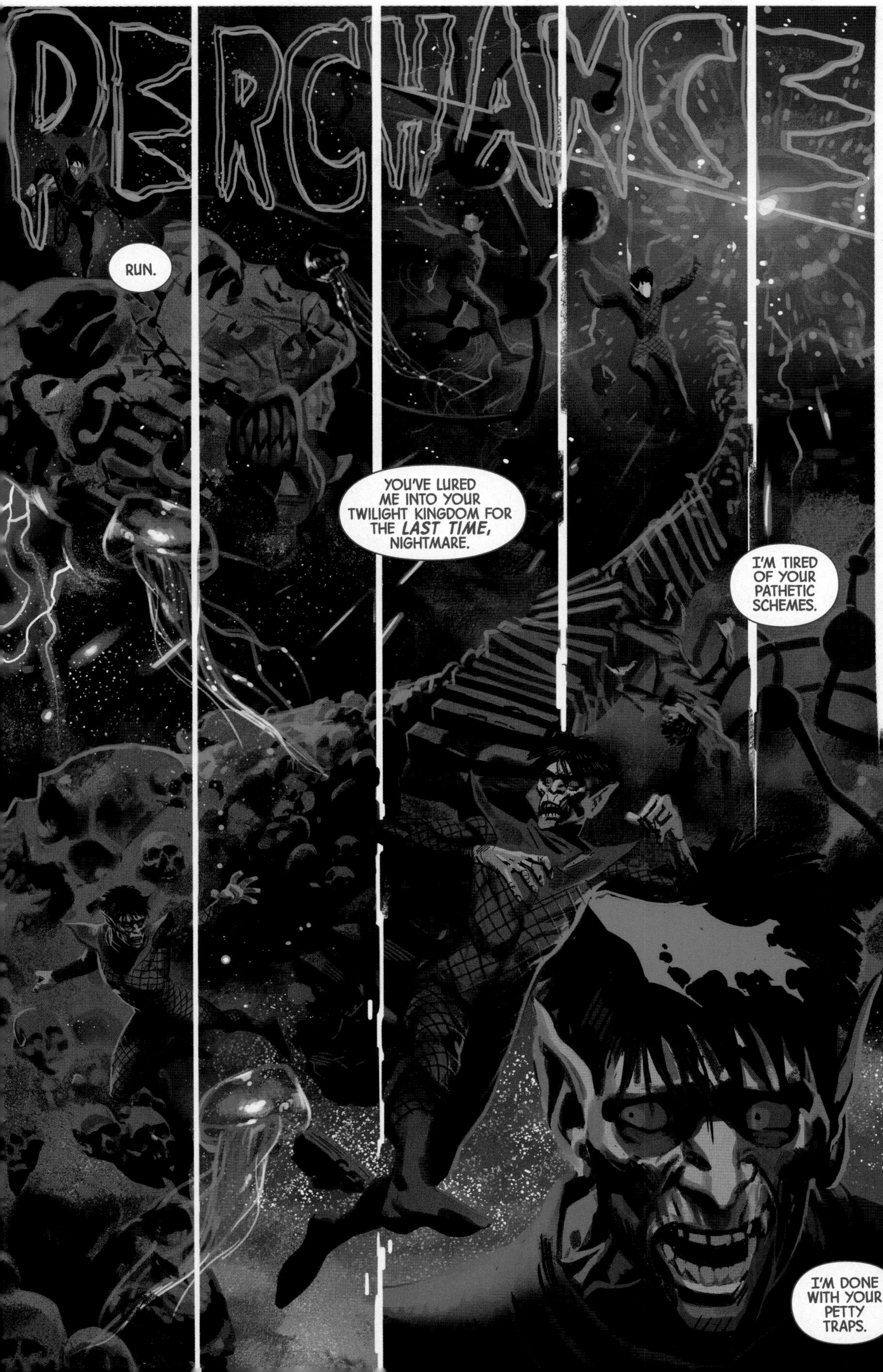
PERCHANCE
RUN.
YOU'VE LURED ME INTO YOUR TWILIGHT KINGDOM FOR THE *LAST TIME,* NIGHTMARE.
I'M TIRED OF YOUR PATHETIC SCHEMES.
I'M DONE WITH YOUR PETTY TRAPS.

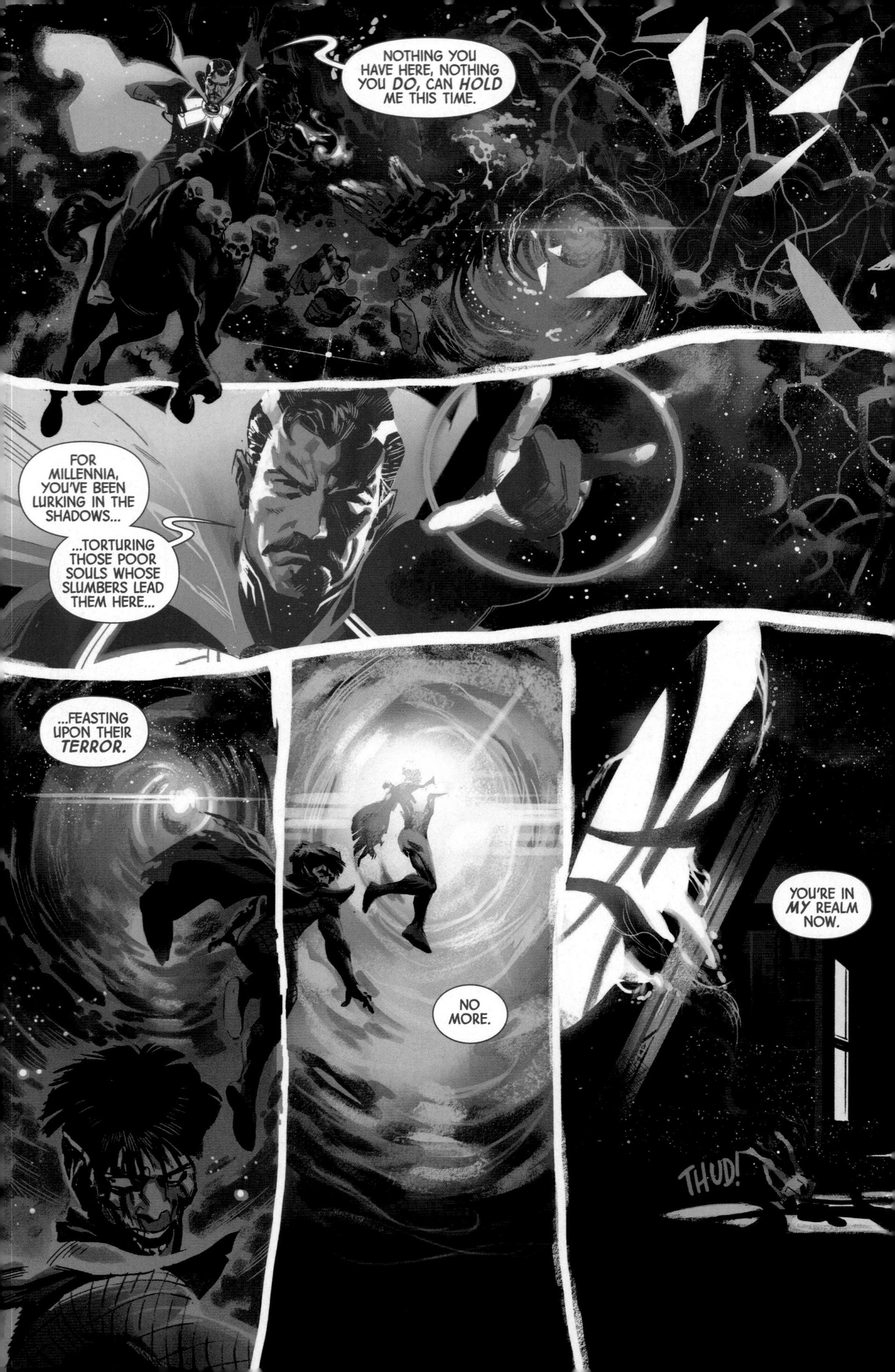
NOTHING YOU HAVE HERE, NOTHING YOU DO, CAN HOLD ME THIS TIME.
FOR MILLENNIA, YOU'VE BEEN LURKING IN THE SHADOWS...
...TORTURING THOSE POOR SOULS WHOSE SLUMBERS LEAD THEM HERE...
...FEASTING UPON THEIR TERROR.
NO MORE.
YOU'RE IN MY REALM NOW.
THUD!

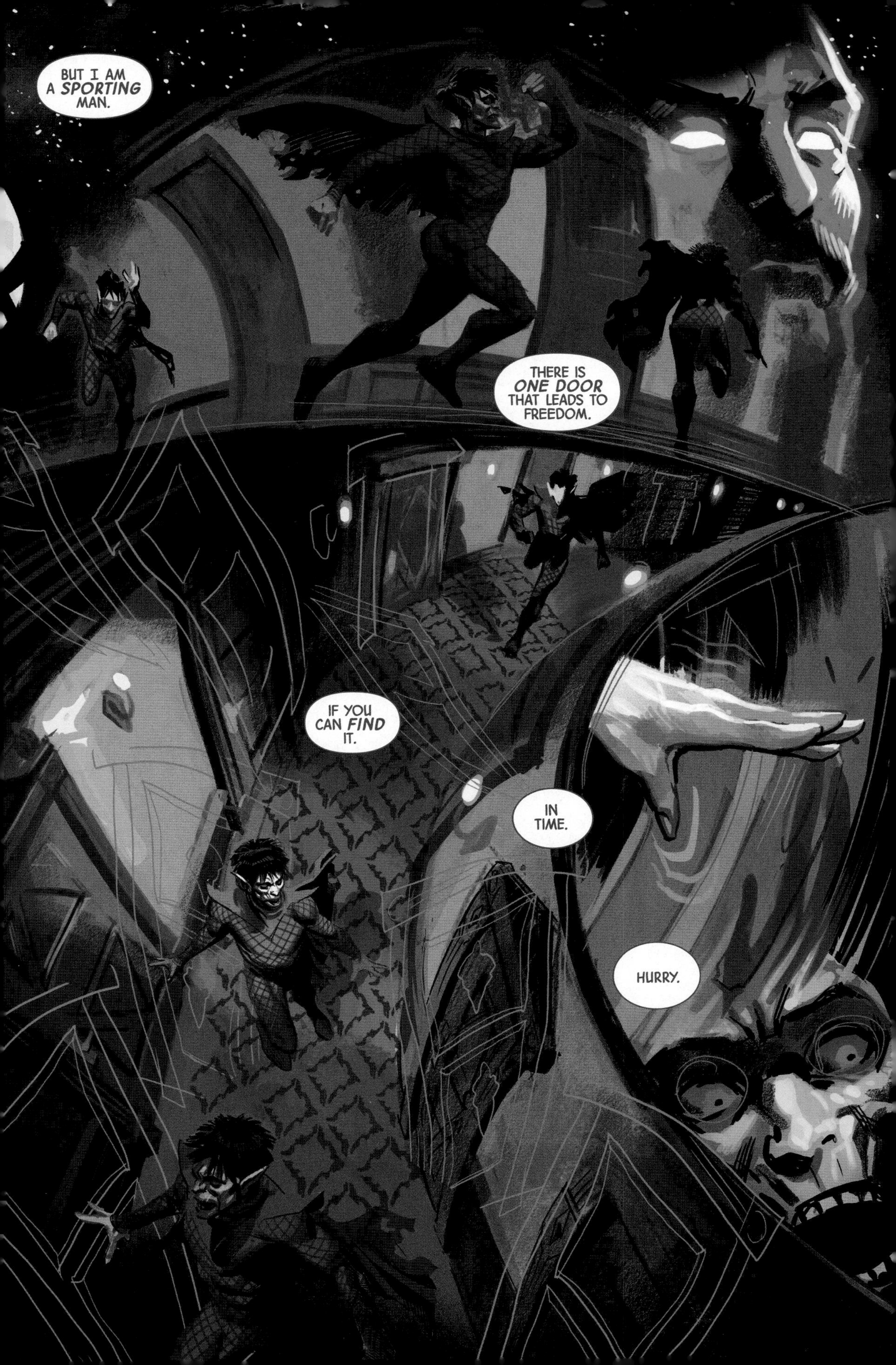
BUT I AM A SPORTING MAN.
THERE IS ONE DOOR THAT LEADS TO FREEDOM.
IF YOU CAN FIND IT.
IN TIME.
HURRY.

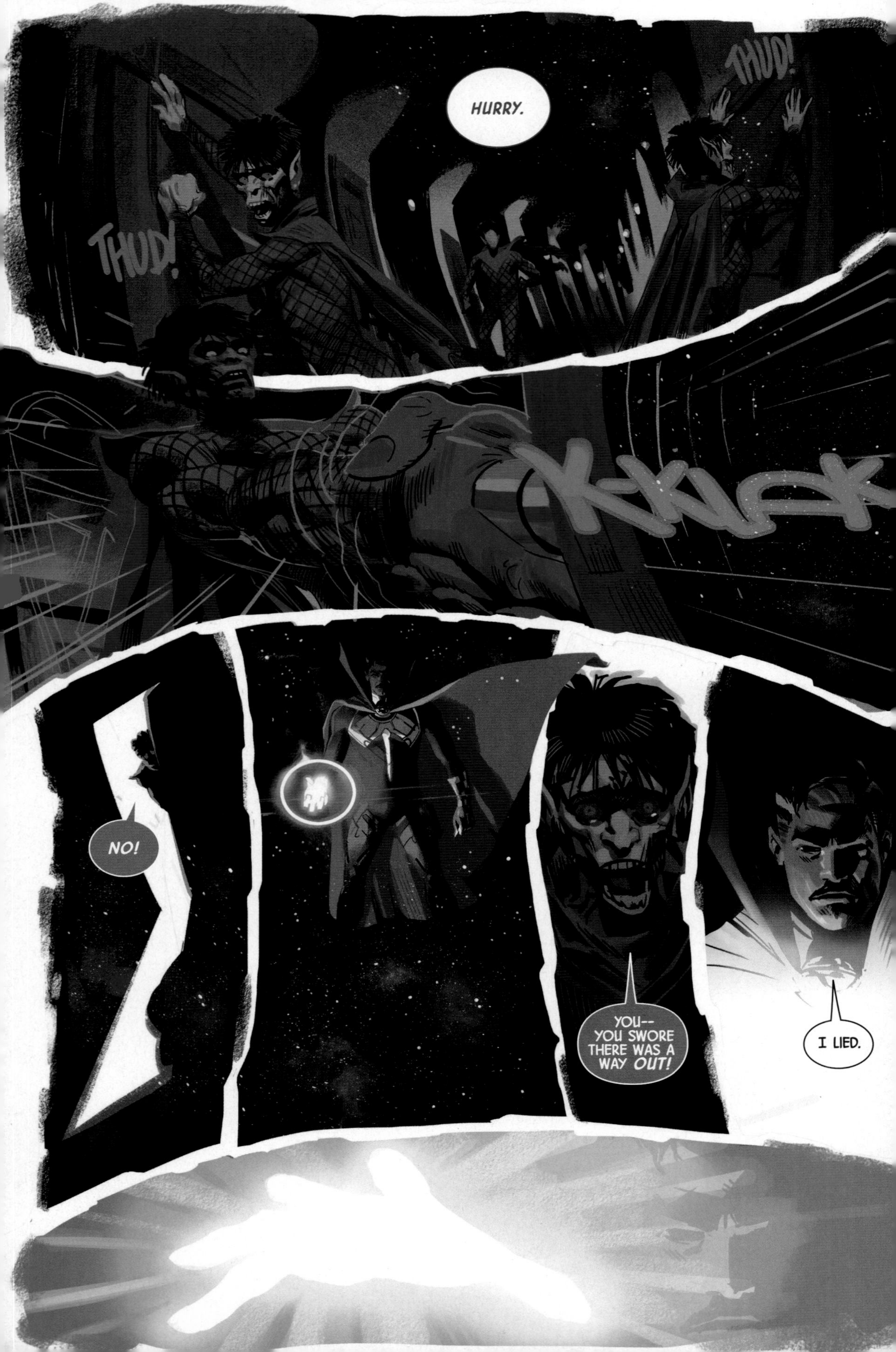
HURRY.
THUD!
THUD!
K-KLAK
NO!
YOU--
YOU SWORE
THERE WAS A
WAY OUT!
I LIED.

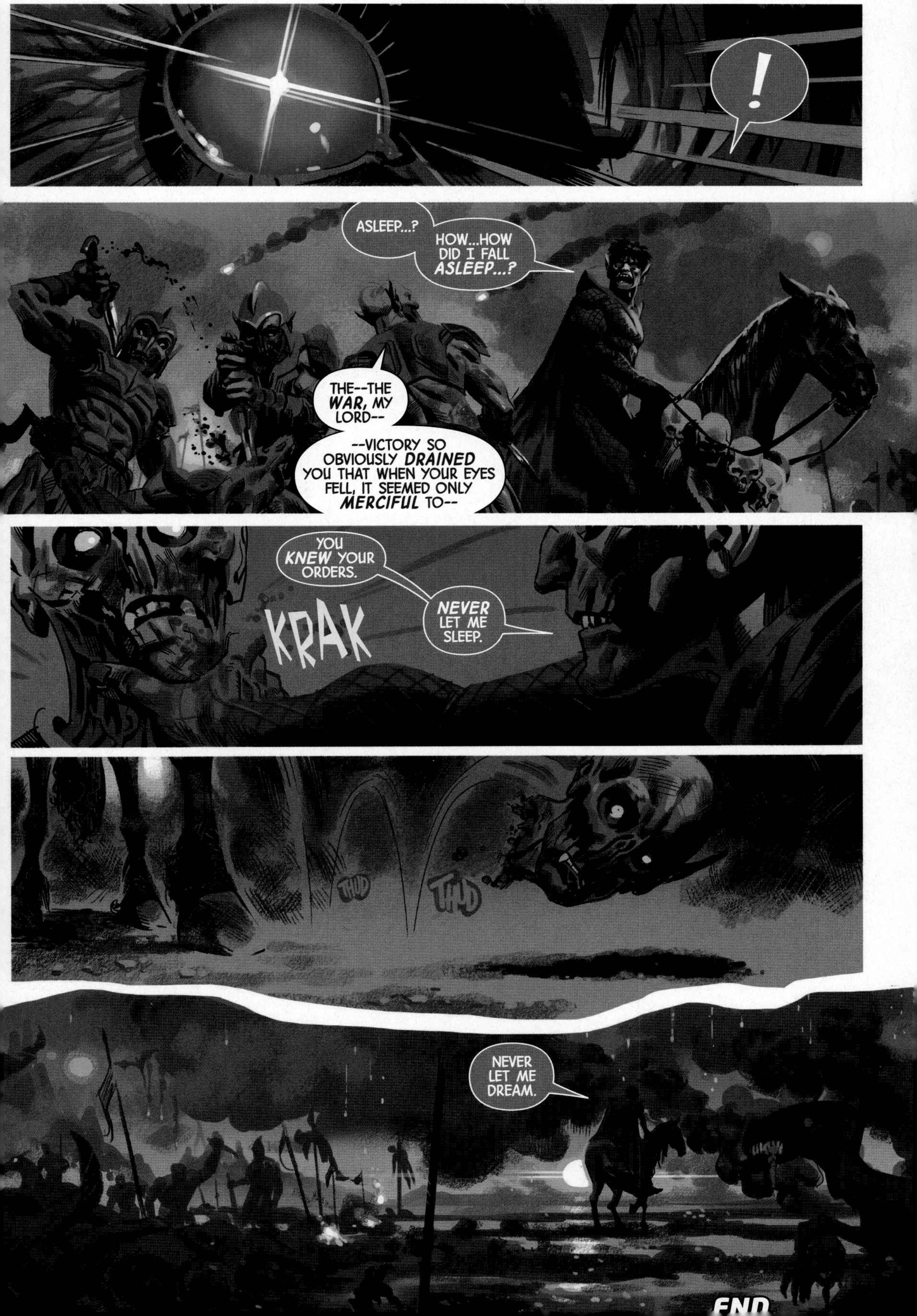
!
ASLEEP...?
HOW...HOW DID I FALL ASLEEP...?
THE--THE WAR, MY LORD--
--VICTORY SO OBVIOUSLY DRAINED YOU THAT WHEN YOUR EYES FELL, IT SEEMED ONLY MERCIFUL TO--
YOU KNEW YOUR ORDERS.
KRAK
NEVER LET ME SLEEP.
THUD
THUD
NEVER LET ME DREAM.
END

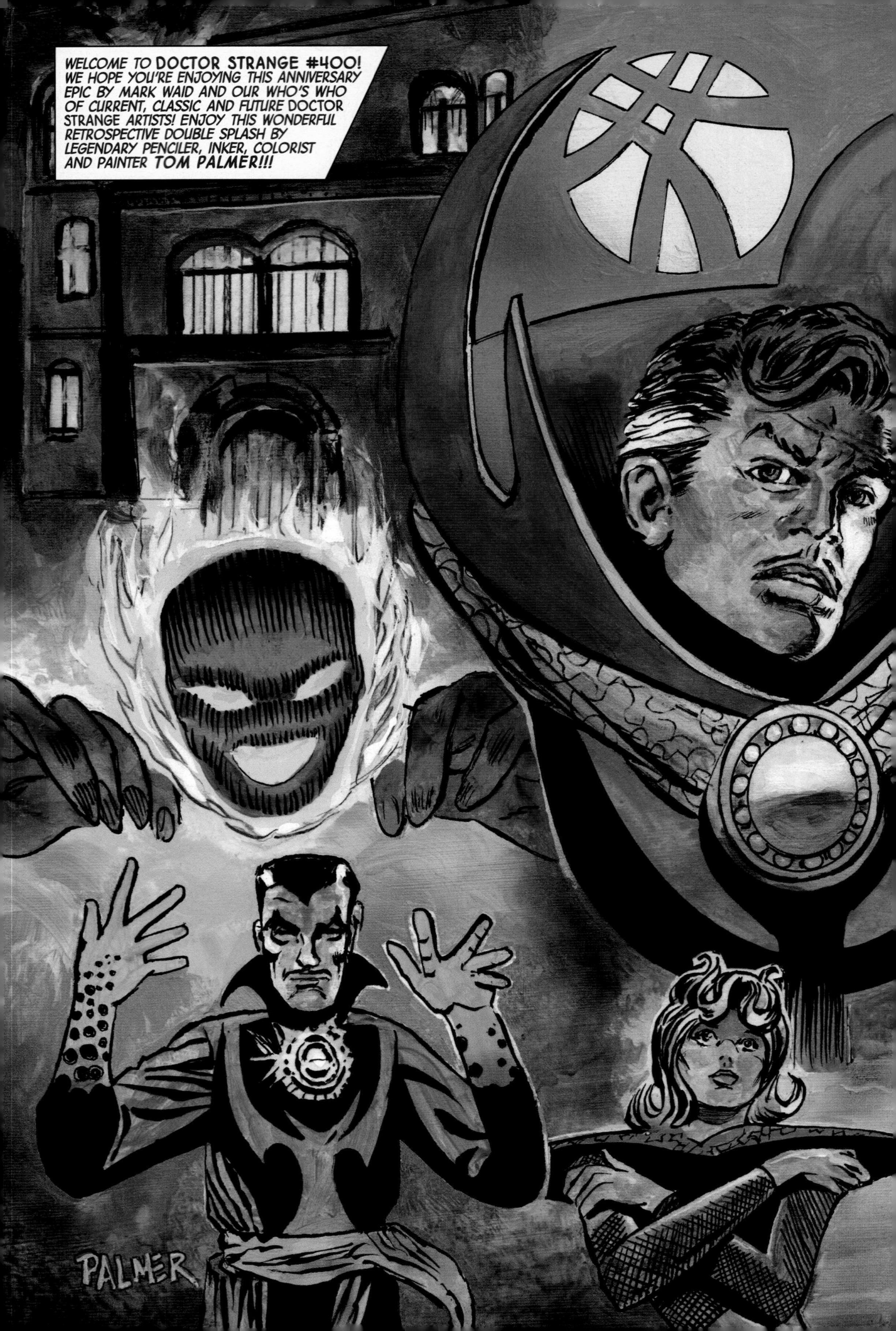
WELCOME TO DOCTOR STRANGE #400! WE HOPE YOU'RE ENJOYING THIS ANNIVERSARY EPIC BY MARK WAID AND OUR WHO'S WHO OF CURRENT, CLASSIC AND FUTURE DOCTOR STRANGE ARTISTS! ENJOY THIS WONDERFUL RETROSPECTIVE DOUBLE SPLASH BY LEGENDARY PENCILER, INKER, COLORIST AND PAINTER TOM PALMER!!!
PALMER

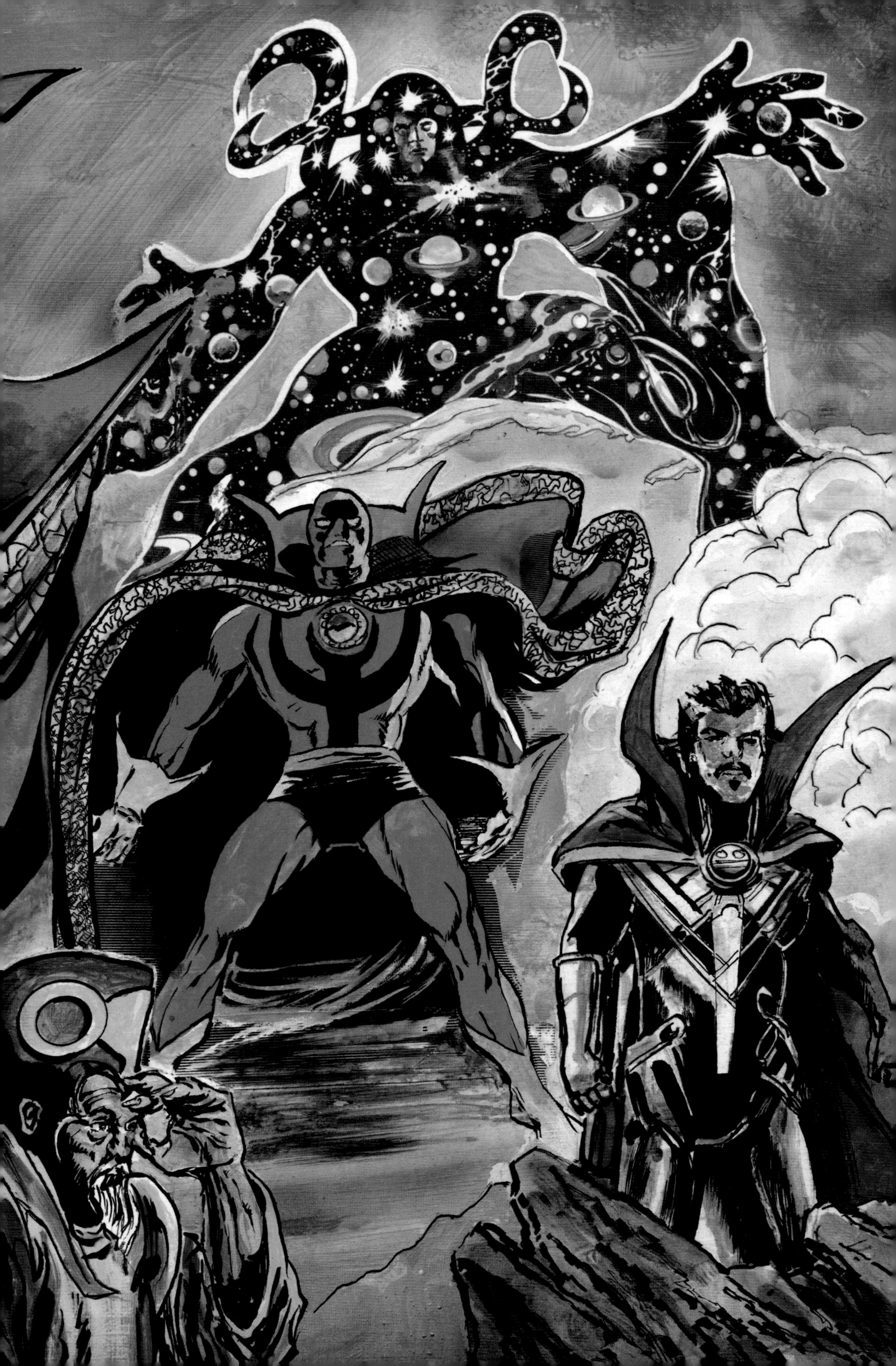

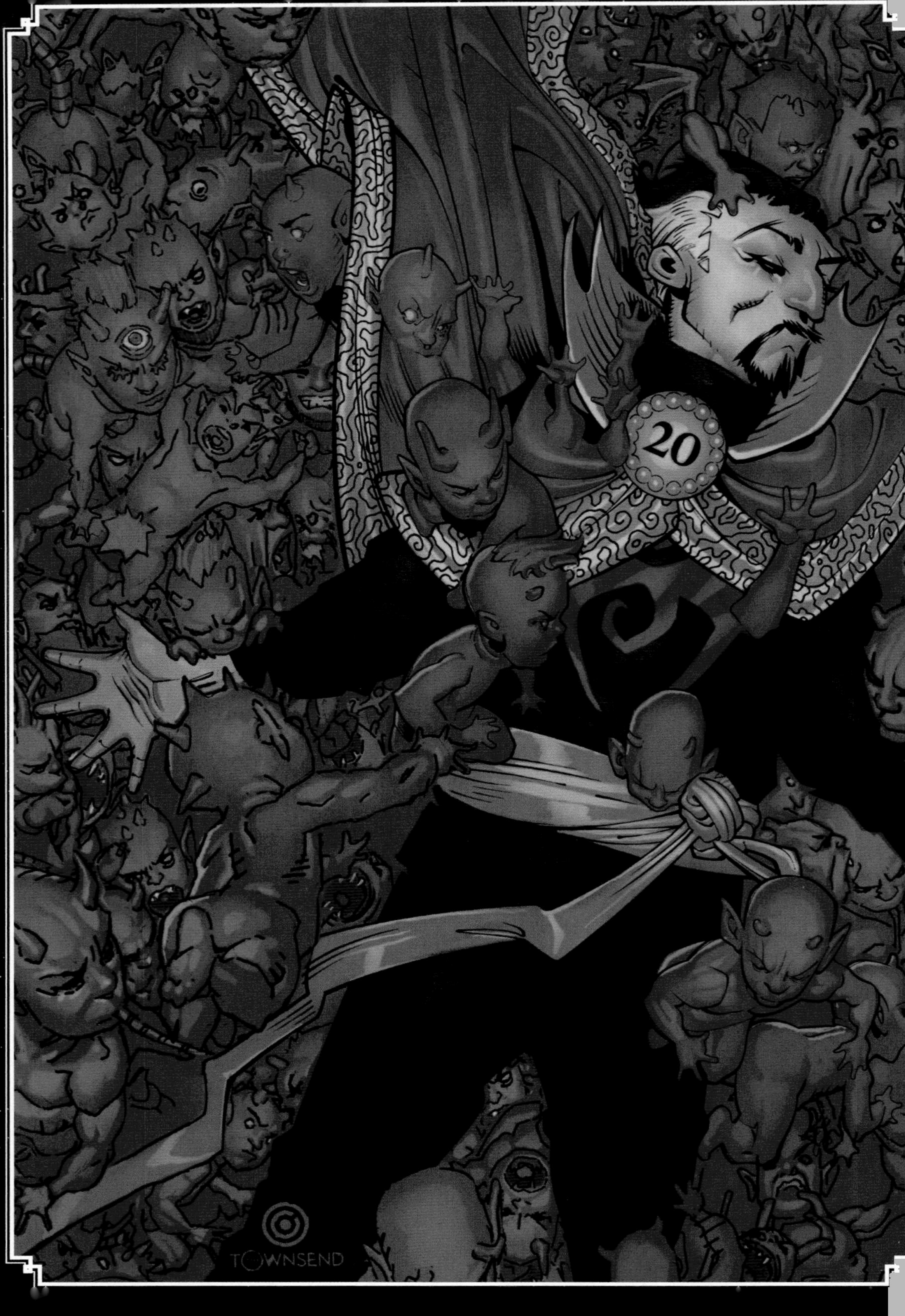
20
TOWNSEND

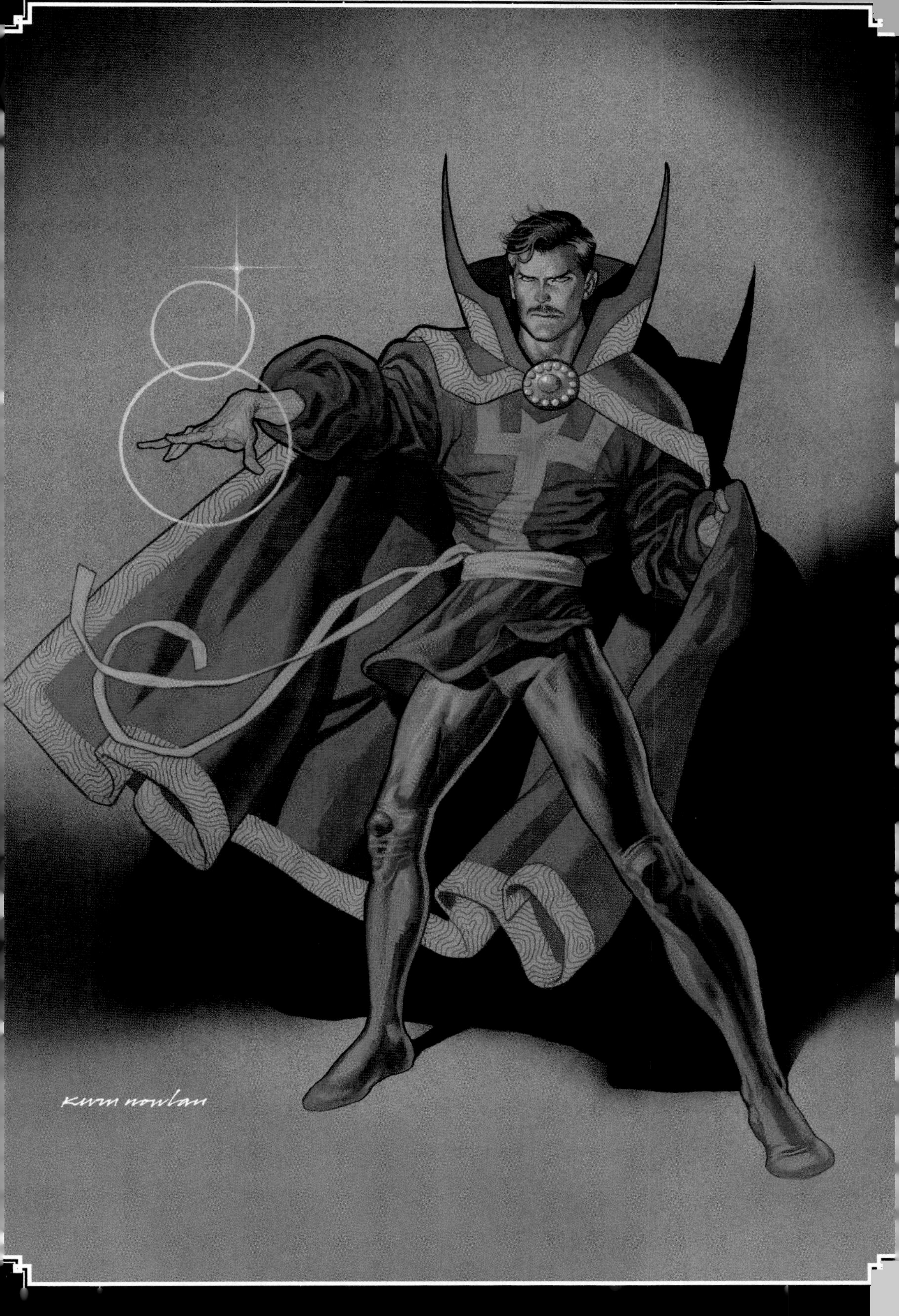
kevin nowlan

Frank Miller &
Matthew Wilson
10 REMASTERED VARIANT

Joe Quesada, Kevin Nowlan &
Richard Isanove
10 VARIANT